CN00923104

BEING A BUDDHIST NUN

BEING A BUDDHIST NUN

The Struggle for Enlightenment
in the Himalayas

———

Kim Gutschow

HARVARD UNIVERSITY PRESS

Cambridge, Massachusetts

London, England · 2004

Library of Congress Cataloging-in-Publication Data

Gutschow, Kim.
Being a Buddhist nun : the struggle for enlightenment in the Himalayas / Kim Gutschow.
p.   cm.
Includes bibliographical references and index.
Contents: Gendering monasticism—Locating Buddhism in Zangskar—The Buddhist
economy of merit—The Buddhist traffic in women—Becoming a nun—Why nuns cannot
be monks—Can nuns gain enlightenment?—Monasticism and modernity.
ISBN 0-674-01287-9 (alk. paper)
1. Buddhist nuns—India—Jammu and Kashmir.   2. Monasticism and religious orders for
women, Buddhist—India—Jammu and Kashmir.   3. Monastic and religious life
(Buddhism)—India—Jammu and Kashmir.   4. Enlightenment (Buddhism)   I. Title.

BQ6160.I42J365 2004
294.3′657′08209546—dc22   2004040573

To the nuns of Zangskar, who
protect the unprotected,
aid the suffering, and
are an inexhaustible treasure for all sentient beings

Contents

Illustrations and Maps

Preface

My first trip to Zangskar was almost as grueling as the second. In late September of 1989, I'd been riding high atop bags of cement, coughing frantically from the combined effects of altitude and cement dust. The fine cement dust billowed out at every bump as our truck slowly crawled along the deeply pockmarked and unpaved jeep track which served as Zangskar's primary travel artery when free of snow between June and November each year. My brother had already threatened mutiny earlier in the day, as we sat perched in the low wooden box above the driver's cabin, with little to shelter us from the freezing wind and stray branches in the predawn darkness. Just after he had told me, "I'm not a piece of meat, you know—I think it's time to get off this truck," the drivers had pulled in for a brief breakfast stop. They had generously invited us into a friend's home to share their breakfast of chapattis and refried vegetables. Yet when their truck had broken down shortly afterward, we had taken our packs to the road and flagged down the first truck going the full 450 kilometers into Zangskar. I couldn't help wondering if we'd abandoned the first truck somewhat too hastily as we sat in the back of the heavily loaded cement truck, which wheezed and gurgled up the snaking track to the top of the forbidding 14,500-foot Pentse La pass. Despite many stops to quench the engine's thirst and cool its overheated radiator, by evening we had arrived deep into the central Zangskar valley. After we were disgorged at a half-built hydroelectric project—which remains under construction today, fifteen years later—we walked the last 15 kilometers into Padum, Zangskar's central village.

My second trip into Zangskar, in May of 1991, was on foot, while the Pentse La pass lay under several meters of snow. Busy avoiding the cement dust the first time around, I hadn't really noticed the meandering plateau at the top of the pass. This time around Phuntsog, my guide, and I were up to our thighs in snow with every second step. His unlucky horse, which was carrying my pack, trembled and panted with each step, as its scrawny legs plunged thigh deep into the snowy crust barely grazing its belly. Phuntsog had been right to want to stop at the unroofed stone shelter we'd passed earlier that day. I had wanted to push on, not realizing the distance that lay ahead before we would drop off the pass, because my backpacking instincts had warned me against sleeping on top of an unprotected pass. "What was I thinking, trying to lead rather than follow, in a landscape I don't know," I chastised myself, as Phuntsog signaled to an island of dry ground no more than ten meters long and half as wide, where we would spend the night. After tethering and unloading the horse, I was grateful that Phuntsog had had the foresight to bring a bottle of kerosene and some kindling. Amid the boulders and small islands where the snow had melted, I set off to scrounge for dung, which spluttered and smoldered in our damp fire. When I expressed surprise at finding dung here, amid the high peaks and a day's walk from a village in either direction, Phuntsog explained that we were camped near the high grazing pastures which would be filled with yaks, cattle, and *mdzo*—the sturdy crossbreed—in a month's time after the snows had melted. For now, the pass was desolate and the snow lay thick and gray as the temperatures dropped to freezing. After Phuntsog set the salt tea to boil, he unwrapped the scarf covering his thin religious text and began to read prayers that would become ever more familiar to me in the coming years. I took out my journal and began to think.

We had set out at 5 A.M. from Phuntsog's house in Tashitongdze, the last village before the pass. Although the political boundaries of Zangskar technically start atop the Pentse La pass, Tashitongdze and two other Buddhist hamlets encircling the monastery of Rangdum are informally considered part of Zangskar rather than part of the predominantly Shiite Suru Valley which lies between Rangdum and Kargil town farther to the north. I'd reached Kargil a few days earlier by bus, after traveling westward along India's border with Pakistan for some 250 kilometers from the town of Leh, which lies somewhat closer to the Tibetan border. A popular destination for backpackers and dharma bums, and a critical army base for the defense of India's contested northern borders, Leh is home to the only commercial airstrip in the Himalayan region of Ladakh, which forms the eastern half of the Indian state of Jammu and Kashmir. After flying to Leh from New Delhi only ten days earlier, I had arrived in Kargil, a frontier bazaar conveniently situated halfway along the single east-west highway that ran from Leh to Srinagar, the state capital. The cheap hotels and pleading tourist wallahs had changed little in the two years since I'd first come to Kargil on my way to Zangskar.

On that trip I'd arrived in Kargil with my brother during Muharram, a festival held to honor Ali, the most famous martyr and founder of the Shia sect of Islam. Like Kargil's women, we had stayed indoors, helpless spectators to the religious delirium into which the festival participants willingly plunged themselves. Gangs of young men paraded through the streets, flagellating themselves with iron braids and field scythes, bearing placards depicting Khomeini and shouting slogans castigating America. As I listened to the weeping and wailing that emanated from nearby balconies, I was both fascinated and repelled by the religiosity around me, so different from the Sunni Islam I'd once studied in Cairo.

This time I'd come to Kargil alone, long before the Pentse La pass was open to vehicles. The local tourist officer had politely suggested that I join a group of schoolteachers from Dras who were planning to walk into Zangskar. After I met up with the teachers and negotiated a berth in the taxi they had booked for the first leg of their trip, I went to purchase a few provisions for the journey—Maggi soups, tea, sugar, and dried milk. As I hastened to the taxi stand the next morning, I was relieved to see four Buddhist nuns from Zangskar, who helped alleviate my awkward exchanges with the young men, whose own sisters would never dare to travel alone, on foot, into the wilds of Zangskar. The classical Tibetan I'd studied in a Harvard classroom was not much help in parsing the drivers' Dardic dialect. Yet I could communicate with the nuns in both Tibetan and their own Ladakhi dialect, which I'd studied in the two previous years I'd visited Ladakh. Despite their flimsy sneakers and thin polyester monastic robes, the nuns sported army-issue bedrolls, backpacks, and glacier goggles which they'd been loaned by cousins serving in the military. Their backpacks were stuffed to the brim with gifts and clothes after their winter pilgrimage in India, where they had attended the Dalai Lama's teachings in Dharamsala and visited the Tibetan communities in South India. As they were unable to find a berth in any of the Tibetan nunneries, they were looking forward to rejoining their own tiny assembly of nuns in Zangla village.

After the taxi left us at the first major snowbank covering the road, we set off on foot. For the next few days, I could barely keep up with my companions as I struggled under my heavy pack. Stuffed with too few clothes, far too many notebooks, and the odd assortment of novels and essays, including both Thoreau's *Walden* and Emerson's essay on self-reliance, I was miserably unequipped to be running over 14,000-foot passes. I crashed through the delicate snowy crust again and again, while my companions nimbly skated across the frozen snowfields and darted from rock to rock across the streams and steep scree slopes. The nuns were solicitous during our tea breaks, chatting amiably as the designated tea brewer would whip out her pot, remove the small bundles of green tea, salt, butter, sugar, dried cheese, and *rtsam pa* or roasted barley flour. Providing just the right mix of salt, carbohydrates, and fat, the staples of the Tibetan diet—salty butter tea and barley flour—perfectly quenched both thirst and hunger during high-altitude exertions. Our first night was spent in a stone shelter, where I shared my Maggi soups with the nuns before we each slipped into our sleeping bags. By the time we reached Tashintongdze, at the base of the Pentse La pass, the nuns had decided to take a rest day until their blisters healed, while I foolishly decided to plunge ahead with Phuntsog, whose horse and services I'd hired for the remainder of the journey into Zangskar.

That is how I came to be stranded on top of the pass with little food, no tent, and a rapidly dwindling supply of dung. While Phuntsog had been reading his text, the sky had turned an ominous shade of gray. When he stopped to make dinner, a thin barley gruel, it began to snow. I absorbed my first lesson in the power of *mantra*. The flakes fell softly at first but gathered momentum as the dense, wet flakes fell thickly into the fire. I felt slightly guilty rolling out my Thermarest pad and down sleeping bag, while Phuntsog laid out the horse blankets and wrapped himself in a full-length sheepskin cloak. While I awoke, shivering, through the night to brush the snow off my wet bag, Phuntsog snored deeply in his blizzard-proof sheepskin. Long before dawn, we awoke from the cold and agreed that it was time to retreat. Packing up and loading the horse in short order, we set off back the way we had come to Phuntsog's house in Tashitongdze.

After a few days of rest and recuperation while the storm abated, we set off once more to walk over the pass. This time, we left Tashitongdze at 1 A.M., walking under the light of the full moon, to take the best advantage of the crust. At the top of the pass we spent a night in the stone shelter we'd passed up the last time, and the next day we marched easily over the pass and down into the upper reaches of Zangskar's northern valley, where we stayed with Phuntsog's relatives in Abran village. After making our way down the Zangskar valley for the next few days, we reached Padum, the administrative center, where I met up with my friends from Zangla nunnery. They were attending a religious teaching just outside of Padum at the Dalai Lama's summer palace. Monks and nuns had come from throughout Zangskar to attend the week-long teaching on the graduated stages of the path to enlightenment. When the nuns from Zangla begged me to come teach English at their nunnery, I promised to come visit after I'd explored the nearby nunnery in Karsha village, which also housed the region's largest and wealthiest monastery. I managed to secure an interview with several of the Karsha nuns and their teacher, the Minister or Lonpo of Karsha. As an aristocrat and a scholar, the Lonpo was also a teacher at the local high school who quickly grasped the scope of my research project.

After I explained that I hoped to study the interactions between nunnery, monastery, and village while living at the nunnery, the Lonpo asked about my personal motivations. I told him that I did not intend to become a nun, but was hoping to apprentice myself to the nuns in order to write a dissertation about life at a Zangskari nunnery. Although the Lonpo and the nuns had never heard of Harvard or even Boston, they understood my Ph.D. to be something akin to their Geshe degree, the highest degree attainable at the great monastic colleges within the Gelug school of Tibetan Buddhism. The Lonpo explained that the nuns would confer as an assembly before coming to a decision—my first experience of the monastic democracy that was used to adjudicate any serious decision that the assembly might face—and indicated that our interview was over. A few days later I got a message from the Lonpo indicating that I was welcome to begin my residence at the nunnery, and I shouldered the pack to walk the easy 10 kilometers across the valley to Karsha.

When I reached the empty nunnery, it seemed forlorn; the entire assembly of nuns was in Padum. Yet this proved to be a blessing, as it gave me ample opportunity to scout out my solitary surroundings and begin to appreciate how little time the nuns actually spent in community rituals, given their busy lives. After the nuns returned a week later, I was introduced to the full assembly during the next monthly prayer meeting. I cooked for myself the first few days and slept on the roof of the cell I'd been offered, having been driven out of the cell by the mice. Yet this paved the way to my friendship with Skalzang, whose cell opened out onto the roof where I'd been sleeping. After she invited me to share her morning tea and meals for a few days, we became roommates and I took the role of purchasing food supplies in Padum periodically, to supplement what I could purchase in Karsha. Sleeping on the roof afforded me the nightly pleasure of a darker, deeper sky than I'd ever seen, split by a lustrous Milky Way and punctuated by nightly flashes of distant lightning refracted from monsoon storms taking place hundreds of kilometers south, in the first ranges that sprang from the Indian foothills. The Lonpo told me that the intermittent flashes of light were believed to be sparkling jewels guarded by a dragon, whose roar could occasionally be heard as the storms came closer.

While the ethnographic trope of arrival is well worn and invariably humbling, its unique nature has a profound influence on how ethnographers are received in their chosen communities. When I first settled at the nunnery, neither the nuns nor I were clear that the arrangement would last more than a few weeks. In retrospect, either side could have terminated the arrangement at any point without much loss of face. It was important that I humble myself to the assembly and be prepared to perform the multitude of menial tasks that any apprentice nun would be required to perform. Slowly the nuns gained some idea of what I'd be doing as I observed the daily routine at the nunnery, which was hardly as onerous or as rigid as I'd first expected. Over the next months and years, we eased our way into a friendship, both professional and personal.

Because I visited the region each year for fourteen years, my relationship with individual nuns and the villagers evolved from rather naive trust to a more complex relationship of dependency, appreciation, and respect. My early foibles and our mutual vulnerabilities have become a cause of laughter rather than chagrin with the mellowing of time. As an unmarried student, I had more in common with a group of studious nuns than with my agemates in the village, most of whom were married and mothers several times over. By living at the nunnery rather than in a village household, I had access to dozens of households which held close relatives of the nuns. In embracing the postmodern multi-sited approach, I have tried to spend time in all nine of Zangskar's nunneries and travel throughout the remote valleys and the most urban and touristed settings. Between 1991 and 2001 I spent a total of thirty-nine months in Zangskar and Ladakh, which included three winters in Zangskar and three precarious trips down the frozen Chadar gorge. As nuns, monks, and villagers observed me over the year and judge how well I deported myself with respect to their village rules and local culture, they became less taciturn and more willing to talk freely about their personal situations. While I have no illusion that my ethnography has helped the nuns very much, I have had the opportunity to raise funds for Karsha and Zangskar's other nunneries for the last decade. In this regard, my fieldwork has diverged from the more common tendency of ethnographers to immerse themselves in a fieldsite or sites for a single stretch of time.

All of the events described herein were discussed publicly, although almost none have been recorded in writing. Although I have changed some names and places to protect the individuals concerned, in many cases I have left names intact to preserve individual histories.

All of my interviews were conducted in Zangskari, a west-Tibetan dialect that I learned in the field after studying classical Tibetan for two years at Harvard. Most Zangskari laypeople and monastics speak only Zangskari and perhaps a bit of Urdu if they have a government job, or classical Tibetan if they have spent time in the Tibetan monastic education system. The Buddha urged his disciples to teach in their local languages rather than in the elitist, classical languages of Pali and Sanskrit. In this vein, I have pared down the use of local Zangskari vernacular and avoided excessive use of classical terms to make this account more widely accessible. I have used the standard Tibetan orthography and the standard Wylie system of transliteration.

My greatest debt of all is to the Karsha nuns, who blessed me with their surprising compassion, unflagging patience, and amazing humor even at moments of utmost exhaustion. They taught me lessons I will never forget but will continue to learn from and practice. Deepest thanks to my girlfriends and agemates at the nunnery over the years—Skalzang Lhamo, Garkyid, Skalzang Drolma, Dechen Angmo, Lobsang Angmo, Nyima, Palkyid, and Skalzang Tsomo—for their constant humor and kindness. I will never forget the amazing grace and wisdom of my grandmothers, Abbi Yeshe, Abbi She She, Abbi Lobsang Drolma, and Abbi Norbu, while my adopted tutors and aunties at the nunnery—Ani Putid and Ani Tsering Drolma—fed me and watched over me as carefully as they had their own apprentices. I also thank the nuns of Zangla, Pishu, Tungri, Dorje Dzong, Skyagam, Stagrimo, Shun, Satak, and Sani, who shared countless cups of tea, meals, and stories which helped broaden my perspective on Zangskari nuns. The Karsha Lonpo was the ideal Tibetan teacher, who offered oral instruction on Tibetan history, Tibetan medicine, and Tibetan astrology. An extremely erudite monk and a teacher by profession, he combined Tibetan oral transmission with the Socratic method in pointing me toward further avenues of study.

The late Geshe Ngawang Tharpa of Hongshed, the late Geshe Sonam Rinchen of Khams, and Geshe Ngawang Changchub of Lingshed offered cogent advice on ritual practice, while Sonam Gyaltsen, Meme Phagsang, Tsewang Manla, and Sonam Phalchung shared invaluable local knowledge on Tibetan medicine, ritual pollution, and expiation. The households which opened their doors to me include those of Shelling, Drongspon, Bragkul Yogma, Dragkul Gongma, and Tiur Gongma in Karsha; Yulang Gongma, Ufti Goyog, Rinam Hilma, Rizhing Gongma, Zenab, and Shamas in Padum; Ldan and Tragang in Leh; T. T. Namgyal in Hemis Shugpachan; and the Onpo of Lamayuru. I appreciate conversations with local scholars, including Tashi Tsering of Tungri, Tundup Namgyal of Karsha, Sonam Dorje of Nubra, Soso and Sonam Angchug of Ule Tokpo, Ali Naqi of Kargil, Dr. Musa, Dr. Lhadrol of Leh, Tashi Rabgyas and Gyatso of Sabu, Dorje Tsering of Leh, and Meme Tsewang Norbu of Phye. In Ladakh, my witty companions otherwise known as Friends of Fluffy (the donkey) sustained me through the winter doldrums.

Nearly the entire manuscript has benefited from close readings by Michael Aris, Nur Yalman, Arthur Kleinman, Sarah Levine, Dennis Donahue, Ashok Rai, Joyce Seltzer, Elizabeth Gilbert, and the anonymous reviewers. Nur, Arthur, and Michael were exceedingly generous mentors at Harvard, and Michael graciously hosted me during research trips to the Oxford archives until his untimely death in 1999. The Harvard Society of Fellows provided intellectual companionship and late-night meditations on indulgence versus renunciation. Martijn van Beek, Rob Linrothe, Don Lopez, Isabelle Onians, Sherry Ortner, Henry Osmaston, Judith Simmer-Brown, Stanley Tambiah, and Unni Wikan each made critical comments on earlier portions of the manuscript which refined my scholarship in important ways. I also appreciate readings by John Crook, Pascalle Dollfus, Katie Getchell, Clare Harris, Adrie Kusserow, Martin Mills, and Isabelle Riaboff; early encouragement from Bill Fisher, Michael Herzfeld, Sally Falk Moore, and Mary Steedly; and final proofreading by Megan Crowe-Rothstein and Millicent Lawson. My friends in the Berkshires deserve my eternal gratitude for getting me through the loneliest hours of writing. Generous funds from the Jacob Javits Foundation, the Mellon Foundation, Harvard's Department of Anthropology, the German Research Council, the National Institute of Mental Health, the Wenner Gren Foundation, and the Milton Fund helped bring the research and writing to a conclusion.

My family's greatest gift has been to show that a life in two worlds is possible. Thanks to Helga, Peter, Kristina, and Kai Gutschow for their enthusiastic visits to Zangskar and Ladakh. I am grateful to my brother Kai for the lovely maps and to my uncle Niels and aunt Wau Gutschow for bringing the Global School of Architecture to Zangskar. I will never forget the Kyirong nuns for their Avalokitesvara *mandala*—a turning point that initiated my new life with Ashok, who helped me see this book to its completion.

BEING A BUDDHIST NUN

1

Gendering Monasticism

The annual springtime ritual of transferring merit to the ancestors was winding down in a village located in the Zangskar region of the Indian Himalaya. Most of the villagers had turned out to participate in a rite which would benefit their ancestors in whatever rebirths they might inhabit. While assemblies of monks and nuns chanted Buddhist prayers of blessing *(smon lam)*, the abbot and senior ritual officiants of the local monastery performed Tantric mediations. The monks had collected a few bone fragments from the nearby ancestral cremation pyres and sprinkled them with sacred water and mustard seeds to purify the body, speech, and mind of the deceased, individually and collectively. The bones were then pulverized and mixed with silt and water to make a clay which was packed into tiny molds in the shape of a funeral reliquary or stupa. These figurines *(tsha tsha)* were then carried up to a distant spot on the hillside as a precaution against inadvertent human defilement, where they would sit until they dissolved back into the elements from which they had emerged. Under the direction of a few monks, the village headman and his assistants mixed barley dough, water, barley beer, and unrefined cane sugar into a dough. They shaped the unwieldy paste into a triple-tiered communal offering cake which resembled a large sand castle in taste as much as touch. After every man, woman, and child had received a crumbled allotment of the blessed cake *(tshogs)*, the adults began to decant the barley beer into a motley collection of serving vessels from a huge vat on the perimeter of the ritual grounds. By the time the gibbous moon finally rose late in the night, the villagers had been replenishing each other's cups for some time and the talk had become boisterous. Eventually makeshift drums—metal jerry cans sold as army surplus and now empty of barley

1

beer—were hauled out. Some girls began to beat out a ragged rhythm of local songs while several men dragged the youngest and boldest men out to dance.

Known locally as "virtuous offering" *(dge tsha)*, the ritual provides villagers with a Buddhist memorial for their ancestors. It serves as a springtime communion for past and present members of the village as much as a reminder of Buddhist bonds of *karma* and interdependence. It is also considered to purify the village fields after dark winter months rife with bitter and destructive energies. As with any act of Buddhist generosity, the making of offerings and chanting of blessings with no thought of selfish gain produce merit, the symbolic effect of virtue. In accordance with the Mahayana doctrine of universal compassion, this merit can be dedicated to any and all suffering sentient beings, both absent and present. Yet like many Buddhist rites, there are pragmatic means to ensure that some of this merit reaches a more specific destination. Every villager who makes a ritual donation can submit the names of several ancestors, who are named in the course of the rite. The clay reliquaries stand for the ancestors, individual and collective, who will benefit from the rite. Like most public festivals, the villagewide ancestor rite does not emerge ex nihilo. It is produced by a lengthy choreography of reciprocities which require merit and material exchanges. The competitive nature of this giving process reinscribes the very logic of difference that Buddhist doctrine seeks to transcend.

The ritual reproduces an ideology of merit and difference. In this ideology, social difference implies moral difference. Those at the top of the system—the monks—are assumed to be benefiting from prior virtue. Their virtue or merit has enabled them to acquire the status of monk and the Tantric power sufficient to purify and transfer merit to the ancestors. These actions are critical, because future rebirths depend largely on the amount of merit and demerit an individual has accumulated. In the local calculus of rebirths, a male human body ranks highest. Being born in one of the heavens such as the western Buddhist paradise *(nub lde ba can)* is almost as desirable. Some monks joked that my life in America—all bliss and not much merit—was just such a paradise. Yet like the gods who are bound to fall from their indolent paradise once they have exhausted their merit, I too would face an uncomfortable shock in my next rebirth if I failed to make merit in this one. They implied that—unlike the gods, who have little chance to make merit—I could make enough merit to secure a male rebirth through generous donations to the monastery. When I told people I hoped to be reborn as a woman, and ideally become a nun rather than a monk, they laughed in disbelief. The most senior nun at Karsha nunnery, Ani Yeshe, could not understand my desire to be a female teacher in my next life. She said it would be far more desirable to be reborn as a monk, or a recognized reincarnation known as a Tulku *(sprul sku)* "on a little throne." Nobody in this region, male or female, had ever expressed a wish to be reborn as a female.

While the villagers danced, drank, and flirted under the light of the stars and moon, the assemblies of monks and nuns each withdrew to a separate house for their obligatory feasts. The nuns were weary and hungry after chanting ritual prayers of blessing all day in the hot sun. Yet they recognized the privilege of being invited en masse to a ritual feast. They would be served a scrumptious meal of rich foods bought through the generosity of those who had made merit with donations. The nuns filed into the empty guest room and sat down cross-legged on the symmetrical rows of rugs arranged around the border of the room. Almost without thinking, they arranged themselves according to the habitual monastic seating order they maintain during most formal or public proceedings. Abbi Yeshe, the eldest, seniormost, and founding member of the nunnery, took the highest spot and the other nuns filed into their places, shifting easily to accommodate a nun above or below as needed. Each nun took out her wooden bowl from inside the folds of her upper robe. Like the texture and style of her robes, her bowl's unique color or design instantly signaled the status and identity of its owner. Abbi Yeshe pulled out the dark bowl of Bhutanese teak she had brought back from Tibet decades earlier.

After some time, the hostess arrived with a flask of steaming butter tea. She began by filling Yeshe's cup at the "head" of the seating order. She poured the tea with her right hand, holding her left hand outstretched with palm upturned in the customary gesture of politeness for offerings made to a higher-status person. As a laywoman, she held these village nuns in particular esteem. They had chosen an ascetic life to which she had once aspired, but to which she was now resigned to send her daughter or perhaps a granddaughter. The nuns asked about their host's experience in managing the festival this year. Had the donors been stingy or generous? The ritual expenses more or less than expected? Having just completed their elaborate three-week Great Prayer Festival, the nuns were attuned to the pitfalls of ritual fund-raising. Each year, turn by turn, one nun was chosen to solicit donations from throughout Zangskar for the nuns' festival. As in the past, this year's steward had outdone herself in providing her community with lavish meals prepared by the two junior monks hired as cooks. One of these young monks-cum-cooks, Tashi, popped his face into the room.

Yeshe jumped off her pillow to offer her seat to young Tashi, whose rakish baseball cap still bore streaks of flour from his duties as nunnery cook. The lengths to which Yeshe went to place herself below Tashi seemed almost absurd. As he moved without hesitation to the head of the row, Yeshe hastily shifted down the row, so that they would not share the same rug. He placed his wooden cup next to hers, but she quickly reached to move her cup off the table they now shared. Temporarily stymied, as there was no other table within reach, Yeshe found a small block of wood and elevated Tashi's cup triumphantly. Everyone laughed at this exaggerated and seemingly ironic display of deference, yet nobody questioned it, least of all Tashi. When the hostess brought the food, Tashi was served first, and none of the nuns took a bite of food until Tashi did. Yeshe had been ordained by the head of the Dalai Lama's own Gelugpa sect in Tibet before founding Karsha nunnery and serving as its chantmaster and CEO for many years. Yet she subordinated herself to a callow teenager without a second thought. In my eyes, Buddhist hierarchy was made concrete even as it was caricatured.

Although it takes time to understand all of the practices that systematically discriminate between nuns and monks, their effects are visible every day. Unlike more ambiguous village seating orders, monastic seating arrangements are relatively fixed. Village seating orders are governed by four set principles, usually, but not always, administered in descending order: monastic over lay, male over female, high caste over low, and age over youth. By contrast, monastic seating orders are governed by two major rules with clear precedence: first, male over female, and only second, by seniority or office. When not fulfilling a monastic office, every monk or nun has a set place in his or her assembly. Monastics sit above those who have joined the assembly later and below those who have joined previously. However, the entire assembly of monks presides over the assembly of nuns. In this calculus, any monk outranks any nun, regardless of seniority or office.

The rule placing monks above nuns is said to date back to the Buddha himself. Yet its validity comes from centuries of repeated subordination as much as from the Vinaya or canonical monastic discipline where this rule

is stated. Although the Buddha admitted that women can gain enlightenment just as men can, he only accepted women into his monastic order on
one caveat. He specified that all nuns be subject to the authority of monks
by the "eight heavy precepts" *(lci ba'i chos brgyad, garudharma)*. The first
and foremost of these eight rules dictates that a nun who has been ordained a hundred years must bow down to a monk ordained for only a day.
This stricture was the only one of the eight that the Buddha's aunt rejected,
albeit to no avail. These rules gave monks the right to discipline and ad-
monish nuns, while forbidding nuns from doing the same to monks. Ever
since, female ordination has presupposed a necessary if not willing subordination. Some feminist nuns may balk at being seated below monks, and
scholars may debate the historical legitimacy of these rules. Yet none have
been able to undo their desired effect. That Buddhist monks gained more
power and prestige than nuns across Asia is well known. Yet the role of
merit, purity, and ordination in sustaining this dominance has been insufficiently understood.

A Tibetan proverb tells us:

> In enlightened thought there is no male and female
> In enlightened speech there is no near and far.

This saying suggests that the distinction between male and female is as
much an anathema to enlightened thought as the distinction made between those near to and far from one's heart. In other words, all beings
have equal potential for Buddhahood, regardless of whether they are male
or female, friend or foe. Doctrinally, gender is a relative truth which must
be ultimately abandoned as an illusion on the path to enlightenment. Yet
practice finds it to be an inescapable obstacle. The Buddhist practices considered in this book create the very forms of social difference which doctrine ultimately denies. But how has this tendency to hierarchy been so
consistently misrecognized?

The nuns' eye view of Buddhism offers a perspective on monasticism
from the bottom up rather than from the top down. Because the nuns'
viewpoint privileges popular practices and local informants over classical
doctrine and textual expertise, it is often either ignored or denigrated.
When I first came to study Buddhism in the Zangskar region of Indian
Jammu and Kashmir, villagers could not understand why I was at the nunnery and not at the monastery. Like scholars, the laypeople assumed that
the study of Buddhist monasticism could best be pursued at its preeminent

institution, the male monastery. By situating myself at the nunnery to see what the nuns' lives entailed, I saw a little-known side of Buddhist monasticism. As my sojourn with the nuns extended from months into years, I became increasingly aware of how different and yet interdependent the nuns' and monks' lives were. Pursuing a dialogical strategy in which informants' concerns advance the research agenda as much as my own, I found my notebooks soon filled with the economic organization of rituals rather than the Buddhist concept denoted by such rituals. Both monks and nuns were more concerned with donor lists and dung collection than with doctrinal debates. Tantric rites were more likely to be fueled by a quest for purity and prosperity than for enlightenment. Merit or virtue was more likely to be measured in terms of butter and barley than in terms of meditation or motivation. The emphasis on material organization led me to theorize that ritual was work which required strategic manipulation of social resources, as much as devotion or symbolic mediation.

Indeed, Buddhist asceticism is premised on reciprocity and sociality as much as on renunciation and individuality. Buddhist monastics are hardly secluded or uninvolved in local socioeconomic relations, except in times of ritual retreat. Many nuns and monks have little time for solitary meditation, given the pressing demands of their clients, the laypeople. In Zangskar, both monks and nuns strategize to maximize both merit and material rewards in serving the laity. Yet their roles within the economy of merit differ vastly. Monks perform rituals and ceremonies through which they have secured a vast endowment from the laity. The monastic enterprise is based as much on the management of property and wealth as on ritual performance and meditation. By contrast, nunneries have little or no endowment and their members are rarely called to perform public or household rituals. Defined as ritually inferior and impure, nuns choose the monastic life to make merit, but lack the ritual means for subsistence. As a result they must make selfless sacrifices for their families, with little time for advanced study. As dutiful daughters, they work on family farms short of labor. As sacrosanct celibates, they must prove their piety and willingness to work for the laity and monks. As subordinate sisters, they serve the monks in many realms, both personal and political. Buddhist monasticism is structured around the same division of labor and dualities of sex that lay communities are.

Buddhist asceticism reflects the society it was supposed to renounce. While nunneries in Zangskar provide a relative degree of autonomy, they impose their own form of servility. Prospective nuns submit to monks at nearly every stage in the ritual process of renunciation, from first tonsure to final expulsion from the nunnery. Nuns who commit to lifelong celibacy may reject the social mandate of marriage. Yet they cannot transcend the social "traffic" in women, as their parents earn merit and the promise of service in exchange for sending a daughter to the nunnery. Nuns reject the high status that marriage and motherhood offer, but they cannot avoid the burden of gender roles. Their shorn heads and androgynous robes signal a lofty intent to renounce sexuality and maternity. Yet their ascetic discipline cannot absolve them from the dangers and defilement of the female body. Although women were accepted into the monastic order by the Buddha, they have faced obstacles and constraints from the start. Their subordination within the monastic order prevents them from reaching the highest status or attainments.

Buddhist practices of merit making, purification, and ordination have reinstated the very social hierarchies that the Buddha disdained. Merit was intended as an inexhaustible symbol of virtue accessible to all regardless of status. In practice, it functions as symbolic capital in an ideology where prosperity is equated with virtue. Purification rituals were scorned as anathema by a doctrine which declared that no one can purify another. Yet Buddhist monks have amassed enormous endowments through their wide spectrum of expiatory and purificatory rites which guarantee the health and prosperity of persons, houses, villages, and space. The nuns' order was instituted so that women might seek merit and enlightenment rather than serve monks or their families. Yet South Asian nuns have been systematically subordinated by the loss of full ordination and the monks' refusal to reinstate this privilege.

The power and prestige of monks rest on a willing and knowing supplication on the part of nuns. This blindness of practice explains why nuns accept and reproduce the conditions of their inferiority. While nuns may misrecognize the effects of their deference towards monks, their stance is hardly unconscious. Both laypeople and nuns consciously pursue merit and purification in order to achieve a better rebirth. The practice theory advocated by a number of anthropologists may help elucidate the habitus of merit making that reproduce social hierarchy. Yet the theory does not tell us enough about the nuns' agency or their strategic subversions of existing hierarchies.[1] Nuns may strategically defer to monks in order to make merit, even as they resist other more powerful forms of subordination. Pragmatic rituals reify and legitimate the religious efficacy of monks, while also providing laypeople with leverage over patronage. Both nuns and monks pursue merit, even as they systematically misrecognize its potential to reify status and power within an ostensibly egalitarian monastic assembly. To paraphrase Bourdieu, ritual practices have a logic of their own which sacrifices the rigor of doctrinal truths.

The anthropology of Buddhism has addressed some of the contradictions between doctrine and practice. Although putatively interested in practice, much of this work betrays a subtle bias toward doctrine. Earlier holistic approaches have tried to classify Buddhist practices into static schemas by isolating enlightenment from more pragmatic goals like merit or prosperity.[2] By contrast, my analysis emphasizes the overlapping nature of these categories. It suggests that merit is an aspect of many Buddhist practices, including the soteriological as much as the pragmatic. Nuns and monks perform a wide range of practices on behalf of the laity, which establish reciprocal ties between the groups. The pragmatic nature of many Buddhist rites gives monks a central role in mundane economic and social affairs.[3] Simultaneously, the dependency of nuns on their families reduces their power and prestige. The lay and monastic realms are hardly as discontinuous or disjointed as formerly assumed, nor is the male monastery separate from its helpmate, the nunnery. The centrality of monks in political and economic processes is testimony to the enduring patronage that has sustained Buddhist monasticism.

Questions of method have disrupted the anthropology of religion in several ways. While cultural anthropologists investigate the nature of the term *culture,* religious studies scholars fret about the category *religion.*[4] Ethnography has come under attack for perpetuating a mythical objectivity which Donna Haraway (1988: 590) once called the "god trick of seeing everywhere from nowhere." Simultaneously, religious studies scholars have destabilized the "god trick" of the category religion itself as well as the crypto-theology conducted in the name of religious studies. The postcolonial efforts to remove lingering stains of orientalism and positivism in both fields unmask religion and culture as disciplinary categories and social formations of considerable import. Yet the methodological critiques are not without their own problems. In ritual studies, the unilateral focus on domination or resistance undermines subjectivity and agency as much as symbolic or interpretive approaches tended to ignore power and class.[5]

Although the irreducibility of categories like ritual, religion, and culture has come under attack, it is not yet clear what new terms will replace them. In the anthropology of religion, postmodern debates over method and discourse have exposed master narratives as outmoded, while still trying to avoid the fallacy of substituting other, equally problematic narratives of decline or progress in their place.

These critical perspectives have investigated the links between Buddhist studies, orientalism, and colonialism. Colonialism was implicated in the race for knowledge and power in Kashmir as in Tibet. The first translation of Buddhist texts brought back by colonial officers or lay Protestant missionaries reflected classic orientalist concerns. To paraphrase Don Lopez, the translators took charge of representing Oriental beliefs because they believed the Orient to be incapable of representing itself.[6] Where possible, classical texts were preferred to modern informants, who were regarded as ignorant or mistaken. Painting a picture of historical decline and corruption, Victorian scholars displayed a consistent preference for classical or Theravada Buddhism over later forms such as Mahayana and Tantric Buddhism. The "primitive" and pristine Buddhism found in Pali texts was hailed as a triumph of Protestant reason and restraint, in contrast to the more idolatrous and ritualized practices of Tantric and Tibetan Buddhism. Yet Western scholars alone are not to blame. Many Tibetan scholars also emphasize the trope of historical decline and the centrality of Buddhist textual knowledge disseminated by a monastic elite.

Some modern scholars still essentialize Tibetan Buddhism as baldly as the Victorians once reified what they called "Lamaism." The tendency to read Tibetan texts for clues about actual historical practices has hardly destabilized texts from the center of such analysis. This is partly due to the difficulty of doing ethnography in Tibet and the Indian and Nepalese Himalayas for the first three quarters of the twentieth century. Largely secluded from researchers up through 1959, Tibet became even less accessible after the Chinese takeover and subsequent Cultural Revolution. With the flight of the Dalai Lama and other religious elites into exile after 1959 and the closure of Tibet's borders, scholars were left in the awkward predicament of studying Tibetan Buddhism outside of Tibet. In the wake of the Cultural Revolution, an entire religious economy was systematically dismantled in Tibet, as thousands of temples were destroyed. Given the persistent Marxist critique emanating from China, many scholars were hesitant to study the social or economic relations of Tibetan monasticism.[7]

A lengthy debate about the definition of Tibetan peasants as serfs under-scores the political axes which were being ground. At the same time, a salvage mentality drove some Buddhist scholars who translated Tibetan works whose Sanskrit originals had been lost since the Muslim destruction of Buddhist libraries in North India in the twelfth century. The dearth of historical sources in both India and Tibet helped propagate a textual exegesis which emphasized internal literary meanings over social or historical context.

The sociological study of Buddhist practices lags far behind. Recent scholarship still privileges textual analysis over the ethnography of ritual practices even while attempting to overcome the classic bias toward texts. A literary hermeneutic still dominates much of recent Buddhist scholarship.[8] Even the scholarship dedicated to practice has omitted ethnographic description of rites in favor of liturgical and literary translations, often de-void of in-depth social or economic context. Although diaspora studies have come to the foreground, the imaginary but vanished "traditional" Tibet still holds pride of place. The actual social and economic relations which continue to produce ritual practices in exile are occasionally noted, but insufficiently theorized. The reinvention and reconstruction of rela-tions of patronage and tradition are exciting new areas of study. This re-vival of Tibetan culture, however, has both nurtured and been fed by uto-pian or romantic imaginings of Tibet as Shangri La.[9] While some critics may argue that these images have little to do with Buddhist practices in Ti-bet, others recognize Tibetan agency in fostering this myth-making pro-cess. Tibetans in exile consciously choose to sell Buddhism as a chicken soup for the alienated Western soul in order to advance any number of po-litical agendas.

The spotlight on Tibet tends to overshadow the regional variants of Ti-betan Buddhism such as that found in Himalayan Jammu and Kashmir. Modern scholars have overlooked the continuing presence of Buddhism in Mughal India by ignoring the fact that Zangskar and Ladakh were both su-zerain to the Mughal empire.[10] This book restores the centrality of these peripheral kingdoms to the history of Buddhism in India. Himalayan Bud-dhism is often regarded as a corrupted or less authentic version of a van-ished template that once existed inside Tibet. Alternatively, the Buddhism of the Himalayas is seen as more shamanic and less civilized than Buddhist India.[11] In either case, Himalayan Buddhism is studied through the lens of exemplary Buddhist paradigms, a view Edward Said has soundly attacked.

The misrepresentation of Himalayan Buddhism as an untamed cousin of Tibetan Buddhism can be corrected by shifting the terms periphery and center. By situating itself among the nuns of Himalayan Kashmir, this ethnography radically reverses previous foci. The emphases on local and vernacular practices at the nunnery take precedence over classical and textual knowledges at the monastery.

Until recently, nuns were deemed largely irrelevant to the story of Buddhist civilization in Tibet or the Himalayas. The scant references to nuns in local Zangskari or Ladakhi sources merely hint at the presence or absence of nuns in any era. Just as a single potshard hardly signifies a community with a single pot, a singe reference to nuns in the eleventh century does not imply a community of one. Clearly further research is needed before confirming the role of nuns in Himalayan Kashmir. Zangskari histories record a landscape conceptualized as demonic and female being subdued by male adepts. These phallic metaphors record the Buddhist conquest through the male and monastic eyes. Where are the nuns or female adepts in this process? The exclusion of nuns from modern Buddhist scholarship is due to oversight as much as to oblivion.[12] Travel literature from the British Raj omits nuns in a territory catalogued so exhaustively in other ways. This may be due to the Victorian bias against insolent informants as much as to a Pali text vision of what nuns should look like. The textual bias persists as scholars continue to ignore ordained nuns who work in the fields or don't always wear monastic robes. Other scholars have mistaken ordained nuns for lay renunciants, as both are called *jomo (jo mo)* in the local vernacular. This confusion overlooks the fact that local informants clearly distinguish the difference between the two groups. While ordained novices are part of a monastic assembly and perform public rituals, elderly renunciants have no formal ritual roles or assembly. Yet even local idiom can perpetuate the elision of nuns, when it fails to recognize that nunneries are also solitary places or *dgon pa,* the generic Tibetan term for a monastic residence.[13]

When not neglected or degraded, Buddhist nuns are discounted as lesser monastics. It is still assumed that nuns have less valid motivations than monks do. The popular assumption that nuns are women unable to find or keep a husband hardly reflects the current generation of nuns across the Himalayas.[14] Not a single nun out of the more than one hundred nuns I interviewed in Zangskar over the last decade was divorced or a single mother. Only one had been a widow. While some remote Himalayan nunneries may house widows or divorced women, many of the rural and urban nunneries across the Himalayas from Kashmir to Bhutan are filled with young women who join the nunnery long before they come of marriageable age. Nuns are as likely as monks to spend their youths in celibate apprenticeship before seeking lifelong ordination in the Tibetan tradition. The poverty and hardship nuns endure imply a motivation which matches or exceeds that of monks.

The systematic elision of women's experience and agency in the study of Buddhist monasticism requires an analysis that does far more than just "add women and stir."[15] The history and practice of monasticism must be rewritten to include both nuns and monks. Taking women seriously as an analytic category means far more than adding a few nuns into the historic record. It requires reanalyzing the historic record and the central role of Buddhist practices that have excluded or subordinated women. This book's analysis of merit making, ordination, and purification practices fulfills only a part of this agenda. This work interrogates the simplistic assumption that nuns are lesser monks by arguing that gender and sexuality are inescapable aspects of monastic life. It also explores why monks and nuns have such different social and economic power. In this regard, it moves away from previous monographs on nuns which tended to isolate nuns from lay society or from monks and argues that it is impossible to study the status of nuns without considering their relations to monks and the laity.[16] In Zangskar, nuns and monks pursue reciprocal engagements with one another as much as with lay villagers. The social status of nuns emerges through such reciprocities and obligations to both sacred and profane realms. Their subordination is reinforced in both ritual and mundane settings. The study of Buddhist practices reveals what doctrinal discourse on gender and enlightenment have occluded.

Donna Haraway notes that "passionate detachment"

> requires more than acknowledged and self-critical partiality. We are also bound to seek perspective from those points of view which can never be known in advance, which promise something extraordinary, that is, knowledge potent for constructing worlds less organized by axes of domination.[17]

I use passionate detachment as a metaphor for a perspective which combines a passionate feminism with Buddhist detachment. In situating itself firmly at the nunnery, this ethnography assumes the Buddha's proverbial middle way between feminist and Buddhist perspectives. It accepts poststructuralist feminist perspectives as well as Buddhist perspectives on interdependence, indeterminacy, and subjectivity. The evidence of experience suggests that nuns have a "different voice" in Buddhist society. Taken alone, their perspective is as partial or incomplete as the more normative view of Buddhism that only referenced monks. By switching the focus from monks to nuns, this book unveils the assumption that the monks' perspective is unmediated or objective. Most important, the description from the nunnery can yield startling insights into how Buddhist practices have perpetuated social difference.

Buddhist literature has produced a range of discourses about the relationship between sex and enlightenment. A single question—is it possible to achieve enlightenment in the female body—has elicited variable responses in almost every era. Yet Buddhist practices like monastic endowments and merit making have perpetuated a consistent preference for monks over nuns. The ideologies of merit and purity have prevented nunneries from earning as much patronage as monasteries have. The ritual practices which produce merit and purity illustrate the sheer impossibility of transcending difference and rank. Doctrine may view duality as conventional and ultimately illusory; practice knows it to be real and necessary. Many Buddhist practices reproduce an implicit hierarchy between nature and culture, female and male, and profane and sacred. While the female body signifies defilement and constraint, the male body suggests purity and potential. Ritual practices reinstate the subordination or subdual of female nature. These discourses both authorize and undo Buddhist institutions. Buddhist monasticism is founded and founders within an ideology that contains the seeds of its own contradiction.

In the Buddha's words, enlightenment is achieved by the cessation of desire. Like a doctor treating a patient, the Buddha explained the cause, cure, and treatment of a universal disease he identified as suffering. The ethical treatment for this suffering prescribes a path of three trainings—morality, meditation, and wisdom—which form the basis of the three vows *(sdom gsum)* that Tibetan Buddhists are supposed to adopt: individual liberation *(pratimoksa),* universal liberation *(bodhisattva),* and esoteric liberation *(tantra).*[18] The accumulation of virtue *(dge ba)* or merit *(bsod nams)* is central to the practice of morality. Although Tibetan Buddhism has broadened or relativized the definition of this path, it has hardly discarded merit or purity as an ethical foundation.[19] Most Tantric ritual includes a standard Mahayana dedication of any merit to all sentient beings. The standard Tantric liturgy *(sadhana)* evinces a clear commitment to purity and merit, as two of its seven stages *(yan lag bdun)* focus on purification and the dedication of merit.[20] The ideal Mahayana figure who perfected merit, purity, and compassion was known as *bodhisattva* in Sanskrit or the "hero [with] a perfectly purified mind" *(byang chub sems dpa)* in Tibetan. Although this hero could adopt antinomian acts and a radical array of guises in the Tantric tradition, he or she cannot deny ethical causality. Placing others before self, the *bodhisattva* might choose to act in ways that took on the karmic burden of what appeared as misdeeds, but only in the service of reducing the suffering of sentient beings. Even such antinomian acts preserve the primacy of merit because they should be undertaken only to prevent others from harming themselves or others. As such, dualistic notions of right and wrong were transcended while an ethos of nonharming and merit was sustained.[21]

Merit is the effect of virtue in the Buddhist ideology. It is central to the Buddhist theory of morality and agency. The law of *karma*—which literally means action—posits that only intentional acts produce an effect. This allows individuals to author their destiny at every moment, through conscious acts of body, speech, and mind. Because conscious acts have causal consequences, individuals create their present as well as their future reality and rebirth. Every action *(las)* produces and is produced by its fruit or effect *('bras)*. These actions produce the effect of merit, demerit, or are ethically neutral. In the Tibetan formulation, the ten virtuous acts *(dge ba bcu)* which produce merit simply comprise abandoning the ten nonvirtuous acts *(mi dge ba bcu)* which produce demerit—namely, killing, stealing, sexual misconduct, lying, slander, using harsh words, idle gossip, being covetous, hatred, and wrong views.[22] Since total abstention from nonvirtuous acts is almost impossible, merit making offers a useful antidote to the buildup of demerit.

Tibetan Buddhists engage in constant attempts to build up their store of merit. Yet merit making is hardly confined to what Cicero would recognize as virtue. The wide spectrum of Tibetan merit-making practices range from the most mechanical—circumambulation, repeating mantras, spinning prayer wheels, and raising prayer flags—to the most esoteric—the construction and deconstruction of visible and invisible universes called *mandala*. In addition to three paradigmatic ways of making merit—generosity *(sbyin pa, dana),* morality *(tshul khrims, sila),* and meditation *(bsgom pa, bhavana)*—Tibetan sources add a fourth, the power of blessed substances *(rdzas).*[23] Merit is produced by a range of ritual acts which extend far beyond the standard list of ten virtuous deeds.

In the Theravada ethics, demerit can never be undone, but can be balanced by the merit of positive deeds. In this view, murderers must suffer at least one rebirth in hell for their negative act. Yet Tantra offers a powerful antidote. It supplies purifying practices which wipe out the stain of negative *karma* before it takes effect. The ritual remedies which can eradicate negative *karma* include remorse, receiving teachings, reciting mantras, making images, making offerings, and even hearing the Buddha's words. One Tibetan ethicist, Tsongkhapa, lists almost as many means of getting rid of negative *karma* as there are ways of accumulating it.[24] The Tibetan narrative of the Tantric adept Milarepa suggests that the sin of killing an entire family can be eradicated with Tantric practices that also achieve enlightenment in a single lifetime. Tibetan Buddhist ethics thus retain a fundamental paradox. It emphasizes virtue and merit even as it supplies Tantric practices for eliminating negative *karma* that nonvirtuous acts produce.

Although merit is central to most Tibetan Buddhist ritual, it is not the only factor influencing events. *Karma* is an ultimate cause *(rgyu)* which operates in conjunction with secondary causes *(rkyen).* Unlike merit, which is stored over lifetimes, such secondary causes operate in a more immediate manner within a single lifetime. These contributing causes—like astrology, nature, diet, and demonic influence—may appear independent even as they are subsumed within the law of *karma.*[25] As such, individual merit does not cause or prevent a natural disaster or the "planetary attacks" *(gza'i gnod)* that cause epilepsy, for instance. Yet a stockpile of good fortune *(rlung rta)* or Tantric blessing *(sbyin labs)* can make an individual less susceptible to these forms of harm or disease. Tantric purification and expiation are intended to protect persons from the accidental and relentless negativities in the universe. As merit declines in salience, Tantric blessing and purity rise.

The Buddhist concept of *karma* was intended to offer an ethical alternative to the Hindu theory of *karma* and *dharma.* In Hinduism, *karma,* or ideal action, is adjusted according to individual nature *(svabhava)* as well as the social *dharma* of caste. The Buddha and his followers revised this relationship by insisting that *karma* was generated by volitional action, independent of caste or gender. Purification was no longer the exclusive realm of the Brahman priests, but an act accessible to each and every individual. The *Dhammapada* argues that no one can purify another, because purification only takes place by the self alone. In theory, an entire religious profession was cast aside in one sweeping phrase. In practice, purification is a central aspect of Buddhist ritual. Internal purification through morality, meditation, and wisdom has never obviated the need for external purification by monastic ritual. Indeed, the agency and authority of Buddhist monks are premised as much on the expiation of impurity and demerit as on their continual recurrence.

The Buddhist ideology of merit sees present status as an index of past virtue. Indeed, happiness or wealth implies previous rectitude and purity while suffering or poverty suggests previous misdeeds.[26] The rank or status of every sentient being is determined by its accumulated storehouse of merit and demerit. The infinite varieties of rebirth are classed into six broad "families of existence" *('gro ba rigs drug):* god, demigod, human, animal, hungry ghost, and hell being. In local idiom, the sum total of all deeds, good and bad, is added up after death by the Lord of Death, Yamantaka, in order to determine the next rebirth. Every rebirth contains an allegorical message, in folk idiom. I was once cautioned before a fasting ritual that falling asleep during the rite could earn me rebirth as a domestic beast forced to work without rest. Alternatively, killing the smallest louse or flea was to risk being reborn as a bug. Excessive desire is said to lead to rebirth as a hungry ghost or "smell eater"*('dri za)*. These sorry beings have grossly distended stomachs, signaling endless hunger and thirst, as well as horribly narrow throats through which no food but only smells can pass. Offerings of burnt barley flour *(su ru pa)* and juniper incense *(bsangs)* are said to give such ghosts temporary relief. A thief might be reborn as a pauper, and a generous donor may be reborn as a prince. Yet gender provides one of the most insidious allegories of all.

In Tibetan idiom, women are seven lifetimes behind men. Women must accumulate the merit of seven additional lifetimes before they can be reborn as men.[27] The proverb persists despite a rather dubious logic which begs several questions. If it always takes seven more rebirths, how can any woman ever be reborn as a man? Could excessive virtue propel a woman into a male rebirth in the next rebirth, allowing her to skip the other six rebirths? Why do women categorically have less merit than men if gender is irrelevant to enlightenment? The question of whether it is possible to gain enlightenment in the female body has plagued authors since the time of the Buddha. While doctrine offers numerous contradictory answers to this question, Buddhist practices are far less ambiguous. Buddhist merit-making practices suggest that women are triply handicapped. Their lesser store of merit from past lives explains not only why they suffer in this life but also why they have fewer opportunities to improve their prospects for the next life. Ritual practices surrounding childbirth and fertility of house and field specify the female body as inferior or impure. Household and village rites of expiation and purification reinforce a gender hierarchy in which the female is defective or inferior.

The bottom line is clear. No Buddhist in her right mind desires a female body. The fifteenth-century Tibetan ethicist Tsongkhapa offers a teaching which indexes sex, race, and family according to moral virtue. His chapter on *karma* explains that a body with sufficient virtue will be easily recognized as being of "consummate color" and "consummate lineage" and consummate gender or male.[28] The implicit sexism and racism of this Tibetan perspective on merit have been studiously overlooked thus far. Tsongkhapa's text does not identify which color or lineage signals virtue, yet it unambiguously finds the male body to signal virtue. Male bodies are rewards for past merit or virtue; female bodies are to be reviled and rejected. Many of my informants in Zangskar repeated this view when they expressed the wish to be reborn as a male. Villagers make merit by donating to monks in the hope of being reborn as males or monks at the top of the social hierarchy. Most laypeople seem uninterested in deconstructing a system of patronage from which they hope to benefit one day.

While all Buddhists need merit, there are many different ways to earn it. In local idiom, it takes merit to make merit. In fact, merit and capital are concentrated at the top of a hierarchy which is at once social and moral. The amount of merit produced by a given act of generosity is relative to the amount of merit of the donor and the recipient of any act of generosity. As such monks, who have the most merit, are also the most worthy recipients of gifts. Indeed, the more virtuous the monk, the greater the merit accrued by the donor. Ironically, those monks seen as the most virtuous— like the Dalai Lama—acquire the largest streams of wealth. They are given palaces which they will never inhabit, even as nearby nuns struggle to subsist. The lay donors and monastics caught up in the economy of merit systematically misrecognize this concentration of wealth. Of course, villagers can and do decide to give to the poor or other worthy recipients.[29] Yet such donations have yet to displace the steady flow of patronage toward the richest monks or monasteries. The Thai monk Buddhadasa once attacked this problem in merit making as follows:

> What is called merit or merit making is for those caught up in the world because it tempts people to lose their way in the grasping of the senses. . . . Indeed of all the things that tempt people to be led astray and preoccupied nothing exceeds merit making. Nothing is so destructive of human freedom.[30]

This is a strong condemnation of a central Buddhist practice followed by laypeople and monastics around the world. To unravel the paradox of merit and hierarchy, one must look at Buddhist monasticism from the bottom up and inside out. Wealth is neither necessary nor sufficient for making merit through generosity *(dana)*. If the self and its attachments are given away, generosity need not involve wealth at all. Yet such purity of motivations is difficult to attain. Numerous parables imply that a small gift of pure detachment earns more merit than a large gift without the proper motivation. Yet numerous practices index social or economic capital to the symbolic capital of merit. More often, making merit reinforces social hierarchies. While the rich and monks can earn merit by donating or performing elaborate ritual spectacles, the nuns, laywomen, and the poor lack the ritual skills or wealth to earn merit in such prestigious ways. The latter may make merit through mechanical means such as praying, prostrating, circumambulating. Of course, rich men or monks can and do fast, while even the poor can make small ritual donations. Yet there are real constraints within the economy of merit. Nuns lack the ordination status and the training to perform certain rites. In the end, merit making reifies the very forms of social difference that doctrine denies.

Although there is evidence of subversion and evasion, there is less resistance than might be expected in the local economy of merit. Nuns and laypeople might grumble at having to perform chores for the monastery, but they rarely refused. Social critics who were outspoken about government corruption showed little impetus to reform the monastic order. Corrupt or promiscuous monks were defamed in private but tolerated in public. Monks accused of adultery or rape were disrobed and fined, but with minimal public outrage. Cases of lapsed celibacy hardly shook the authority of the monastery. There were few public denunciations such as those which wracked Buddhists in Boulder or Catholics in Boston more recently. The hegemony of monks, however, is always partial and contingent. The competition for social and symbolic capital seems to be intensifying. In Zangskar and Ladakh, monasteries are hemorrhaging monks, while nunneries are packed to overflowing with new recruits. Although the ratio of nuns to monks continues to rise, it is far too early to tell if the glass ceiling within monasticism will disappear.

CHAPTER

2

Locating Buddhism
in Zangskar

The last surviving founder of Zangskar's largest nunnery has told the story of her pilgrimage to Tibet many times. There are not many monastics alive today who, like Yeshe, have had the privilege of being ordained in Tibet by the state's third-highest ecclesiastic at the time, the abbot of Ganden monastery and head of the Dalai Lama's own Gelgugpa sect. Only a few short years after Yeshe's journey, Chinese shelling reduced Ganden monastery—which housed over five thousand monks in 1959—to a pile of rubble while the Dalai Lama and thousands of Tibetans, including the abbot of Ganden, fled to India. Although a war between India and China closed the border in 1962, refugees have continued to make their way out of Tibet to join a community of exiles who live in scattered settlements across north and south India, including Yeshe's home state of Jammu and Kashmir. Within the space of a single generation, the millennium-old traffic between Tibet and Kashmir was largely shut down. Buddhist monks from Ladakh and Zangskar no longer travel to Tibet itself for advanced studies, but set out for lengthy sojourns in monastic institutions reestablished by Tibetan refugees in India that resemble but do not replace those of historic Tibet.

It was early spring in 1956 when Ani Yeshe and her companions set off for Tibet from their homeland of Zangskar in the newly created Indian state of Jammu and Kashmir. Yeshe, Deskyid, and Angmo left Karsha village with a monk who was to become the first abbot of the nunnery they founded upon their return. Their lengthy preparations included weeks of grinding grain and churning butter which they would carry on their trip, working in other people's fields to raise money, and borrowing additional sums from relatives. The three Karsha nuns left their homes in late November after the harvest was finished, each carrying a bedroll, thirty kilos of flour, ten kilos of butter, hard biscuits, Tibetan tea, rock salt, lumps of cane sugar, spices, and a bit of cash—somewhere between two hundred and five hundred rupees. The flour and butter weighed heavy during the steep climb up the Shingo La and the Rohtang La, so they left half of their food supplies with Lahauli villagers living just below the Rohtang pass. They planned to return by the same route and pick up the food the following spring. Taking just enough to tide them over in times of need and to have an offering at Lhasa's Jokhang temple, they set off for the hot and dusty plains. Lacking Hindi but clearly dressed as renunciants, they earned free passage from conductors who gave up trying to communicate with them. After traveling clear across the subcontinent, they turned north into Sikhim and headed for the border of Tibet at Phari, known for its roaming bandits and dangerous winds. Yeshe still recalls the frostbite she got on the Tibetan plateau in January. They could not understand how Tibetan villagers could be so stingy until they got to Lhasa and saw the hordes of pilgrims who had come and begged along similar routes before them. Yet the generosity of the Lhasa urbanites amazed them. Every monastic attending the prayer festival received daily rations of barley flour, butter, and tea, regardless of provenance or sectarian affiliation.

When they finally reached the frozen cluster of whitewashed cells at Ganden monastery in central Tibet, the nuns sought out a monk who was purported to hail from their fatherland *(pha yul)* of Zangskar. When they reached the cell of Ngawang Tharpa, neither the nuns nor their host could know that he was fated some thirty years later to become the most beloved abbot of a nunnery they had not yet founded. Their dusty robes and emaciated faces may have betrayed their lengthy journey over treacherous passes, frozen rivers, and the scorching Indian plains. Although Ngawang invited them into the lodgings he shared with a Tibetan monk, the nuns declined his invitation to stay for a meal. They knew that the room could not be Ngawang's own, given the sophisticated Tibetan furniture and rugs which littered the cell. Having given him the eagerly awaited news from home, they asked him for a tour of the monastery.

Like them, Ngawang had left Zangskar with just enough butter for the journey, although it had been nearly fifteen years ago. He had worked for months to earn money and butter for the journey, gathering and then selling or bartering local plants used as dye. He came to Tibet in stages, relying on the generosity of strangers. After working as a laborer building roads in Kulu and stopping to do prostrations in Bodhgaya where a kind Englishwoman gave him a monk's robe, he landed in Sikhim. With his supplies exhausted, he stopped to read texts for a rich Tibetan merchant. The patron gave him some advice on finding a companion from his homeland. He left his tattered Zangskari boots by the roadside as a signal to passing countrymen. Soon enough, a trader from Ngawang's hometown stopped and offered to accompany him to Shigatse. After joining several of his countrymen at Tashilhunpo monastery, Ngawang went on to study for his Geshe degree at Ganden monastery, despite the fact that he was in his thirties. He also took a job tutoring a burly Zangskari monk who served as one of the Dalai Lama's bodyguards *(ldab ldob)*. He met the Dalai Lama several times and finally completed his Geshe *(dge bshes)* degree by defeating Lhasa's foremost monks in debate. When he returned to Ganden for a blessing, he had been invited to receive further oral teachings *(lung)* on the Tantric deity Vajrasattva *(rdo rje chang)*.

After finishing his tale, Ngawang accompanied the nuns through Ganden's chapels, explaining how the Tibetan ethicist Tsongkhapa had founded Ganden and the Great Prayer Festival they were soon to see in Lhasa. The nuns were relieved to hear they had reached Lhasa in time for the festival, when any merit they made would be multiplied a thousand-fold. Ngawang suggested that they join an upcoming ordination ceremony which the abbot of Ganden would perform during the festival. When Yeshe protested that she was unworthy, Ngawang insisted that her merit would outweigh any ritual mistake. Thus Yeshe and her two companions—as well as two other Zangskari nuns also in Lhasa—were ordained along with several hundred young monks by the abbot of Ganden. Amid the pomp, Yeshe noted that her Zangskari contingent outnumbered the four Tibetan nuns also receiving ordination that same day. The nine nuns sat at the tail end of the assembly in Lhasa. They were dwarfed by a sea of monks who sat between them and the raised dais where a quorum of monks sat in resplendent robes. After the ordination, Yeshe and her companions returned to Zangskar. They had to struggle over two formidable passes in the late spring. Getting up long before dawn to walk on the crust of the snow, they broke through to their waists after the sun rose and the crust would no longer hold them. They ate the rations they'd stored in the village below the Rohtang La while waiting for the weather to clear for a safe passage over the pass. They wept when they saw their familiar valley.

On the day that they arrived in Karsha, Yeshe's father rode down to the river in a rare show of deference to his daughter, now a nun. Her father dismounted and allowed Yeshe to ride back into her village like a new bride. For the next few weeks, the nuns were feted by villagers eager for news of the outside world. In their nine-month pilgrimage to Buddhist holy sites in India and Tibet, Yeshe and her companions had seen more of the world than many of the village women would see in a lifetime. Their unusual ordination by the head of the Dalai Lama's own Gelugpa sect gave them a new religious status. It also inspired them to found the first full-fledged community of nuns in Karsha village. While their village had been Buddhist for over a millennium, there is no record of its ever having housed a community of nuns. Even more surprisingly, after five short decades, Karsha has become the largest and most ritually active nunnery in Zangskar. The desire of women to follow the celibate path was hardly lacking.

This book is about the nunnery they founded and its survival. It describes the choices and constraints faced by many of the nuns who have come after Yeshe. It is framed by an important premise. To understand how and why women still become nuns in the early twenty-first century, it is important to appreciate the society being renounced. In fact, nuns can no more reject their society or culture than they can cast off the female bodies they inhabit. The impossibility of escaping sexuality and gender makes the rejection of maternity and femininity all the more interesting. The choice of celibacy can only take place within a social context. As such, monasticism offers less a rejection of society than its radical transformation. The community of nuns explored herein represents an alternative society rather than its antithesis.

The social, economic, and political dynamics which produce the economy of merit are critical to understanding Buddhism in Zangskar today. Buddhist monasticism requires a network of social and cultural practices as much as a self-generating set of beliefs or texts. These practices are concerned with reciprocity as much as with ritual or renunciation. The monastic enterprise is based as much on political and social conditions as on individual and collective discipline. What is involved in being Buddhist in Zangskar today? Although Buddhism has been threatened and nearly extinguished in Kashmir, it has produced a flourishing civilization within the remote reaches of this region. Although more than half of the people living in eastern Jammu and Kashmir practice "Tibetan Buddhism," most are not Tibetan refugees. The villagers in Ladakh and Zangskar have ancestors who have been making merit and tilling monastic land for generations. By what historical accident have they come to be citizens of India and its state Jammu and Kashmir?

How Zangskar Landed in Jammu and Kashmir

Straddling the world's highest mountain chain on the "rooftop of the world," Zangskar lies just west of a valley—Kashmir—long regarded as both gateway and jewel of the Indian subcontinent. After being plundered for centuries by Hindu, Turkish, Tartar, Mughal, and Afghan rulers, Kashmir came under the rule of the powerful Sikh emperor Ranjit Singh by 1819. Ranjit Singh was assisted in his conquest of Kashmir by one of his own vassal princes, a Dogra ruler named Gulab Singh. Gulab Singh had a rapacious appetite of his own for conquest as he overran the kingdoms of Zangskar, Ladakh, and Baltistan to the east and north. Gulab's forces finally overextended themselves and his most famous general, Zorawar Singh, perished on the Tibetan plateau in 1842. Shortly afterward, the Sikhs became overextended in their war with the British in 1846. Gulab Singh cleverly allied himself with the victors—this time the British—and managed to purchase the entire territory which the defeated Sikhs were forced to cede to the British.[1] The birth of Jammu and Kashmir allowed Gulab Singh to tax Zangskar and Ladakh as ruthlessly as Kashmiris had been taxed before. His forceful policies of extraction in Zangskar led inhabitants to seek work in neighboring Lahaul, before the Permanent Settlement of 1908 allotted land to individual tillers. The British and Dogra rulers acquired a vast archive of knowledge about Jammu and Kashmir as they tallied every resource—natural and man-made. The calculation of wealth, caste, and religious affiliation late in the British Raj would have fateful consequences for the subsequent partition of India.[2]

By the time of Partition in 1947, Jammu and Kashmir was as large as the United Kingdom minus Wales. The state capital, Srinagar, was just under half the size of Delhi, the capital of the British Raj, in 1921. Even more than most of the 500-plus princely states who wound up in either India or Pakistan, princely Kashmir was ridden with internal inconsistencies at the time of partition. Albeit ruled by a Hindu maharaja who presided over the Hindu-majority area of Jammu, just over half of the population lived in the Muslim-majority Kashmir Valley. Yet half of the state geographically lay to the east, where Buddhists predominated. The maharaja dithered indecisively about whether to join India or Pakistan when a large group of armed tribesmen from northwest Pakistan stormed into the Kashmir Valley in late October of 1947.[3] After signing the article of accession to India, the maharaja saw his lovely kingdom torn apart by two armies who had until recently served the same ruler. A group of Gilgit Scouts hoisted the Pakistani flag on November 1, before raising recruits and proceeding to march up the Indus River in the direction of Ladakh. By the time of the cease-fire in January of 1949, it was only daring ingenuity which had kept Zangskar and Ladakh from falling into Pakistan's hands.[4]

The entire defense of Ladakh and Zangskar hung on a slender thread for most of the war between India and Pakistan. A brave major from the nearby region of Lahaul, Prithi Chand, marched through blizzards from Srinagar to organize the defense of Ladakh. Although it took Chand's forces almost twenty days to reach the capital of Ladakh, Leh, on foot, they quickly organized the construction of an airstrip—using men and donkeys but no machines—and arranged for the defense of the region as a force of five hundred Gilgit raiders advanced on the city. By late May the Gilgit forces were within thirty kilometers of the capital. On May 24, the first Indian plane landed in Leh—albeit only by tying an extra engine on the wing of what one major general I interviewed called a "hyper Dakota." The plane bore General Thimmaya, who only stayed an hour for fear of being stranded in an exceedingly vulnerable spot. When a few Indian reinforcements arrived under the command of Lieutenant Kaul—a man with only one year's service—Leh was nearly lost, but Chand, Kaul, and their brave but inexperienced men managed to defend Ladakh with the help of locals like the fifteen-year-old Ladakhi colonel, Tsewang Rinchen. July saw the arrival of added Indian troops who had marched on foot from Manali, some 450 kilometers south of Leh. Yet the tide of the war only turned from defense to offense in late October of 1948, when the Indian army finally retook the Zoji La pass from the raiders. When Indian forces retook the town of Kargil on November 24, the line of defense finally stretched from Leh to Srinagar. But unrecorded in most war histories and unbeknownst to the soldiers defending Ladakh, a small force of Gilgit raiders had penetrated deep into Zangskar, where they would be lodged until June of 1949—six months after the UN cease-fire.

When three dozen Gilgit raiders arrived in Zangskar during the sixth Tibetan month (August?) of 1948, the locals were alarmed. As the news of the soldiers' presence spread like wind between the villages, people began locking up their houses and fleeing to the high-pasture huts. In Karsha as elsewhere, villagers stored their valuables—religious scrolls, statues, sacred texts, jewelry, brass utensils, and other ritual implements—in boxes which were buried beneath piles of manure in the stables. Several of the women chose to wear their dowry jewels or turquoise headdresses when fleeing their houses. While a few able-bodied men stayed behind, most of the villagers fled to the tiny stone shelters on the high pasture where the livestock are taken to graze. Entire villages remained anxiously in cramped quarters, waiting for news from below.

Abbi Yeshe still recalls how a few of the Gilgit raiders came up to the high-pasture huts where she had gone with her family. When her father spotted the soldiers in their gray uniforms, he ran to tell Yeshe to hide. Grabbing all the butter she could and stuffing it into her wicker basket, Yeshe ran off with her friends, the daughter and wife of the local Zaildar, or tax collector. They ran up the riverbed and hid behind a huge boulder, where they tried to bury the skins of butter under stones. Yeshe saw her father come out of the hut, greet the soldiers, and then begin gesticulating toward a distant plain which housed abandoned fields named after the wife of the epic hero Gesar. As the soldiers trotted off, the villagers fled to the nearby village of Yulang far down on the plain, fearing the wrath of the soldiers whom they had just duped.

Several nuns told tales of surprising kindness in the soldiers that is unheard of in the ongoing terrorism wrought in Kashmir today. Yeshe described how an elderly lady in Yulang—the grandmother of a younger nun named Garkyid—was so frightened when the soldiers arrived that she jumped into the grain storage bin *(bang nga)*. When the soldiers removed the stone covers of the bin and saw her turquoise headdress, they ripped it off but did her no further damage. Kundze told how the soldiers came to her house in Yulang shortly after her mother had given birth to her brother. Although her father begged his wife to flee, her mother didn't want to leave the house because of birth pollution. Her fear of violating ritual proscriptions was greater than her fear of soldiers. When the soldiers broke into her house, her husband jumped off the balcony and ran away. The soldiers who came into the bedroom saw her cradling something under the blanket, which they assumed to be her jewelry. Ripping off the blanket, they saw her infant. In response they merely patted her on the shoulder, before leaving with the guns they had propped near the door. Dechen explained that her grandmother, a widow with no sons, was not afraid to deliver her obligatory share of firewood to the soldiers stationed at the old Dogra fort in Ufti village. Although other houses sent a male member to deliver the monthly firewood tax, Dechen's grandmother recalled that the soldiers always let her warm her hands at their hearth. There were no stories of rape or other horrific abuses which had plunged other border regions into panic and terror during this same period.

Yeshe's most vivid memory was of the way in which the soldiers took one goat from every house in Karsha before killing the animals in cold blood. The Gilgit raiders faced little resistance from the frightened villagers, who supplied them with the beer and meat they demanded. The soldiers lived for some time in Karsha, where their most prominent resident, the Zaildar, collected five sheep and ten kilograms of butter from every household under his jurisdiction.[5] Eventually, a small party of Gilgit raiders forced the Zaildar, his assistant, and the headman from nearby Langmi to accompany them to Kargil, where they would negotiate the new taxes to be paid henceforth. As the men traveled up the beaten track toward the Pentse La pass, they may have suspected that they were being taken to their deaths. When they tried to escape one night just beyond the tiny hamlet of Lungmur, the Zaildar was shot while the assistant had hidden himself by the river bank. He was soon surrounded and forced at gunpoint to carry the body until he was waist deep in the river, where he too was shot. The Langmi headman saw these events from behind a boulder, before he crept off and fled back home, where he quickly spread the news. The king of Padum and the two highest monks in the valley, Bakula Rinpoche and Stagna Rinpoche, had already fled Zangskar shortly after the soldiers' arrival. Yet the king of Zangla continued to cooperate with the Gilgit raiders. In late fall, when the streams had subsided and it was safe to proceed along the treacherous Jumlam route with its 108 river crossings, he sent a group of men on foot to Leh. The men returned in midwinter leading a group of Indian soldiers down the frozen river gorge. After defeating an advance party of Gilgit raiders in a skirmish at the mouth of the Zangskar river gorge in Pidmo, the Indian soldiers marched to Karsha.

Yeshe described the arrival of the column of Indian or "Hindustani" soldiers in Karsha village as vividly as if it occurred yesterday. The women, who were so excited they had not slept all night, came up onto their roofs in their finest dresses to welcome the soldiers with smoldering plates of juniper incense and pots of their freshest curd. The monks came to the roof of the monastery with cymbals clanging and long horns blaring, greeting the soldiers like a visiting dignitary or high monk. After being hosted in Karsha for a few days, the soldiers marched across the valley, where they commandeered a house in Pipiting. In the meantime, the Gilgit raiders had fled to the Stagrimo monastery perched high up an open hillside above Padum. From this vantage point, they proved virtually unassailable for the next few months. With the clandestine support of Muslims in Padum, the raiders fended off occasional attacks from the Indian side. Several informants described the stalemate that ensued. The Indian officers took secret bribes from Muslims in Padum not to harm the Gilgit raiders, while the commanding officer of the raiders defected before being summarily shot by Indian forces. In early June of 1949, a platoon from the Ladakhi Home Guard under the command of Ladakh's hereditary Minister or Kalon, Tsewang Rigdzin, marched over the Pentse La pass to announce that a cease-fire had been declared six months earlier. The Kalon forced a few civilian collaborators who had joined the raiders to be extradited to Pakistan, against their own will and that of their families. The Gilgit raiders readily surrendered, pleased that their dreadful sojourn in Zangskar was over. The war in Zangskar was over as quietly as it had begun.

The Politics of Being Buddhist

As the generation that lived through Partition is passing away, the events that split the state of Jammu and Kashmir have been overlaid by other more recent wars. In the space of only half a century, India has fought four wars with Pakistan (1947, 1965, 1970, 1999) and one six-week war with China in 1962. By the beginning of the twenty-first century, Jammu and Kashmir lay fragmented between three nations: India, Pakistan, and China. India holds one-half (39,000 square miles) of the state, while Pakistan claims a third (30,000 square miles) and China another fifth (17,000 square miles). At present, the Indian state of Jammu and Kashmir lies nestled up against both the Tibetan plateau and Pakistan's Northern Areas. The only border exempt from warfare in this century lies to the south, against the neighboring Indian states of Himachal Pradesh and the Punjab. The eastern border of Jammu and Kashmir runs along Tibet's Northern Plain or Changthang, coming within a few days' walk of the holy Mount Kailash, home to Tantric protective deities as well as to the Hindu deity Siva. To the west and the north, the Line of Control drawn between India

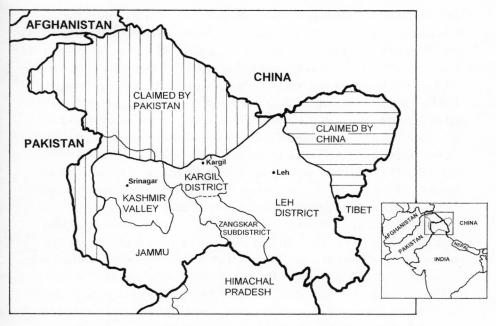

Map 1. Jammu and Kashmir State. The political boundaries of Jammu and Kashmir are contested by three countries, India, Pakistan, and China. Four distinct regions of Indian Jammu and Kashmir can be identified: Kashmir Valley, Jammu, Kargil District, and Leh District (the last two are also known as Ladakh). *(Kai Gutschow)*

and Pakistan divides two armies poised to recapture territory each claims as its own.

Jammu and Kashmir remains one of the most diverse and contested states in India. The state can be divided most crudely into four geographic areas split by both terrain and religious makeup: Kashmir, Jammu, Kargil, and Ladakh of Leh District. The western half of the state includes the Kashmir and Jammu valleys, each encircled by a mountain range. Kargil and Ladakh lie in the isolated and eastern part of the state, tucked between the folds of the Greater and Lesser Himalayan ranges. The inhospitable terrain has been a mixed blessing. While the forbidding ranges and high passes have kept Islamic terrorism at bay, they have also hindered development and infrastructure. More than half of the state's ten million inhabitants live in Kashmir Valley, which is now over 99 percent Muslim because of the exodus of Hindus in the wake of terrorism and militancy after 1989. Slightly less than half the population resides in Jammu, which was 66 percent Hindu in 1981. Kargil District and Ladakh—officially known as Leh District after 1979—each account for only 1 percent of the state's population but together make up half of the state's land mass. Both Kargil and Leh districts each have populations around 115,000, albeit with symmetrical religious breakdowns.[6] While Kargil's population was three-fourths Muslim—mostly Shia—and one-fourth Buddhist in 1981, Leh District was four-fifths Buddhist and one-fifth Muslim. The southern half of Kargil District, known as Zangskar, is home to a population of 12,000 people, of whom 95 percent are Buddhists and the remainder are Sunni Muslims.

Both religion and region are more salient and resilient forms of identity than the nation or the state.[7] In Zangskari idiom, there is little expression of allegiance or identity with the nation as an imagined community. *Yul* can mean land, village, or the homeland of Zangskar. Yet it is rarely used to refer to India or even Jammu and Kashmir. The terms Indian *(rgya gar pa)* or Kashmiri *(ka jul pa)* are used to signal others who live south or west of Zangskar. A trip to Delhi is known as "going to India," while a trip to Srinagar is referred to as "going to Kashmir." More abstract notions of belonging to the state or nation have less relevance in a culture dominated by regional, village, or household-level identities. Local idiom also preserves a sharp boundary between faiths. Buddhists are called "insiders" *(nang pa)*, while non-Buddhists, especially Muslims, are called "outsiders" *(phyi pa)*.

Globalization has not meant homogenization in the multicultural and polyglot state of Jammu and Kashmir. Urdu is the official state language, but the inhabitants of Leh and Kargil speak a range of Tibetan and Indo-Iranian dialects including: Ladakhi, Zangskari, modern Tibetan, Balti, Shina, and Brogpa, which can be written in Tibetan or Arabic. Ethnic identity is fiercely contested because of the affirmative action laws which made certain groups eligible for the highly contested status of Scheduled Tribe (ST). The eight official tribal groups declared in 1989—Balti, Beda, Bot, Drokpa, Changpa, Gara, Mon, and Purigpa—made up almost nine-tenths of the combined population of Leh and Kargil districts, but only a tiny fraction of the state population.[8] While federally mandated quotas set aside jobs and university seats for the members of these tribal groups, such quotas also perpetuate the stereotype of tribals as uneducated or "backward" in metropolitan discourse. The tribal label has exacerbated caste and class divisions, as the wealthier members of these groups manipulate a label intended to help the most vulnerable. Caste replicates class, as blacksmiths and other outcastes still lack a voice within their Buddhist communities and its dominant institution, the monastery.

Religion remains a powerful and divisive force. Yet it is cross-cut by further divisions of sect, class, and language. Despite the political rhetoric of communalism, Buddhists and Muslims in the region are hardly homogenous groups. Buddhist and Muslim farmers in Zangskar may have more in common with each other than with urban elites of the same faith in Leh or Srinagar. Shia farmers living in rural parts of Kargil District may have little social traffic with Sunni elites in Srinagar, who share neither their language nor their poverty. Yet politics is hardly irrelevant. The Muslims in Leh and Kargil Districts may have disavowed a more radical Islamist stance, yet their politicians adopt an identity politics that pits Muslims against Buddhist. Both the Buddhists and the Muslims perceive themselves as minorities or subalterns in relation to the state or the nation. While the Buddhists in Zangskar live in a district and a state dominated by Muslims, the tiny community of Sunnis in Zangskar is surrounded by a sea of Buddhists in a district dominated by Shias. Finally, the Shias who predominate in Kargil District hardly count within a state largely run by Sunni elites. Both Buddhist and Muslim communities in Zangskar and Ladakh have been marginalized by state and national governments. Their common struggle against systematic neglect and corruption has merely intensified their mistrust of one another.

The international news portrays Jammu and Kashmir as a theater of conflict, between two nations, two religions, or the liberal and extreme wings of a single faith. The Muslim villagers who face intermittent shelling along the 740-kilometer Line of Control (LoC) between India and Pakistan bear little love for Pakistan. Yet the psychological toll of imminent warfare over the last decades has scarred civilians as much as military personnel. The soldiers from both nations posted along the Siachen glacier share the dubious distinction of having survived a battlefield where most of the deaths come from altitude or cold. A year after India and Pakistan each tested nuclear bombs in May of 1998, then Chief of Army Staff Pervez Musharraf masterminded an invasion of troops which penetrated deep into Indian territory, eluding detection for almost three months. When Indian soldiers were finally alerted by local herdsmen, Pakistani troops had seized nearly 1,500 square kilometers of Indian territory. Although the

Pakistan government initially denied knowledge of the invasion, Indian intelligence reports confirmed dead soldiers wearing uniforms from Pakistan's Northern Light Infantry. Three short months after Pakistan's prime minister Nawaz Sharif signed a cease-fire with India under pressure from Washington, Musharraf deposed Sharif and shamed him for being "soft" on Kashmir. More recently, the American war on terrorism has unearthed reports of numerous terrorist training camps in Pakistan, which have drawn Arab and Afghan mujahedeen into the Kashmir struggle since 1989.[9]

The storyline of regional conflict hardly does justice to the highly constructed nature of religious and political identities in the region. Most Buddhists and Muslims in Zangskar and Ladakh remain largely united in their opposition to the freedom fighters who are trying to "liberate" Kashmir from India. Graffiti scrawled on walls along the road to Leh city in 1989 sent an unambiguous message: "Kashmiri Dogs Go Home." Local politicians capitalized on Ladakh's Buddhist and marginal identity while pushing for autonomy from Kashmir. Although the movement soon alienated Buddhists from Muslims, it hardly reflected a primordial split between Buddhists and Muslims.[10] Local politicians deliberately used violent incidents between Buddhist and Muslim youths to further the autonomy movement. When the police shot two Buddhists in the courtyard of the local monastery in 1989, Buddhist youths went on a rampage, destroying Kashmiri and government buses, taxis, and other property. The Ladakhi Buddhist Association then imposed a three-year social boycott on Muslim stores, punishing collaborators with beatings or fines. Yet villagers resisted and subverted the process. Although Ladakh finally received some political and financial autonomy by being granted Hill Council Status in 1995, the development of the region continues to lag.

The Zangskari autonomy movement was plagued by even less consensus.

> Zanskar area is ban for tourists from 10 August 1995. So please go back or you face the consequences. We are not against you. We are doing only against the public administration for our various demands. It's the decision of all Zanskar people.

The politicians who wrote this proclamation hardly canvassed numerous fellow villagers who earn their living from the tourist industry. Although some villagers subverted the plan to expel all tourists from Zangskar, several stone-throwing youths surrounded a hapless group of tourists at the government-sponsored Dak Tourist Bungalow. When the Indian army took the tourists over the pass to Kargil, the press garbled the headlines as a story of Buddhist "hostages" in Zangskar.[11] Yet the medium helped the message, as Zangskari leaders could announce their local demands—including autonomy from Kargil, the completion of an all-weather road from Leh to Padum along the Chadar gorge, and a separate voting constituency in the state assembly. Monks and village headmen studiously conscripted villagers to serve in the daily sit-in protests *(dharna)* held in Padum, Zangskar's headquarters. Those households who refused to send a member were fined. Although sporadic protests continued, a decade later none of the demands had been fulfilled. As in Ladakh, the movement was spearheaded by communalist Buddhists—some of whom were allied with the right-wing Hindu party known as the BJP which has ruled India since 1996.

The split between Buddhists and Muslims in Zangskar has only escalated in recent years. Buddhists took to the streets in protest when three monks were killed by Kashmiri terrorists along the desolate highway leading into Zangskar in 2000. While Buddhist politicians rallied to decry the militants, the army took note and established semipermanent camps in Zangskar for the first time. The same year a grazing dispute pitted Muslims against Buddhists in Padum and its environs, where Muslim households usually finish their harvest sooner than Buddhist ones. This is due to Muslim inheritance practices, which have left individual households with fewer fields. Tensions came to a head when several Muslim households ignored customary law by letting their livestock graze before the Buddhists had finished their harvest. When some cows accidentally strayed onto the ripe fields owned by Buddhists, Buddhists pelted the cows with stones. The Muslims demanded reparation and the Buddhists refused to pay, insisting that Muslims first pay for crops the cows had eaten. Neither side gave in and individuals on both sides began refusing to attend each other's weddings. In 2002 a physical scuffle between Buddhist headmen and Muslim shopkeepers over a plot of government land escalated the communal conflict once again. Even development projects have taken a communal flavor; Muslim leaders were noticeably absent from celebrations inaugurating the construction of the Chadar road to Leh in the summer of 2002.

These communal struggles in Zangskar and Ladakh have spawned increased conservatism and hardened the boundaries between Buddhist and

Muslim communities. Yet not without resistance. As in Sri Lanka or Egypt, the effort to restore a "corrupted" faith to its original and pristine purity evokes nostalgia as much as conflict.[12] While mullahs in Kargil push more orthodox forms of Islam, Ladakhi politicians are attempting to cleanse Buddhism of its aberrant practices.[13] Politicians have used the radio to push for bans on polyandry, beer drinking, and ancestor worship. Yet such attempts have largely failed in rural areas despite heavy pressure from monks and urban elites. The summertime circumambulations of fields in Leh and its environs have been purged of alcohol, and wintertime ceremonies commemorating the dead *(shi mi)* have been curtailed for being un-Buddhist. Yet the same rites still inspire inebriation and merit making in Zangskar. Polyandry has died a more natural death, albeit mostly due to economic opportunity. A rising number of nonagrarian jobs have led to a decline in polyandry as much as in the numbers of young men who still seek out the monastic life.

Monastics and Modernity in Zangskar

The monastic vocation remains a matter of renunciation as well as reciprocity. Roughly 2 percent of Zangskar's population are monks or nuns, who live in eight monasteries and nine nunneries.[14] While there are three Kagyud monasteries, the remaining five monasteries and all nine nunneries follow the Gelug sect. Zangskar supports one of the highest ratios of nuns to monks in the Himalayan realm. The fact that one-fourth of Zangskar's monastics are nuns may be due as much to local sponsorship as to the lack of other opportunities for educated women. Moreover, the agrarian economy depends on the valuable labor of nuns who sustain their family farms as much as the Buddhist economy of merit. The monasteries of Zangskar have more land and wealth than any household or local institutions in Zangskar. While individual monks are some of the wealthier members of society, nuns fall among the poorest.

Both the monastery and the nunnery offer social mobility, albeit less cash than a civil service job. Nunneries offer women a religious and scholastic path that is barely possible in lay life. Although women have taken up jobs in nursing and teaching, these positions remain highly restricted because of the failing state economy, inflation of educational standards, and corruption. Nunneries offer numerous opportunities for travel, religious study, and making merit. Yet enrollment in the nunneries suffers due to limited financial support, lack of residential cells, and limited educational resources. Rural nunneries have a hard time recruiting advanced teachers or obtaining modern Tibetan textbooks, while cosmopolitan Tibetan nunneries in other Indian states or Nepal are so overcrowded they tend to reject most applicants from Zangskar or Ladakh outright. Yet feminist initiatives have provided funding and impetus for new nunneries, or an expansion of existing ones across the region.

Although the monks' career is desirable, it has declined in economic value given the recent rise in tourist and government jobs. The rewards of monasticism include a decent modern education in the local monastic schools funded by a federal agency known as the Central Institute for Buddhist Studies (CIBS). This agency has only recently begun to support a single nunnery school in Ladakh. The most ambitious monks leave Zangskar as soon as they can secure a coveted spot in one of the Tibetan exile monasteries, which still maintain dormitories for "west Tibetan" students as they did in historic Tibet. Those monks who excel in scholastic or ritual training may be chosen to study for the advanced Geshe degree or for a ritual tour abroad making *mandalas*. Yet all monks who go south for study will be exposed to a cosmopolitan Indian life rather removed from their rural Himalayan culture.[15] Many of the monks fail to return to Zangskar, and those that do often experience some culture shock or simply leave the order of monks.

The ideals of voluntary celibacy and asceticism are losing ground in Zangskar's modernizing economy. Disenfranchised young men from rural backgrounds who once chose the monastic vocation may decide to serve their country instead of their religion. The military and civil service are the region's largest employers, although petty trade and tourism offer cash incomes as well. The demand for military recruits rose after the Kargil war of 1999. As radio announcements spread the message that educational standards for new recruits had been dropped from tenth to eighth grade, scores of desperate young men jumped to apply. Those who had not forged their educational certificates and who passed the cursory literacy and physical exams were lucky enough to earn a place in the local branch of the Indian army known as the Ladakh Scouts.

The cash economy is exploding. When I first arrived in Zangskar in 1989, it was rare to see a single truck arrive in Padum in late autumn. By the year 2000, taxis and scores of newly arriving trucks ferried locals across the valley daily between Karsha and Zangskar's administrative center, Padum.

Padum town has mushroomed as new construction springs up every week of the busy summer building season. More and more families have at least one member earning a cash income. Trade, tourism, and the military are dominated by men; women tend to work in teaching, nursing, and midwifery. Unlike Leh District, where women run most of the roadside vending stalls, Zangskari and Kargili women rarely work as informal vendors.

The military may provide camouflage fatigues, status, and swagger, but the tourist industry offers young men cash and hip clothes. Traders who once brought stone pots and apricots from Baltistan and wool or salt from Tibet have been replaced by backpackers and spiritual seekers bearing gifts of worn-out fleece jackets and trekking boots. Clad in neon-colored Patagonia, these outsiders march resolutely through the landscape or speed by in Tata Sumo jeeps. They are a source of amusement and income for most elderly locals, with whom they can barely converse. Padum alone offers proper tourist hostels and enough youths whose English can facilitate more meaningful cross-cultural exchanges. The tea stalls which dot the more remote valleys are run by monks or by students on summer vacation. Leh town caters directly to the international backpacker with cyber cafés, hashish, endless German pastry shops, rooftop garden cafés serving the standard fare of everything from falafel to pasta. Yet Zangskar has yet to make many accommodations for tourists outside of the desultory smattering of shops and decrepit hotels in downtown Padum. The ongoing militancy in Kashmir has curtailed tourism somewhat as adventure companies cancel trips through Kargil, yet the region has continued to gain tourist fame.[16] Several tourists were brutally massacred in the remote valleys between Srinagar and Zangskar in the mid-1990s, while a lone German was abducted and executed by Kashmiri militants just over the Pentse La pass in 2000. The local tourist officer estimated that between six thousand and twenty thousand tourists visited Ladakh every summer in the 1990s, of which perhaps an eighth travel to Zangskar.

Capitalism and consumption are spurred on by Bollywood celluloid and Indian media as much as tourism and trade. Older markers of status have fallen into disuse as have the unpaid vocations of monk, doctor, or astrologer. Traditional markers of status like seating arrangements and deference are rapidly disappearing as cash and consumption become new indices of wealth and power. The conspicuous purchases of motorcycles, televisions, and glass windows are as much competitive displays of power and wealth as ritual donations once were. Traditional hierarchies are collapsing as aristocrats and royals—whose power is largely symbolic—make way for the nouveau riche and government functionaries. The public sector employs people with every conceivable skill or education level. When the first Zangskari villagers became civil servants in the 1950s and 1960s, only aristocrats and educated elites dared apply. There is somewhat more meritocracy now, although the lack of a decent public education system continues to stymie many locals from civil service jobs. In 1992, only one-third of the three hundred civil servants in Zangskar were local, according to one government servant I interviewed. Most of the Zangskaris held menial or semiskilled jobs at the bottom of the salary scale, while Kargilis and Kashmiris held many of the higher posts. Yet education has brought cash incomes and a breakdown of caste boundaries. Discrimination against outcastes like blacksmiths does remain in social and ritual contexts. As more members of the outcaste households advance in their civil service jobs, other villagers are forced to rely on them for basic services like electricity and veterinary visits.

Graduating from secondary school remains exceedingly difficult, given the lack of teachers, books, and skilled instruction in the public schools. Those who do graduate may have passed through bribes or outside tutoring rather than through bookishness. Half of the teachers in Zangskar's thirty-four schools were Zangskari natives in 1992.[17] The teachers who do not live locally often leave Zangskar in November on foot only to return in late May or June, depending on whether the erratic helicopter service arrives. For the Shias from Kargil—who don't eat in Zangskari homes because of pollution beliefs—there is little incentive to stay during the harsh winter months. Most schools are closed for almost half the year as a result of teacher absence, festivals, or agrarian work like harvest and spring watering. The Kashmiri teachers, who are most fluent in the official language of instruction, Urdu, usually cannot speak much Zangskari. Almost 95 percent of all students fail their tenth-class exams.[18] Yet even the few who pass face stiff competition from the glut of graduates in Kargil town—who also have a home advantage in networking or bribing the district officials who administer job openings.

Social mobility and development remain a distant dream for many residents of Kargil District, one of the least populated and poorest districts in India. Funds and materials have been siphoned off by corruption, resulting in a lack of the most basic amenities, including roads, electricity, communication, and medicine. Although educated Zangskaris have bid successfully for development and construction projects, corruption and graft have produced shoddy work. A twenty-year-old hydroelectric project in central Zangskar is yet to be completed, while the three diesel generators serving the central valley of Zangskar often fail for months at a time. A phone system was set up in Padum in 1999, although it only transmits outside Zangskar when its solar-powered satellite system is functioning. Most villagers rely on solar energy and kerosene to power their lamps, radios, and the few televisions found in the central valley. Radio provides news and culture; television offers a slew of bizarre images which cannot undo the everyday reality of poverty and disease.

Deaths from infectious and preventable diseases such as tuberculosis and pneumonia are commonplace. Infant mortality hovers around 250 per thousand, and one-third of all children under the age of five are likely to die.[19] The nearest allopathic dispensary usually requires several days' travel on foot. The single "hospital" in Padum offers a rudimentary set of concrete rooms, no ward, no operating theater, and rarely a resident doctor. Medical shipments arrive once every summer, and many clinics run half the year without supplies.[20] Qualified doctors and nurses are even more scarce. The single doctor in residence is often underqualified or out of station, while the handful of medical assistants and nurses, as well as scores of midwives, usually have no more than two years of postsecondary school training in Urdu. Many doctors and medical assistants do not stay in Zangskar through the winter, when many fatalities occur. Patients often die before the requested emergency helicopter arrives from Leh. While Padum has a sporadic helicopter service during the winter that is often canceled in inclement weather or fog, Leh has daily flights to surrounding Indian cities like Srinagar, Jammu, or Delhi.

Given the inadequacy and unavailability of biomedical treatment, many Zangskari patients prefer to rely on traditional doctors *(am chi)* and healers. Patients can seek a range of complementary treatments from monks, astrologers *(rtsis pa)*, oracles *(lha pa)*, doctors *(am chi)*, and exorcists *(dbon po)*. Each of these discourses of healing—religious, astrological, oracular, and magical—draws on shared idioms about bodily imbalances and a broad Buddhist discourse about causality. *Karma* offers an underlying causality which operates in conjunction with secondary causes *(rkyen)*, such as luck *(spar kha)*, diet, season, astrological causes, demonic forces, and witchcraft. Each of the specialists above may draw on a specific hermeneutic to interpret the secondary or contributing cause of a given ailment. Yet none of the ritual specialists has an exclusive right to any ritual discourse. Monks perform divinations and exorcisms, while astrologers may advise on the appropriate time to take medicines or may perform ritual healings. Unlike in Thailand—where the divide between monks and other ritual specialists was rather clear-cut in Tambiah's (1970) model—Zangskari ritual specialists offer eclectic and overlapping services. There is little attempt to isolate the monks' Tantric rites from more pragmatic ritual services. Indeed, Tantric power is precisely necessary to overcome the array of contributing causes which result in misfortune.

Monks offer the widest array of complementary treatments. They remain the ritual specialist of first choice because of their ritual prowess and range of possible treatments. These treatments include making merit, ritual prophylactives, propitiation, and exorcism. While traditional doctors move from "gentle" herbal mixtures to "fierce" remedies like acupuncture or moxibustion (applying a burning root to the skin), monks begin with peaceful or merit-making rituals before proceeding to more wrathful Tantric rites. The most skilled monks can invoke the highest Tantric protectors to empower ritual expiations and exorcisms—often performed by shamans in other Buddhist societies. The panoply of ritual services which monks provide ensures their income as much as their social power.

Buddhist Landscape and Society

Imagine a landscape of stunning beauty, amazing breadth, yet nearly depopulated. Contorted folds of rock, scree, and sandstone give way to ragged escarpments of snow and ice. Remote glaciers and snowfields feed meandering streams that trickle down narrow gorges and arid glacial fans before joining the larger rivers. Trapped within the Himalayan rain shadow, the region receives its scant precipitation as winter snowfall, when temperatures can drop to −50 degrees Celsius.[21] Blinking, from an airplane, one could miss the pockets of cultivation entirely. The entire population of Ladakh and Zangskar lives clustered in tiny oases of terraced fields neatly built up around accessible tributary streams. Less than 1 percent of Zangskar's area is inhabited or cultivated. Zangskar's 12,000 inhabitants live scattered across over 100 hamlets in a region twice the size of Rhode Island.[22] Lying between 3,300 and 4,500 meters, most hamlets range in size from 40 to 400 people, although the main administrative center has up to 800 permanent residents.

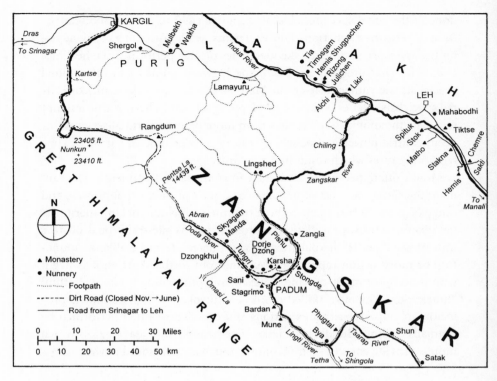

Map 2. Zangskar. The main monasteries and nunneries of Zangskar as well as Ladakh are identified. *(Kai Gutschow)*

Encircled by peaks and passes, Zangskar's territory is a virtual fortress. The central valley lies around the confluence of two major rivers which form the mighty Zangskar River. The Zangskar flows 150 kilometers northward before joining the Indus, or Lion River, as it is known in Tibetan. While the Doda River flows southward into Zangskar from the Pentse La pass which forms the northwest boundary of Zangskar, the Tsarap River flows more than 300 kilometers northwest from the boundary between Ladakh and the neighboring state of Himachal Pradesh. All of the passes into Zangskar would dwarf the highest peak in the continental United States, Mt. Whitney.[23] This rigorous and mostly uninhabited terrain makes traffic into and out of Zangskar difficult. The only vehicular road into Zangskar is a 250-kilometer, unpaved track over the Pentse La pass, which is open between July and November. Much of the travel between Zangskar and Ladakh outside the summer season proceeds on foot over high passes that are impassable during the deepest winter. In January and February, Zangskar is only accessible by the precarious "Ice Way" or Chadar *(bya rdar)*, which consists of the partly frozen surface of the Zangskar River gorge. The harrowing but unforgettably beautiful journey traverses the Zangskar gorge for 120 kilometers of ice sheets of varying hue, stability, and liquidity. A steady traffic of traders traverses this risky route in search of a winter escape from Zangskar.

Zangskar's ethos of self-reliance and communal solidarity relies on the relatively even distribution of wealth. The local economy of merit and monasticism has resulted in nearly universal access to land and water. Unlike elsewhere in the Himalayas, where land changed hands between villages quite frequently, cultivated land was rarely sold or given in dowry until recently. As a result, most village residents own fields only in their own village.[24] Zangskar's population was far less stable in the twentieth century. The number of inhabitants tripled, from roughly 4,000 to 12,000 people.[25] It nearly doubled in the last third of the century between 1971 and 1991. Yet the number of households increased far more slowly during the twentieth century, from roughly 1,000 households to 1,900 households. The area cultivated rose even more slowly than the households.[26] Thus the average household holding dropped from 3.2 acres in 1908 to 2.8 acres in 1981. Much of the newly cultivated land is located in recent settlements built after 1908. The most arid settlements shrank in the last century, while those with more water, like Yulang or Rinam, expanded. The difficulty of building new irrigation channels and the scarcity of water, as well as a collective approach to resources, limited growth overall. Creating new fields requires the unanimous decision of the entire village, because each new field will need a share of water from the streambed, which is considered a collective resource.

Communal but scarce resources like water, fodder, and fuel are distributed according to custom and collective schemes. Elsewhere in India, scarcity of resources has often led to radical concentration of wealth in the hands of few. Yet in Zangskar, subsistence for all has taken precedence over accumulation for few. Unlike in the American West, Zangskari settlers did not grab upstream rights at the expense of those downstream. Rights to fodder and water cannot be bought or sold by residents, or alienated from the village and its residents. Outsiders rarely secure rights to common property unless they marry or move into the village. The allocation of common property rights reflects the distribution of wider social and political rights. Although hierarchy and competition exist, they are highly mediated by consensus. Village headmen set annual limits on the amount of wild plants *(bur tse, tsher mang, kyi lce)* that each household may harvest every year for fuel or as fodder.[27]

Since the three major rivers run in deep gorges and floodplains are shifting or salinated, most villages are irrigated by their own tributary stream, although two villages may share a larger stream. Every village has its own schema of water allocation which serves the topography and demography. A skeletal principle of "hydraulic solidarity" binds all the farmers into a communal scheme which allocates water according to need rather than greed.[28] Depending on the size or scale of the system, water is distributed by household, field, or channel. These schemes can be adjusted with the democratic participation of water user groups by season, day, or even hour. The flexible and democratic allocation of water ensures that the users can make their own decisions regarding readjustment of the system. In the village economy, water use is a zero-sum game in which fair play is constantly monitored. Breaches are punished swiftly with customary fines, adjudicated by the headman and his assistants. An ethos of sharing overrides competition, and consensus prevails over division. Only the largest villages in nearby Ladakh elect local officials, called the Lords of the Water *(chu dpon)*, who adjudicate water disputes or infractions. Although antagonisms and disputes are not unknown, these are resolved through village-level meetings.

Even building supplies are collectivized according to village residence. Every village resident has the right to collect rocks, stones, and silt from the surrounding landscape, although government contractors may use rock and silt lying in "wasteland" outside village boundaries. Zangskari houses resemble fortresses, with their heavy, hand-built walls made out of stone and sun-baked mud bricks. Doorways, doors, and window frames are made from hewn timbers; roof beams are hand-hewn poplar trunks. The floors are mud while ceilings are made of tightly latticed poplar branches covered with willow branches, straw, and mud. The standard floor plan of many Zangskari houses consists of two to three stories, with the lowest floor housing livestock stables, cold storage rooms for beer and butter, hay storage, and the winter quarters or *yog khang*. This room—the lowest and innermost for warmth—serves as the winter kitchen and residence for the entire family. It is insulated against the subzero temperatures by a live form of central heating: the livestock in their adjacent stalls. The second floor houses the "summer kitchen," storage rooms *(mdzod)*, guest rooms, compost toilet, an open courtyard for festivals, and the family offering room *(mchod khang)*. The offering room usually houses the altar for the guardian deity, ritual texts, and other ritual paraphernalia. In recent decades, rapid increases in wealth have led to the use of imported construction materials such as machine-hewn beams and lintels, glass windows, wooden floor planks, concrete, and steel. There has also been a rise in the use of imported labor, with Bihari and Nepali laborers working on most of the larger construction projects in central Zangskar.

Barley and Butter, Trade and Tourism

Butter and barley are as critical to local subsistence as monasticism is. The four-month growing season must support the lay population as well as the community of monks, who do almost no work in the fields. The major crops grown in Karsha, as elsewhere in Zangskar, are barley, wheat, and peas, although mustard seeds are grown at lower elevations.[29] Lucerne and alfalfa crops *('ol)* are grown between fields on strips of land, while most houses also have a small poplar plantation *(lcang ra)* for construction and a vegetable garden *(tshas)*. Crops are watered, plowed, sown, weeded, harvested, transported, threshed, winnowed, washed, dried, roasted, and ground by human, animal, or water power. Before the streams freeze in winter, the fields are plowed and the stables are emptied out. Dung is collected in autumn and spring as fuel for cooking. The busiest seasons—harvest, plowing, and first watering season—require intra-household labor exchanges *(las 'byes)* or the hiring of day laborers, usually from the village. Unlike in Ladakh, Biharis or Nepalis are seldom hired for agricultural work. Machine threshers are mostly used by wealthier Muslims in Padum. Buddhists are averse to these machines because the mechanical thresher produces finely ground straw which is believed to stick in the throats of livestock. Most households roast and grind only enough barley and wheat for the coming winter, but also have grain stores where they keep unroasted grain to cover at least several years of drought. The winter is a time for carding wool, spinning, weaving, and other tasks like making baskets, sacks, twine, rope, shoes, and repairing household objects, as well as extensive meditation and devotional practices.

Most households maintain livestock herds of five to thirty sheep and goats, along with more than a dozen cows, crossbreeds *(mdzo, mdzo mo)*, yaks, horses, and donkeys. Livestock cultivation provides essential by-products such as wool, dung, butter products, and meat to the Zangskari livelihood. Every summer, most households in Zangskar send their flocks to the high pastures *('brog sa)* directly behind their villages or to the rough shelter built near the passes leading out of Zangskar. Every household or group of households chooses a young woman to milk and tend the live-stock all summer. The crude stone shelters afford a rich diet of curds and milk, as well as the freedom to live among girlfriends and the male visitors who frequent these huts on their journeys in and out of Zangskar. Yet the work is backbreaking as fifty cows are milked and fed, the milk is turned to yoghurt, and huge vats of yoghurt are churned into butter each day. Households who do not send a member to the high pasture will re-ceive a payment of butter from the caretaker.[30] The family collects several kilos of butter per month, while the caretaker keeps any additional butter and cheese she produces. This butter is sewn into sacks made from sheep or cow bladders and stored for consumption during the winter, when fat is a crucial part of the diet. Sheep and goats are not taken to high pasture but are kept near the village to avoid wolves or other predators. The fines imposed upon the owner of any animal caught grazing in the fields are imposed by a villager appointed each year on rotation called the Lorapa *(lo ra pa)*.

The additions of subsidized wheat flour, rice, salt, and sugar from the Punjab have changed the Zangskari diet, although most households are largely self-sufficient in terms of grains, butter, and meat. The average Zangskari diet is still based on homegrown staples with no less than six different types of flour: roasted barley flour *(rtsam pa)*, roasted pea flour, roasted barley and pea flour *(tshos mo)*, toasted pea and barley flour *(yos phye)*, unroasted barley flour *(tsal phye)*, and unroasted wheat flour *('gro phye)*. The roasted flours are tossed skillfully into the mouth with a spoon and washed with tea, beer, buttermilk, butter, or yogurt. The unroasted flours are cooked into soups, stews, mash, porridge, and gruel with water and salt, dried cheese, or meat. A few locally grown vegetables—radishes, turnips, onions, potatoes, cabbages, peas, mustard greens, and spinach—complement the dairy and starch. Most households buy subsidized rations such as rice, salt, and wheat flour, and staples such as cooking oil, spices, tea, salt, and lentils. At the end of winter, villagers must rely on home-grown produce as the ration stores often run short just before the passes open. The Indian economy provides Amul butter, Nestlé ghee, Lifeguard soap, Nutri soya protein, Taj Mahal tea, flashlights, batteries, matches, televisions, and radios, while the global economy offers Coca-Cola, Yankee caps, and Phillips radios. This economy requires extensive reciprocal arrangements between lay households as well as between laity and monastics. The following story illustrates the importance of customary law in regulating these arrangements. While I heard it from several informants, here is how I imagine it took place.

The Nun Who Stole Some Water

The darkness in Karsha village was illuminated by a sliver of moonlight as a figure picked its way slowly through the steeply terraced fields. Skirting stalks plump with barley corns, the figure wound its way uphill through the well-worn footpaths which followed the network of tiny channels which bring water to the furthest fields. Proceeding along a path he had walked countless times before in his lifetime, Paljor's feet adjusted to the familiar bumps and turns while his mind was thinking of how cursed he was to have so many fields along the nighttime channels, which required this infernal chore of watering while his neighbors were busy sleeping. Lost in dreamy thoughts, he did not immediately register the odd sight in front of him. At his feet lay a glistening pool of water, shimmering in the moonlight. Although the field looked like it had just been watered, he couldn't see a soul, not even a hungry ghost. He bent to his knees and examined the field more closely to make certain he was not dreaming. Sticking his fingers into the sticky earth, they came up oozing with mud.

Although there are thousands of fields and hundreds of subsidiary irrigation channels in Karsha, Paljor knew that this field did not lie along a night-time leat *(mtshan gyi yur ba)*. It was important to know how the water flowed through the fields, because it determined whether a given field would receive water during the day or night. Although Paljor was sure this field was only supposed to receive water in the daytime, it was moist now with the signs of recent watering. He walked around the fields to check for further clues. It was soon apparent that the watering had been intentional and deliberate. The "mouths" *(rka)* of the channel along the edge of the field still lay open to allow water to flow into the field. The subsidiary channel which circled the perimeter of the field had clearly been "opened" at the point where it met the channel running up the hillside to the main leat from the river. Even the main leat, which should have been dry as a whistle at this time of night, bore telltale signs of moisture. Yet none of the other fields nearby had been watered. He could read these signs as easily as he could read the Diamond Sutra text in his altar room. He knew what he had to do, although he hated to do it since it was forbidden in ordinary circumstances. Grasping a few stalks of barley, he ripped them out by their roots and laid them down over the wettest portion of the field. This act of witnessing was proof that he had observed the theft of water firsthand. As he walked home, he thought about who might have watered this field surreptitiously.

He realized that the field belonged to one of Karsha's most respected citizens, the hereditary Minister or Lonpo *(blon po)*, whose family once served the king but now only had an elevated status due to their aristocracy. Why would such an upstanding and wealthy family commit the unthinkable crime of stealing water, even in this time of drought? Paljor then recalled that the field was tilled by a village nun, who served as a caretaker of the Lonpo's family temple. This woman, a native of Ufti village, was called a "village nun" *(grong pa'i jo mo)* because she had taken up five precepts but was not ordained. Without ordination, she could not join the community of Karsha nuns who used the Lonpo's temple for their monthly rituals. She lived alone in the Lonpo's ancient temple, lighting the butter lamps most days, when not home in Ufti during the busy agricultural seasons. While living in the Lonpo's temple, she was also required to take care of the large herd of sheep and the single field, which belonged to the Lonpo but was set aside to cover temple expenses. Every day, she took the flock of sheep out to pasture, milked them, and returned them to the makeshift stable attached to the old temple. This summer's drought had forced her to take the sheep to higher and more distant pastures every day before bringing them back for the evening milking, leaving precious little time for watering the Lonpo's field. Paljor reckoned that the nun had decided to steal some nighttime water because she had missed her turn during the day.

The next morning, Paljor got up before dawn and made his way to the headman's house, wearing a bright pink silk sash and relatively clean woolen robe to mark the formality of his visit. As was customary when making a visit, he stood and called out under the kitchen window until the headman poked his head out of the house. Groaning, the headman wondered what could be the matter so early in the morning. Grazing rights? Yet another case of adultery? He made a mental note to give a Buddhist homily on carnal desire at the next village meeting and waved Paljor to come in. After taking a spot on the rug near the hearth, Paljor waited as the headman's wife set a cup of scalding sweet tea before him. When both men had finished their course of sweet tea and had started on the course of butter tea, Paljor explained what he'd seen last night in the fields. The headman listened carefully until Paljor had finished, then put on his cloak and left to collect one of his assistants *(kotwal)*. The three men headed out into fields under a pale pink sky. They proceeded to examine the spot where barley stalks were laid horizontally. While the soil was still stained with water here, the rest of the field had begun to dry. They all agreed: the watering rules had been violated.

When they returned, the headman called for the other assistants and the Lonpo, who arrived rather puzzled and irritated. When the headman asked him if anyone in his house had been out watering last night, the Lonpo said no. When the headman reported what he'd seen, the Lonpo turned a shade of crimson. He argued that the nun who tilled the fields, Ani Drolma, might have been confused about the watering restrictions. She might even have been out of the village when the system of alternating daytime and nighttime channels first was imposed. The headman decided it would be best to call Ani Drolma herself. By the time Drolma came down from the temple, the accusations were flying fast and furious. In her humble patchwork robe, Ani Drolma sat down at the foot of the row, a respectful distance from the angry men. Ani Drolma eventually admitted that she had watered the field the previous night, pleading ignorance and confusion. The headman's assistants refused to believe her excuses, and argued that the Lonpo and Ani Drolma should be fined, although they could not agree on the sum. The Lonpo was incensed as he watched these young men berate the elderly renunciant, without any shame. Although the Lonpo insisted that Ani Drolma was guilty of an oversight rather than an infraction, the headman decided to call a village meeting.

The headman and his assistants continued to debate the matter over many cups of barley beer *(chang)* and tea. The headman wisely knew it was best to present the matter to the village, but his assistants were eager to punish the Lonpo, who was far too privileged, they felt. By the time they left the headman's house, their anger and lack of sobriety had sharpened into a simple resolution: they marched up the cliff, intoxicated with adrenaline and beer, to confront Ani Drolma, who was doing her daily prostrations. The rabble of angry young men began to taunt her. How could she not have known about the watering scheme when none of her neighbors were watering their fields last night? Had she not lived in Karsha already for quite a few years, tending the Lonpo's sheep and field? They suggested she pay a monetary fine, but she replied that she had no money. They argued that she had become rich in sheep, since taking over as temple caretaker. They reminded her that the original flock of eleven sheep which she had received from the Lonpo had grown to over two dozen now, fat from grazing on the Karsha hillsides. One brash man suggested that she donate one of the sheep from her flock as payment for the fine, but Drolma argued that this would be an excessive payment for a water infraction. Several other nuns had come out of their cells as the commotion escalated. One of the men went into the stable and emerged with a struggling sheep. As the nuns helplessly stood by, the young men led the sheep down the cliff, whooping and shouting.

The village men killed the sheep later that night after many more bottles of distilled barley beer *(a rak)*. While villagers expressed indignation at Ani Drolma's theft of water, they also knew the Lonpo and Drolma had been fined without due process. When the headman saw the sheep dismembered in the kitchen where his assistant stood with the blood literally on his hands, he was visibly upset. He sent a message of apology to the Lonpo and called all the village men to a customary feast of meat dumplings *(mog mog)*, in order to redistribute the slaughtered meat fairly among the entire community. The Lonpo's wife was livid with rage when she heard that a sheep dedicated to the eleven-headed statue of Avalokitesvara in the Lonpo's temple had been slaughtered. Hysterical with rage, she exclaimed that the village men had "eaten shit" *(rkyag pa zas song)* by eating the meat of a sheep dedicated to the *bodhisattva* of compassion and thus protected from slaughter for its life. She cursed the assistants to miserable rebirth for their senseless deed. Ani Drolma simply locked the temple, to protect her precious stores of butter, and returned to her home village.

The Karsha nuns, who were now locked out of their assembly hall, went to complain to the Lonpo. The Lonpo's wife refused to listen to their pleas, so they went to the headman in despair. A village meeting, to which each household was forced to send a member by customary law, was called to resolve the affair. The assistants argued that the Lonpo's caretaker had broken the village water rules. The Lonpo complained that Drolma had been falsely accused and as an added insult one of his sheep had been stolen as well. The community of nuns complained that Drolma frequently locked the temple when she returned to Ufti, disregarding their "right" to hold assemblies in the temple. The villagers claimed that the temple actually belonged to the village rather than to the Lonpo, despite the fact that his family had been hereditary caretakers for centuries, a duty they had been given by the early kings of Zangskar, the Lonpo claimed. The Lonpo's wife threatened to tear down the temple with her own hands before handing it over to the village.

After several days of meetings, all who wished had spoken and yet no resolution was in sight. A few senior monks from Karsha intervened to settle the dispute. The monks recruited the Naib Tahsildar, who was head of the revenue department and the highest officer in Zangskar. By checking at the land records office, it was determined that one of the Lonpo's fields was indeed set aside for the upkeep of the temple, indicating his right and duty to act as caretaker. Yet the Lonpo decided henceforth to abandon the practice of setting sheep aside for a caretaker and resolved to light the butter lamps using his own family. Ani Drolma returned to Ufti with her share of the sheep. The villagers were not punished for stealing the sheep, because it was argued that Drolma had broken customary law with her theft of water.

This case illustrates the importance of water and barley and local authorities within the Buddhist economy of merit. The dispute offered a "diagnostic event," in which traditional authority and power were up for grabs.[31] Aristocrats, commoners, and monks struggled over basic economic and symbolic resources. The dispute arose out of an ambiguity in which power and authority were renegotiated. The Lonpo, villagers, and headman struggled for the right to water as much as to worship. Although the Lonpo's sharecropping scheme for the temple was abandoned, the Lonpo's and the headman's traditional legitimacy was retained. While the Lonpo appeared temporarily disempowered by the young men who killed his sheep, he retained his rights to the temple. Yet the nuns gained little or nothing in a conflict they had observed firsthand. The nuns were observers but second-class participants in village democracy.

Ritual and Reciprocity in Village Life

Perched high up against the buttress of peaks which encircle the broad valley, Karsha village is one of the largest and oldest villages in Zangskar. Its earliest traces of Buddhism include a rock carving of Maitreya and an abandoned, fortified settlement that may date to well before the tenth century. The village is home to 450 laypeople, 85 monks, and 22 nuns. It lies tucked up against two symmetrical red cliffs which are split by a small riverbed. The river flows down from snowfields that grace the higher peaks of the Zangskar range, far behind the village. Rather appropriately in symbolic terms, the nunnery lies on the more bulbous left-hand cliff, while the monastery is perched atop the more aggressive and upwardly thrusting cliffs on the right. The monastery and nunnery face each other as much as they look down upon the village roofs far below. The nuns and monks look out over the smooth, glaciated contours of Zangskar's central valley, where every shift in season, month, and hour yields shifting shades of rock or snow. The early morning pink turns to beige, before yielding to burnt sienna, pale brown, dark orange, and even flaming pink.

The nunnery and monastery permit a balcony view on the theater of village life. The flat roofs of every monastic cell afford a marvelous view of the procession of animals and people across the desolate landscape. The arid desert yields few trees which would block the panoptic view from the two monastic institutions. A smattering of houses and shops are bunched around the base of the Karsha ravine, where a small stream is dispersed into a fine web of irrigation channels that feed a butterfly-shaped swath of fields far below. Most village houses are within shouting distance or sight of one another. Like Bentham's famous panopticon, the village layout offers easy surveillance of everybody's comings and goings. The most intimate details of the community are known less through incessant gossip as through inexorable visibility. There is no place to hide within the fields and paths that many villagers will tread until death. Gaits and clothing offer clues which can be read from miles away. Like the terrifying trap and paradisiacal tease of Hilton's Shangri La, the Zangskar valley is both a haven and a prison.

Although the village of Karsha is broken down into three neighborhoods—Tiur, Nangkar, and Phikar—it is the household which largely defines membership in the village. The household, rather than the individual, is the major corporate unit in village life. The head of the household—usually the senior male, but the senior female if he is not present—represents its members at most village rites or public meetings.[32] Households, rather than individuals, are the units which engage in sharing water and other material resources on the village level. Every household, regardless of the number of inhabitants, has similar duties and rights in the village. The rights of residence include regulated access to sustainable resources like water, fuel, and fodder. The obligations include paying monastic taxes in labor and goods, raising funds for or contributing donations to ritual events, and attending village work schemes for planting trees, repairing irrigation ditches, or repairing religious edifices like stupas.

The village ritual calendar is structured around rites performed by the monastery (see Table 2.1). The monastery's ritual calendar creates and affirms the social body of Buddhists within the village as well as the wider region. Situated within a state and district that is predominantly Muslim, Zangskari Buddhists affirm their communal identity by attending or donating to the monastery's rites. The highly choreographed ritual events which punctuate the calendar create social solidarity as well as social differentiation. On the one hand, the monastery's rituals affirm village or regional membership through the obligatory services and donations they require. Almost every single ritual requires some butter, barley, or fuel which has been produced or gathered by local villagers or from the surrounding region. Those who contribute to a given ritual receive merit as well as membership in the body of patrons who are ritually blessed by the monastery. On the other hand, these rites also emphasize social and economic differences through an elaborately choreographed spectacle of donation described below. While some of the more self-reflexive rites at the monastery that purify the monastic body or wider space (such as the construction of *mandalas*) are hardly attended by the laity, others (such as the wintertime fasting ritual) draw large crowds who come to make merit as much as status.

Many of the rituals in the village and monastic calendars are pragmatic rites dedicated to village and household purity and prosperity, which also ward off disaster and misfortune. The significance of some of these may be declining as local household economies are supplemented by nonagrarian vocations. However, every household remains partly dependent on its fields and local produce. Survival through a Zangskari winter is hardly possible without local products like barley, butter, or dung. The success of agricultural ventures is considered to be highly dependent on ritual protection, even by the more educated members of the community. In times of drought, villagers still call for ritual services as quickly as they may petition the local public works department for a new irrigation channel. The rituals supplement rather than give way to technological innovation. I believe that the rituals remain popular because they allow monks to renew their legitimacy and villagers to renew their commitment to the community. Last but not least, they allow the newly wealthy to secure a more tradi-

Table 2.1 Annual rites held at Karsha monastery

Months 1–12, Days 15 and 30. Renewal of monastic vows *(bkra' shis gso sbyong)*.

Month 12, Day 30, through Month 1, Day 9. Great Prayer Festival *(smon lam chen mo)*.

Month 1, Days 7–9. Fasting rite *(smyung gnas)* in upper assembly hall.

Month 1, Day 9. Long-life initiation *(tshe dbang)* for villagers.

Month 1, Days 13–14. Heruka empowerment and mandala *(bde mchog gi grub mchod dang dkyil 'khor)*.

Month 1, Day 15. Heruka burnt offering *(bDe mchog gi sbyin bsreg)*.

Month 1, Days 16–22. Vajra Bhairava empowerment and mandala *(rDo rje 'Jigs byed kyi bdun sgrub dang dkyil 'khor)*.

Month 1, Day 22. Vajra Bhairava burnt offering *(rDo rji 'Jigs byed kyi sbyin bsreg)*.

Month 1, Days 21–24. Reading the Tibetan canon *(bKa 'gyur)* in the lower Labrang.

Month 1, Day 25. Offerings to the underworld spirits *(klu bsangs)* for snowfall.

Month 2, Day 1. Spring day feast for village.

Month 2, Day 8. Banishment of enemy forces *(dgra lha phar byes)*, juniper offering for Dalai Lama *(rgyal ba'i lha bsangs)*, expiatory prayers *(bskang gsol)*, and reading of the Prajñaparamita *('Bum)*.

Month 2, Day 13. Unveiling of monastery's relics, "offerings of the 13th" *(bcu gsum mchod pa)*.

Month 5, Days 25–29. Propitiatory offering *(lnga pa'i lnga mchod gyi bskang gsol)*.

Month 5, Days 28/29. Gustor Festival with dances *('chams)*, expiatory offering *(gtor rgyab)*.

Month 6, Days 3–5. Fasting rite *(smyung gnas)* at the monastery's Maitreya temple.

Month 6, Day 15, through Month 7, Day 30. Summer rains retreat *(dbyar gnas)*.

Month 6, Day 26, through Month 7, Day 2. Guhyasamaja empowerment and mandala *(gSang ba 'dus pa'i dbang, dkyil 'khor)*.

Month 6, Day 29. Expiatory offering *(bskang gso)*.

Month 7, Day 2. Guhyasamaja burnt offering *(gSang ba 'dus pa'i sbyin bsreg)*.

Month 7, Day 29. Expiation *(gtor rgyab)* to conclude the rains retreat.

Month 9, Day 22. Celebration of the Buddha's descent from Tushita heaven.

Month 10, Day 25. Commemoration of Tsongkhapa's birthday *(dga ldan lnga mchod)*; propitiatory offering *(skang gsol)*.

Month 10, Day 29. New Year's feast and tossing of ransom figure *(glud)*.

Month 11, Days 17–18. Propitiatory prayers *(skang gsol)* dedicated to a fifteenth-century Karsha saint *(slob dpon rDo rJe Rin Chen)*.

Month 11, Day 29. Propitiatory prayers *(skang gsol)* and expiatory offering *(gtor rgyab)*.

Note: All dates are provided in the Tibetan calendar. This calendar is made up of twelve intercalated lunar months, each of which is roughly thirty days long, with intercalated days dropped or added as necessary according to the movement of the moon.

tional means of authority in a rapidly changing economy. In this regard, it is hardly surprising that most of the village festivals and monastic rituals in the village calendar continue to be celebrated. While some may grumble about the onerous weight of obligatory contributions to the ritual calendar, most villagers recognize the necessity of providing a means to merit as well as status.

Besides those events listed in the monastic calendar (Table 2.1), Karsha village also celebrates certain popular festivals which are largely funded and organized by the laity, although they may include the participation of monastics. The villagewide festivals include the three seasonal renewals of the altar for the village god *(yul lha tho spo byes)* held during the New Year around the winter solstice, on the first day of the second Tibetan month near the spring equinox, and during the seventh Tibetan month around the autumn equinox. There is also a week-long celebration of the New Year festival *(lo gsar)* to mark the transition from the tenth to the eleventh Tibetan month; the wintertime Mani recitation *(ma ni tung 'gyur)* during the eleventh and twelfth Tibetan months; the villagewide reading of the *Prajñaparamita (yul pa'i bum)* on the full moon of the twelfth Tibetan month which is also known as the water ritual *(chu'i skyu rim)*, because it is believed to bring snow which melts into irrigation water; the "opening of the earth door" *(sa kha phe byes)* for fertility at the end of the first Tibetan month; the villagewide archery festival *(mda rtse)* at the end of the second Tibetan month; the springtime merit-making rite for the ancestors *(dge tsha)* at the end of the fourth month; the circumambulation and purification of the fields and a reading of the *Prajñaparamita* on the tenth day of the fifth Tibetan month; and the whitewashing of the village stupas on the full moon of the fifth month. In addition to these seasonal rites, the laypeople of Karsha village also celebrate two monthly rites which affirm Buddhist sentiment as much as neighborhood membership. On both the tenth and the twenty-fifth day of every Tibetan month, the members of Karsha's three neighborhoods gather in a designated household to read religious texts (the *Padma thang yig* on the tenth, which is dedicated to the Tantric adept Guru Rimpoche, and the *brgyad stong pa* or *Prajñaparamita* in eight thousand lines on the twenty-fifth).

Each of these popular festivals is organized by several village households who must take their turn *(gnyer pa)*. Each ritual has its own rotational system which rarely overlaps, so that a given household should not be responsible for more than a few rites a year. With almost a dozen popular festivals, and roughly fifty member households, Karsha village requires its member households to steward a larger rite once every five years. In some cases, the ritual is celebrated separately by each of the three neighborhoods in Karsha, each of whom has its own stewards for the given rite. The system of stewardship serves as a local tax, which is used to provide ritual protection as much as an opportunity for collective drinking and gossip. Only those households which fulfill their obligation to organize these village festivals are entitled to the material benefits of village membership—access to irrigation water or dung. Most of the smaller festivals are funded by simple collection schemes in which every household in Karsha contributes a set amount of grain, butter, breads, or other substances. The steward is responsible for collecting the goods, brewing the barley beer, and preparing the foods or ritual cakes to be consumed during the course of the rite. Organizing a larger village festival or a monastic ritual like the wintertime fasting rite *(smyung gnas)* is much more onerous and may require the steward to raise funds across Zangskar for months in advance of the rite.

The largest collective rites in the village and monastic calendar usually require that one or two households be chosen as stewards *(gnyer pa)*, by rotation, from the village community. The stewards spend months soliciting donations in cash and kind before the actual ritual, where these gifts are used to feed monks, nuns, and the donors themselves who have come bearing their donations. Donors make merit as much as status through contributions which are pledged during highly visible fund-raising parties known as "begging beers" *(dri chang)*. Each village household is invited to send one member to this party organized by the steward in villages across Zangskar. The steward serves only beer and no food until the guests have become sufficiently lubricated, at which point they are asked to stand a pledge a donation to the upcoming ritual that the steward is organizing. The public recital of each pledge—of grain, butter, cash, or other foodstuffs—makes each donor's contribution visible to all present, not just the steward, who carefully records each pledge in writing. Having made their intentions visible to all, donors are dutifully bound to attend the ritual weeks or months later, bearing their pledged gift in hand. At that time, the donors are invited to an elaborate return feast in the steward's house or rented quarters. These feasts are often graded according to the generosity of the donor, such that the biggest donors may be served special meals in separate, more ornate rooms than the mass of ordinary donors. Finally, the biggest donors may be singled out in the course of the ritual with prominent seats or other special accommodations.

The ranking of donors reifies minutely graded differences among donors in what may seem to be an egalitarian and democratic process. Although merit is available to all who attend or donate to a ritual, it is hardly distributed evenly among the participants. The highly visible manner in which donations are pledged and made reifies social as well as spiritual hierarchies. Merit making exacerbates differences in rank between rich and poor, or male and female, as the latter usually have fewer resources to earn merit in the most visible or spectacular fashion. When donors earn merit they also earn symbolic capital. For Pierre Bourdieu, symbolic capital is a denied form of capital whose origins and relationship to more material forms of capital are often misrecognized.[33] Although merit making may appear to run counter to the accumulation of wealth—by affirming the Buddhist virtues of nonattachment and universal generosity—paradoxically, it affirms a highly individual form of both status and wealth. Doctrinally, donations are supposed to be disinterested acts of generosity that are less dependent on material wealth than on inner motivation. In practice, however, donors earn both merit and status in direct proportion to the size of their gifts, regardless of their undisclosed private intentions. Bourdieu held that one of the classic means of exhibiting or producing symbolic capital was highly prestigious and visible forms of gift giving— exactly the sort of donations that accompany many Buddhist rituals in Zangskar. For Bourdieu, supposedly disinterested gifts or noninstrumental acts are precisely symbolic forms of capital because they act as a form of credit which secures the procurement of further capital, scarce labor, or other social debts. By giving to a festival once a year, donors secure far more than an implicit promise of repayment when their turn to sponsor the festival arrives. Donors also earn a highly legitimate form of status, which is convertible to social as well as material wealth. Although the excessive pursuit of merit or symbolic capital can lead to economic ruin, a noticeable lack of merit usually signals a lack of prestige. This is hardly surprising when one considers the frequency and pervasiveness of ritual donations that support Karsha village's annual calendar, to which we now turn.

The Ritual Calendar: A Year in Karsha

Buddhists believe that any merit made during the first Tibetan month is multiplied a thousand times. This rush to make merit finds the Karsha monks sitting all day in prayer for their ten-day Great Prayer Festival, besieged with donations from all over Zangskar. The hundreds of villagers who come bearing voluntary gifts or obligatory taxes of butter, grain, wood, cash, and other provisions are rewarded with pomp and spectacle. There are numerous maroon-clad monks sitting, as if frozen to their seats, in the dank lower hall where temperatures are only slightly above zero, while in the upper hall, hundreds of villagers fast and prostrate while reciting Gelongma Palmo's invocation of Avalokitesvara. The close of the fasting festival is heralded by the unfurling of medieval *thang ka* (a representation of a deity, in this case embroidered on a forty-foot piece of cloth) and the solemn procession of monks who bear the monastic relics from the lower to the upper assembly hall. Later that month, the monks will create and dismantle two symbolic universes known as *mandala (dkyil 'khor)*, made of sand. On the full moon of the first month, the monks invoke the Tantric protector Cakrasamvara *(bde mchog)* with a *mandala* and a burnt offering *(sbyin sregs).*[34] Only a week later, a second *mandala* is constructed and then dismantled with a burnt offering to invoke another major Tantric protector worshiped by Gelugpa monks, Vajrabhairava *(rdo rje 'jigs byed)*. Few laypeople attend either of these rites, which are intended primarily for the monks who have taken these protectors as their meditational deities *(yi dam)*. Later in the month, the monks gather for several days to read the Buddha's teachings known in Tibetan as the Kangyur *(bka' 'gyur)*.

Several rituals are conducted in the first month to appease the underworld spirits or *klu,* who are connected to snowfall, water, and fertility. One of the most senior ritual experts at the monastery, Zurba Tashi, performs a month-long set of ceremonies for these vexatious spirits. He embarks on a three-week fast to purify himself for his ritual performances by forgoing onions, garlic, spices, meat, and beer, because the *klu* are believed to be sensitive to certain food and smells, as well as other human impurities. While in ritual seclusion, he subsists on the dairy and grain products supplied by village girls who come to prostrate and receive a blessing for their fertility or the removal of acne and other skin diseases caused by these spirits. On the twenty-fifth day of the first month, when these underworld spirits are considered to awaken from their winter slumber, Tashi performs a propitiary rite at the village altar and spring. He prepares and offers a vessel of precious substances like grain and dairy products and a juniper fumigation *(klu'i bum pa, klu bsangs)* for the *klu,* who are pleased by wealth. He then performs similar rites at most houses in Karsha, making offerings to the individual spirits of the hearth and home *(thab lha, klu)* which regulate household fortunes. The only houses he does not visit are those which have been polluted by a recent birth—animal or human.

A villagewide fertility rite known as the "opening of the earth door" *(sa kha phye'bye)* is held toward the end of the first month, when the subterranean spirits *(klu)* first awaken.[35] On this day, a monk performs a juniper offering at the village altar *(lha tho)* while every household sends one male member to honor the subterranean spirits of earth and water *(sa bdag, klu)* with two offering cakes *(lha bon mchod pa, gtum po lha)*. This gathering involves lewd jokes, ritual songs, a horse race, and a mock plowing ceremony held in the snow, all of which invoke human and animal prosperity, harmony, and fertility. The person chosen to be fool for the day has his face painted with a mixture of barley beer and flour, as all male members of the village gather to consume copious quantities of barley beer. After the horse race, villagers bring a local yak to the monastery's "mother field" *(ma zhing)*, attach a plow, and then proceed in a virtual plowing, parting snow rather than soil. On "spring day" *(spyid tshe)*, which is the first day of the second Tibetan month, the monks perform a juniper offering at the village altar for the village's guardian deity *(yul lha)* while members of each household propitiate their own clan deities *(pha lha)* at home. The household propitiation of the clan's deity involves a simple prayer, juniper offering, beer libation, and a meal of pea flour cakes *(bag pa)*, meat, butter, and beer which should only be consumed by family members. On this day fire and other items should not be borrowed from other houses, and the altars are cleaned and restored with new juniper sprigs. Later that day villagers gather at the steward's house to consume copious quantities of barley beer and to greet the abbot of the monastery, who receives their gifts of blessing scarves and cash. The villagers are also treated to a meal cooked by the monastic stewards, as a form of thanks for their annual services on behalf of the monastery. This meal used to consist of blood sausage and beer until 1987, when such unorthodox offerings were banned in favor of rice and porridge. It proved impossible to ban the beer, which is prepared by lay stewards, not the monks. In Zangskar at least, the entire system of monastic patronage and merit making is heavily lubricated by barley beer.

The monastic treasury or Labrang *(bla brang)* rotates its personnel and honors the Dalai Lama and Tibetan warrior gods *(rgyal ba lha bsangs, dgra lha phar byes)* on the eighth day of the second month. Some monks offer juniper smoke to an effigy of a warrior *(dgra lha)*, which harks back to the more militaristic side of Tibetan monasticism. Others perform an expiation *(skang gso)* for the monastic protectors. The remainder of the assembly reads the Perfection of Wisdom Sutra in one hundred thousand lines before the formal rotation of the Labrang personnel. While the sacristan of the Labrang is rotated among junior monks each year, the three senior monks who serve as stewards *(gnyer pa)* are rotated every three years. The Labrang stewards must present account books showing all credits and debits in their management of the monastery's properties and permanent endowments, while the sacristan brings out all ritual items out from the storeroom to be itemized before he is rotated out of his position. In this fashion monks are held accountable at the end of their terms for whatever monastic property they have managed. On the thirteenth day of the second month, the monks display the monastery's sacred relics, ordinarily kept under lock and key in heavy metal boxes lying in the monastic storerooms. Villagers gather in the upper assembly hall to receive a blessing from the fantastic relics. A tooth believed to originate from the Buddha's elephant is displayed along with clothing from a seventeenth-century Panchen Lama. Later in the second month the villagers of Karsha organize their annual archery festival. Laywomen and laymen gather separately for several days to feast and dance at the two stewards' houses. They congregate each evening at the festival ground to watch the archery and dances, where the entire assembly of monks is hosted one evening. As the earth warms up, the human manure is carried from the household and monastic compost toilets to the fields and earth is spread on fields to hasten the melting of the snow. A group of young monks is sent to collect the obligatory taxes of horse dung or firewood, which are owed by every member household in Karsha and its neighboring villages. The young monks mix the dung with water, shape it into bricks, and set them in the sun to dry, before they are delivered to the monastery later that spring.

On an auspicious day chosen in the third Tibetan month by the village astrologer, the Labrang stewards inaugurate the spring plowing season by plowing the monastery's "mother field" and making offerings to the subterranean spirits. All the households are then free to plow their own "mother field," where they will make additional offerings to appease the troublesome spirits *(klu)*. Each household appeases the spirits with its own offerings of juniper incense and small libations of cake, beer, and butter, which are poured directly into the furrows behind the plow. While the most literate member of the family reads two texts *(gNam sa snang brgyad, bKra shis brtsegs pa)*, other members share the designated fertility cakes *(gtum po lha)* with the beasts of burden. Every yak, cow, crossbreed *(mdzo)*, and donkey receives a taste of the cake and a dab of butter for health and fertility. The Labrang stewards also tend to the monastic herd of yaks, cattle, and horses. Between the fourth and seventh months, the livestock are taken and tended at high pastures *('brog sa)* by a group of women on hire. Either nuns or laywomen are hired to take on the grueling job of milking and herding the monastery's vast herd. For a few thousand rupees, they spend almost five months, churning thousands of gallons of milk into butter. While there is a certain freedom associated with being at the high pasture—far from the prying eyes of village elders—the women who work for the Labrang have little time to join the nightly song and dance fests that their girlfriends host.

In the last few years, the monks have stopped tilling their monastery's fields in Karsha, perhaps in deference to monastic discipline or simply because it proved too laborious. Most monastic fields are leased by hereditary sharecroppers, although a few are leased out on a more ad hoc basis in Karsha village. Under state revenue laws, these ad hoc arrangements can be converted to permanent tenancies after three years. Villagers are also paid with hay to water the vast alfalfa pasture which lies between Karsha and the neighboring Langmi village. This pasture receives a disproportionate share of water in the local system of water allocation. The monastery's pasture receives its own allocation of water from the Langmi streambed—even in times of severe drought—while it is highly unusual for pasture rather than fields to receive a separate allotment of irrigation water. In exchange for this unusual arrangement, Karsha monastery and those households which own adjacent fields send an obligatory donation of grain to the fifteenth-century Dorje Dzong nunnery above Langmi village. This payment implies that the pasture or even the fields may have once belonged to the nunnery.

The ritual marking of the transition from winter to spring, and from death to life, continues late in the fourth month. The celebration of the ancestors is known as the "virtuous offering" *(dge tsha)* ritual. On a day chosen by the local astrologer, monks are called to purify and transfer merit to the villagers who died the previous winter as well as the deceased more generally. As noted in Chapter 1, the head monk pounds the human bones which have dropped from the cremation pyre and mixes them with clay to make votive figurines *(tsha tsha)*. The full assemblies of monks and nuns chant blessings for the dead, while a few monks cook a meal for the monastic assembly. The headman and his assistants prepare an offering cake consumed by the villagers, who attend the ritual en masse. The consumption of food and alcohol continues through the night and into the next day as donors are feasted in the steward's house.

Like every village in Zangskar, Karsha hosts a springtime circumambulation rite ('bum skor) to purify village space. This ritual cleansing of the fields is believed to guarantee a "clean harvest" (ston thog lha mo) and prevent the jackdaws from eating the seedlings. Late in the third month, a party of Karsha monks circumambulates the fields of Karsha, Yulang, Sendo, and the five villages just west of Karsha. The circumambulation— on horseback—is a high-spirited affair of impromptu races among the younger monks. The monks make at least thirty-one stops during their procession at sacred spots, temples, and some donor houses.[36] The two main officiants, the abbot and his assistant, repeatedly perform their elaborate ablution (khrus), sometimes without dismounting. This ablution involves pouring saffron water from a ritual vessel (bum pa) over a mirror (me long) in which the deities, beings, and landscape are reflected and ritually cleansed.[37] Throughout the circuit, villagers make merit by hosting monks with tea, food, and donations of barley flour, which is measured out according to the status of the recipient. A second circumambulation takes place on the tenth day of the fifth month to purify Karsha village alone. On this day, monks, nuns, and villagers from the three subsections of Karsha (Tiur, Nangkar, Phikar) and the nearby hamlets of Yulang and Sendo gather in their respective temples to read the twelve volumes of the Prajñaparamita ('Bum).[38] Within each subsection of Karsha and the nearby hamlets two households are chosen as stewards to solicit food and beer. When the reading is complete, monks toss out ritual effigies (glud) at each temple to purify the space, before the abbot, the chantmaster, and ritual assistant perform a further circumambulation, carrying Buddhist relics. They ride through Karsha's fields in a clockwise fashion, stopping at the four directional stupa (mchod rten) to perform ritual ablutions that purify village space.

The monastery's major festival, known as "ninth [day] offering" or Gustor (dgu gtor), has been held during the high summer since the late 1980s. It was formerly held at the end of the eleventh month in midwinter, until the Dalai Lama's brother—Ngari Rinpoche, who is the honorary head of Karsha monastery—decided to move the festival to the late fifth month. A series of avalanches which killed several pilgrims en route to the festival prompted the switch. Villagers still journey from all over Zangskar to attend the monastic dances *('chams)* and the annual unveiling of the monastic protectors *(chos skyong)*. The abbot and head officiants offer the protectors ritual propitiations *(bskang gsol)*, while a chosen set of monks rehearses the dances for a week preceding the festival. The two-day festival involves a choreography of ritual dances which are performed on the first day without costume and only on the second day in full silk regalia with enormous papier-mâché masks, some of which have been brought from Tibet. The second day of the festival also involves a ceremonial parade of the monastery's four sacred animals—yak, horse, sheep, and dog—as well as a ritual visit of two villagers dressed up as the "old couple" *(rgad po, rgad mo)*, the village's mythical ancestors, who wander about making lewd jokes and collecting small sums in exchange for a blessing.[39] During an intermission between monastic dances, the new grooms and brides are called to dance in the monastic courtyard while the audience showers them with blessing scarves and token bits of money. The festival is a heady event which draws both elderly and youths in search of suitors, gossip, and spectacle. Given the lack of telephones and convenient transport, large festivals remain a convenient spot to network with villagers from far-flung valleys.

Despite the lack of rain in Zangskar, monks follow the "rainy season retreat" stipulated by the Buddha. One-half of this retreat takes place during six summer weeks *(dbyar gnas)* from the full moon of the sixth month to the end of the seventh month. The other half of the retreat is conveniently situated in the depths of winter when there is little else to do. The *chos grva* retreat is held from the beginning of the twelfth month to the full moon of the first month. On the first day of the summer retreat, the monks who will undertake the retreat take a set of vows *(bka' len)*—including fasting after noon—which are binding throughout the retreat. Very few monks take these vows, as most are too busy with managing monastic affairs or property to be able to attend this retreat. Halfway through the summer retreat, at the beginning of the seventh lunar month, monks spend a week invoking the third major Gelugpa protector, Guhyasamaja *(gsang ba 'dus pa)*. They invoke the deity after consecrating the monastic space *(sa'i cho ga)* and creating his virtual residence or *mandala*. The rite concludes with the dismantling of the *mandala*, the ritualized offering of the blessed sand into the village streambed as offerings for the subterranean spirits, and a fire offering to pacify the six realms of existence. These rites sanctify monastic and village space, but do not draw many attendees except an occasional donor. During the summer, monks travel far afield performing village circumambulations, purifications, and all kinds of ad hoc rites for earth spirits *(sa bdag gdon sgrol)* and other ill-tempered spirits.

At every point in this seasonal calendar, production and consumption rely on ritual markers. On an astrologically specified day in the seventh lunar month, a ceremony *(srub lha)* inaugurates the harvest of first fruits from the fields. The Labrang sends one of its monks to perform a juniper offering at the village altar, which is decorated with freshly cut sprigs of alfalfa, barley, wheat, and peas, blessing scarves, and libations of beer and butter. Along with the village deity, every household honors its clan deity with a similar libation ceremony on this day. The ceremony also marks the first day on which villagers may use their scythes to harvest the alfalfa and other grasses grown for fodder.[40] For two days villagers are conscripted in a vast haying operation in the monastery's fields. A set of villages is chosen for this job each year on rotation, either Karsha/Yulang/Sendo or the five villages west of Karsha. Every main house must send one person to work on the monastic fields, where these helpers are plied with food and beer to keep up their spirits. Along with dung taxes and obligatory porterage services, haying is one of the few chores that all households in the area perform for Karsha monastery.

The close of the monastery's summer retreat is marked with a feast *(dga' yas)* for the monastic assembly held in the three villages who share a single headman—Karsha, Yulang, and Sendo. In Karsha, the monks perform a dramatic expiatory offering *(gtor rgyab)* to atone for any inadvertent ritual mistakes during their retreat. A group of officiants, headed by the abbot, proceed out of the monastic courtyard into the village, where they offer a large blood-red offering cake *(gtor ma)* at a crossroads whose direction has been specified astrologically. The villagers continue to harvest their crops as they ripen, first peas, then barley, and finally wheat. The crops are pulled up by hand to harvest the stalks, which serve as valuable fodder for livestock in the winter months. On a communal day set by the headman and his assistants, every household in the village begins to carry the stacked sheaves of grain from the fields where they have been drying to the threshing circles. Only when all houses have finished carrying their crops out of the fields are monks invited to perform a brief ritual *(sku rim)* to bless the individual threshing circles. After this day, villagers are permitted to bring back their yaks, cattle, and horses from the high pasture, where they have been grazing. From now on, the livestock is allowed to roam freely through the fields, feasting on any remaining stalks. All the households begin threshing *(kho g.yu skor)* together, sharing cattle between themselves as necessary. The cattle are yoked to a central pole in the threshing circles and driven over the straw in circles to loosen the grain. The crops are then winnowed, the grain is blessed, and the villagers and monks carry their crops to the earthen storage tanks *(bang ba)* while the chaff is taken to the stables.

When harvest is nearly complete, in the eighth lunar month, the assembly of monks and three Labrang stewards set off to collect alms and rents from the sharecroppers. The monks then circulate through every main house in Karsha and its environs to perform an atonement and blessing of the crop. Senior officiants are called to perform this atonement *(bskang gsol)* with burnt offerings that propitiate the household and wider protective deities with a share of sacrifice. The total amount of grain that goes up in smoke during these burnt offerings across Zangskar totals 12,000 kilos.[41] Monks retreat from manual work in the winter by farming out their livestock to village households for feeding and care. On the twenty-second day of the ninth Tibetan month, they celebrate the Buddha's descent from heaven with a day-long prayer, and on the twenty-ninth day of the same month, they hold a set of ritual dances *('chams)* in Padum together with the Kagyud monks from Bardan to ward off the wintertime forces of darkness.[42]

On the twenty-fifth day of the tenth month in mid-December, the Ganden Namchod rite commemorates the fifteenth-century reformer Tsongkhapa. Butter lamps are lit throughout the monastery and village, while the abbot and key officiants perform a propitiatory offering *(bskang gsol)* in the disciplinarian's room to celebrate the famous reformer. The post of disciplinarian *(dge skos)* and the inner and outer retinue of posts at the monastery are then rotated. The incoming disciplinarian is welcomed into the monastery like a new bride, with gifts of blessing scarves, new clothes, utensils, and cash. Draped with offering scarves, the new disciplinarian reads the monastery's law code *(bca' yig)*, which was composed by the fifteenth-century Gelugpa reformer Sherab Zangpo and his disciple Lopon Dode Rinchen.[43] The Labrang hosts the entire congregation of monks to a celebratory meal of rice, vegetables, and flat breads baked by nuns from Karsha.

The farmer's New Year or Losar *(lo gsar)* celebrations take place at the end of the tenth lunar month. The farmer's new year is positioned around the winter solstice while the Tibetan new year is held in late February or March. The farmer's new year presents a ritual renewal of house and field rife with pre-Buddhist elements. On the twenty-ninth and thirtieth days of the month, laypeople renew the village and household altars *(lha tho)* with juniper sprigs, blessing scarves, and five different colored cloths *(snyen dar)*. They gather to offer a libation of barley beer and dough ibex (a wild antelope which was hunted and ritually sacrificed by Zangskar's first inhabitants, who left petroglyph images of it).[44] After a monk offers juniper incense and a short honorific text *(lha bsangs)* to the village and regional guardian deities, the village men retire to the steward's house to eat and drink till night falls. Every household propitiates its own clan deity *(pha'i lha)* with a lengthy prayer and a sacred meal of beer, roasted barley flour, meat, breads, pea cakes, dough ibex, dough sheep, and offering cakes *(lha bon mchod pa)*, consumed by all household members.[45] Each house decorates a pair of live sheep—a ram and ewe known as its "God Sheep" *(lug lha)*—with a stripe of maroon dye and five colored cloths. The sacred sheep are brought into the household altar room, where they are fed barley beer and food. Their movements are divined as omens from the household deity. Although the rite bears traces of former animal sacrifices, a Buddhist injunction holds that the two sheep should never be killed, but must die a natural death.[46]

A ritual day of the dead simply called "dead people" *(shi mi)* is held after dusk on the last day of the year. Traces of ancestor worship linger in the ritual offering of food to departed ancestors. Every household sends a female member to the wintertime cremation grounds *(dur khrod)*, where the women set out food offerings for the deceased and share the remainder with all who gather. All items must be eaten or abandoned, as it is inauspicious to return to the world of the living with food for the dead. Later that evening, the members of the house gather in their lower kitchen *(yog khang)* to worship the gods of the clan and the hearth with a sacred song and fertility symbols which are drawn on the walls and beams. These symbols are found across the Himalayas—both dough ibex and circular white dots of butter or dough. The traditional paean praises parts of the house: the golden dough ibex on the kitchen shelf, the central poplar pillar, the golden mother beam, the roof lattice of pearls, the roof of barley dough, the great starry eye or smokehole, the eight supporting beams in four directions, and the various deities of the underworld, place, and sky who guarantee household prosperity.[47]

A meal is held only for members of the household to which strangers cannot be invited. A small dough effigy *(glud)* is sculpted of two figures astride a yak in sexual embrace—the man riding forward and the woman riding backward. This figure and a burning firebrand *(me tho)* are taken from the house to a crossroads, where they are left as ransom or substitute offerings for the demons and hungry ghosts with loud shouts of "kya ho, kya ho."[48] The children who have taken this ransom out must answer a series of riddles before they are admitted back into the house. They return with a huge block of ice or snow *(gser ri pho long)* signifying fertility and wealth, which is supposed to ensure that the home, stable and grain silo will be full for the rest of the year. With its large kitchens, treasury, storehouse, and responsibility for managing the monastic endowment, the monastic building called the Labrang serves as a virtual household for the entire monastic assembly. The Labrang kitchen is decorated with dots and dough ibex, and its cooks serve an honorific meal for local sharecroppers on the last day of the year, when an effigy and firebrand are tossed into the streambed. After the sharecroppers are fed a meal of rare delicacies—fried meat, deep-fried dough, and stewed vegetables—they watch the monks prepare a small human effigy of an old man with a pointy cap, surrounded by small butter lamps *(ting lo)*. An older monk then sings the same paean to the roof and pillars that is recited in village households. At the close of festivities, the ibex will be fed to the crows, who represent the symbol of the monastic protector, Mahakala.

The eleventh month begins with the New Year dramas featuring ritual reversal and other classic elements of carnival. Gender roles and norms are turned upside down as young men cross-dress during a mock wedding.[49] Two boys are dressed up as bride and auntie, while a girl decked out as mother of the bride wears a traditional headdress *(pe rag)* adorned with horse dung instead of the usual turquoise and amber. A villager is dressed up as a monk during a dramatization of how Buddhism civilized the valleys earliest inhabitants. When a hapless youth fell into the huge vat of communal barley beer one year, the villagers exploded with laughter.[50] For the first ten days of the new year, two laymen wearing wooden masks tour the village making prophecies, addressing villagers as "my child." They are the same old man and woman *(rgad po, rgad mo)* who will appear at next summer's Gustor festival as the village ancestors or Zangskar's first inhabitants. Village households invite each other for reciprocal feasting and visits are made to friends at the monastery. The old couple and two troupes perform evening dances on frozen stages of snow. The troupe of boys are called grooms *(bag po)*, wearing full-length woolen robes *(gon cha)* and black hats decorated with wooden beaks. The troupe of girls *(kha tu ma)* formerly dressed in Balti costume, depicting a popular sixteenth-century queen of Ladakh who came from Baltistan.[51] As Baltistan is no longer accessible since Partition, the girls dress as Kashmiri or Lahauli teachers, chasing the boys with sticks. On the ninth day of the eleventh month, offering cakes *(gtor ma)* are tossed to the demons, and villagers return to the tedium of normal life once again.

Around the winter solstice, village households celebrate the rites known collectively as "sun returning rites" *(nyi ldog sku rim)*. The name for solstice, "sun returning" *(nyi ma log byes)*, reflects the careful marking of the solstice points at the southern- and northernmost points on the eastern and western horizons.[52] Every household chooses its own version of these rites depending on the health, wealth, and fortune of its members. On the eighteenth and nineteenth day of the eleventh month, the monastery holds a two-day propitiation *(bskang gsol)* to honor the death of its fifteenth-century reformer, Dode Rinchen. On the full moon of the twelfth month, the members of Karsha's three subsections gather at a steward's house in each section to read the *Prajñaparamita* and burn a set of dough effigies *(be le, glud)* for the demons. The effigies—a man and a woman astride a horse, a child, and several butter lamps—are burnt rather than tossed as other effigies are. The children take turns jumping over the fire, recalling the midwinter Persian custom of fire jumping.[53] The monks are then confined to the monastery for six weeks of winter retreat *(chos grva)* in order to memorize ritual texts or to meditate for the entire twelfth month and the first half of the first month, when the Tibetan new year begins the ritual calendar all over again.

The Nunneries in the Economy of Merit

The nunnery's ritual calendar (see Table 2.2) hardly intersects with the ritual calendar just described. Indeed, the cycle of ritual activities at the nunnery is largely peripheral to the village, outside of its Great Prayer Festival and fasting rite. Most of the nunnery's rituals are modest rites which make merit for donors and contribute to the welfare of all suffering sentient beings. Unlike the monks' more spectacular and pragmatic rituals, nunnery rituals rarely involve spectators at all. All of the regular rituals in the

Table 2.2 Annual rites held at Karsha nunnery

Months 1–12, Day 10. Deity yoga, alternating each month between Heruka or Vajrayogini visualization *(bDe mchog bla ma mchod pa, rNal 'byor ma'i bdag 'jug).*

Months 1–12, Day 15. Monthly renewal of Mahayana vows *(theg chen gso sbyong)* consisting of 42 rites *(sku rim)* and 12 prayers *(smon lam).*

Months 1–12, Day 25. Deity yoga for Vajrayogini *(rnal 'byor ma'i bdag 'jug).*

Month 2, Day 13. Unveiling nunnery relics and offerings of the 13th *(bCu gsum mchod pa).*

Month 2, Days 26*–31.* Assorted textual recitations *('bum, mdo mang, sman bla mdo mchog).*

Month 3, Day 8. Ritual atonement *(sdung bshags).*

Month 3, Day 30, through Month 4, Day 20.* Great Prayer Festival *(smon lam chen mo).*

Month 4, Day 8. Purification of mountains and valleys *(ri khrus lung khrus).*

Month 4, Day 15. Thousand auspicious offerings *(bskal bzang stong mchod).*

Month 4, Days 13–16. Gelongma Palmo's fasting rite *(smyung gnas).*

Month 4, Day 16. Long-life initiation *(tshe dbang)* for villagers.

Month 5, Day 8. Tara prayers *(sgrol mchog).*

Month 10, Day 15, through Month 3, Day 30. Daily winter prayers *(smon lam, sku rim).*

Month 10, Day 25. Birthday of Tsongkhapa *(dga ldan lnga mchod).*

Month 10, Day 29, through Month 11, Day 3. New Year celebrations *(Lo gsar).*

Month 12, Day 10. Vajrayogini burnt offering *(rDo rje rnal 'byor ma'i sbyin bsreg).*

Note: All dates are provided in the Tibetan calendar. Dates marked with an asterisk vary according to astrological indicators.

nunnery calendar are funded by local donations, with some supplemental foreign sponsorship. The wintertime burnt offering *(sbyin bsreg),* on the tenth day of the twelfth month, honors the nunnery's main meditational deity, Vajrayogini *(rdo rje rnal 'byor ma).* Because nuns are considered unqualified to perform burnt offerings even to their own meditational deity, a set of senior monks is invited to perform the fire sacrifice. The monastery's ritual assistants arrive a day early to help prepare a new set of collective offering cakes *(gtor ma),* which are locked into a wooden offering box where they will remain until the following year. The bulbous cakes— decorated with finely carved butter adornments—represent the entourage of meditational deities which nuns visualize in their daily practices. Every nun who has undergone a Vajrayogini empowerment renews her own offering cakes in her room during this period.

The nunnery's meager endowments limit the scope of the ritual calendar but not the devotional intensity of the nuns. Thrice a month, the nuns gather for all-day prayers in their nunnery. On the tenth and twenty-fifth of each Tibetan month they honor their guardian deity, Vajrayogini, but the full moon is spent renewing their Mahayana vows *(theg chen gso sbyong)*. Although nuns, as novices, do not hold full ordination vows and cannot recite the discipline of full liberation *(pratimoksha)* that fully ordained monks do, they do renew their Mahayana vows with a full day of prayer and fasting, so rare among the busy monks. Well before dawn, the steward *(gnyer pa)* rises with a few other nuns she has recruited the previous evening while mixing the bread dough. The steward and her assistants cook the tea in the dark kitchen before they knead the dough and pat it into palm-sized flat breads *(gro dkar)* baked on a thin stone over the scorching dung coals. While the breads are baking and the huge pot of tea comes to a boil, the ritual assistant prepares the altar and the communal offering cakes which will be consumed by mid-day.[54] Long before the sun rises, the other nuns arise and gather at the assembly hall, collecting their sleepier colleagues on the way. When the entire assembly has gathered, the chantmaster signals the beginning of the rite with a sonorous low-pitched prayer. The prayers rise in volume as the light gains outside.

The first set of prayers are performed kneeling in imitation of the ordination ritual with lengthy prostrations. When the first prayers are over, each nun receives a steaming helping of salt tea in her wooden bowl. In memory of the Buddha's offering bowl, every nun has her own wooden bowl, to be used during ritual assemblies and stored in the assembly hall. The first tea—a "gift" from the steward which has less than the prescribed two kilos of butter—is not heralded by a conch like most tea services for the full assembly of nuns. By the time the sun has risen, the ritual assistant goes to the roof of the nunnery to blow the conch, signaling the service of the morning tea. The steward spends most of the day behind the scenes in the kitchen, keeping the praying nuns supplied with a steady flow of salt tea, roasted barley flour or *tsam pa,* and perhaps a meal of rice and vegetables if there are funds.[55] The prayers continue until noon, when the nuns eat the designated meal and sample the offering cakes *(tshogs)*. The meal is eaten in a ritually proscribed manner: they must remove their hats and remain seated during the entire meal. Each nun makes a bit of dough from *tsam pa* mixed with tea from her cup, and squeezes this dough between the five fingers and palm of her left hand. The resulting impression, or *chang bu,* is rolled over one's clothes to remove all defilements *(sgrib)* before being tossed to the floor, where it will be gathered by the steward and tossed outside as food for dogs. After tossing the *chang bu,* each nun will fast until the next morning as the Buddha's discipline once specified.[56] As the hypnotic chant of the prayers continues long into the afternoon, the younger nuns often become drowsy and are the targets of deftly flung barley corns, to much laughter. While ritual work is exhausting, many nuns prefer it to the monotonous drudgery of work in the village. As celibate and thus childless women, their services are much required in the domestic economy where women rule hearth and home.

Gender, Kinship, and Marriage

Although men dominate the public arenas of trade, law, and civil service, women manage most of the allocation of household labor and wealth in Zangskar.[57] While women and men have power in their own realms, they share each other's duties frequently. Women can take part in politics or trade, while men contribute to household chores like cooking and washing. Men and women work side by side in fields and kitchens, weeding, watering, washing, and cooking. Both men and women cook, wash, clean house, sew clothes, spin wool, weave baskets, and process food. Both men and women do most field chores, although women do more of the weeding. Women wash and roast most of the grain, although both men and women thresh, winnow, and grind grain. While women dominate in dairy preparation, men are in charge of slaughter and meat preparation. While men spin coarse yak wool from a drop spindle to make rugs, blankets, and sacks, women spin the finer sheep and goat wool using the hand-twirled spindle *(phang)*. Despite considerable overlap in gender roles, transgression spells disaster. There are two tasks forbidden to women: plowing and weaving.[58] A local proverb notes that "If women were to weave or plow, the mountains would fall down." While gender roles have considerable overlap, there are clear and incontrovertible distinctions between male and female bodies, as we see in Chapter 7.

Zangskari identity is shaped by descent as much as residence, both of which carry certain obligations. Alliance and descent still affect the rise and fall of households and individual fortunes today. Zangskari kinship is similar to the Tibetan in reckoning identity through the idioms of descent and residence.[59] There are two dominant kinship idioms which children receive: "bone" *(rus)* from their fathers and "flesh" *(sha)* from their mothers.[60] Both idioms, flesh and bone, denote conceptual categories rather than a corporate group. Both children are known by the bone they receive from their father rather than by the flesh they receive from their mother.

Those individuals who share the same bone share a common patrilineal ancestor, real or fictive. A subset of those who share the same bone are those who also share a guardian deity, known as the "father's relatives" (pha'i spun).[61] This group or patriclan provides its members with a shared status and offers assistance at times of death and birth, when the household members are polluted. When women marry, they sever their ties to their natal household by giving up their affiliation to their father's guardian deity and patriclan, but retain their father's bone.

The rules of exogamy, which exclude all bilateral kin up to a depth of five or seven generations, usually require that men marry a woman of a different bone. Ideally, the household bone remains continuous as it passes from father to son, but this is not always possible in a generation with no sons. In the absence of sons, a daughter will inherit the house and her father will seek a groom (mag pa) with the same bone. It may be difficult to find an unrelated candidate. If the new incoming husband has a different bone than his wife, their children will inherit his bone and a new bone will be introduced into the household. The husband may also choose to install his own guardian deity (pha'i lha), in which case the household no longer belongs to the original patriclan. The ceremonial installation of the husband's new guardian deity ties the house to the husband's and his father's patriclan. Alternatively, the new husband may abandon his natal household deity and patriclan, and reside under his wife's household deity (bu mo'i lha yog la bzhugs). In this case, the house deity and patriclan affiliation remain the same, but the bone of the children will shift. As a result, the members of a single pha spun occasionally do not share the same bone. Alternatively, members of the same bone may worship different household deities.[62] In Ladakh, the idiom of bone has become defunct and the pha spun is an assembly of households who join or leave at will.

Every household has a shrine (lha tho) for its guardian deity, either on the roof or inside the upper story of the house in the altar room or some other hidden sanctum. This shrine is usually a white-washed block of stones, adorned with a vessel of barley holding arrows that symbolize the members of the family. In the absence of a stone cairn, a vessel of barley grains holding arrows represents the shrine to the guardian deity. The guardian deities of the patriclan and of the village are both considered to be worldly gods ('jigs rten pa'i lha) who have not yet transcended the cycle of death and rebirth. Legends suggest that such gods are pre-Buddhist spirits which were converted to Buddhism in a distant mythical past. By contrast, the monastic protectors, who have escaped the cycle of death and re-birth as other-worldly gods *('jig rten las 'das pa'i lha)*, are a step higher on the cosmological scheme. This rich pantheon of protective deities is propi-tiated by members of the relevant unit, household, village, or monastery. While laypeople can make offerings of beer and first fruits to the house-hold and village protectors, only monks and nuns make offerings to the Buddhist protective deities *(chos skyong, srung ma)*.[63]

The status of the patriline determines a person's rank in society most broadly. All of the patrilines can be ranked into one of three groups: roy-alty and aristocracy *(rgyal po, sku drag, rigs ldan)*; commoners *(mi dmangs, dmangs rigs)*; and outcastes *(rigs ngan)*. Like caste, these three strata deter-mine many aspects of individual identity including with whom one may eat, marry, or have sex, as well as the degree of deference one is owed and owes others. In Karsha as elsewhere in Zangskar, roughly nine-tenths of the population fall into the commoner stratum, while a handful of aristocrats (2 percent) and untouchables (8 percent) make up the remainder.[64] Al-though the three strata are not supposed to intermarry, have sexual con-tact, or share a cup, commoners and aristocrats can bend these rules. Aris-tocrats often intermarry with commoners, and often eat and drink at commoner houses, although they rarely share the same cup.

The untouchables consist of three groups: blacksmiths, Beda, and Mon. The latter two groups are believed to be descended from immigrants to the Zangskar. They cannot share food or sex with members of the other two strata. They often live at the outskirts of the village, and face considerable social discrimination, although they can have sizable farms and modern jobs. They are forbidden from joining the monastic orders and cannot of-fer cooked food to the monastics.[65] The prevalence of caste in Zangskar is apparent in the custom to give alms in the form of raw grain, unlike the cooked food offered in Southeast Asia. At villagewide festivals *(khrom)*, untouchables must always bring their own cups, for their touch would pol-lute the cups and utensils shared between commoners. Utensils and indi-viduals can be purified with ritual fumigation or ablution after a breach of commensality, although sexual pollution is a far more severe and irrevoca-ble transgression.

In Sri Lanka as elsewhere in South Asia, men can sleep around: "It does not matter where a man goes; he may sleep with anyone, but the woman must be protected."[66] In Zangskar, by contrast, cross-caste philandering is not permitted for either men or women. Ritual pollution, like AIDS, is sexually transmitted to both sexes. One nun told a tale about her sister, Tandzin. Tandzin was once happily married, with three children, before her husband began a secret affair with a woman from the Beda caste. Tandzin's husband was suddenly rejected by his village when his mistress had a child and declared him the father. The villagers stopped sharing their cups and utensils with him and no longer visited his house. Although Tandzin's husband never cohabited with his mistress, and their child died shortly after birth, he was ostracized by his commoner friends. He no longer could claim his ordinary place in village seating orders, but was relegated to a place near the door with other untouchable villagers. His wife, Tandzin, was also socially ostracized, as neighbors began to decline to share their cups with her. In desperation, she left her husband and returned to her natal home with her children, where they have lived since. She has never returned to her husband's village, and it is unclear whether her ritual pollution will affect her children's prospects for marriage.

It is clear that caste pollution can be passed from philandering husband to wife. However, it is also transmitted through commensality or cohabitation for generations. Tandzin's husband's mistress was the daughter of a man named Norzang, who had contracted pollution from his mother's sister. Although Norzang's parents were both commoners, their untimely deaths sent him to be raised by his maternal aunt and her husband, who was from the neighboring region of Manali. When it emerged that this man was an untouchable from the Beda community, both the aunt and Norzang's entire household were ostracized from village life. When Norzang's younger brother became mute in childhood, villagers speculated that his disability was caused by the polluting effects of the aunt's husband from Manali. Norzang and his brother were both considered untouchables long after their aunt and her husband had died. While Norzang's brother married a woman from the blacksmith caste and had four children, who all became untouchables, Norzang married a commoner woman, hoping perhaps to transcend his low status. Nevertheless, Norzang and his daughters have remained untouchables in the eyes of their village. Despite Norzang's legitimate claim to commoner status, via his parents, both his daughters have been treated as untouchables. Caste and gender discrimination are rarely discussed, although they are extremely important in local society.

Besides caste, the house remains the most important symbol of individual identity. As the crucible within which alliances are anchored and identities are forged, the household socializes and prepares children for future roles in society. It is oriented toward both the past and the future, by nurturing the traditional wisdom of the elders as much as the desires of its younger members. An individual's position in the household—father, mother, son, daughter, bride, or groom—determine many of the wider social roles in village life. Yet it is households rather than individuals who negotiate labor exchanges, social obligations, or ritual duties. Residence takes precedence over descent in terms of inheritance and identity. Both adopted and illegitimate children have rights to inheritance in their father's house, if the father agrees to raise them. Such children will be regarded as sharing the household bone or lineage, regardless of their birth—unless they are untouchables. Marriage is conceptualized as a relation that occurs between households and only secondly between individuals. There is relatively little intermarriage between Ladakh and Zangskar—despite the similar culture. While Zangskari wives have been considered rustic or uncouth by the urbane Ladakhis, Ladakhi wives have been seen as too sophisticated to settle in remote valleys.

Brothers still share a wife more often than wives share a husband in Zangskar. As elsewhere in the Tibetan Himalaya, a mélange of marital and residential rules has been flexibly oriented toward a single goal: keeping landholding intact.[67] Patrilocal and matrilocal marriages make use of monogamy, polyandry, and polygyny in order to thwart the splitting of a household or to produce a legitimate heir.[68] Although laws have outlawed polyandry and primogeniture since the 1950s, these social practices continue. Younger siblings have only recently begun to claim their legal right to a share of their father's property. Until recently, the oldest son inherited his father's estate, while younger brothers often became monks, traders, outmarrying husbands, or homesteaders who claimed new lands. In recent decades, the increased job opportunities have enabled younger brothers to earn a separate livelihood without dividing family property. The younger sons may build a new house on family lands, which some continue to share with their brothers and others choose to split up. The increased tendency to split estates has led to smaller parcels and increased disputes over water and other rights.

Daughters, by contrast, rarely claim their rightful inheritance. Their dowry is regarded as a substitute for their forfeited share of property. Under customary law, those daughters without brothers can inherit their father's estate and marry matrilocally. Yet the deed to the estate is rarely put into their name. After their eldest son's marriage and maturity, he receives the title to his grandfather's estate. By keeping the property in male hands, the household staves off any attempts by in-marrying husbands to claim the land as their own.

When the parents are aged, they may retire to an adjunct or "little house" *(khang chung)*, with some livestock and "food fields" *(lto zhing)* that will be reabsorbed by the main house *(khang chen)* upon their demise. Before shifting to their little house, the parents hold a public ceremony to divide all movable wealth between the main and subsidiary houses. The entire village is invited to this ceremony and hosted with beer and bread. In front of the crowd, the parents read out a proclamation *('pho deb)* listing each household item they have ceded to their son and his wife, to avoid future arguments. The local revenue officer may be called to adjust the land deed in the name of the sons, if they wish to split the estate. The elderly parents and the eldest son may continue to till the son's fields jointly. When his parents move into the little house, the son takes over the ritual obligations his estate owes the monastery and the community. He must now steward and sponsor the village rituals until his eldest son relieves him of this burden.

Both polyandry and monasticism require individuals to subordinate their personal desires toward the collective good of the household. Sons and daughters submit to the good of the household just as monks and nuns subordinate their personal desires in favor of the community. Nuns are even less likely to receive or claim a share of the family property, although they may be given usufruct rights. In such arrangements, nuns till a few fields in exchange for food handouts from the family estate. Monks earn their subsistence through ritual performances and the monastic endowment. The accumulation of private property is perfectly legal under the monastic law followed by Tibetan Buddhists, as Schopen (1995) has shown. In this regard it is hardly surprising that Zangskari monks accumulate considerable moveable wealth throughout their career. In contradiction with the monastic laws laid out in their Mulasarvastivadin Vinaya, however, Zangskari monks often deed their moveable wealth to the monastery, family members, or disciples shortly before their death. After their death, their remaining possessions are auctioned off among the community of monks, and the proceeds from this auction are immediately distributed among the members of the monastic assembly. The same procedure—auction and distribution—is followed among the community of nuns, although the objects auctioned are fewer and command less value, reducing the total amount distributed back to the community. For both monks and nuns, the monastic cell is owned by the lay household which built it or maintains it in readiness for the next family member who will take up monastic life. Cells may be bought and sold by the laity, or loaned to distant relatives already at the monastery.

Monasticism versus Marriage

Nuns are exceptional in Zangskar because they forgo the central rite of passage that most young women undergo: marriage. Marriage is more than a crucial rite which moves a young woman along from youth to adulthood. It binds households and their members with an exchange of women and goods. The conspicuous exchange of feasts given by the bride's, the groom's, and other village households crystallizes the critical values of Zangskari culture: generosity and reciprocity. The departure of a young bride from her natal home and her subsequent arrival at her new marital home is an event witnessed by the entire village. Most villagers are expected to attend certain key feasts as well as offer a symbolic welcoming gift in the form of a blessing scarf to the new bride. Overall, weddings cement relations between wife-giving and wife-receiving households as much as they cement the relations between the community of adult women. The new bride is welcomed into the village collective through a series of feasts coordinated by sets of households throughout her husband's village. She will be expected to offer similar foods when it comes her time to hold such a feast on the next ritual occasion. In short, she is being both feted and instructed in the customary norms surrounding village feasting. By contrast, the arrival of a young woman at the nunnery and her departure from her home are hardly recognized by the wider community. Women who join the nunnery receive neither a dowry nor any other gifts from the village, although their household does receive a symbolic payment to compensate the house for the loss of its member, as explained in Chapter 4.

Interestingly, monastic assemblies in Zangskar do maintain one ritual that maintains the flavor if not the form of a wedding. The ritual passage of a monk or nun to chantmaster or, for monks, to disciplinarian resembles the giving of the dowry during the wedding. The monks and nuns who take up the role of chantmaster receive a stack of gifts and well wishes from their relatives and villagers, just as a new bride does before departing from her natal home. The monk who is being sworn in as chantmaster or disciplinarian invites one representative from every household in Karsha to attend the ceremony. Every guest brings a small gift of cash or clothes, and a blessing scarf. The size of the gift signals the donor's wealth and proximity as kin. In front of the entire assembly, the new chantmaster is draped in a mountain of blessing scarves until he or she looks like a new bride. The gifts of robes and utensils are not packed away like the bride's dowry, but are carried to the nearby monastic cell by an apprentice. As in weddings, all those bringing a gift are hosted with a return feast. The new chantmaster usually offers guests meal, barley beer, and distilled alcohol in his own quarters while the assembly of monks usually also hosts the entire community of laypeople for a drinking party down in the village. This example of village reciprocity is developed in the chapter on monastic economics, to which we now turn.

CHAPTER

3

The Buddhist Economy of Merit

For Ani Yeshe and her companions, the pilgrimage to Tibet was the beginning of a profound transition in their own lives as much as in their village. Over the next four decades, Yeshe and her colleagues developed what was perhaps the first nunnery in a village that had been Buddhist for over a millennium. Karsha housed one of the largest and oldest monasteries in Zangskar, several religious edifices funded by Zangskar's most illustrious kings and queens, as well as an Avalokitesvara temple and stupa believed to have been founded by successors of the legendary tenth-century Tibetan translator Rinchen Zangpo. Clearly the village was a religious center in Zangskar, with ample evidence of patronage. Why, then, was there no record of a nunnery in the past millennium? The answer is due as much to the lack of records surrounding nuns and their institutions as it is to the social and economic constraints nuns face within the Buddhist economy of merit, which are explored in this chapter. When Yeshe returned from Tibet in 1956, she settled back into the tiny monastic cell she shared with a distant aunt, Ani Angmo. While there were only a handful of cells on the cliff surrounding the Lonpo's Avalokitesvara temple at that time, forty years later the cliff was covered with monastic cells and a brand-new assembly hall, which supported a community of over twenty nuns. The struggles that Yeshe and her disciples faced in developing this community of nuns elucidate the wider constraints on women throughout the region who wish to develop a community of nuns or pursue the spiritual life in the absence of such a community.

In the first summer after Yeshe and her companions returned from their Tibetan pilgrimage, they had little time for religious retreats. Although their vows were supposed to guarantee a lifetime of renunciation, there

77

was little opportunity for meditation or study. From the time the spring snow thawed until the last of the harvest was stored in the houses before the winter, the nuns had hardly a moment to apply themselves to their newly held discipline. Without the institutional support of a nunnery or the ritual expertise which might provide a means of livelihood, they had little choice but to work on local estates for a wage. Yearning to dedicate themselves to their preliminary Tantric practices, they waited patiently for the frozen lull of winter. In the first few winters, the nuns performed the requisite hundred thousand prayers and prostrations, throwing themselves to the floor until elbows and palms were rubbed raw. As they visualized the vast, interdependent emptiness described in their texts, they began to think in wider terms than the laywomen in their village. They emerged from their cells with a vision it would take decades to complete.

After their return from Tibet, Yeshe and her companions received their devotional instruction from a few elderly monks at Karsha monastery. Their first abbot, the monk who had guided them to Tibet, taught them a basic devotional text known as the Guru Puja (bla ma mchod pa). For the first several years they held only one formal ritual a year, on the full moon of the fifth Tibetan month. They gathered for four days, fasting most of each day so as to conserve the meager supplies of barley and butter they had saved up for the rite. Eventually a Tibetan monk who had taken refuge in Karsha suggested that they gather once a month to renew their eight Mahayana Precepts (theg chen gso sbyong). The nuns agreed, but still needed additional material resources for the rite. Ani Angmo, who had been to Tibet with Yeshe, asked her father for a donation. He gave each nun five rupees as a loan, which they accepted with the understanding that future interest "payments" on this loan would fund the monthly rite, henceforth. The nuns received their first permanent endowment with this gift, while Angmo's father (and household) would receive merit in perpetuity as long as the rite continued to be held. The offerings that each nun brought to the ritual as her interest payment are still in effect today in the form of the monthly ritual payments—a kilogram of butter, five kilograms of barley flour, a handful of tea, and a pinch of salt as payment on a five-rupee loan—for the tri-monthly rites held at Karsha nunnery on the tenth, fifteenth, and twenty-fifth of each month. Additionally, every nun who joins the nunnery accepts the so-called "empty exchange" (stong deb) of five rupees in exchange for agreeing to manage and fund her share of the nunnery's tri-monthly rituals, turn by turn. After a few more years Yeshe and her companions were bold enough to hold a Great Prayer Festival, along the lines of the one they had seen in Lhasa. Although this festival is practiced by Karsha monastery and countless other Gelugpa monasteries across the Buddhist Himalaya, it was not common for nuns to hold such a spectacular rite. Overcoming some resistance from suspicious villagers, the Karsha nuns convinced some monks to teach them the ritual for the first few years. Once they had mastered the ritual texts, the nuns no longer invited the monks but continued the rite under the leadership of their abbot.

By the early 1970s the membership of Karsha nunnery had grown to over a dozen nuns, who still lacked a temple of worship. With the help of several powerful monks, the nuns were able to galvanize local villagers behind the construction of a new temple. While the process of fund-raising and construction was driven to its conclusion by persevering nuns, the initial catalysts were charismatic monks. A key monk was Geshe Zodpa, considered an incarnation of the Tibetan saint Milarepa and also the first Ladakhi to become the abbot of the famous Tibetan monastery Tashilhunpo, albeit in exile. A charismatic public leader and Tantric expert, he conducted a week-long esoteric "Wheel of Life" or Kalachakra initiation for Zangskari villagers in 1972 and was elected honorary abbot of Karsha. Many of the nuns who joined the nunnery after Yeshe first renounced lay life and were ordained as novices by Geshe Zodpa. When Geshe Zodpa gave the week-long empowerment into the "Profound Teachings of Vajrayogini" *(rdo rje rnal 'byor ma'i zab khrid)* in Karsha in 1975 and 1978, he initiated many Karsha nuns into their central Tantric practice. He only admitted novice nuns and a handful of fully ordained monks into these initiations of the Highest Yoga Tantra.[1]

Eventually, the nuns invited the venerable Geshe Zodpa to attend their full moon ritual, held in the Karsha Lonpo's ancient Avalokitesvara temple. Moved by their perseverance and mindful of the temple's aristocratic owner, Geshe Zodpa suggested that they build a new assembly hall where they might assemble in peace. It would take fifteen years to complete the task. For three years, the nuns hauled rocks from the nearby ruins of Karsha's earliest settlement. They also collected dirt, silt, and water from the streambed far below to make mortar and plaster. By the time the most senior monks at Karsha monastery performed the earth ritual *(sa'i cho ga)* to anoint the construction process in 1978, the membership of the nunnery had risen to fourteen. The rite enabled the local religious establishment to authorize the nuns' religious construction, while also propitiating

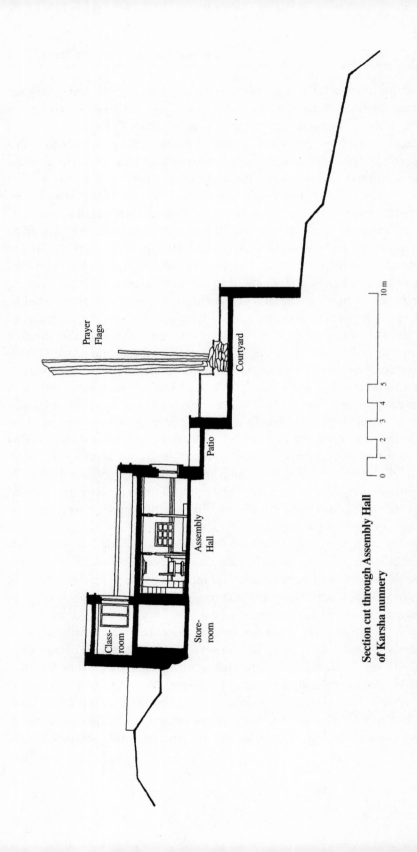

Section cut through Assembly Hall of Karsha nunnery

Prayer Flags

Courtyard

Patio

Assembly Hall

Store-room

Class-room

0 1 2 3 4 5   10 m

First-floor plan of Karsha nunnery

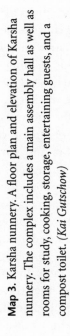

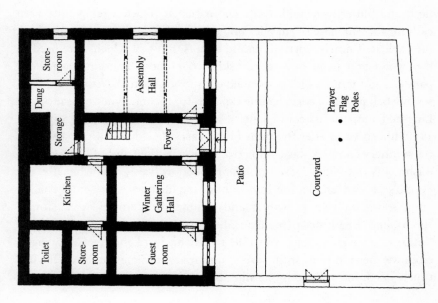

Map 3. Karsha nunnery. A floor plan and elevation of Karsha nunnery. The complex includes a main assembly hall as well as rooms for study, cooking, storage, entertaining guests, and a compost toilet. (*Kai Gutschow*)

local spirits of soil and place *(sa bdag, gzhi bdag).* Over the next few years, the construction process continued sporadically, whenever there was time or labor on hand. Nuns solicited help from the villagers who offered their labor, hauling construction supplies up the cliff to the construction site, and cooked meals for local carpenters and stonemasons, who often worked free of charge. Begging beers were held in various villages to solicit labor, cash, and gifts of trees which yielded wooden beams and roof lattices. Store-bought construction supplies like glass, concrete, and wood to frame doors and windows were purchased on credit by a local monk named Tsetan. After Tsetan spent several years in the company of women, he eventually abandoned his monastic robes. He took not just one but two wives, the first a laywoman and the second a nun.[2]

After four years of hard labor, the nuns had exhausted their own supplies and the generosity of nearby villagers. The nuns traveled further afield to solicit donations for several winters, continuing the construction sporadically in summer months. Begging on foot for donations in cash or kind, they traveled through many of the Buddhist villages of Zangskar and the neighboring region of Ladakh. While some Ladakhi villagers turned the nuns away empty-handed, the Zangskari villagers seemed far more welcoming and respectful of nuns. The fund-raising was laborious, as they received no more than a cup of flour or spoon of butter at each house. The flour and butter were sold in the Leh bazaar to Tibetan refugees to earn cash for the purchase of supplies not available back in Zangskar. All in all, they solicited nearly thirty thousand rupees, most of which were used to buy wood and paint and to pay skilled laborers, including carpenters, painters, and monks who performed consecration rituals. Painting the assembly hall proved a considerable expense, for the renowned artisans from Lingshed monastery required hefty wages for two months of work. In 1990, fifteen years after the nuns began carrying stones for construction, the nunnery complex was completed. Known as the Land of Oral Accomplishments *(bKa 'spyod sgrub gling),* or colloquially as Chuchizhal after the Lonpo's nearby temple, the Karsha nunnery includes an assembly hall, a guest room for visitors, winter and summer kitchens, assorted storage rooms, and a bathroom (see map 3). Shortly after its completion, Geshe Zodpa returned to Zangskar in 1991 to give his third and final Vajrayogini empowerment to nuns from several nunneries in Zangskar. Since his untimely death in 1997, no monk in Zangskar has offered a Vajrayogini empowerment. The nuns who have received the empowerment are deemed unfit to transmit the teachings because of their inferior Tantric training.

Merit Making and the Production of Difference

Why did it take the nuns almost half a century to accomplish a feat that monks might complete within a single year? Why must nuns travel all over Ladakh and Zangskar to build a tiny assembly hall, when a set of Zangskari monks can build a small palace for the Dalai Lama during the space of summer? The answer to these questions is due as much to a historical lack of permanent endowments as to the fact that nuns perform a very different set of services for laypeople than monks do. Unlike Thailand, where monks concentrate on salvation, death rites and other forms of collective merit making, Tibetan Buddhist monks perform a wide spectrum of ritual activities of a soteriological, instrumental, and propitiatory nature.[3] Monks engage in Tantric meditations which secure symbolic power and efficacy that make them ideally suited for pragmatic rites which protect and secure the individual life cycle, the household, and villagewide fertility and prosperity. Tantric power also helps monks harness the energies of local spirits who can help ward against danger, disease, and natural disaster that can be triggered by accidental human defilement or mistakes. By contrast, nuns are called to perform more mechanical acts of generalized merit making, which have fewer instrumental or pragmatic functions. This chapter examines the economy of merit within which nuns and monks operate on behalf of their village clients to produce merit and other ritual effects.

What is the role of gender in the local economy of merit? An analysis of the relationship between merit and social status makes it clear that merit functions as a form of symbolic capital in this economy. Both historical and current patterns of patronage systematically favor monks over nuns in the Buddhist economy of merit. The preference for giving to monks determines past endowment as well as present resources for ritual training and status. Although both nuns and monks are supposed to follow a discipline of detachment, they serve laypeople in different capacities. Monks provide ritual expertise, while nuns offer a general source of merit as well as adult labor.

Nuns embody the ideals of voluntary poverty that the Buddha outlined, not because they choose to but because they must. Renunciation may be a full-time occupation for monks, but it is an unpaid vocation for nuns. Both monks and nuns uphold their links with their natal households. Yet monks do so out of personal sentiment; nuns do so out of need. Sending a daughter to the nunnery is akin to placing her in a community college without any scholarship. She may have access to ritual knowledges, peers, and pilgrimages which take her far beyond her provincial village life. Yet she is tied to an institution close to her natal village, so that she can work at home to earn her daily bread. Although nuns take up celibacy and religious training as early and as passionately as monks do, their institution offers few advancements or sources of income. Devoting their youth to helping parents and villagers, senior nuns may wind up neglected in their old age.

By contrast, sending a son to the monastery is like enrolling him in an Ivy League or Oxbridge college on a full scholarship. He will earn a handsome stipend at an elite institution which provides him with ample opportunities for privilege and profit for the rest of his life. No matter how impoverished or provincial, a monk receives a training that enables a lifetime of ritual employment and support. Even when feeble or incapacitated, elderly monks are supported until their deaths. For the most ambitious monks, the local monastery is merely the gateway to advanced religious studies at Tibetan or Indian institutes and perhaps a ticket to the West. Those monks who are less scholastically inclined may hold jobs managing the monastic endowment and its business ventures. The ritual experts graduate into ever more obscure offices for which the qualifications are less clear but the remuneration ever more handsome.

Much of the inequity between monks and nuns is due to the concentration of wealth and status produced by merit-making practices. Merit and morality are indexed to wealth and status in the economy of merit. Those with wealth and power are said to have accumulated a good deal of virtue or merit in past lives. In theory, Tibetan Buddhism promotes a radical nonduality. The Mahayana doctrine of emptiness ultimately denies all forms of conventional duality. As a result, every self is similar by virtue of its emptiness. All selves are identical in lacking a permanent or independent existence.[4] The lack of innate existence implies an interdependence between all selves, which is the basis of universal compassion. The *bodhisattva*—who truly understands the nonduality as well as the emptiness of self and other—takes a vow to dedicate herself or himself toward the liberation of every other sentient being. In addition, the Tathagatagharba (literally, womb or seed of the Buddha) sutra explains that every individual has the same seed of Buddhahood, an already pure and perfected mind.[5] Such a profoundly egalitarian vision suggests that all humans have an equal potential to Buddhahood. Despite the radical theories of nonduality, debates continued to simmer about whether or not the female body had the potential for Buddhahood. The very debates about whether it was possible to gain enlightenment in the female body suggests an inconsistency within Mahayana thought.[6] Early Mahayana texts noted that women could not become irreversible *bodhisattvas* or Buddhas, while later Mahayana texts prevented women from taking rebirth in celestial lands such as the Pure Land. Since these lands were only populated by male bodies, women could not take birth there unless they despised their female nature.

The Sutra on Changing the Female Sex comments:

> The female defects—greed, hate, and delusion and other defilements— are greater than the male's . . . You should have such an intention . . . Because I wish to be freed from the impurities of the woman's body, I will acquire the beautiful and fresh body of a man.[7]

Some Mahayana texts resolved the problem of gender and duality by arguing that the defective female body should be traded in for a more usable male body by someone aspiring to Buddhahood. It was only in the later Mahayana sutras like the Vimalakirti Sutra and the Sumati Sutra that goddesses scold disciples representing these earlier views for being mired in discriminatory thinking. The Vimalakirti Sutra includes an oft-cited passage about a debate between a goddess and Sariputra, who is made to stand in for the outdated sexism of the earlier schools of Buddhism, collectively called the Hinayana, or "Lesser Vehicle" by those favoring the Mahayana or "Greater Vehicle." The goddess first showers Sariputra with flowers, before observing his vain efforts to remove them. When she scolds him for his simplistic but discriminatory attitude that disciples should not wear flowers, he taunts her by asking her why she is still in the female form if she is so enlightened. She literally returns the insult by transposing their bodies and asking him where he now sees the female body. When he has no answer, she explains that just as he only *appears* to be trapped within the female body, so too are all women. This is why the Buddha said there is no distinction between male and female. She then returns him to his male body. Yet the very evidence of this textual discussion suggests that disparagement of women among Mahayana adepts was hardly unknown. Other texts offer ample evidence of ingrained attitudes about the imperfections of the female body.

The Mahayana pursuit of six perfections *(paramita)*—generosity, ethics, patience, effort, meditation, and insight *(dana, sila, ksanti, virya, dhyana, prajna)*—emphasizes a hierarchical or progressive view of enlightenment. The first of the six perfections, generosity, is supposed to be extended equally to male or female, rich or poor, friend or foe. Yet a graded hierarchy of recipients develops in practice. The more meritorious the recipient, the greater the merit accrued by the donor.[8] Monks—who are considered most virtuous and most detached—become known as the greatest field of merit. Nuns, by contrast, are lesser fields of merit because they are considered more in need and less detached. Their poverty is a sign not of detachment but of desperation. In this view, nuns inhabit innately inferior bodies because of their lesser stockpile of merit. As a result, donors prefer to sponsor monks because they earn more merit than if they sponsored nuns. The persistent poverty of nuns relative to monks becomes self-replicating.

For donors, merit making is both strategic and moral. There is considerable incentive to be generous, particularly on public or ritual occasions. Most donations are hardly disinterested, especially those made as "payment" for completed or expected ritual services. Monks are the preferred ritual officiants because they have greater purity and Tantric prowess than nuns. While pragmatic gifts in exchange for ritual services earn somewhat less merit, they secure other, more immediate and pragmatic goals such as purity, prosperity, and protection from misfortune. The public nature of many rituals encourages an inflationary cycle of spending, of ever more spectacular gifts and rites. The purchase of rituals enables a competitive arena in which monks compete for donors and the opportunity to perform ritual services. The ranking of monks by donors perpetuates a concentration of wealth among the monks. The practices of merit making produce a circular logic, in which wealth and merit remain firmly associated with monks rather than nuns.

Even within the assembly of monks, a hierarchy emerges. The most detached or meritorious monks receive the most donations. In Zangskar as elsewhere in the Buddhist world, donors struggle to outdo each other in giving to a select group of monks, while ignoring nuns or mediocre monks.[9] When the Dalai Lama and his younger brother, Ngari Rinpoche, tour Zangskar, they are overwhelmed with gifts of butter, woolen clothes, jewels, and cash. They may turn over some of their booty to local social welfare institutions or schools, yet they must also accept many of the gifts for the merit to accrue to the donors. Thus even though Ngari Rinpoche has lived abroad, traveling in exclusive circles with Richard Gere, he dutifully sends a representative to Zangskar every few years to collect his share of the grain and cash offered to the Gelugpa monasteries of which he is honorary head. The irony of sending tithes to a Tibetan lama who only visits by helicopter is lost on local Zangskaris. Even the nuns at Dorje Dzong nunnery—who live in barren cells and are desperate to find a religious teacher—have yet to receive any financial or educational aid from their symbolic spiritual patron, Ngari Rinpoche. Yet they are happy to make merit by giving the Rinpoche or his representative humble gifts when either comes to visit.

How can the Buddhist economy of merit celebrate the renunciation of material rewards while it produces such a strong concentration of wealth? In ethical terms, neither wealth nor poverty is rejected; it is their deleterious effects that are seen as harmful. It is attachment—not riches or rags—which is dangerous. Both poverty and wealth are not threatening in themselves so much as conditions which could breed greed or avarice. Because wealth indicates past virtue and merit, it is both legitimate and desirable to have wealth.[10] In fact, wealth is useful because it provides the opportunity to make merit through disinterested generosity; only those who have wealth can learn to renounce it. At the same time, wealth is theoretically rejected by those who aspire to pure renunciation. In practice, however, monks need hardly reject wealth or property, as this chapter shows. It is not coincidental that Siddhartha was a prince before he became a Buddha. In practice, the prince who renounces his kingdom to become a monk earns more merit than a poor commoner. A wealthy donor is considered to earn more merit by giving up all his possessions than the pauper who has little to offer. In theory, the merit accrued is supposed to be proportional with the donor's ability to give. In practice, however, most people act as if the absolute size of the gift alone determines the amount of merit earned.[11]

Individual motivation is supposed to counter this inherent circularity within the economy of merit. The higher the perfection or motivation of the donor, the greater the merit accrued by even the smallest gift. A legendary story of the Indian king Asoka is used to illustrate that intention matters more than the absolute size of the gift.[12] When Asoka, late in his life, has exhausted all other means of giving, including the state treasury and his personal wealth, he gives the monastic assembly half a myrobalan—a tiny astringent fruit. The modesty of this gift—which even the poorest layperson could give—is that which restores Asoka's kingdom, because it is given with pure devotion. However, even this case assumes that only those who give away entire kingdoms can benefit from humble gifts. Asoka's gift takes its deeper meaning from the fact that he has already given away more wealth than any pauper could own. The tale also reinforces a numerical counting of gifts, as the final tally of gifts Asoka has given are said to equal that of the famous donor of the Buddha's lifetime, Anathapindika. It thus reinforces the lesson that those who know great wealth can learn detachment but those who know only poverty are unlikely to become exemplars of generosity.

Buddhist doctrine barely deconstructs the social hierarchy it produces. Mahayana doctrine explains the continuing existence of poverty and misfortune as the fault of innumerable imperfect sentient beings. Even though *bodhisattvas* have perfected the attitude of generosity, sentient beings continually create the causes of their own suffering. In this social allegory, outer status reflect an inner morality of defilement and delusion.[13] When a hungry ghost sees the ocean as dry, it is hardly the fault of the ocean but merely caused by the hungry ghost's own sins. Indeed, despite an abundance of food, hungry ghosts are doomed to hunger because their own throats are too narrow for any food to pass. This is why they are known as "smell eaters" *(dri za)*—because they can only consume smells. Similarly, when women suffer woeful bodies and other humiliations, these are perceived as punishment for past misdeeds. The ethic of compassion offers a motive for helping suffering beings even as the ethos of *karma* determines this suffering to be self-created. The practices surrounding merit both legitimate and produce social difference.

Tibetan Buddhism offers a plethora of private and mechanical forms of merit making—including meditation, chanting, circumambulation, prostration, and spinning prayer wheels. These individual means of making merit have led observers to characterize Tibetan and Himalayan Buddhism as fundamentally asocial and antirelational.[14] Ortner (1978), in particular, has focused on the atomized and individualistic nature of Sherpa merit making in comparison with Thai practices. Sherpa monks collect alms only once a year, compared with Thai monks, who collect alms daily. However, this lower frequency of alms is counterbalanced by the considerable sums and labor owed annually to monasteries and the multitude of voluntary donations which support monthly and incidental rituals. In Zangskar as in Sherpa society, frequent and ongoing village and household rites rely on extensive reciprocities and networks between the monastic and lay spheres. Ortner's ritual analysis largely overlooks the reciprocal relations between households and the monastic realm which fund the rituals she describes as individualistic.[15] This book looks at the material relations which produce ritual and demonstrate the strategic reciprocity so essential to Himalayan Buddhism.

Of all the forms of merit making, generosity is the most paradigmatic in many Buddhist societies. The scholarly rankings of merit-making practices in Theravada societies each conclude that giving trumps other forms of merit making, such as ethical action.[16] A number of possible reasons are given for this fact. Giving is more easily quantifiable than the abstention from nonvirtuous acts. Moreover, giving is the most strategic form of merit making, because it provides public prestige or status. Even within the realm of giving, spectacular gifts like the endowment of a temple rank far higher than more mundane, daily gifts like offering alms to the assembly of monks. My Zangskari informants often agreed that building a stupa or temple—an enduring source of merit for others as well as for the donor— was the most meritorious act. Some, however, scoffed at the idea that merit-making acts could be categorically ranked, pointing to the importance of intention or motivation in the gift. One nun pointed to the inflation of donations required to produce merit. While a handful of grain used to be sufficient, monks are disappointed unless one offers some cash, she noted. Even she alluded to the importance of gifts that produce self-replicating or permanent sources of merit, like endowing a ritual or a temple. Unlike virtuous acts of concentration or patience, which can be shattered in a moment of distraction or laziness, generosity offered to the monastic order can generate merit in perpetuity, long after the donor and his or her sentiment have vanished. Only investments in the Buddhist assembly have the power to reproduce and redirect a specific quantity of merit on a periodic but enduring basis.

The monastic code followed by all major schools of Tibetan Buddhism, the Mulasarvastivadin Vinaya, offers ample evidence of how and why lay donors can make merit in perpetuity with certain endowments. The text elaborates and justifies the monks' acquisition of enduring resources. It uses a vignette about donors who saw their own constructions collapsing in the space of a lifetime and therefore sought a method of making more enduring gifts to the assembly which might outlast the lifetime of a donor. In response, the Buddha granted monks the right to collect permanent endowments and loan them out at interest to donors. By keeping the principle intact but using only the interest as a source of funds for monastic expenditures, such endowments literally became "that which is not consumed" *(mi zad pa, aksaya nivi),* as they are glossed in Tibetan.[17] Although interest-bearing loans were forbidden to individual monks, the collective treasury *(spyi mdzod)* of the monastery was explicitly encouraged to loan out its endowments in this fashion.

Initially, the return on these loans was supposed to be used only for monastic constructions. Yet the Vinaya and other sources suggest that these loans were soon extended to cover any ritual that would benefit the Buddha, his teachings, or the monastic assembly. For example, a fifth-century inscription from the famous Buddhist site Sanci records a monetary gift whose interest would be used to feed a single monk and light four lamps in a nearby temple.[18] By extending the concept of permanent endowments to landholdings, the Vinaya gave monasteries an even more lucrative source of monastic maintenance, sharecropping. Here again, the Vinaya carefully explains that if the order allows its seeds to be sown on a layperson's fields, or permits its fields to be sown by laypeople, a portion of the harvest will accrue to the monks.[19] The solution to the problem of permanent endowments had its own problems—such as finding suitable lenders and sharecroppers who were neither too rich nor too poor. Those who were too poor might take the monastic loan but be unable to repay. Sharecroppers who leased the land might refuse to pay the rents. However, the monastery could retaliate by throwing the sharecropper off the land, while it had less coercive power in the case of faulty loans. Thus it came to pass that an institution dedicated to spreading an awareness of the impermanence of worldly things rapidly acquired a vast set of worldly goods by which to permanently fund its ritual expenditures.

How did this system of endowments produce a permanent stream of merit for individual donors? The Vinaya explains that gifts designated as permanent endowments could be used to fund ongoing ritual activities, in perpetuity. The interest from such endowments could be used to build a temple, light a lamp, or perform an annual, monthly, or daily ritual. A specific ritual or prayer, called Ngowa *(bsngo ba)* in Tibetan, might single out a named beneficiary to whom merit could be directed in perpetuity.[20] In theory, any gift could provide an endless and self-replicating source of merit for a named donor. Yet this process had its own limitations. In practice, merit was only produced if the monks maintained the ritual or the religious edifice the donor had sponsored. If the monks dispersed and no longer managed the endowment and its associated rituals, the donor would no longer earn any merit. Similarly, if a temple was built but remained empty or unused, it ceased to generate merit. As such, donors had good reason to support the permanent maintenance of a community of monastics and their rituals.

The stupa or reliquary—usually housing a monk's physical remains or texts—was another self-generating source of merit which required far fewer resources to maintain. A stupa provided an enduring source of merit for the donor or other named beneficiary as long as it was maintained and worshiped. Inscriptions along the base of early Indian stupas show that they were constructed largely for the purpose of transferring merit to a relative or other beneficiary. The practice of merit transfer by constructing stupas was more extensive and more a monastic rather than a vulgar lay practice than has been previously thought. Not only were monastics more likely to be donors than laypeople, but also nuns were as likely to be donors as monks up through the fourth century C.E.[21] Yet while the construction of stupas for deceased monks was openly encouraged, the construction of stupas for deceased nuns was not. In one canonical tale, a monk openly destroys a stupa built to commemorate a deceased nun.

Scholars have been loath to accept the popularity and pervasiveness of the practices of merit transfer because they contradict Buddhist doctrine. On the one hand, such practices are premised upon the belief that merit will flow permanently to a self which doctrine has characterized as impermanent and illusory. On the other hand, merit is believed to flow toward a named other, although the doctrine of *karma* suggests that merit is earned by the self alone. Merit-making practices have been justified by the suggestion that merit is not transferred from the donor to other selves, but is earned by those who rejoice in an act of merit. As such, merit is still earned by the self alone, even if those selves are now deceased ghosts *(preta)* or gods doing time in one of the other six realms of existence. As long as such beings rejoice in an act of virtue, they can earn merit. By removing the notion that merit is transferred, this explanation maintains the doctrinal consistency of *karma*.[22] Yet it also maintains a fictive continuity of self—between a former ancestor and her or his reincarnation as a ghost. Regardless of how merit transfers have been justified doctrinally, they have had a pervasive and profound influence on the economy of merit in Zangskar as in other Buddhist societies.

The Transmission of Buddhism from Kashmir to Tibet

The permanent endowments of land, cash, and other perpetuities to Buddhist monks have perpetuated the concentration of wealth within the monasteries of Zangskar. Donations to monks often signal piety as much as prestige. By gifting land to a monastery, which was sharecropped by local peasants, kings were able to finance the monastic realm, consolidate their power over peasants, and expiate their sins in a public and prestigious manner. Endowing or building monasteries could enhance the power of the ruler as well as the indebtedness of both monks and peasants. As in Bali and Thailand, rituals were always a performance and an enactment of power.[23] The calibration of gifts and ranked seating of donors during the public festivals held at the monastery suggest its role in affirming social hegemony. Yet the nunneries never achieved such power in local society. While monks and wealthy donors continue to consolidate their joint power, nuns and poorer strata remain excluded from the highest ranks within this economy of merit.

Buddhism in northwest India developed through a set of historical exchanges between Tibet, Kashmir, and the Himalayan kingdoms of Ladakh and Zangskar. This fluid and transnational development saw Buddhist teachers crossing back and forth between Tibet and the Himalayan borderlands for much of the second millennium. Each region was reinvigorated at critical junctures. Kashmir and its Himalayan kingdoms were home to a flourishing Buddhist culture when Tantric texts and techniques were first brought into Tibet between the eighth and twelfth centuries. After the destruction of Buddhist universities in India in the late twelfth century, Tibet became the cultural center for the more peripheral Buddhist kingdoms of Zangskar and Ladakh. Finally, after the twentieth-century destruction of Buddhist monasteries by the Chinese, the Himalayan kingdoms of Zangskar and Ladakh are once again a cultural center for monastic and ritual practices.

According to the northern Buddhist sources, Buddhism was first introduced into Kashmir during the reign of the third-century Indian emperor Asoka by Ananda's disciple, Madhyantika. Yet the twelfth-century

Kashmiri chronicle by Kalhana, the *Rajatarangini,* notes that Kashmir's first Buddhist monastery *(vihara)* was founded by King Surendra, four generations before Asoka's conquest of Kashmir. Surendra's monastery was located "near the country of the Dards" in a city called Sauraka, which may refer to Suru, a valley north of Zangskar lying just east of the Dardic region of Dras and its neighboring valley, Kashmir.[24] The presence of a royally funded monastery in the Suru Valley helps explain the presence of a forty-foot-high Kashmiri-style rock relief of Maitreya in the Suru Valley, outside a fortified town named Kartse Khar or White Peak Castle. Both the Suru and Dras rivers flow together to join the Indus River, which was already a well-traveled trade route by this time, as petroglyphs from the first millennium B.C.E. in Zangskar and Ladakh's Dardic areas attest.[25] A Kharoshti inscription along the Indus River in Khalatse records the presence of the Buddhist Kushan empire by the first or second century C.E. A stupa in Zangskar dedicated to the legendary Kushan king Kanishka suggests a possible connection with the Kushans which has yet to be explored.[26] Immense rock carvings in Suru, Zangskar, and Ladakh attest to a flourishing Buddhist culture in this region with certain Kashmiri connections by the sixth or seventh century.[27]

The sources for this Buddhist history are fragmentary, and records regarding nuns are almost nonexistent. Yet one thing is certain. By the end of the first millennium, neither the monks nor the Buddhist patrons of Kashmir deemed nuns worthy of much comment or sponsorship. While the monks' order spread rapidly across Central, East, and South Asia during the first millennium, the nuns' order was hardly promoted. Tibet produced one of the most elaborate monastic civilizations in Asia. By contrast the nuns' order seems never to have been transmitted to Tibet, although it did spread from India to Sri Lanka and China by the 4th century C.E.[28] Individual nuns may have traveled between Kashmir and Tibet, but there is no record of a quorum of nuns establishing a formal order in Tibet. Buddhist experts still offer widely disparate figures—by as much as three centuries—for dating the disappearance of the nuns' order in India. While some scholars continue to mistakenly claim that the nuns' order died out in the fifth century C.E., there is archeological evidence from Gujarat testifying to the presence of fully ordained nuns as late as 723 C.E.[29] Literary evidence testifies to the presence of fully ordained nuns in the Indo-Tibetan borderlands east of Kashmir Valley until at least the eleventh century. Why did the nuns' order die out in India and why was there no effort to reinstate it? Why did kings and nobles take such risks to reestablish the monks' order but make so little effort in the case of the nuns' order?

Tibetan sources provide significant detail about the transmission of the monks' order to Tibet between the eighth and the tenth centuries. Kashmir was well known as a flourishing Buddhist center after the seventh-century Tibetan king Songtsen Gampo (ruled 618–650) supposedly sent his minister Thonmi Sambhota to Kashmir to acquire an alphabet.[30] A later Tibetan king, Khrisong Detsen (ruled 755–797), managed to build Tibet's first monastery and establish the monks' order only by enlisting the help of Santaraksita—the abbot of India's famous Vikramasila university—and Padmasambhava—a Tantric adept from a western Buddhist land of Uddiyana (modern-day Swat, Pakistan).[31] After the abbot and the adept managed to subdue the jealous ministers, angry priests, and evil demons, the monastery was completed in 779 c.e. and Tibet's first seven monks were ordained.[32] The monastery was then given a permanent endowment of nearly 100 estates whose profits were used to provide monks with annual supplies of barley, butter, horses, clothes, paper, ink, and salt.[33] After roughly sixty years, Tibet's monastic order appears to have been wiped out during the social chaos which followed the collapse of the first Tibetan empire in 841 c.e. Sometime during the following century, a quorum of monks who had fled to peripheral regions gathered to reinstate the monks' order in Tibet. The "later diffusion" *(phyi dar)* of Buddhist teachings into Tibet after the tenth century from Kashmir and other Indian regions reestablished the power and primacy of monks in Tibetan society.

As the site of a Buddhist renaissance between the tenth and twelfth centuries, Kashmir was a fertile ground for the scholars, artists, and translators who transmitted Buddhist texts and teachings into Tibet. While Tibet's early fortunes waned, new kingdoms arose in the western Himalayas lying between Kashmir and Tibet. Known in Tibetan as Ngari *(mnga' ris)*, the region which lay south and west of the famed Mount Kailash was the site of several new kingdoms founded by descendants of the first Tibetan dynasty. The great-grandson of the last king in Tibet's early dynasty, King Skyide Nyimagon (ruled 923–950), made several successful conquests and alliances with local clans in order to consolidate a new dynasty in the area. After marrying a queen known as Zangs khama, he divided his kingdom between three sons, Palgyigon, Tashigon, and Detsugon.[34] Although the exact boundaries of each kingdom are in debate, many of the sources agree that the eldest son received Ladakh, the second son received Purang and Guge, while the third son received Zangskar, Lahaul, and Spiti. The kingdoms of the two younger sons—Guge and Zangskar/Spiti—were merged soon after because one of the two sons died without issue, possibly Detsugon.[35] Zangskar remained under the suzerainty of the Guge kings for some time, although the chronology is unclear on how long.[36]

The Guge kings are famous in Tibetan history because their most illustrious scion, Yeshe Od (947–1024), played a key role in the transmission of Buddhism into Tibet. Yeshe Od, who was the son of Tashigon, sponsored twenty-one youths to study Buddhist texts in Kashmir, including the famous translator Rinchen Zangpo (958–1055). Although all but two of the young men died of fever in Kashmir, Rinchen Zangpo and Legspa Sherab eventually translated many of the Tantras in the Tibetan canon from the Sanskrit, after their return from Kashmir. The Guge king's grand-nephew, Byangchub Od, was responsible for inviting the great Indian pandit Atisa to Guge in 1042. While we hear a great deal about Atisa and Rinchen Zangpo and their revival of monastic discipline and temple foundations, the records are almost silent on the question of the nuns' order during this time. A twelfth-century biography of Rinchen Zangpo reports that his sister became a probationary nun *(dge slob ma)*—a preliminary stage to full ordination, which can only be granted by a quorum of fully ordained nuns.[37] This text provides evidence for fully ordained nuns in Guge as late as the eleventh century. One must also note that full ordinations are occasionally given by monks alone, although this is not canonical. Such unorthodox ordinations explain reports of fully ordained nuns in later Tibetan texts from the fifteenth century.[38]

A fifteenth-century Tibetan source records that the Guge king, Yeshe Od, established the custom of women becoming nuns *(bud med bstun ma byed pa'i srol btsugs)*.[39] It is not clear, however, whether this meant full ordination—which requires a full quorum of at least six nuns in a border area like Guge—or if these nuns were ordained by monks alone. His daughter, Lha'i Metog, established a community of nuns *(bstun ma'i sde)* and became a nun herself. The text explains that both she and her brother Nagaradza had "gone forth completely" *(rab tu gshegs)*, which implies full ordination, especially since Nagaradza was said to be undergoing his second and thus full ordination at the age of twenty-nine in this instance. Both Metog and her brother built temples and established an endowment for a monastic assembly before taking ordination. The presence of a full monastic quorum would be necessary for a valid ordination of either monks or nuns.

Yet artistic evidence complicates this scenario. A wall painting at Tabo monastery in Spiti, founded by King Yeshe Od in 996, shows a set of horizontal friezes which include monks, laypeople, and female renunciants who may or may not be full nuns.[40] The women depicted in the painting are not wearing the monastic robe (chos gos)—unlike the monks immediately below them in the frieze, who are labeled as Gelong (dge slong, fully ordained). The women also have longish hair rather than shaved heads, and they kneel with their hands clasped in devotion like laypeople, rather than sitting cross-legged with their hands in a religious gesture as are the monks and bodhisattvas. Further research may confirm that nuns in this period may not have shaved their heads or offer evidence that the Guge king only extended the order of nuns after the founding of Tabo.

The literary evidence for fully ordained nuns in India continues in the late tenth century. According to a fifteenth-century Tibetan history, a Kashmiri princess, Gelongma Palmo, transmitted an important fasting rite to Yeshe Zangpo (Jnanabhadra), who ordained Rinchen Zangpo in 971 C.E.[41] Despite the importance and significance of Palmo's rite, the historical text offers almost no biographical information on the rite's founder, Gelongma Palmo. Although a long and illustrious set of disciples transmitted Palmo's liturgy and teachings, the details of her life were unknown to the fifteenth-century Tibetan historian who wrote the Blue Annals (deb ther ngon po). The fasting ritual known as Nyungnas (smyung gnas) is still practiced far beyond Palmo's homeland of Kashmir, in Tibet, India, Mongolia, China, Europe, and North America. While there are several liberation tales (rnam thar) of Palmo's life, there has been no full-length critical study of her life in English.[42]

Born a Kashmiri princess, Palmo longed to avoid an impending marriage to one of four royal suitors. She prayed to the bodhisattva Avalokitesvara to grant her leprosy.[43] Tricking her brother into thinking that she had her parents' permission to become a nun, Palmo left home with an elephant and two loads of gold. She arrived at a nearby monastery, where the abbot first dismissed her but then relented after he realized her royal background. She was accepted into the monastery and took full ordination as a Gelongma (dge slong ma), before distinguishing herself in debate when she defeated three Buddhist experts, a scholar (dge bshes), a Tantricist (sngags pa), and a mediator (sgom pa). After Palmo became the abbot of her monastery, she was struck with leprosy and withdrew to her retreat chambers to meditate. The monks grew suspicious when they found blood dripping from her cell and accused her of having a miscarriage. They threw her out of the monastery, and she wandered for a few years until she found a cave, where she vowed to fast until she attained a vision of Avalokitesvara. Sending off her servant, Gelongma Palmo undertook extensive austerities until she had a vision of the Eleven-Faced Avalokitesvara, who cured her leprosy. Gelongma Palmo then flew off to the Buddha fields but returned to earth to meet her faithful servant and recite her ecstatic song of liberation at her old monastery. While most of the astonished monks prostrated in recognition of her accomplishments, those that did not went straight to hell:

> Chattering fools . . . who disparage women out of hostility,
> Will by that evil action remain constantly tortured
> For three eons in the fathomless Raudra hell,
> Wailing as their bodies burn in many fires.[44]

Gelongma Palmo's story suggests that disparaging women was hardly unknown to Tantric practitioners, despite their vows to honor women. Her tale offers a special paradigm within the Tibetan genre known as full liberation stories *(rnam thar)*. Out of the hundreds of such tales that have come to light, hers is one of the few whose protagonist is a nun. As such, it is important to consider how her tale presents the female body and a woman's life in a favorable or different light than other liberation tales. The monks in the tale reflect the female body as impure and vulnerable, while Palmo proves it to be a critical teaching tool for liberation. Palmo courts her own pollution and disease as a means rather than an obstacle to reaching enlightenment. Indeed, her liberation out of the disease of leprosy extends rather than reverses the discourse of impurity that stigmatized the female body.[45] Palmo explicitly embraces her own polluted state while ignoring the general contempt for the female body she faces. Palmo's use of her diseased body as a skillful means to gain enlightenment recalls the unorthodox methods practiced by Tantric adepts such as the eighty-four *Mahasiddhas*. While the male adepts must humble themselves to women and outcastes, Palmo is humbled by proud monks within a Buddhist institution. The tale betrays a Tantric disdain of the monastic realm, yet it preserves the ideal of celibacy as Palmo remains a celibate nun. Unlike other enlightened women from Tibetan literature who practice sexual yoga with male consorts, Palmo achieves her liberation on her own, albeit inspired by the *bodhisattva* Avalokitesvara.[46] Palmo defeats three Buddhist experts who represent the more conventional and patriarchal Buddhist paths before she embarks on her singular and unconventional quest for enlightenment. The blatant suspicion she encounters from the monks is noteworthy because it points to the deliberate discouragement even the most skillful nuns faced in the monastic realm.

> To the north of the middle-lying Bodhgaya, near the place where the Ar-
> hats dwell, the Himalayan Tise, and the banks of great and sluggish flow-
> ing Sita [Sutlej?] River, in that illustrious, hidden land Zangskar, a land of
> spreading fruit trees and ripening millet, a country white in the *dharma*
> where virtue is accomplished, a province of honest speech and rare de-
> ceptions, a land of Urgyen Padmasambhava's prophecies and scrutiny,
> where one *dharma* king follows another awaiting their turn, in the royal
> seat of the northern realm, lying elevated above the valley, the white lin-
> eage of gnya' khri [Tibet's early dynasty] is practicing the *dharma*.[47]

This medieval inscription from Karsha village is one of many sources which relates Zangskar to wider Indian and Tibetan Buddhism. Peasant never meant primitive in Zangskar. Lying close to the trade routes which brought Buddhism from Kashmir to Tibet, Zangskar is supposed to have been visited by many of the important figures in Buddhist history. Oral legends and literary sources depict the landscape as an imaginary palimp-sest where only the faithful can see the traces of a heroic past.[48] A plain of rubble bears the impressions of legendary slingshot battles which the Tibetan superhero Gesar fought with local demonesses and his enemies from Chinese Turkestan. The Indian yogi Naropa (956–1040) is believed to have left impressions of his dagger and staff in his meditation cave at Dzongkhul in Zangskar, while the Tibetan saint Marpa (1012–1096) founded Strongde monastery when his boat landed on the shores of the lake that once covered Zangskar. Rather than plumbing the historical accu-racy of these beliefs, it is best to understand them as part of the historical imagination by which Zangskar is related to broader Buddhist epics.

Written sources state that Karsha's earliest edifices date back to at least the eleventh century.[49] An eleventh-century monk known as Phagspa Sherab (1045–1115?) or the Zangskar translator, a disciple of the translator Legspa Sherab, is believed to have founded Karsha and Phugthal monasteries. He is known to have translated several key Tantras, spent a lengthy time in central Tibet, and participated in the famous Guge Council of 1076 which standardized Tantric practices.[50] Karsha, Phugthal, Stongde, Mune, and Lingshed monasteries were all converted to the Gelug school of Buddhism in the fifteenth century. These conversions were undertaken by a charismatic Ladakhi monk named Byangsems Sherab Zangpo (1395–1457), one of the foremost disciples of the Tibetan monk Tsongkhapa (1357–1419), who founded the Gelugpa school of Tibetan Buddhism.

Sherab Zangpo received numerous permanent endowments of land in Zangskar, including the villages of Karlang, Trahan, and Tzazar, which he used to fund nascent temples at Tzazar and Dorje Dzong, a site above Trahan village. While the temple at Tzazar was soon abandoned due to negative omens, the Dorje Dzong temple became home to a community of monks and later nuns. Phugthal monastery received a large land grant when its head monk paid the ransom money to spare the life of the Zangskari king, Tshang Gyalpo, who had been captured by invading Mongol forces under Mirza Haider in 1534. In the seventeenth century, an uncle and nephew from the royal house of Zangla, along with several Zangskari doctors, became disciples of the first Panchen Lama, Lozang Chokyi Gyaltsen. Because the doctors became personal physicians of the first and third Panchen Lama, Lozang Palden Yeshe (1738–1780), as well as the illustrious fifth Dalai Lama, Ngawang Lozang Gyatso (1617–1682), a few Zangskaris gained considerable influence in the Panchen Lama's court.[51] The Kagyud monasteries of Bardan and Stagrimo were founded in the early seventeenth century due to the influence of Ladakh's foremost Kagyud lama, Stagtshang Raspa, while Dzongkhul monastery became a flourishing Kagyud meditation retreat under the Zangskari yogi Ngawang Tsering (1717–1794).

By the close of the twentieth century, Zangskar was home to eight major monasteries and ten nunneries. Of the eight monasteries, five follow the Gelug school—Karsha, Stongde, Phugthal, Mune, and Rangdum—and three follow the Kagyud school—Bardan, Stagrimo, and Dzongkhul. Together the monasteries housed a population of roughly 325 monks in 2002. By comparison, the ten nunneries in Zangskar housed 125 nuns.[52] Nine of Zangskar's nunneries follow the Gelug school—Karsha, Zangla, Tungri, Dorje Dzong, Pishu, Skyagam, Shun, Bya, and Manda, while only Sani follows the Kagyud school. Nuns comprise one-fourth of the resident monastic population, a remarkably high ratio in the Himalayan realm. Yet their numerical strength belies their social marginality in the local economy of merit.

We know even less about the history of Zangskar's nunneries than we do about its monasteries. Two of the oldest nunneries in Zangskar, Dorje Dzong and Tungri, appear to have been monastic complexes only later occupied by nuns. A local Zangskari history notes that a Zangskari queen and her son set aside several fields in the villages which were to be used by the fifteenth-century reformer, Sherab Zangpo, as a meditation site that became known as Dorje Dzong. Local legend confirms this and notes that after the Maitreya statue began to take on female characteristics, including breasts, nuns began to inhabit the retreat complex. This mysterious transformation is said to have been due to a charismatic nun, Yeshe Lhamo, who flew straight out of the temple window when she gained the rainbow body of liberation. The same nun is also said to have copied the *Prajñaparamita Sutra* in eight thousand lines by hand, with beautiful illustrations and introductory folios written in gold ink. The text, which is now housed in Karsha monastery and stands almost four feet tall, lacks a colophon and any reliable date. Yet it points to a mysterious female author whose talents and patronage offer tantalizing clues to the prominence of nuns in Zangskar. Certainly, this nun must have benefited from a wealthy, local patron or was perhaps of aristocratic descent herself.

After Dorje Dzong, Tungri is the second-oldest nunnery in Zangskar. Although the cliff-top temple in Tungri was first founded by an illustrious Ladakhi monk, Stagsang Raspa (1547–1651), the abbot of Hemis monastery and advisor to Ladakh's greatest king, Serge Namgyal (ruled 1616–1642), it is unclear when nuns began to settle on the cliff. By local legend, a few fields were set aside as an endowment for the local temple founded by Stagsang when he visited Tungri in 1613 on his way to visit the birthplace of the great Tantric adept Padmasambhava in Uddiyana, now in Pakistan. The lama stayed for two years in Zangskar, ignoring repeated requests to return to Ladakh by his patron, King Jamyang Namgyal (ruled 1595–1616). The fields dedicated to Stagsang's nascent temple in Tungri were legally owned by Hemis monastery—Stagsang's home monastery—in Ladakh. Thus taxes were sent annually to Hemis down the frozen river gorge each winter. When the Tungri villagers carrying the tax fell into the river and drowned one year, the Ladakhi king sought his payment but the villagers refused. The small army sent to collect the tax was routed by the villagers, who foiled the invaders by diverting the frozen stream over their fields.[53] As the soldiers tripped and fell on the ice, the Zangskari peasants—with their special leather boots—soon sent the Ladakhis running for cover. The villagers continued to pay the taxes to Hemis monastery until the

Dogra rulers plundered the temple and restored the land to the tillers in the nineteenth century. As a result, the Tungri nuns lost their large landed endowment, which used to take three days to plow. Of all the nunneries in Zangskar, only Dorje Dzong and Tungri—temples that were first occupied by monks—have sizeable permanent endowments of land.

Zangla and Pishu nunneries were founded sometime in the nineteenth century, possibly by royal patrons from Zangla, but with no fields or other permanent endowments. The Pishu nuns follow an eclectic mix of Gelugpa and Nyingma practices including a meditation known as *gcod* in which the human body is symbolically dismembered and offered up, which was founded by the Tibetan heroine Macig Labdron.[54] Karsha nunnery was founded in the mid-1950s by Yeshe and her companions, while a nunnery in the remote valley of Shun was established sometime in the 1970s. Due to the hazards of winter travel along a frozen gorge, Shun was split into two parts—Shun and Satak—in the 1980s, but reconvened as a single monastic community in 2000. Skyagam was founded in the early 1990s by a group of villagers whose daughters all took novice ordination from the Tibetan monk Dragom Rinpoche. Bya and Manda are hardly full-fledged nunneries, but are merely conglomerations of nuns' cells built in the late 1990s which have yet to establish a ritual calendar. At one time there were nuns' communities following the Kagyud sect at Padum and Shilatse which may have dated back to the end of the seventeenth century.[55] The Shilatse community was built around an eighteenth-century chapel painted by Zhadpa Dorje (1747–1816), but disbanded when their nearby village was decimated by a devastating landslide in the late 1980s. The Padum nuns left Zangskar to join their teacher in Bhutan around the same time. Since the early 1990s, a group of Kagyud nuns has established a small retreat center above Sani at Starkhungsa, a site founded by one of Zangskar's foremost mediators, Ngawang Tsering (1657–1732). All of the nunneries are under the spiritual authority of monks and few have any extensive endowments.

Land as a Source of Merit and Wealth

The monastery continues to benefit from its permanent endowments and patrons, even today. Land has been a principal source of power and income in Zangskar's history. Although pastoralism has always supplemented agriculture, land provides an enduring income and a means of ensuring loyalty to those in power. Kings offered land grants to nobles and monasteries in exchange for political allegiance. For rural sharecroppers, these land grants offered a means of subsistence and social mobility. Kings might grant an entire village to a monastery or spiritual leader as a permanent endowment and enduring source of merit. In the struggle for power between petty kings, corrupt ministers, and wealthy aristocrats, land and monasteries were critical. Monks often took center stage in political dramas—by ransoming kings, hiding queens in flight. In return for their assistance to the royalty and local princes, monasteries were rewarded handsomely with land and other endowments. Nunneries were largely overlooked in these political schemes.

After lands were donated to a monastery, the monks earned rents while the donor earned merit and the sharecropper earned a livelihood. Peasant sharecroppers earned a guaranteed and inheritable right to till the land and keep a percentage of the crop, provided they fulfilled their obligation to pay fixed rents and other services to their overlord. If the sharecropper fell into debt and could not pay his rents, he ceded his rights to the land. At the same time, the monastery or overlord could not unilaterally raise the rents or remove the land from the tiller. For most peasants, the rents were paid in fixed amounts of grain or butter, while other services might include labor on the lord's estate, porterage services (*'u lags*), and military duty. When entire villages or estates were transferred to a monastery or famous monks, the sharecroppers simply paid their existing rents to the monastery. Through these permanent endowments of land and labor, the monks became ever more involved in worldly and economic affairs—collecting rents, taxes, and other subsidies.

Another way in which the monastery received land was by gifts of single fields. These gifts might transfer the ownership of the field to the monastery permanently or temporarily, for the duration of the donor's lifetime. In either case, the tiller earned merit and retained usufruct rights along with some share of the crop. Permanent endowments of land provided a continual and inheritable stream of merit and subsistence for the household, and an enduring source of wealth for the monastery. The tiller could also cede marginal lands to the monastery in times of labor shortage, or simply for the duration of the donor's lifetime. The monastery, in turn, leased such marginal lands to the poorest, landless peasants, for whom land was a valuable source of social mobility. In Zangskar, landless peasants were those who had fallen into debt, migrated from Tibet, or were simply disenfranchised younger sons not eligible for inheritance under primogeniture. Such peasants leased marginal estates from the monastery, which they could pass on to their children. Because usufruct rights were inheritable, an industrious family graduated from the landless to the landed class in a single generation, albeit burdened by heavy monastic rents. Since breaking new ground and digging irrigation channels required a huge amount of labor, and crop returns were likely to be low until sufficient manure made the soil more fruitful, these sharecroppers earned barely enough to cover rents. As a result, even the poorest households had little incentive to expand existing estates unless absolutely necessary.

By withdrawing land and labor from the private sector but keeping it in production, the monastery perpetuated the subsistence economy and effectively prohibited the spread of capital to a broad merchant class. Private accumulation was stifled as well as suspect in this economy of merit, which allowed monasteries to accumulate a vast surplus of land, labor, and other capital in addition to controlling long-distance trade. The scarcity of water and arable land was instrumental in checking capital accumulation among an urban or middle class. The few merchants who do appear in historical records were hardly able to challenge the economic and political power that monasteries wielded. Even today, the monasteries own the largest estates in Zangskar, while controlling labor and capital in the local economy.

Landholding, polyandry, and monasticism kept population growth to a minimum until the twentieth century. Along with kinship arrangements which aimed at limiting each household to one marriage per generation, celibacy also placed a brake on natural increases in population. The monastery siphoned off surplus sons while others settled new lands or became monastic sharecroppers. Monks had considerable social mobility, especially for rural sons from the poorest households who might otherwise be destitute. While sons who came to the monastery renounced reproduction and inheritance, they earned status, power, and wealth. Although member monks came from all ranks of society, except the lowest or outcaste stratum, each monk received an equal share from the monastic income. Although opportunities for advancement did not completely ignore previous social status, the monastery was a virtual meritocracy in a stratified society. Every monk could aspire to the highest posts in the monastery as well as the most education he could master. Regardless of their background, monks might serve as educators, bureaucrats, administrators, doctors, astronomers, or jurists. Those monks with the quickest minds might advance rapidly within their local monastery before setting out for education in the distant Tibetan monasteries. Others, more inclined toward worldly pursuits, might find ample careers in monastic finance, trade, or other business ventures. In exchange for gifts of land and service, the monastery provided jobs, social welfare, and ritual protection for its populace.

Buddhist monasteries in Zangskar today provide extensive social, economic, and ritual services to their society. Unlike nunneries, which function largely as places of refuge or retreat, the monasteries still maintain extensive estates and political power. Monastic endowments support an array of socioeconomic services, including providing loans, keeping land records, acting as judiciary, and providing educational, medical, artistic, and ritual services to local villagers. Monasticism has encouraged a high literacy rate, as well as numerous and sophisticated artistic, philosophical, and medical achievements. The monastery has become the repository of movable wealth, including ritual objects and religious art. With a fleet of monks constantly traveling between stations across the region, the monastery offers communication, travel, and transport services for many rural villagers.

The twentieth century was a watershed in providing private ownership and more opportunities for economic expansion than any previous century. When the Kashmiri maharaja promulgated the Permanent Settlement Act in 1908, tillers earned individual deeds to their lands, although monasteries and Muslim trusts were exempt. By granting land to the tillers, the law erased all overlords except the monastery in theory if not always in practice. In 1998 monasteries owned roughly one-tenth of all cultivated land, and one-third of all households sharecropped some monastic land, if only a fraction of an acre.[56] The monasteries and overlords held much less land in Zangskar than in Tibet and elsewhere in North India. Although royal and aristocratic families had to relinquish parts of their estates after the passage of the Large Landed Estates Abolition Act in 1950, there were only a handful of such cases in the entire region. Rather surprisingly, only twenty-one households in Zangskar and Ladakh had landholdings which exceeded the upper limit set by law of 22.75 acres.[57] Because of the intervention of Bakula Rinpoche in Ladakh, monastic institutions were exempt from this upper limit.[58] While individual landholdings remain clustered around the average holding of just under three acres, Karsha monastery owns nearly a hundred times as much land. There are still very few excessively land poor or land rich households.

Most monastic landholdings are sharecropped by two different types of households: full sharecroppers and freeholders. The first group consists of the poorest tenants *(chun pa)*, who have no land of their own but till a large estate owned entirely by the monastery. These tenants serve the monastery in a variety of capacities—acting as cooks for rituals or portering ritual materials between villages. Most pay a standard rent of 400–600 kilos of grain, which may account for almost half their total harvest. The rents are paid annually in grain, although cash and other foodstuffs may be substituted during years of drought. In extenuating circumstances, rents may be forgiven until the following year, when they must be repaid with interest, usually 25 percent. Loans taken out for seed are paid at the same interest rate. The poorest of such tenants may fail to keep up their estate. Those with little livestock and thus not enough manure may experience a decline in field quality and harvest. If the crop can no longer suffice for the rents and subsistence, the family may abandon its estate and the monastery must find a new tenant.[59] Because land is in short supply, there are usually families willing to take up the burden.

Freeholding *(rang bad mkhan)* households can also sharecrop a field or two, which their ancestors may have donated to the monastery. While such households own most of their land, their ancestors may have donated one or two fields to the monastery in the past, which gives them inalienable and inheritable rights to till these fields as long as they pay the required rent. As with full tenants, the annual rent *(khral)* is paid in whatever crop is sown—barley, wheat, or peas. Each field is cropped in rotation—barley, wheat, then peas—to allow the legumes to return nitrates to the soil. The rent is fixed by the size and quality of the field and does not vary with the harvest. Because tillers keep any excess crop, they have an incentive to put labor into the fields in hopes of increasing their yield.[60] The rents on individually sharecropped fields ranges between one fifth and one third of the harvest. In Karsha village, the monastery owns several fields leased out every year to villagers on an ad hoc basis. This arrangement is known as "half support" *(phyed gzhi)* because the tiller often pays up to half the crop to the monastery. When the monastery auctioned off the rights to till these fields to the highest bidder in 2002, they received some bids in excess of half the crop.

Karsha monastery is far more than just a landlord. Besides rents, the monastery collects a wide range of goods and services from the households under its ritual protection. Its monastic dominion *(dgon pa'i mnga' 'og)* encompasses a broad sweep of Zangskari territory where the majority of its landholding and sharecroppers are located. This area, known as the Northern Realm, owes extensive labor services and other taxes to the monastery. The traditional boundaries of this realm stretch up along the northern side of the Stod River from Pidmo to Abran. Most of the houses own fields sharecropped from Karsha monastery and all of the villages have a resident monk from Karsha serving as ritual officiant. In exchange, the villages provide labor services during ritual occasions and annual taxes of fuel for the monastic hearth. The labor obligations which these villages owe include portering butter for the winter fasting festival, carrying their firewood taxes by horseback (until recent years, when the monastery has rented a truck), and portering ritual paraphernalia between Karsha and Padum or Sani during ritual performances in these villages. Other portering obligations have lapsed since the advent of trucks and improved transport services in Zangskar after 1980.

Every household in the villages throughout the Northern Realm and in three villages opposite Karsha monastery owes an annual tax of firewood (tshogs shing). This tax is collected by the assembly's disciplinarian (dge skyos) in the late fall. The households in the villages closest to Karsha, like Yulang and Sendo, and five nearby villages (yul tsho lnga)—Rizhing, Hongshet, Langmi, Tetsa, and Kazar—pay a special kind of fuel tax. Half of the group (Karsha, Yulang, Sendo) owes horse dung one year while the other half owes firewood, in rotation every year. This system ensures the sustainability of the thistle bushes which provide the firewood and guarantees the monastery its most precious fuel, horse dung. Although the amount of thistlewood is fixed at one bushel per household to prevent over-gathering, the amount of dung paid by each household is adjusted according to the number of horses it owns, at a rate of three bushels of dung per horse. The dung is mixed with water and fashioned into dung bricks by a group of young monks every spring, before villagers transport it to the monastery later in the spring.

Karsha monastery also owns fields outside the formal boundaries of the Northern Realm, such as in the royal villages of Padum and Zangla, which are home to Zangskar's two surviving royal houses. Although the residents of these two villages no longer pay much rent to their local king, they still pay their monastic taxes. The king of Zangla owes five hundred kilos of grain to the monastery's wintertime Great Prayer Festival, while the king's former subjects in Tshazar owe one thousand kilos of grain annually dur-ing the monastery's summertime Gustor festival.

The Monastic Corporation and Its Collections

Hardly a place of quiet renunciation, the monastery is best understood as one of the wealthiest corporations in Zangskar. Its assets, debits, and investments are micromanaged by a fleet of skilled monks who rotate through various offices in the monastery. Monks serve their duties in a vast web of ritual posts which cover even the most remote valleys in the region. From the moment a monk joins the assembly until the day he graduates from the highest office as abbot, he must serve in a variety of offices. In his junior years, he serves in the "inner and outer retinue" *(nang 'khor dang phyi 'khor)* as cook, bearer, trumpeter, or ritual assistant.[61] After serving at least a decade in mundane posts, monks graduate to more senior posts like steward, chantmaster, disciplinarian, ritual master *(rdo rje slob dpon)*, or abbot. Besides stewarding the treasury or Labrang, the most labor intensive of economic posts, those monks with business acumen are chosen to man-age the monastery's economic ventures, including shops, a hotel, and other construction. Monks are also sent out on three-year terms to reside as rit-ual officiants *(mchod gnas)* in villages throughout the monastic domain. These ritual officiants attend to the daily ritual needs of villagers and per-form offerings at the local village chapels *(lha khang)* scattered across the land. Ex-abbots *(zur ba)*, who have cycled through all these posts, have the most time to pursue spiritual and ascetic goals.

At Karsha monastic resources are managed by an internal treasury known as the Labrang *(bla brang)*. The Labrang functions as a treasury and venture capital firm for the monastery's endowment. Four monks serve three-year terms, on rotation, as stewards *(gyner pa)* of the treasury. Over-seeing the monastic assets is a full-time job, which requires continuous and judicious management. The monastic rents must be collected each fall and delivered into the monastic coffers, where they may be consumed, stored, or loaned out to villagers in need of advances. The monastery also owns a herd of over thirty cows, yaks, and crossbreeds which provide be-tween 400 and 450 kilos of butter per annum. This butter is used for ritual expenses and entertainment, or sold to the nuns and local villagers when they run short.[62] The monastery also owns poplar groves throughout the region, whose wood is used in construction or sold for profit. The stewards also manage hostels for traveling monks in Padum, Kargil, and Leh. The stewards and the monastery's governing members may use their assets and additional taxes to fund construction projects, such as a new palace built for the Dalai Lama in 1997. The palace, which cost 470,000 rupees, was never occupied and was later rented out as a schoolhouse. It is a shining example of how excess wealth is concentrated among the most meritorious monks and wealthiest institutions.

Besides its movable wealth in art, statues, jewels, and sacred wall hangings *(thankas)*, the monastery also has a tidy sum of liquid capital, which is loaned out to laypeople. The monastery offers short-term loans at a 20 percent annual interest rate to shopkeepers or contractors. Most of the shopkeepers borrow up to one or more lakhs (100,000 rupees), which are usually paid back within one to three years given the steep interest rates. In case of default, the monastery has little sanctioning power beyond public shame and confiscation of assets. In the case of one unlucky sharecropper whose land and house were both owned by the monastery, the monks lost the entire principal they loaned him. When they came to confiscate the furniture he'd bought for his failed restaurant, they discovered that he'd already sold or ruined all that was of value. According to the steward who oversaw the loan, the monks "took pity" on him and did not confiscate his livestock, his only asset they did not own. The monastery may choose to suspend loans for a year or two if it is involved in a large capital venture or if too many loans are defaulted. Corruption is not unheard of, although offending monks are rarely sanctioned. Several years ago, the monk in charge of finances was accused of doctoring the books. The monastery's governing body *(dbu chos)*—consisting of the abbot, ritual master, chantmaster, disciplinarian, and Labrang stewards—has since regulated the monastic finances but the offending monk was never expelled. The monastery once ran a shop in the village, which it abandoned after it was discovered that the monk in charge reported consistent losses and pocketed much of his profits. He also received a reprimand but no other formal sanction.

Collecting rents from the sharecroppers is a major undertaking for the Labrang stewards every autumn. Because there are several hundred households which sharecrop fields scattered over thirty hamlets, the job requires careful organization.[63] Every fall, after the farmers have threshed and winnowed their harvest, the Labrang stewards proceed across the landscape visiting each monastic tenant. Going door to door, they collect rents and alms at every household. Since the rents are fixed by field, the monks measure out the required rent in a perfunctory manner using the monastery's own wooden measuring cups or boxes *(bre, 'bo)*. Although grain is the standard payment, a householder may give butter, meat, or cash in years of drought. The grain is poured into yak-hair sacks which are sewn up and sealed with wax. As farmers have become more wealthy, sealing is less necessary, one steward explained. After measuring the rent, the monks are hosted with a rich repast. The villager will deliver his rent later in the winter at his own expense, when agrarian activities have ceased. His payment will be recorded by the Labrang stewards before being set aside for storage, distribution, or consumption. The total sum of rents collected each year amounts to roughly 11,000 kilograms of grain.

Another set of rents are collected from five villages near Karsha monastery—Karsha, Yulang, Rizhing, Stongde, and Kumig—by the *manipa* stewards. The name *manipa* comes from the Urdu term *mana*, a measure (half a pint) which may have been used to measure the rent in the Dogra era. The total rent collected from the five villages is roughly 1,800 kilograms of grain per annum.[64] Two monks who are chosen as *manipa* stewards to collect these rents every fall proceed to every tenant which sharecrops *manipa* fields, to measure the rent. Later in the winter, the stewards announce the day on which the taxes are due from two villages across the river, Kumig and Stongde. The tradition of delivering the taxes from these villages dates to long before the cement bridge was completed across the river in 1998. In the dead of winter, when the river is at its lowest ebb, the sharecroppers ferry the allotted rent in big burlap bags on the backs of horses and yaks. Until 1990 the horses and yaks tramped up to the storehouse right through an ancient assembly hall whose glorious wall paintings date back to before the fifteenth century. The *manipa* stewards still greet their taxpayers with a special feast of barley, pea flour, fried meat, butter, and enough beer to last the entire night. The rents from the three other villages are delivered by villagers at their own expense without a feast, although the two *manipa* stewards may invite the tenant in for a private meal. Every three years, when the manipa stewards are rotated, there is an audit of all rents, loans, and expenditures.[65]

Ritual sponsorship of festivals used to be a far more complex and onerous process than at present. In the past, the permanent endowments for each ritual were managed separately by individual monks, on rotation. Monks were chosen to steward or produce a given ritual with fields or livestock they leased out to individual tenants and by soliciting donations using begging beers. Each steward was responsible for collecting rents and donations to fund ritual expenses for a set number of years. Because most ritual expenditures had outgrown historical endowments, the stewards were forced to hold ever more begging beers to raise additional cash, food, and other materials used in the course of the ritual or festival. When the titular head of Karsha monastery, Ngari Rinpoche, visited Zangskar in 1987, he took a long hard look at the financing of rituals. The custom of holding raucous drinking parties to lubricate donors' generosity had led to a "compassion fatigue" among villagers who were besieged almost constantly for monastic donations. In response, it was decided that the monastic treasury or Labrang would sponsor most of the rituals in the monastic calendar henceforth, and set aside liquid assets as necessary.

Yet many village festivals such as the fasting rite, springtime ancestor rites, and circumambulation of the fields are still managed by lay stewards who solicit ad hoc donations. The monastery's wintertime fasting rite is stewarded by two lay households drawn from the sharecroppers settled in the twenty-seven hamlets that make up its northern domain. These stewards spend an entire year collecting the resources for the largest lay ritual in the monastic calendar—which may involve as many as five hundred participants and thousands of donors. While begging beers are used to raise most of the donations, a set of permanent endowments and taxes also fund the festival. One such endowment consists of a nineteenth-century loan of silver rupee coins to roughly 175 sharecropping households throughout the northern domain.[66] Every household which received such a loan still brings an interest payment (*skyed*) of 10 kilograms of grain to the festival steward each year, who uses it to produce almost five hundred liters of beer for visiting donors.[67] Most of the major houses in the region which accepted the loan in the nineteenth century still make this payment every year as a sign of status and antiquity.

The formalized collection of alms gives peasants an annual opportunity to make merit while providing monks with yet another source of income. In local idiom, the homology between the words for merit and alms—Sonam (*bsod nams*) and Sonyom (*bsod snyoms*)—reflects the close association between the two concepts. Indeed, alms are given in exchange for a specific ritual which dedicates the merit to the donor or his household. In local idiom, the ritual of dedication, called *ngowa (sngo ba),* transfers merit earned by giving alms to the donor and other sentient beings. Local informants believe that the ritual transfers both merit and blessing to countless visible and invisible beings, including bugs or worms and even underworld spirits *(klu)* who may have been injured by the symbolic or real harm of agricultural activities like plowing, weeding, and harvesting. Explicit in this account is the recognition that many of the gods and spirits to whom merit is being transferred have the power to protect or to harm human beings. As such, the villagers adapt a classic transfer of merit to others without regard for the self to a reciprocal exchange in which merit is traded for ritual protection. The only monks who are qualified to perform this rite during the collection of alms are the abbot and the ritual master *(rdo rje slob dpon)*.

The entire assembly of monks splits into two groups, each headed by two Labrang stewards, to tour the length and breadth of Zangskar. One group travels north to upper Zangskar and the other travels to lower and central Zangskar, rotating each year. The monks collect alms and taxes throughout the monastic dominion *(dgon pa'i mnga' 'og)* in the villages where Karsha monastery posts a ritual officiant *(mchod gnas)*. In each village, the party of monks is hosted with an elaborate meal and butter tea before the abbot or ritual master performs the *ngowa* rite. Afterward, the family pays its rents and gives its annual donation of alms, which usually falls between ten and thirty kilos of grain. The alms are divided among the monks later in the winter when rents are delivered by tenants.

Since nuns are not authorized to perform the *ngowa* rite, they do not earn the same amount of grain or respect in the process of alms collection. In fact, the nuns beg for alms in a rather different fashion from the monks. They travel individually in an informal and somewhat ad hoc fashion. Groups of two or three nuns may decide to go alms collecting spontaneously, unlike the more formalized groups of monks. The nuns may wander through villages, stopping at households where they have a relative or an acquaintance, rather than going to each household systematically as the monks do. Their collections are pitifully small compared with those of the monks. A party of nuns may receive a plate of grain or half a finger-length of butter, while the party of monks usually receives ten kilos of grain, one kilo of butter, and an elaborate meal at a similar house. Unlike the monks, who are hosted by total strangers, the nuns may find it difficult to secure a decent meal or a place to sleep in valleys far from home. Many nuns have confessed that they were embarrassed *(sngo byes)* to collect alms, because they have no ritual services to offer in return. Such statements emphasize the reciprocal nature of alms giving in Zangskar, which is contrary to the doctrine of disinterested generosity.

Because the monks collect their alms and rents in a more formalized fashion, it is difficult for villagers to avoid the monastic gaze. The poorest peasants may shirk giving to nuns, but it is virtually impossible not to give to monks, even in times of hardship. Indeed, making merit by giving alms is even more imperative in times of drought or other misfortune. Merit offers hope in times of worry, security in times of abundance. Because the alms are given inside the house in full view of half of the monastic assembly, the monks have the power to shame a stingy household. The canonical purpose of the rite, the Mahayana transfer of merit, is lost among the more pragmatic reasons for giving alms—local respect, protection from misfortune, and blessings of the assembly. Since alms are given in uncooked grains, even outcastes can earn merit. At the same time, monks can perpetuate the caste rules about commensality by studiously avoiding any gifts of cooked food from outcaste households.

The monastery uses the grain collected in rents and alms to fund its expenditures and to support its member monks. Roughly one-half of all the grain collected annually by the monastery goes directly to the monks, while the other half is stored and used to fund rituals, feed guests, or pay workers. The grain used for ritual and guest expenses is ground into flour by the *manipa* stewards with the assistance of local nuns or laywomen. Over five thousand kilos of grain are washed, dried, and roasted by the women before being ground into flour under the supervision of three *manipa* stewards.[68] The grain must be hauled down to the streambed for processing into flour before it is hauled back up the cliff to the monastic storerooms. Although monks earn their living by ritual services, they each receive roughly 55 kilograms per year from the monastic coffers. All monks except for the governing body receive the same share of grain, which is distributed on two occasions: during the ceremonial changing of the monastic offices on Tsongkhapa's birthday and during the summertime Great Prayer Festival.[69] About three-fifths of the handout comes from alms and the remainder from rents. When the Labrang empties out its grain coffers every decade to prevent rot, monks receive an additional dividend of grain. In 1995 when the storage banks were emptied, each monk received over sixty kilos of grain. Besides actual handouts of grain and flour, most monks are fed by the monastery kitchen during communal rituals, which may account for one-fourth of the days in any given year. On other days, monks prepare their meals individually using food and store-bought supplies. Any cash donations to the assembly of monks are divided, and each monk receives a share *(skal ba)* of the offering. The amount collected by an individual monk at Karsha over an entire year may range as high as several thousand rupees, while the average nun at Karsha will collect no more than a few hundred rupees in the same time period.

Nunneries in the Economy of Merit

Unlike monks, nuns cannot subsist on monastic endowments or ritual earnings. A room of one's own at the nunnery offers a reprieve but little escape from the daily demands of farm and field. Nuns cannot escape household poverty even after they join an institution dedicated to the renunciation of worldly tasks. While monks can subsist off their ritual income, nuns spend most of their time helping relatives to secure their livelihood. Both nuns and monks may have taken vows to avoid worldly pursuits, but only nuns must work as domestic servants. This is due largely to the lack of permanent endowments at the nunnery. This lack has changed dramatically since the 1990s with foreign sponsorship. Although funds have supplemented the earnings of individual nuns, they do not make up for the landed endowments the monasteries have.

Although Dorje Dzong, Karsha, and Tungri nunneries each have several fields which are sharecropped out to villagers, they provide barely a pittance of grain once the harvest is divided among the assembly of nuns. The largest nunnery in Zangskar, Karsha, has two fields, which provide each member nun roughly two kilograms of grain a year.[70] While these two fields were given many years ago, the land is still listed in the owners' name in the local land records office. As such, they only represent temporary endowments which may expire after the death of the head of household. The nuns tilled the fields themselves until increasing aridity made them less viable after 1997. They are now leased to local villagers, while the timely death of the nuns' last cow has absolved them of any need for fodder. The nuns still own "shares" in three cattle, which provide a small yield of butter annually. Karsha nunnery also owns more than forty goats, which are farmed out (two per nun) among the twenty nuns, who send them to their relatives' homes. The family consumes the goats' milk and butter and keeps any offspring, in exchange for an annual delivery of butter on two ritual occasions. Every nun must deliver a kilo of butter to the nunnery twice a year: during the Vajrayogini burnt offering *(sbyin sregs)* and during spring-time Thousand Offerings for an Auspicious Era. When a nun dies or leaves the nunnery, her family returns the two goats.

Foreign sponsorship has brought cash income but not the three most critical resources in Zangskar—land, water, and fuel. An American nun named Lekshe Tsomo was instrumental in getting sponsorship from a Canadian dharma center named Gaden Choling in 1990. By the year 2000, the Canadian center provided small funds (under $300) to most of the nunneries in Zangskar, to purchase collective and individual rations. I have delivered this aid annually, collected accounts, and written fund-raising letters to sponsors. Besides enabling the purchase of butter, tea, salt, and other foodstuffs, the funds have been used to build rooms, a greenhouse, a toilet, and a debate courtyard.

Unlike the monastery's ritual calendar, many of the nunnery's rites are funded by voluntary donations. Because there are no rents of grain or village taxes of firewood or butter, nuns must collect ritual expenses as well as dung or firewood themselves. Located in one of the richest villages in Zangskar, Karsha nunnery receives enough donations to fund a fairly expansive ritual calendar. By contrast, the other nunneries in Zangskar simply don't celebrate rites for lack of funding. Even the rites they do celebrate are curtailed for lack of endowments.[71] Nuns must gather the needed goods themselves or solicit them within the village. Every nun in the assembly must serve her turn as a steward for both monthly and seasonal rites. The skill of the stewards and the generosity of the villagers largely determine the length and extent of the ritual calendar. When the entire assembly of nuns gathers thrice a month at Karsha, one or two nuns steward the rite by soliciting barley, butter, and other foodstuffs from their families.[72]

Most Zangskari nunneries elect a member nun, on rotation, to steward the most onerous ritual of the year, the springtime Great Prayer Festival *(smon lam chen mo)*. The steward spends most of the previous year collecting donations for this festival throughout the length and breadth of Zangskar. She will hold numerous begging beers at which she solicits donations in cash and kind. Households customarily give generously of that good which is in surplus. Those with access to uninhabited willow groves give wood, those short of grain give butter, and those short of cash give their labor. Pledges of cash are preferred because this allows the steward to manage the necessary expenditures more efficiently. The steward will shop in advance the summer before the festival is held, while the passes to neighboring regions are open. She purchases the supplies of vegetable oil, kerosene, dried eggs, rations, and spices before the winter comes and the shops run out of necessary supplies. She also travels on foot up and down the three major river valleys of Zangskar, going door to door, collecting dried cheese, butter, and grain in alms. During the late fall and early spring, she collects dung in order to shore up the supply of fuel required to run the monastic kitchen continuously for almost a month. At least a month before the festival begins, she will ask several village women to assist her in making beer. For a few weeks, her monastic cell will smell like a brewery as she cooks and prepares hundreds of kilos of barley into fresh, aromatic barley beer, the staple of any ritual festival.

From the day the Great Prayer Festival begins until its conclusion three weeks later, the nunnery is a beehive of activity. Every day, the steward manages a multitude of tasks as she feeds the entire assembly all day long in lavish style.[73] The steward usually hires two monks to serve as cooks for the duration of the festival, a job that earns some status and good pay. While nuns pray continuously through the day in the assembly hall, the kitchen and guest rooms are filled with a stream of villagers from all over Zangskar who arrive bearing donations in cash and kind that were solicited months earlier. The donations made by each guest are recorded in a notebook by the steward and her assistant before being handed over to the kitchen. The guests are hosted with tea, a standard meal, and all the beer (chang) they can consume. From dawn to dusk the sponsoring nun (gnyer pa) must attend simultaneously to the lay guests, the cooks' proceedings, and the nuns. Every evening, the nuns are fed one last time with a hearty soup while the rowdy villagers celebrate long into the night drinking, singing, and dancing.

The festival continues in this way for three or more weeks, until the donations have run out. After the last day of the nuns' festival, the steward hosts the cooks, water bearers, barley beer servers, and other assistants with a festive meal and pays them in both cash and kind for their services. When Yeshe and the founding nuns first instituted the festival in the 1960s, they barely solicited enough donations to hold a five-day festival. Recent years have seen the festival increase to twenty days with a corresponding rise in nuns' earnings.[74] Yet nuns still earn only a fraction of what monks collect during their Great Prayer Festival, although it is only half as long.

During the course of their Great Prayer Festivals, both the nunnery and the monastery sponsor the three-day fasting ritual *(smyung gnas)* founded by the Kashmiri nun Gelongma Palmo.[75] Because the fasting rite is held in the midst of the wider prayer festival, each is relatively well attended and funded. Yet the fast held during the fourth month at the Karsha Lonpo's ancient Avalokitesvara temple just outside the nunnery pales in magnitude and power to the one held at the monastery three months earlier during the first Tibetan month. The difference in material resources collected by each institution reflects the blessing power and status of each institution. While the nunnery's fast might involve twenty to thirty participants and up to one hundred individual donors, the fast held at the monastery involves over four hundred ritual participants and several thousand donors.[76] The fast near the nunnery is stewarded by two local houses who spend two months in organization, while the monastery's fast is stewarded by two households who spend a year soliciting funds and collecting other endowments.[77]

The number of participants in a given ritual often reflects the degree of merit or blessing power generated by the rite. A fast attended by hundreds of participants generates more collective merit and blessing power *(dbang)* than one which is sparsely attended. This may be one of the reasons that the fast at Karsha monastery consistently draws hundreds of participants while a fast held at nearby Dorje Dzong nunnery draws few if any participants each year. The fact that donors happily contribute to the Dorje Dzong fast even when there are no participants clearly illustrates a preference for donating over ritual asceticism. Tantric initiation given by the Dalai Lama is considered to produce far more merit or blessing power than one given by a less well known monk from Zangskar. This helps to explain why pilgrims will travel for days at considerable expense to attend a week-long initiation given by the Dalai Lama. The same is true for ritual donations. Gifts made to the Dalai Lama or other highly meritorious monks are believed to generate more merit than donations to a few impoverished nuns at Dorje Dzong. In all of these cases, merit making generates cyclical inequalities between those who already have wealth and status and those who do not.

Merit and Resistance

The extensive alms, rents, and donations paid to the monastery and to a lesser extent the nunnery beg the question of what, if any, lay resistance there may be. Why do households continue year after year to donate their money, labor, and harvest to the richest corporation in their society? Why do villagers across Zangskar continue to pay alms and taxes to a monastery which were initiated under legal conditions which have long since become obsolete? The answer has as much to do with prestige as with merit.

The production of prestige is as central to the Buddhist economy of merit as it was to Geertz's depiction of the Balinese cockfight.[78] Paraphrasing Geertz, both donors and stewards lay themselves on the line, through the medium of merit, for all to witness. Public opinion and private fear of shame may be sufficient incentive for most villagers to make some donation, however small. But why do villagers keep making such extensive donations and why do they seem to be in competition with each other? Donors and stewards are competing for prestige as much as they are seeking merit. They know that they will be judged according to their generosity and skill in producing a ritual event. The visibility of donations is heightened by the system of public pledges during the begging beers, return feasts for the donors, and endless gossip. While there is little explicit coercion of donors, the size of a donation is expected to be commensurate with the donor's income. Those individuals who make donations far above or below what is expected are singled out for recognition or reprobation. The stakes are highest for the wealthiest individuals, who have the most status to lose or gain from their donations. To be judged avaricious is to lose face in the eyes of fellow Buddhists. Stinginess is a social stigma which can only be cured with greater shows of generosity. Losing face as a donor may precipitate other hardship, especially in times of need. To be judged ungenerous may mean a loss of patronage or assistance from within the social and kin networks so critical in a subsistence-based economy. The public nature of giving and receiving fuels the escalation of donations in Zangskar.

The reciprocal arrangements between donors and stewards reflect the wider reciprocities which bind households to one another and to religious institutions. The public pledging and careful accounting of all donations at major festivals produce a public and permanent archive of information about generosity. Households store account books recording ritual donations for festivals they stewarded as palpable reminders of what they may be expected to donate in subsequent years. An especially generous donation may carry a subtle expectation of a higher return gift or other favor. Ritual donations produce symbolic capital to the extent that they produce credit which the donor can call back at a later stage. Such credit or promise of support, in the form of gifts or labor, is critical to Zangskar's agrarian economy, which is perpetually short of labor.[79] While stewards and donors sacrifice their time and wealth to produce a ritual event, they gain considerable social capital in the form of prestige and credit. While stewards take a risk in floating many ritual expenses on credit, they rarely fall into total financial ruin. The greater the risk they take in producing a lavish ritual, the more prestige they earn in the end.

Exit rather than voice appears the dominant mode of resistance to the Buddhist economy of merit. Villagers may complain about their rents, but they continue to make donations and serve the monastery in the interest of making merit. Dissent is private and uncoordinated, and hardly celebrated within a society where generosity is the first and foremost virtue. Those who resist making donations or alms do so silently. Villagers cannot shirk the obligatory rents to the monastery without losing their rights to till the land. The monastery may use the threat of ritual sanctions to coerce villagers into making voluntary donations to ritual events. In one instance of a dispute between two villages over firewood collecting rights, the members of one village simply refused to bring their share of firewood to the annual ritual reading of the Tibetan canon at Sani. After calling both sides in the dispute to a meeting, the monks officiating the rite threatened to stop performing funeral rites unless the dispute was resolved. The villagers hastily dispersed to make amends and then returned with the firewood as the monks had requested.

Villagers who regularly resist making donations or alms are chided in public as well as in private. The economy of merit relies as much on informal village gossip as on ritual threats. Both rich and poor who consistently give too little can be ostracized with public scorn or private epithets like calling them witches. Poorer peasants, especially, suffer small but significant losses in status in a society where poverty is already regarded as a sign of moral failure. As such, those who are poor are doubly damned for being "stingy," while those who are rich are expected to be even more virtuous than the poor. Regularly avoiding donations in this society entails some form of ostracism and slander. People attempt to ward off evil gossip (*mi 'kha*) with a specialized ritual discourse of purifications, astrological predictions, and expiatory rites. Surprisingly, even Muslim households sponsor some Buddhist rites, suggesting that status is as important a motive as merit. Until recently stewards of the monastery's largest fasting rite regularly invited Muslims to a separate begging beer—where tea is served in lieu of alcohol. Yet the recent escalation of tensions between the Muslims and Buddhists may soon make this interfaith ritual sponsorship obsolete.[80] Although their ritual clientele may be shifting, monks have yet to lose their salient role in local village rites.

Ritual Roles for Nuns and Monks

In general, monks are seen to deliver more ritual bang for the buck than nuns do. Some informants felt that more merit was made by having monks perform a rite. Others noted that monks have more Tantric prowess than nuns. As a result, monks are overwhelmingly called to perform expiations and propitiations. Unlike nuns, who usually have only a single meditative deity, senior monks can call upon a host of Tantric deities to placate the nasty and unpredictable sprites that plague human life. Yet the innate purity of the monk seems as important as his advanced ritual training. The presumed purity and strength of the male body are believed assets when dealing with demonic agents. If a human life is hanging in the balance, households will spare no expense or trouble to find the purest and most skilled ritual virtuoso.

As Pierre Bourdieu notes, "Rites take place because, and only because, they find their raison d'être in the conditions of existence and the dispositions of agents who cannot afford the luxury of logical speculation, mystical effusions, or metaphysical angst. It is not sufficient to deride the most naïve forms of functionalism to be rid of the questions of the practical functions of [ritual] practices."[81] Ritual efficacy is not unlike medical efficacy: the more powerful the monk, the more effective the rite. As a result, monks are called to perform most ad hoc personal, household, and villagewide rites. It is monks rather than nuns who are called upon for the expiations, propitiations, and ablutions that secure individual and family health and wealth. Bodily rites that monks perform include expelling demons, calling spirits, and subduing ghosts. Individuals and households who have been attacked by illness, misfortune, slander, or envy may request healing rites which involve tossing, burning, or burying ritual effigies, firebrands, and thread crosses (brgya bzhi, rgyal mdos, lha gsol, dgu mig bzlod). Most families engage monks seasonally to expel evil, ensure fertility, purify subterranean spirits, offer thanks, and ward off negativity.[82] Additionally, entire villages might conscript a set of monks to ward off floods, droughts, avalanches, or hailstorms. Monks are called to bless many human ventures, including the construction of houses, stupas, planting trees, or digging new irrigation ditches. Many rites like the monthly fumigation rite *(bsangs)* or the "four hundred [offerings]" *(brgya bzhi)* both bless and cleanse. Monks are preferred in warding off ritual pollution or securing good fortune because they are presumed to be both pure and fortunate. Monks are the only ones who perform more elaborate household rites that capture wealth or defeat enemies *(g.yang 'gugs, rnam rgyal stong mchod, dgra lha phar byes, rgyal ba lha bsangs)*. There is one set of prayers which is considered as efficacious when performed by a nun: the Tara Puja. Dedicated to a Buddha who vowed to take only female form, Tara, this puja is often commissioned by women suffering from female ailments.

Although there is a clear preference for monks, nuns can and do perform village or household rites on certain occasions. In such cases, nuns are a fallback rather than first choice for ritual performances. Nuns may perform village and household rites in villages where the ritual officiant is away or otherwise engaged. Even here, however, households will only call nuns for the most basic rites like the monthly juniper fumigation *(bsangs)* or honoring of regional deities *(lha gsol)*, but will leave more complex expiatory rites to monks. By the same analogy, while both assemblies of monks and nuns are called to certain villagewide events—weddings, funerals, the ancestor rite, and the *Prajñaparamita* readings—only monks officiate at these rituals. At weddings, only monks perform the ritual transfer *(gyang 'gugs)* of the bride from her old home and only monks destroy the effigy *(zor rgyab)* which prevents demons *(rgyab 'dre)* and malicious gossip *(gnod pa, mi kha)* from following her to her new husband's home. During the springtime ancestor rite, both monks and nuns are called to pray for the dead. Yet only monks consecrate the votive chorten *(tsha tsha)* that transfer merit to the deceased. Both nuns and monks may read the *Prajñaparamita* texts, but only monks circumambulate and purify the crops.

Pragmatic versus Generalized Merit Making

Bourdieu (1990:97) has said: "To understand ritual practice, to give it back both its reason and its raison d'être without converting it into a logical construction or a spiritual exercise, means more than simply reconstituting its internal logic. It also means restoring its practical necessity by relating it to the real conditions of its genesis, that is, the conditions in which both the functions it fulfils and the means it uses to achieve them are defined."[83] Disinterested charity at the nunnery may be virtuous, but pragmatic charity at the monastery is far more strategic. Making merit at the nunnery may improve a sponsor's karmic balance sheet, but making merit at the monastery can have far more pragmatic benefits. Nuns specialize in prayers that generate universal kindness *(snying rje)* or compassion for all sentient beings. Yet given that such suffering beings are innumerable in space and time, no finite amount of prayer or virtue could heal the universe. As such, nuns' prayers are doctrinally valid but bound to fail. More limited aims like health, wealth, and prestige are attainable with limited and directed giving—exactly the opposite of what Mahayana doctrine recommends. In local idiom, the monks occupy the "big monastery" *(dgon pa chen mo)* while the nuns live in a "little monastery" *(dgon pa chung tse)*. Donors who wish to offer the monastic assembly a full tea service and a token cash donation spend roughly five times as much at the monastery as they do at the nunnery. Yet the size of the donation translates into the quantity of symbolic capital a donor earns. Consider the postcremation offerings, which are supposed to be held every seven days during the forty-nine days before rebirth is said to take place. The wealthiest households might offer seven full tea services at both monastery and nunnery, including a cash sum for each monk and nun. More modest households might only offer seven services at one institution, probably the monastery if they can afford the butter and cash. The poorest families may choose to only make weekly offerings to the much smaller nuns' assembly. In terms of social prestige, those who give most generously are rewarded, while those who give too little may be shunned.

Ritual performances provide most monks with a necessary income in cash and kind. Because Zangskari monks live and eat separately in their own rooms rather than at the monastic kitchen, they require an income to furnish their rooms and purchase food. Yet the regularized repetition of paying monks for services erodes their ascetic and impoverished status. The economy of merit operates in a such a way that donors consistently prefer to spend lavishly on the wealthiest monks. The most skillful or meritorious monks become ever more wealthy, until the ascetic ideal is all but lost. While some monks grasp at conspicuous status symbols, others compete to earn more powerful patrons. As the dis-ease of desire spreads, monks soon decorate their cells with glass windows, opulent furnishings, gas burners, and even televisions. The cells at the nunnery appear barren and desolate in comparison. When the monks' realm becomes as driven by consumption as the profane, patrons may shift donations elsewhere in disgust. Corruption and greed may be purged by a state-sanctioned cleansing or lay reforms. Yet soon enough, the innocuous drift toward wealth and power begins once again.

Throughout the historical and geographical spread of Buddhism, the shift away from rigid discipline and asceticism has been replaced by periodic "purifications" of the monastic order.[84] Such sporadic reformations have had limited success in every era. The ultimate dialectic between ascetic retreat and worldly engagement is built into the practice of making merit. In a cyclical process, villagers make merit by giving largely to select monks. When these monks have too much wealth, donations decline, until only "truly ascetic" monks are left. Yet soon enough, the cycle begins again, as new monks join the ascetic ranks hoping to earn fame and glory. Indeed, spiritual advancement may only be possible by deliberately flouting the worldly game of merit altogether.

"Women are amputated of the purpose of their action, forced to be disinterested, self-sacrificing, without ever having chosen or wanted this. The path of renunciation described by certain mystics is women's daily lot," observes Luce Irigaray.[85] Self-sacrifice was a radical aspect of the Buddha's doctrine. When the Vedic ritual of sacrifice was internalized by Buddhist monks, an entire class of priests and caste hierarchy became obsolete, in theory if not in practice. The Buddhist renunciants were supposed to fuse the position of patron and priest by internalizing the purification of thoughts and deeds and abandoning external ritual purification. Yet it is nuns more than monks who embody that internalized self-sacrifice today. While nuns rarely perform rites of purification and remain enmeshed in poverty, monks benefit from ritual payments and vast permanent endowments. The marginality of nuns within the economy of merit has led to their servitude as much as the centrality of monks and their ritual efficacy has led to monastic wealth. Nuns may carry water, cut firewood, and perform countless mundane tasks that teach meditative detachment but not Tantric discipline. They may exhibit extraordinary compassion and selflessness, but are not able to apply these skills in esoteric Buddhist rites. Nuns cannot escape this servitude any more than they can avoid the burden of a female body. They struggle to advance on the Buddhist path despite the numerous practical obstacles. Yet it is far too early to tell which of the two sexes will reach the "other shore" first.

Ani Yeshe. Now in her mid-seventies, Yeshe is the last surviving founder of Karsha nunnery. After traveling on foot to Tibet in 1956 to see the Dalai Lama and be ordained, Yeshe returned to Karsha village to help develop a community of nuns. *(Kim Gutschow)*

Karsha nunnery. The white buildings of the nunnery sit on a sandstone cliff high above the village of Karsha and below the jagged ruins of Karsha's first settlement in the ninth century. The slender path snaking up the empty cliff marks the boundary between the sacred realm and the profane. *(Kim Gutschow)*

Karsha monastery. The Karsha monastery sits on an opposing cliff, jutting high above the nunnery and the village. As the largest and oldest monastery in Zangskar, it houses roughly ninety monks. The twelfth-century Labrang (lower left) also serves as a treasury, granary, and residence for visiting dignitaries. *(Kim Gutschow)*

The assembly of Karsha nuns in 1994. The Karsha nuns are assembled in the courtyard, with the profile of the cliff and Karsha monastery behind them. The twenty nuns range in age from seventy-seven to ten. *(Kim Gutschow)*

Bowing and scraping. The nuns at Karsha are bowing and offering white blessing scarves to a revered Tibetan monk who has just graced their nunnery with a rare visit. *(Kim Gutschow)*

Ritual assembly. Most nuns in Zangskar perform esoteric Tantric visualizations during their daily meditations and periodic assemblies. Here, the nuns of Pishu practice a Tantric rite known as *gcod,* or "cutting through," aimed at severing all attachments and desire. *(Kim Gutschow)*

Tantric visualizations. This nun from Pishu visualizes the ultimate act of self-sacrifice and compassion during the *gcod* ritual. Her Tantric meditation includes a visualization in which she offers her body as food for hungry ghosts and other beings. *(Kim Gutschow)*

Offering cakes. Skalzang, one of the ritual assistants, is responsible for preparing the offering cakes needed during collective assemblies at Karsha nunnery. Every offering cake, or *gtorma,* has a prescribed shape, color, and decorative features which signify philosophical concepts. Some cakes are consumed by participants in the rite, others symbolize the deities being visualized, and yet others are scattered for demons and other beings. *(Kim Gutschow)*

Barley and butter. The nuns of Pishu are preparing the dough to make ritual cakes for their Great Prayer Festival. The ingredients—roasted barley flour, milk, butter, and raw sugar—are arrayed in pots around them. While the elder nun on the left sifts the flour and the nun on the right pours out the milk, the head nun looks on. The nuns who organize a given rite must find sponsors to provide the necessary material ingredients. *(Kim Gutschow)*

Demons and dogs. Nyima, a ritual assistant, sets out the offering cake for demons who might obstruct the ritual in progress at Karsha nunnery. The nunnery mascot has been loitering all day for this reward. *(Kim Gutschow)*

Nunnery school. The youngest nuns at Wakha nunnery learn the Tibetan alphabet from an instructor who is only slightly older than her pupils. In addition to an apprenticeship with an elder nun, the youngest nuns attend collective classes in their nunnery to learn grammar, calligraphy, and other subjects. *(Helga Gutschow)*

Apprenticeship. The two youngest and most recent members of Karsha nunnery, Kundzom and Namdrol, recite the latest texts they have memorized. Each has spent the last year living with an elder nun, who tutors them in basic ritual texts. Such lengthy residences with older nuns help knit the nunnery's generations together and strengthen filial bonds among nuns. *(Kim Gutschow)*

Palkyid with child. Nuns offer day care for the children of the village. In forgoing having their own children, nuns are free to take care of countless others in their community. They appear to enjoy these duties as much as the overworked mothers appreciate their services. *(Kim Gutschow)*

Shaving heads. Younger nuns perform many duties for elder nuns, including shaving their heads. Chodron, from Pishu nunnery, shaves an elder nun's head in preparation for an upcoming ritual assembly. *(Kim Gutschow)*

Watering the barley fields. Garkyid stands in her cousin's field, routing the irrigation water to gently flood the month-old barley shoots. The "first watering" is done with great care, because the water will flow through the field in the same pattern for the rest of the growing season. *(Kim Gutschow)*

Bringing dung. Nuns from Dorje Dzong nunnery have walked several hours to deliver bushels of dung to the revered abbot of Karsha nunnery. Since collecting dung is largely woman's work, nuns are recruited to collect dung for monks and village households alike. Dung is a critical heating fuel in Zangskar, where wintertime temperatures can drop to minus fifty degrees Celsius. *(Kim Gutschow)*

Bringing thistle. Thuje carries a load of thistle up the narrow plank which leads to the nunnery rooftop, where it is stored for the coming winter. Thistle is a necessary cooking fuel in the desert landscape. Every nun who has not yet served as chantmaster must collect three loads of thistle as one of her annual chores for the nunnery collective. *(Kim Gutschow)*

Brushing pile. Ani Norbu and Ani Lobsang Drolma brush woven strips of wool to produce the fleecy texture of the Zangskari cloth called *nambu.* From sheep to coat, every step in producing this cloth is done by hand. The warm woolen material is used to make monastic robes, coats, pants, hats, boots, and other pieces of clothing worn both summer and winter. *(Kim Gutschow)*

Construction at the nunnery. The Karsha nuns carry the main beam of their new greenhouse from the monastery plot where it was harvested earlier. After being purchased from the monastery's bursar, the tree was felled and carried up to the nunnery within the hour. Nuns have built their entire nunnery and individual cells by hand using local materials. *(Kim Gutschow)*

Window of a nun's cell. Skalzang stares out of the tiny window on the first floor of her two-story cell at the nunnery. In most Zangskari houses, the windows in the first story are very small to prevent heat loss in the winter, when the entire family may live in the lower story in rooms adjacent to the stables. In the other three seasons, families occupy the upper stories while only livestock remain in the lowest story.

(Kim Gutschow)

4

The Buddhist Traffic in Women

Gender is an inescapable and absolute condition of Buddhist monasticism in Zangskar. Buddhist nuns may renounce both desire and sex, but they cannot transcend their sexuality. Their shaved heads and androgynous maroon robes may signal the lofty desire of detachment, yet they cannot escape their mundanely gendered bodies. Nuns can no more escape the dialectic of difference than they can flee the gender roles in which they are trapped. The few, intrepid women who seek out the celibate life in Zangskar may avoid the traumatic day when they are sent off to a husband's home. But they cannot escape the exchange of women which is the foundation of marriage as a social formation. Nuns are not traded in marriage like their lay sisters, but their families "exchange" them for merit and the promise of service. In the end, nuns are as trapped within the traffic in women as the average bride. Fathers may negotiate their daughter's bride-price, but it is monks who manage the traffic of nuns into and out of the nunnery.

Let us consider who becomes a nun in Zangskar and at what cost. Understanding both the drawbacks and the gains of renunciation helps explain why relatively few women become nuns. Although every woman comes to a Zangskari nunnery by her own unique path, common themes emerge. Jealous stepmothers, philandering fathers, orphans, and powerful teachers are just some of the influences that can lead a woman into the ascetic life. The personal narratives explored below suggest strategies of resistance and cooperation. The ascetic life challenges domestic obligations even as it must accommodate them. Filial piety is expected and encouraged long after daughters join the nunnery. Most nuns toil selflessly as dutiful daughters on their parents' estates to sustain themselves. Some nuns follow their family's expectations in order to join the nunnery; many others struggle against oppressive family dynamics. Yet all nuns must make peace with their village and monastic authorities during their monastic quest.

The Narrow Path to Nunhood

The path to religious renunciation is long and tortuous in life as much as in literature. When a popular narrative about one woman's difficulty in renouncing social obligations was staged locally in Karsha one year, I had ample opportunity to discuss the play with the cast. By the time the play was staged during the monastery's annual Gustor festival for the benefit of a crowd of pilgrims, the Nangsa Öbum play was far more than a performance for local actresses. The all-female cast saw the play as a paradigm of their own fears and regrets about marital choices.[1] The young actresses confided their dashed hopes late into the night after rehearsals. Kunzang admitted that as an oldest daughter, she had been destined to marry the suitor that her parents chose. Unmarried Kesang confessed that she had hoped to join Karsha nunnery rather than be enslaved to a stupid husband. She regretted spending her youth in caring for her parents rather than studying religion *(chos)*. Lhadrol explained that while she had divorced her husband after only a week of marriage because he was so mean, it was already too late for her to learn the Tibetan texts she'd need to know as a nun. Most of the actresses identified with Nangsa's story, regardless of whether they had been married or not. All had heard similar tales of abusive husbands, wicked in-laws, and the difficulty of committing oneself to celibacy. They knew that even if they had attempted renunciation, their aspirations would have been thwarted many times along the way.

"Storytelling . . . reveals meaning without committing the error of defining it," Hannah Arendt tells us.[2] The Tibetan folktale of Nangsa Öbum offers a paradigmatic *bildungsroman* in which the experience of death offers a valuable lesson on life.[3] As in other instances of Tibetan hagiography, Nangsa undergoes numerous hardships and lessons in her search for enlightenment. Yet Nangsa's tale appears fraught with limitations specific to the female body. Her struggle to escape uncompromising social obligations are as important as eluding male figures of authority. Like the male saints Naropa, Milarepa, and Marpa, Nangsa must undergo terrific austerities to prove her endurance. Yet Nangsa's teachers are not just Tantric mas-

ters but her cruel and stupid in-laws. Unlike the male saints who are forcibly humbled by clever masters, Tibetan heroines like Nangsa are almost
too self-effacing. For female adepts like Gelongma Palmo, Mandarava, and
Laksminkara, marriage is such a burden that they must disfigure or deface
themselves in order to escape into the ascetic life. Like Nangsa, they can
only find enlightenment outside the enforced constraints of marriage or
domesticity. A twin theme emerges in these stories: husbands and children
can mean nothing but servitude and sorrow.

The tale of Nangsa Öbum begins in a Tibetan village under the roof of a
devout elderly couple. Although they were very aged, the wife experienced
a vision of Tara in her sleep one night. Nine months later she gave birth to
a daughter they named Nangsa Öbum. When Nangsa grew into a beautiful
maiden, suitors came from many lands but her parents refused them all,
saying she wanted to become a nun. After Nangsa went to the Gustor festival at a nearby monastery, the lord of Rinag chose her as the ideal wife for
his son. When he called her over to propose, she protested that she was not
fit to be a nobleman's wife. The arrogant lord persisted, placed a turquoise
on her head, and declared that he would kill any other man who dared
marry her. The next day the lord appeared at her parents' doorstep, an-
nouncing that he had come to make the bridewealth payments. When he
left, Nangsa wailed that she would rather meditate until she died than
marry. Her parents replied that the lord might kill them all. In the end,
Nangsa was married and bore a son after a year.

Nangsa was terribly unhappy at her husband's palace, where her sister-
in-law, an unmarried and perhaps sexually frustrated spinster, never gave
Nangsa keys to the storeroom and generally made life difficult. One day,
two religious mendicants came to visit the palace while Nangsa was in
the fields harvesting barley. Because she had no access to the storeroom,
Nangsa could only offer them grain straight from the fields. The jealous
sister-in-law struck Nangsa for her impromptu generosity and complained
to her brother. The husband then added injury to insult, breaking three of
Nangsa's ribs. Nangsa suffered his rage in silence rather than offend her
husband or his sister. Shortly thereafter, another religious mendicant (her
future teacher, in disguise) came to the palace. When he sang a parable
about the suffering that beautiful women experience, Nangsa was deeply
moved and, for lack of anything else to offer, gave him the jewels from her
breast.[4] The lord, who had been listening at the door, entered the room, furious over her indiscretion. The beggar leapt out the window while the lord

beat Nangsa senseless, inadvertently killing her. The astrologer who came to perform the death horoscope warned them not to burn Nangsa's body because she would come back from the dead in seven days' time. As foretold, she came back to life a week later, declaring her intention to take up the celibate life.

When Nangsa's in-laws pleaded and her son begged her not to abandon him, she relented. Still miserable, she went to visit her parents and told them of her wish to become a nun. Nangsa's mother said her daughter was ridiculous to ignore her husband and dream of renunciation. She said that a woman who does not follow her husband is like a sheep who does not follow the flock or a patient who does not take her medicine. After her mother threw her out of the house in disgust, Nangsa ran off to the mountains to search for her teacher. Wandering for days, she found his hermitage where she requested religious instruction. The teacher flatly refused and said she was not ready. In response, she pulled a knife from under her skirt, threatening to plunge it into her breast. He relented and initiated her into Tantric practices. Eventually, Nangsa's husband came to recapture her with an army. After killing many meditators, the soldiers captured her teacher and insulted him:

> You are an old dog that has seduced our snow lion! . . .
> Why did you try to rape this white grouse? . . .
> Why did you pull out her feathers and wings?
> You are an old donkey living in a dirty stable.
> Why did you rape our beautiful wild horse?
> Why did you cut off her mane?
> You nasty old bull, why did you have sex
> with our beautiful white female yak?[5]

In retaliation, the Tantric master reached out, moved the mountains, and brought his dead disciples back to life. Nangsa then levitated above the soldiers, mocking their attempts to tame or own her. She told them: "You have tried to make a snow lion into a dog, tried to tame a wild yak and turn it into a cow, tried to saddle the wild mule who lives in the forest, [and] tried to make a rainbow into a piece of cloth . . . You cannot hold me." When the soldiers and her in-laws saw her fly miraculously into the air, they dropped their arms and were converted to the religious life.

What can this tale tell us about the conflict between renunciation and marriage in Tibetan Buddhist culture? For women, the decision to renounce is portrayed as selfish, unnatural, or unreasonable. In Tibet as in Zangskar, daughters are expected to become wives and mothers. While Nangsa chooses the spiritual life, she cannot avoid being traded like chattel to a pestering suitor. Later, she is pursued like a domestic animal who has gone astray. Her husband's family believes she has been seduced and defiled by her religious teacher. By comparing herself to the wild and untamable animals of the forest, Nangsa protests her domestication. Nangsa's efforts at renunciation are in vain until she magically embodies the perfection of wisdom which ordinary Buddhist monks strive to emulate. Yet her miraculous ability to pierce through the delusions of the Rinag clan are much more difficult to achieve in the real world of Zangskari reciprocity.

Who Becomes a Nun in Zangskar?

The decision to take up the monastic life is influenced by a number of circumstances, including place of birth, lineage, family status, number of siblings, and birth order. Eldest or only children rarely become nuns or monks because such children usually are destined to inherit if they are sons or be married off if they are daughters. Not a single nun out of the 100 nuns I interviewed in Zangskar was an eldest daughter, and I met only a handful of monks who were only sons.[6] Common family patterns among Zangskari women who are nuns, besides not being the eldest daughter, include having a parent who died, being raised by stepparents, and having spent time away from their home during their youth. At Karsha nunnery, half the nuns had lost at least one parent in childhood. Being raised by stepparents or other relatives may hinder a girl in securing a good marriage. Two-thirds of the twenty-two nuns at Karsha had lived away from home in childhood, working as nannies or as farmhands for relatives with no children of their own. This experience away from home teaches young girls the stoic self-abnegation which is so essential to monastic life. Yet one cannot leap to generalizations. For every orphaned or illegitimate daughter who arrives at the nunnery, there are similar girls who do not choose the nun's life. Since many women marry in their mid- or late twenties in Zangskar, unmarried women are not pressured to join the nunnery. Up to one-fifth of the adult women in some villages remain unmarried even today.[7]

The popular image of Himalayan nuns as unhappy women who have no better options in life does not hold in Zangskar. Women do not arrive at the nunnery gate "by accident" because of divorce, widowhood, or looming spinsterhood. Those women who encounter bad marriages and other misfortunes are more likely to wind up as elderly renunciants than as nuns. Such renunciants may take up five precepts, including celibacy, late in life, but very few can master the extensive texts and learning required of novices who join a monastic assembly. It is not unusual to hear divorced or unmarried women express a yearning to become a nun, as well as the admission that they lack literacy or the discipline. Although religious conviction can be born in a flash of illumination, a woman cannot join the nunnery overnight. Almost every woman who joins a monastic assembly must dedicate herself to years of textual and ritual tutelage. The nuns' life demands an appetite for intellectual discipline as much as manual drudgery.

Most girls and boys who wind up at the nunnery or monastery are apprenticed to the religious life as children. To the jaundiced Western eye, this narrative can imply unhappy little children who are forcibly dedicated to lifelong celibacy. Yet the reality is rather different. Just as American parents may have high hopes that their daughter will go to Harvard, so too Zangskari parents hope for their sons and daughters to go to the monastery or nunnery. Yet it is up to the child to make that choice in the end. The long delay between this childhood apprenticeship and taking novice ordination during adolescence offers plenty of opportunity for children to experiment with the monastic life. Children either take to the ascetic life or they do not. Those that don't have an inclination to the monastic life may simply refuse to memorize the necessary texts, make trouble, steal, run away, or make their monastic tutors miserable. Other, less confrontational children may simply grow their hair out, elope, or wait until the marriage proposals come in. Despite their parents' best-laid plans, it is not difficult to get thrown out or avoid the monastic life altogether. While parents often pledge children to the nunnery or monastery by cropping their hair, many such children lose interest long before it is time to take tonsure or ordination.

Both caste and class are further barriers to becoming a nun or a monk. Children from the "lowest stratum" (*rigs ngan*) in Zangskari society are ineligible to join the nunnery or monastery, without exception. Although the Buddha himself was against caste, the members of the Gara, Beda, and Mon clans are still unable to join the monastic order in Zangskar as elsewhere in the Himalayas. Local monks and nuns in Zangskar have no trouble justifying the ban on lower-caste monastics. As one nun, Putid, put it pithily, "If a blacksmith were to become chantmaster and sit at the head of the seating row *(gral),* where would we sit?" For Putid, the image of a blacksmith sitting at the head of a seating row was inconceivable. Because such individuals would ordinarily sit at the tail of a row, placing them at the head would force everyone else out of the room, in her view. A more learned monk explained that while it is possible for a lower-caste person to join the monastery, there were no instances of this in Zangskar.

Class is far less of a barrier than caste. Nuns and monks come from all kinds of socioeconomic backgrounds, although many monastics are from the middle or lower end of the income spectrum. The most impoverished families may not be able to afford to send their child to the monastery or nunnery, because they forfeit that child's labor and because of the ritual expenses they owe. Alternatively, the most wealthy or aristocratic families tend to rule out the monastic life in hopes of securing a powerful alliance for their sons and daughters.

Garkyid came to the nunnery with her mother's blessing and a remarkable prophecy. Garkyid's mother, Sonam, was born in the largest house in Rinam, just east of Karsha. She was a precocious child who spoke of a previous lifetime in Karsha, as the daughter of the Zaildar. Just before her birth in Rinam, the daughter of the Karsha Zaildar—who had been betrothed to a man from Lungnag—died. At her death, the astrologer had predicted that she would be reborn in a wealthy house to the east, where Rinam lay. He also predicted that she would face considerable hardship if she did not become a nun. When Sonam recognized her previous house and village, the people were amazed and recognized her as a reincarnation. While she pleaded with her parents to become a nun, they refused. As the oldest daughter, albeit of her father's second wife, she was married off to a man from Yulang. Although she had twelve children, eight died. After some years, she lost her husband as well. Once her eldest daughter was married, she decided without hesitation that her second daughter, Garkyid, should become a nun. Garkyid was sent to study texts with Putid, also from Yulang, until she had learned enough texts to take novice ordination. She is glad she does not have to repeat the suffering her mother has seen in two lifetimes.

Drolma told me about the misfortunes that brought her to the nunnery. Because Drolma's mother was only a mistress and never married, she was forced by custom to relinquish her rights to raise her daughter. Her mother's role as clandestine mistress of several brothers in the same household brought her little respect and no authority over the children she bore. Drolma's paternity was decided by a lottery between the three brothers who had shared Drolma's mother's bed. After Drolma's birth, she and her mother were sent back to her mother's natal village, where she was raised by her mother until the age of four. Following local custom, Drolma's father eventually came to claim Drolma.[8] When he moved to Karsha where he married his elder brother's widow after the brother's untimely death, he and his new wife decided that Drolma might be useful around the house to do chores and take care of his wife's son from her first marriage. Drolma was an outsider twice over in her stepmother's wealthy house, with no rights to moveable property or inheritance. Drolma's father was an in-marrying husband who would never fill his deceased brother's shoes, while Drolma was a sign of his past infidelities. Given little to eat and nothing to wear but rags, Drolma lost count of how many times she ran away to her mother's house before her father took her home forcefully.

Although her mother told her she was being treated badly by her father and stepmother, Drolma accepted their suggestion that she join the nunnery rather than get married. She did not want to wind up a spurned mistress like her mother or as a spinster working for her stepfamily. Despite their considerable wealth, her father and stepmother delayed sending her to the nunnery in hopes of keeping her at home to work. In response, she threatened to run off or even kill herself. Her own half-brother's tragic suicide was still fresh in her mind. Also an illegitimate son, he too had been raised by his father, albeit in a different village. He too suffered abuse at the hands of a jealous stepmother and stepsiblings, who called him a bastard. After being sent to Karsha monastery for his tonsure ceremony, he begged his father to allow him to be ordained but was kept at home to do chores. Finally, despairing of ever being ordained as a novice, he hung himself in the toilet one year, to his family's shock and shame. Drolma eventually ran off to her mother's house threatening never to return, until her father and stepmother finally relented and took her to join the nun's assembly. She is still embarrassed that her seat at the nunnery is below other nuns who are much younger than she. Her father arranged for her to borrow a neighbor's cell rather than build her a new one as would be customary. Her barren and sparsely furnished cell at the nunnery reflects her father's lack of support, despite his house being one of the wealthiest in the village. After years of serving a loveless home, she left the nunnery to go to the neighboring region of Lahaul in 2002.

Tsomo was raised by her mother, who never married Tsomo's father. When her father came to claim Tsomo at the customary age of four, her mother simply refused, because she needed her daughter's help around the house. One of several sisters with no brother, Tsomo's mother had inherited a parcel of land and some livestock, where she raised her daughter until she was sixteen. Tsomo spent several summers working in her father's house, but always fled back home to escape her stepmother's wrath. Tsomo got the shock of her life when her father came to visit one year to announce that a neighbor had sent the "begging beer" (*'dri chang*) for Tsomo's hand in marriage. When she heard the news, Tsomo spun on her heels and took to the red cliff behind the house. She climbed up and up the cliff until she was dizzy, and only stopped when the village and her house were a safe speck far below. While her father and mother called her all afternoon, she remained hidden in the warm comfort of the red rocks and thought about how to avoid the indignities she had seen her mother suffer. While her mother's liaison with Tsomo's father had ended in bitter recriminations, her mother's next affair, with an abusive drunk, was even worse. Tsomo waited until night fell, when she heard the jingle of her father saddling his horse and the familiar clop of the hooves fading in the distance. When she had descended the cliff, her mother agreed to speak to her father, and shortly thereafter allowed her to begin her apprenticeship at the nunnery. Although she shares a cell with her mother's sister—who is also a nun—Tsomo still helps her mother daily on the farm.

Having spent much of her childhood away from home, taking care of her sister's children, Putid had ample opportunity to learn about the trials that a young wife and mother can face. As a child, Putid and her best friend, Tsering, learned to read Tibetan with a kind and learned doctor. Shortly before both girls were to be married, they attended an esoteric Kalachakra empowerment given by Geshe Zodpa in Tungri. Dressed in their finest silk brocade vests, tie-dyed shawls, and jewelry, the two maidens were oblivious to the staring young men and the gossiping elders. Profoundly moved by the teachings, the two girls offered their hair and jewels to Geshe Zodpa—who later helped the nuns raise money for their new assembly hall. After the women returned home from being initiated by Geshe Zodpa into the "homeless state," Putid's parents started to cry. Putid insisted that she would become a nun. Her parents insisted that they had already drunk the begging beer and that her marriage negotiations were well under way, but Putid told them that marriage was nothing but unhappiness and abuse. She'd seen the different lives her sisters led. While her sister who was married suffered long harangues and occasional marital abuse, her other sister, a nun, seemed to fully enjoy her life at the nunnery, despite the work she owed her family and despite her poverty.

Tsering, who was an eldest daughter, faced much greater resistance from her parents than Putid. When Tsering's father came to the nunnery and saw her freshly shaven head and her neck bereft of jewelry he was livid with rage. He told her that he'd been negotiating her wedding for five years, at considerable expense. Thrashing her soundly, he tied her onto the horse in front of him and took her home. Although he hastened to conclude the marriage negotiations, Tsering fled back to the nunnery with her father in rapid pursuit. For a year, Tsering eluded her father time after time until she could bear it no longer. When the snows melted, she fled south over the passes to Dharamsala, in the neighboring state of Himachal Pradesh, where she settled near the Dalai Lama's personal monastery. After several years of study she was ordained as a novice. She has never returned to Zangskar, although twenty-five years have passed.

An elderly nun, Sheshe, grew up as the second of six children in a poor household. Because her parents couldn't afford to feed all their children, they sent her away to live with two of her father's sisters, who were married to the same man and both childless. Sheshe's aunts were rather abusive, perhaps in response to the beatings they had received for being sterile. She recalls that she was hardly allowed to drink a single cup of tea without getting up for nine different chores. Her aunts never gave her proper clothes or shoes, and she recalls being cold and hungry. Her aunt once cut her ankle to the bone with the fire prongs, and she fainted at least once under her uncle's blows. When Sheshe tried to run away for the first time, she was soundly thrashed and told that she would be drowned if she tried this again. Sheshe ran away the next time when she was already a teenager, but she was caught by two men on horseback. On her third attempt, when she was twenty years old, she forded the river to Karsha with the help of a man on horseback and finally reached her parents' house. Vowing never to return to her aunts, she began to memorize religious texts with her brother, a monk. When she begged for years to have her head shaven, her family finally gave in and took her to be apprenticed to an elder nun at Karsha. When she took novice ordination years later, she cried with relief.

Norbu, whose legendary beauty still shines from beneath her wrinkles and shaven head, is the only nun in Zangskar who was once married. Norbu, whose name means jewel, was known for her sweet disposition as a girl. She was one of eight sisters—including Sonam, Garkyid's mother—but in a very wealthy house, and she had more than enough marriage proposals. When she was married off to the distant Ladakhi village of Nyerags, her husband died after seven years of a childless marriage. Norbu returned to her natal house, and eventually married a man whose wife had run off with another man. She was greatly loved by his three children, whom she treated as her own. After nearly twenty-five years of marriage, her second husband died as well. Because Norbu had studied religious texts as a young woman, she began to go regularily to the prayer sessions at Karsha nunnery, where three of her nieces—Garkyid, Thuje, and Dechen—were nuns. Several years later, while on pilgrimage in northern India, she renounced her lay life. She asked Lotsa Rinpoche to shave her head in Dharamsala, and ultimately was ordained by the Dalai Lama himself in Bodhgaya, where the Buddha himself had gained enlightenment more than two thousand years earlier. Her ordination ceremony included hundreds of female renunciants from across the Himalayas. Norbu has only one regret: that she waited so long to become a nun.

What do these stories suggest about why women become nuns in Zangskar? Although there is no single reason that a woman joins the nunnery, some common themes emerge. Family circumstances, poverty, and other hardships during childhood often predispose a child to be selected for the nunnery or the monastery. While some nuns appear to choose the religious life, others are chosen. Some nuns tread a path paved by parental will, while others must scramble and scheme to get to the nunnery. A daughter from a prominent family like Norbu or Tsering faces a different set of possibilities and constraints than an illegitimate and unwanted daughter like Drolma. Nuns from poor or broken homes where labor shortages are evident may have to fight to join the nunnery. Yet even daughters from wealthier homes may be enjoined to marry like Garkyid's mother, Sonam. The circumstances which bring a woman to the nunnery and those that keep her there may have an elective affinity. The sight and experience of suffering in childhood may be a condition as much as a justification for taking up a life of detachment and deprivation. For some nuns, individual adversity is a sign of reduced merit as much as a signal to begin stockpiling merit as soon as possible. Women like Drolma or Sheshe endure countless hardships to secure a seat at a nunnery. Their tales of abuse should be read against a cultural grain where beating naughty children is perfectly acceptable. Moreover, in Buddhist ideology, untoward amounts of adversity signal a lack of merit rather than a cause of counseling or anger management.

In many cases, parents are less interested in opposing than in delaying their daughter's wish to become a nun. Such parents know that they can make merit by sending a daughter to the nunnery, but they also realize that they forfeit some of her labor after she joins. The self-serving wish to delay a daughter's entrance into the monastic assembly is economic as well as Buddhist. Parents may prevent their daughters from rushing into monastic life for fear that the decision is made in haste. As Buddhists, they know the terrible burden ex-nuns or -monks bear in their future rebirths. According to a common belief, a nun or monk who breaks the four root vows—to kill, lie, steal, or have sex—cannot be reborn as a human or in any of the upper realms. Such beings are destined for one of the lower three rebirths as an animal, hungry ghost, or hell-being.[9]

Yet many nuns speak less of "choosing" than of being chosen for the nun's life. Most nuns spoke of the rare opportunity they have earned, because of merit or pasts acts *(sngan ma'i las)*. In local idiom, the requisite conditions for taking up the monastic life—being born in a Buddhist land, appropriate caste, family, birth order, and geography—are the result of past merit coming to fruition. Because merit is like capital, those individuals who are born with sufficient reserves of merit have the chance to take up the monastic life. In local idiom, people speak of a child's quick facility at learning to read or memorize Tibetan texts as a sign of past merit. Conversely, those who fail may justify their abandoning the celibate path through a lack of sufficient merit. As one ex-nun explained, "While I thought it was my *karma* to be a nun, instead I'm a mother. Yet I could not have known so beforehand, because *karma* is written upon our foreheads. Only those who are enlightened can read it."[10] While many children are born across Zangskar every year, only a few persevere and become nuns or monks. Choice and chance easily intercede to upset the lifelong project of celibacy.

Although Buddhists speak of *karma (las)* as destiny or potential, they do not deny agency. To borrow Geertz's (1973) metaphor of culture, *karma* provides the web of meanings from our previous lives by which we are suspended in the present life. Because every action and thought has some consequence, every event—no matter how inexplicable—can be made meaningful. Yet there is no transcendent position outside of the relentless law of *karma* except liberation or Buddhahood. Individuals cannot escape their *karma* any more than they can escape their bodies. Yet every moment offers a liberating potential in which choices help determine the future. Although the present is conditioned by the past, it does not dictate the future. Put into rational choice theory, *karma* is the set of constraints which limit the choices available. Choices are never free but are always constrained by circumstances that are due to past actions and events. *Karma* accounts for one's position, although how one uses that identity shapes present morality and future consequences. In Buddhist doctrine, *karma* may shape choice, but it does not dictate the outcome any more than history, culture, politics, or status would.

Several nuns recited a proverb when I asked them what they valued most about life in the nunnery:

> Everything by your own will is happiness,
> Everything by another's will is suffering.

Although freedom is rarely cited as the main reason for joining the nunnery, it is a powerful draw. The proverb alludes to the belief of individual responsibility for actions and points to one of the main reasons nuns give for taking up the celibate and monastic life: making merit. Many nuns recognize that following the monastic discipline offers the training and the opportunities to make more merit than as a layperson. Taking up the monastic life is a sign of both having merit and making merit. The monastic discipline avoids the ten nonvirtuous actions *(mi dge ba bcu)* as much as the venial distractions of lay life. Most villagers agreed that nuns make more merit than laywomen, but not all accepted that nuns make more merit than laymen. Laymen can make merit on a grand scale by building temples or sponsoring vast rituals, which allows others a chance to make merit as well. Nuns, however, have far fewer material resources to make merit through permanent endowments. Learned villagers added that nuns can and do make merit on a smaller, individual scale through upholding their discipline, reading texts, prostrations, circumambulation, and fasting. As such, nuns have a better chance than laywomen do of avoiding ever more suffering in a lower rebirth. Yet as with any monastic, both nuns and monks also have more merit to lose. As with any capital investment, those who invest in the ascetic life also have the most to lose by abandoning this life.

Besides making merit, the two most common reasons for joining the nunnery were to avoid marriage and maternity. Both of these situations create more suffering in the endless cycle of birth and rebirth known as *samsara (srid pa'i 'khor lo)*. Marriage is considered to offer many chances for suffering through promiscuity, divorce, or marital abuse. Women who initiate divorce may lose their dowry and find their family members unwilling to take them back home. Parents want to see their daughters married so they no longer need to support them. As long as a daughter is unmarried, expressed in local idiom as "not yet through the door" *(sgo mi mthon byes)*, a parent must worry about her marriage prospects. Because custom demands that women wait for marriage offers rather than seek them out, there is pressure to accept an offer lest it be withdrawn. As a result, even the smartest girls who complete their education and are eligible for jobs may be married off without regard for their personal wishes. Poor parents, who can promise little in the way of dowry, may have to settle on the first marriage offer available. For that reason, girls from poorer families have less say in choosing their husbands and less leverage if the husband turns abusive. Yet the nunnery offers a convenient escape from unsuitable marriage proposals that a girl may face. Even as other career options beckon in today's climate, the nunnery offers an autonomy and independence of which wives and mothers can only dream.

According to Durkheim, "We cannot detach ourselves from [the profane world] without doing violence to our nature and without painfully wounding our instincts."[11] But although I asked again and again, I never heard nuns mourn their inability to have children. Many nuns said that maternity was as much a burden as a boon. Although they recognize that motherhood is one of the highest ideals in society, they seem happy not to have children. They may be sublimating their desire, but Buddhist ideology offers another perspective. When I asked one nun if she missed not having her own children, she replied, "Nuns are fortunate *(bsod bde chen)*. They can be mother to many children. They love all children equally and do not grieve over just their own, selfishly, as mothers do." Other nuns told me that "children bring nothing but suffering." How so, I asked? Paraphrasing

Milarepa, one nun explained that when the pain of pregnancy and the pangs of childbirth have died away, there is the sorrow of infant death. Then the children simply grow up to forget their parents. In this view, children bring parents nothing but ingratitude or cruelty. Mothers, in particular, face endless suffering in a society where maternal anemia, miscarriage, infant mortality, and spousal abuse are hardly unknown.

The Risk of Being a Woman

Domestic violence is rarely mentioned except in intimate circles when no men are present. When I spent a "ladies' night" with several girlfriends whose husbands were attending a nearby festival, I heard stories of abuse as well as resistance. As the beer flowed freely that night, women explained how some husbands became abusive with too much of that common vice, alcohol. Yet their stories also implied that they were anything but passive. Strategies of resistance against their husbands included locking the doors against his return or slipping off to stay with neighbors on that night. Laywomen I interviewed presented an image of themselves that was both strong and playful. They also were able to joke about the contradiction I presented to their schema of gender roles. Some marveled that I could travel about so freely, like a man. Others wanted to know why my father, brother, or husband had not insisted on traveling with me to Zangskar. In jest, one woman asked me where I kept my penis or "male badge" *(pho mtshan)*. She joked that I must be keeping it tied to my leg in order to live at the nunnery. Another woman explained that she would gladly relieve me of my hidden member. She would sew the penis onto her own body after cutting off her breasts, so that she could "be a man and drink beer, lounge about, and order women around all day." In the end, almost every woman I interviewed admitted that she prayed to be reborn as a man. This appeared to confirm a rather terrifying truth: the victims pray to be reborn in the sex of their aggressor.

One nun told me: "With a man's body, it does not matter whether you are born into a rich or poor household. No matter where you end up, sleeping by the roadside or drunk on the path, nobody can hurt you. But a poor woman who sleeps on the roadside or outside is lost. She can lose everything." With these words Skalzang explains why the male body is considered invincible and helps clarify the Tibetan word for women, *bud med,* literally, "that which can't be put outside." The female body is less desirable than the male body because it is far more vulnerable—to sickness, abuse, adultery, and rape.[12] In Buddhist theodicy, people draw suffering toward themselves. In this logic, the victim may also become the accused. While it is men who rape, it is women who are blamed. Most broadly, women are considered innately sinful *(sdig pa can)*, because their beauty and sexuality generate lust. Women's greater desire and skill trap men, who are innocent before proven guilty. Moreover, a rape may reflect a prior connection between victim and aggressor. The woman's lust may simply be the precipitating cause *(rkyen)* for a man's depravity. Even nuns, who are not "available" sexually, are vulnerable to rape. The nunnery and monastery were the site of at least one rape and several clandestine affairs during my fieldwork period.

The line between rape and consensual sex seems painfully thin in Zangskari culture. This may be partly due to ambiguity in Zangskari discourse, where a "no" can mean "yes," by those refusing a host's offer of food. Women who transgress the unspoken rules of village custom may be courting danger. My girlfriends rarely walked alone at night, except if they were going to water the fields during the night, but even that was changing. I often walked alone even at night, but was less vulnerable because of my ambiguous male-like position within the local gender spectrum. Yet women are relatively safe and free in Zangskar and Ladakh, compared with elsewhere in North India. Zangskari women are free to travel and work in the fields without chaperones, although they must ask permission to travel from their male family members. Within the watchful eyes of the village, there is little anonymity or secrecy. Because aggressors can always be identified in a rural context, village women are safer than urban women. Yet their freedom always comes at a price.

Although rape, abuse, and adultery are tacitly condoned they are also sanctioned. Both women and men in society exhibit scorn for men who beat their wives. I recall a heated discussion about a man in Karsha who beat his wife in public at the ancestor festival one year, yet only a few villagers were outraged. Customary law has clear rules about fining men for any illegitimate children they sire, but does not distinguish between rape and adultery in these cases. I have heard of men being fined for rape, but only after a child resulted from the union. In this case, customary law did not offer any restitution to the woman for being forced to have sex against her will but only for the child she bore. In this view, women are never forced against their will, but are always consensual sexual partners. An adulterous man is shamed as "one whose errant meddling has left his own bone strewn upon the plain" *(khyed rang rus pa thang la 'khyams bcug mkhan)*. In this epithet, bone stands for the male line embodied in his semen, which should not be scattered indiscriminately. Moreover, the reference to an empty plain rather than to a fertile field suggests that such actions are wasteful and not conducive to proper fertility. The customary fine which an adulterous man pays to the woman's family includes a monetary sum set by the village headman, two rolls of highly prized homespun woolen cloth *(snam bu)*, a few pounds of butter, a blessing scarf, and a purification ceremony held to appease the village's guardian deity and monastic protectors. The woman pays for her part with a loss of reputation and slightly lower marital prospects. The monetary sum and wool are material supports for the child, who comes under the father's care by customary law. If the mother consents, the father will raise the child after the age of five or six in his own house. This arrangement does not always work satisfactorily, particularly when the stepmother mistreats an illegitimate child who is not her own.

Even today being a woman in Zangskar presents dangers. One year, the drinking parties at the nunnery's Great Prayer Festival seemed to get wilder every night. Toward the end of the festival, a group of young men came to drink the beer that the nun stewarding the festival had prepared for her donors. Night after night, I watched these young and insolent drunkards banter with their hosts, the nuns, until they passed out in the guest room or drifted back down to the village. When the jokes became too tiresome one night, I begged off early and went off to sleep in the room I shared with Garkyid, only a stone's throw from the nunnery compound. Declining an offer to be accompanied to my room, I made sure to bolt the door from the inside, knowing that Garkyid would sleep in another nun's room that night. My head was buzzing with barley beer *(chang)* as I dropped off to sleep in the room on the roof. Several hours later, I was awoken by a flashlight shining straight into my face. Starting up, I put on my glasses, and was shocked to see one of the young drunkards staring at me from the room's doorway, which led onto the roof. When I asked him what he wanted, he said he wanted to sleep with me. I began to curse him at the top of my lungs—in English for shock value. He sat there as I began to struggle out of my sleeping bag. Then he laughed, jumped up, and leapt straight off the roof like a cat into the noiseless night. Shaken and indignant, I realized he had climbed up the wall of the cell to the roof, but decided he would not return that night. When I told Garkyid and a few other friends about the intruder the next morning, they told me that I should take care not to walk alone at night even near the nunnery. While I wanted to take the matter to the headman, they assured me that the young man was harmless and would never dare attack an American.

Yet Zangskari women do not have the safeguard that I did. With an uncanny sense of déjà vu, I realized that this was the same man who had raped the headman's daughter almost a year earlier. Angmo was only twenty-nine and unbetrothed, when she was raped by Phuntsog, a neighbor—himself married with three sons and an official assistant *(kotwal)* to the headman. The circumstances of the assault or affair were unclear, but Phuntsog was said to have "wrestled" *(sngal byes)* and is believed to have overpowered her during the raucous drinking which followed the springtime ancestor rite. Nobody knew exactly when Phuntsog caught up with her in the fields. Angmo kept the shameful incident and her subsequent pregnancy secret from everyone in the village, including her own sister, whom I interviewed at length. While it seems unbelievable that Angmo could have concealed her pregnancy from a sister with whom she shared a bed each night, the meager diet, strenuous chores, and the bulky robes worn by most women may have helped hide her growing belly. Sadly, Angmo was too embarrassed to ask her own grandfather, who was a traditional doctor *(am chi),* for a herbal remedy to induce a miscarriage. Lacking the money or the means to take herself to a distant hospital in Leh or Kargil for an abortion, she also avoided seeking an abortion locally from the local nurses in Zangskar.

Angmo grew thin with exhaustion during the last trimester of her pregnancy. Because her family suspected nothing, she could not ask for the fortifying foods that most pregnant women receive. She had done her evening chores of hauling several forty-pound cans of water from the frozen streambed and thrashing fodder off the roof for the animals in the stable the night she went into labor. As the contractions increased, Angmo lay down and she began to cry out, waking her sister who called her parents. Straining through ten hours of labor, she gave birth to a stillborn son but failed to expel the placenta. As she continued to lose blood, her grandfather and a local allopathic doctor were called in to help. For the next twelve hours, the doctors could do little to stanch the blood. When her grandfather wrapped up his medicines and took them out of the room to protect them from the ritual pollution of death, her family knew that her time had come. Her death from retaining the placenta seemed symbolic of the fierce intensity with which she had kept everything inside for so long.

After seeing the doctor rush back and forth, most people in Karsha village knew something was up. Although Angmo had named Phuntsog as the father, she was barely conscious by the time he was summoned. Phuntsog was ordered to bury his son far below the village, as children under ten are not given cremations in Zangskar.[13] Once monks were called to the house to perform the customary death rites, including prayers to transfer merit to Angmo in her next rebirth, villagers began to come to pay their respects. On the fourth day after her death, the entire village gathered in front of her house to receive the customary communal meal. The menfolk and monks carried her body through the waist-deep snow to the cremation ground beyond the perimeter of the fields. Because her death had taken place two days after the subterranean spirits (klu) awaken on the twenty-fifth of the first Tibetan month, her cremation was performed beyond the fields to avoid ritual pollution. As I watched Phuntsog and Angmo's male clansmen carry the corpse through the snow, I wondered what Phuntsog might have been thinking. Did he recall his lustful night with the girl whose body he now carried to the cremation grounds where he had pursued her nine months earlier? Was he thinking of how the village girls had danced in front of the fire, near the spot where her body would soon be cremated? To atone for his adulterous behavior, Phuntsog was required to pay the monks to perform a purification rite at the village altar, in addition to a symbolic restitution of one thousand rupees paid to the headman. Rather than keep the payment—a paltry price for his daughter's life—the headman sent the funds straight to the monastery as a donation for prayers to transfer merit to his daughter.

Over the next months, I observed the interchange between the headman and his assistant Phuntsog. Not only was Phuntsog not fired from his post, but the headman seemed to use the rationality of karma to mitigate the tangled web of suffering. While this event would have been the cause of a lengthy bloody feud in Muslim villages just to the north of Zangskar, the Buddhist ideology of karma dictates a universal law of retribution which obviates the need for human punishment. As such, the headman showed neither hatred nor anger toward Phuntsog in public, no matter how he may have felt in private. During the ancestor rite a few months after his daughter's untimely death, the headman worked side by side with the

Phuntsog distributing communal offerings *(tshogs)*. Although the head-man's daughter had been cremated at the same site just months ago, his calm demeanor showed little trace of malice toward Phuntsog. The head-man's appearance served to restore the ruptured community and affirm the interdependence between his own and Phuntsog's existence. As eldest sons who'd inherited their father's properties, the two men would be neighbors until death. In affirming an ethos of solidarity over retribution, the headman offered a critical lesson in the principle of dependent organi-zation, in which self and other, ultimately, are interchangeable.

The Fellowship of Women

While women will always be subject to the law of patriarchy, nuns have both freedom and safety within the company of women. Many nuns say they became nuns to share in a community of women.[14] One nun recalled that as a child she saw nuns as happy and harmonious. Others say that the community is a welcome escape from the dysfunctional families they hope to renounce. Laywomen often speak of how jealous they are of the way nuns live in the company of women, far from the prying, onerous eyes of men. Life at the nunnery requires a capacity for solitude as much as for co-operative living. As nuns age and their family ties dissolve, they rely on younger nuns to collect dung, carry water, and perform other strenuous chores. Younger nuns, conversely, depend on elder nuns or tutors for food, a home, and other support during their apprenticeship at the nunnery. As a result, women begin and end their life at the nunnery dependent on others. As aging nuns are slowly marginalized by their own families and grow too feeble to work in the village, they rely on other nuns for fuel, food, and labor.

When Yeshe, the oldest nun at Karsha, fell dreadfully ill with hepatitis for several winters—improving somewhat in the summers when vegeta-bles were available—a younger nun, Thuje, stayed by her side. Although Thuje's room was a stone's throw away, she slept every night in Yeshe's room where Yeshe lay delirious with fever and exhaustion. Thuje kept the fire going, cooked, and helped Yeshe get up while she still could. In grati-tude, Yeshe spent the subsequent summer spinning and dyeing the wool which she hired a local man to weave, before sewing Thuje a woolen jacket and boots. By contrast, Yeshe received no help from her nephew's family in the village. Her nephew's wife had never forgiven Yeshe for her sharp tongue from years earlier. When Yeshe almost died the first winter, villagers gossiped that she had eaten the butter which she'd hoarded for several summers. Despite the attentions of Tashi, a ritual expert, and local doctors like Thuje's father, Yeshe's sickness had lingered. Villagers suspected it was her *karma* to be humbled and to have to "eat" the butter they accused her of amassing. Given Yeshe's barren cell and storeroom, the talk of Yeshe's miserliness was less surprising than the speculations on her hidden wealth.

Older nuns find that asceticism is no cure for suffering and sorrow. As they grow old and frail, nuns grow lonely and distressed. While their own relatives may neglect them, they find solace in the network of younger nuns who share in caring for the elderly in their community. By comparison, elderly renunciants without a monastic community may be utterly destitute. I once found an elderly renunciant living in a cave above Padum, too weak to look for dung to burn or even to beg for food. Her cave was equipped with a few broken kettles, and a single stone pot sitting on a cold hearth with no firewood, kerosene, or matches to be seen. In a voice faint with despair, she told me she had eaten only barley gruel that week. Without any cooking oil or other rations, she could soon die of malnutrition. Soon after, a newly founded woman's group in Zangskar began to bring her monthly rations of oil and rice.

Every nunnery has several subgroups made up of nuns who are age-mates or friends. These alliances offer comfort, security, and domesticity. Such groups may spend their days working together in the village, and their nights cooking and sleeping together. These attachments are usually maintained over time and demand loyalty as well as fidelity. A tacit and mutual web of reciprocity rules over the community. When Skalzang was building a second story onto her cell, she asked several friends from the nunnery to help her carry rocks, water, and silt to make the mortar. The work was intense in the strong summer sun, but Skalzang fed her helpers lavishly while her cousin Norbu, a monk who had come to help as a stonemason, entertained them. His witty and raunchy stories kept them in stitches of embarrassed laughter. When one of the nuns, Nyima, quit after a day without any explanation, Skalzang guessed that she had gone to the village to help the elderly couple whom she had adopted as a local family. Years later, Skalzang was still upset with Nyima, especially since Skalzang had worked as a cook during Nyima's stewardship of the Great Prayer Festival.

Although close friendships are sanctioned, sexual intimacies seem to be avoided. Many Western women have asked me if there are lesbian relations at the nunnery. I have yet to find evidence of this in over a decade of fieldwork. While I have been privy to a host of secrets and scandals, including abortions, affairs, rapes, and thefts, I have never heard of sexual intimacy between nuns. Outside of the apprenticeship period, joint living arrangements between unrelated nuns are discouraged. There may be jealousy and anger, yet every nun knows that sexual relationships are a breach of their Vinaya vows. Nuns freely display physical affection for one another, even flirting with and teasing one another. By contrast, homosexuality is openly suspected among monks. Local gossip implies that monks are notorious for both homosexual and heterosexual activity. In Tibetan idiom, homosexuality is a neologism which includes both gay and lesbian behavior: "male lusting after male, female lusting after female, an internal meeting of similar sex organs" *(phos pho la chags pa byed mkhan, mos mo la chags pa byed mkhan, rtags mtshungs nang 'brel).*[15] Although village banter suggests that monks do climb over the monastic walls quite often, there is less talk of sexually frustrated nuns. The bawdy Tibetan tales of Aku Tonpa and his seduction of nuns were unknown in Karsha.[16]

One nun jokes about her wish for a husband: "Why don't you bring us a few husbands the next time you come from America? Do you think they will follow quietly and obediently, or will you put rings through their noses like we do with our calves? Although nuns joke about wanting a nice American husband who will share the housework, they know that celibacy is critical to being a monastic in the "virtuous ones" or Gelugpa *(dge lugs pa)* sect. In Tibetan vernacular, celibacy *(gtsang ma, tshangs ma)* literally means pure, holy, clean, or sanctified. There are more words for abandoning celibacy *(mi tshang par spyod pa, log g.yem, 'khrig pa, grong pa'i chos)* than for maintaining it. Although all monastics practice Tantra to sublimate their desire, nuns appear to have mastered sexual detachment more effectively than monks have. When I asked nuns how difficult it was to maintain celibacy, they turned the question back on me. They implied that if I could manage without sex at the nunnery, why couldn't they do so as well? When I countered that my celibacy was only temporary, they laughed and pointed to those nuns for whom it had proved equally temporary.

Yet they were curious about marriage and sex in the West. When I told them that I was waiting to marry until after I'd finished my Ph.D., they expressed concern that I'd be too old to have children. They were more concerned about my biological clock than I was. Nuns may be innocent in experience, but not in imagination. They are well informed about contraception, sexual pleasure, and pain, albeit vicariously. By the time most nuns take ordination, they have been celibate apprentices for years. All my informants at the nunnery flatly denied having any carnal knowledge. One layperson, a Don Juan type who pursued an affair with a foreign nurse despite having two wives, told me that sex among young people was as common and as satisfying as eating barley soup *(thug pa)*, standard fare in any Zangskari home. Yet his conclusion that there is little shame in illicit liaisons reflects his own appetites more than village norms.

In person, villagers tend to treat both monks and nuns with great respect, although they may gossip in private. Irreverent villagers may accept that monks are sometimes promiscuous, but rarely accuse a monk directly unless they have a witness or proof of sexual misconduct, in the form of a child. The one time I observed a nun being teased with crude sexual jokes, I understood her situation to be rather unusual, as she spent only her winters in retreat and her summers working on her family's farm, which had been largely decimated by an avalanche. Since this nun was the only survivor in her family, it was assumed that she would eventually marry and take over the family's estate as all her other colleagues at the nunnery had done after the avalanche hit. Monks are mocked but rarely shamed for their sexual exploits, given that men are expected to be predators.[17] Sexual misconduct is hard to prove as the Vinaya requires a witness in order to defame an ordained monk. Women bear visible markers of their transgressions. Because monks maintain secret affairs far more easily than women, they may deny accusations even when their guilt is clear.

Celibacy and Its Discontents

Renunciation is as difficult to maintain as it is to attain. The narrow path to celibacy is strewn with obstacles through which only the hardiest souls may persevere. There is shame as well as sadness for those nuns and monks who disrobe. Families may weep over a fallen monk or nun for years. Yet neighbors and friends joke about the ironic irreducibility of desire. Those who commit the sin *(sdig pa)* of breaking a root ordination vow will strive to earn as much merit as possible before their deaths. Nuns and monks who disrobe are not ostracized by their village anymore, although they will be punished by their respective orders. Ex-monastics were formerly punished by the village in order to expel the impurity of their sin from the village sphere. Until recently, monks who committed adultery were first disrobed, then tarred, and often banished from the village.[18] After being stripped of the last vestiges of humanity, his clothes, and transformed into a live "ransom" *(glud)*, the fallen monk would be cast outside the village as food for the demons, similar to the offering cakes *(gtor ma)* cast out in rituals. Although many defrocked nuns and monks marry each other, others wind up with a lay spouse who was formerly divorced or unable to find a suitable marriage partner. Of the six disrobed nuns who have left Karsha in the last fifteen years, four are married to former monks, one is married to a divorced layman, and one, who had an affair with a married man, lives as a single mother with her parents.

When a nun in a Zangskari village once became pregnant by a monk from a nearby monastery, she was immediately disrobed as soon as her pregnancy was noticed. Once she gave birth to a son, she began to clamor for the father to be disrobed as well. When the case was brought before the village council, the woman accused the monk, stating to everyone's surprise that their sex had been performed the "foreign" way, that is, fellatio. The monk simply denied his involvement and refused to accept the son as his own, although many suspected that he was the father of the child. He had been observed coming or going at odd hours from the nun's family home in the village and from her monastic cell. Eventually the offending monk fled to Ladakh, where he found a new monastic teaching post, still wearing the robes of a fully ordained monk. The ex-nun persisted and went to Leh to complain to his employers that he should have been disrobed in Zangskar long before. Although his job teaching at a monastic school technically required that he be a fully ordained monk, his employers insisted that they did not have the authority to disrobe him. The ex-nun returned to Zangskar in dismay. When her erstwhile companion was seen in Zangskar later that summer, a posse of monks tried to catch him. He hid in a friend's room and fled back to Ladakh the next day. The ex-nun went again to Ladakh to call her lover to task. Although his blood type turned out to match her son's, it was one shared by half the Ladakhi populace as well. The monastic council in Karsha finally admitted that they had no jurisdiction over him anymore since he had left the monastery and paid his exit fine. Although they said they would disrobe him if he ever returned to Zangskar, he later disrobed and married on his own. He has had several children with another ex-nun. Such incidents do not appear to shake the villagers' faith in the monastic order but only in certain candidates who are eventually considered disqualified from the monastic life.

Another nun, Sonam, returned home to take care of her aged parents and their decrepit but vast estate in Rinam. Although still in robes and putatively celibate, she began to spend more time with her girlfriends in the village than with her colleagues at the nunnery. Attending their dancing parties, she soon learned the words to sing and the controlled rhythms by which to sway her hips and shoulders as gracefully as her age-mates did. She did not go unnoticed by flirting boys and visiting monks. To her mother's shame, she was pregnant a year later by a monk from a nearby monastery. Although he'd fled to Ladakh, he returned the next summer to work as a carpenter. They were married in a brief ceremony, although he spends little time at home with Sonam and barely sees his two sons. While Sonam and her husband have been given a few fields to till—because her brother inherited most of the estate—her husband has not shown much enthusiasm for the farming life thus far.

Angmo was seduced back to the mundane village realm as well. After she joined the nunnery, her father became severely bedridden, and so she returned home to live with her parents in the village. Although Angmo had become a nun in hopes of getting on in life and escaping domestic servitude, it seemed her destiny was to grow old and single in her parents' house. Her neighbor, a married man who had been observing her from afar as she went to fetch water each day, eventually propositioned her. When he asked if she wanted to join him on a pilgrimage to attend a Kalachakra initiation in India at almost no cost, she jumped at the chance. Although her mother and her friends warned her about the neighbor's lecherous ways (he was rumored to have children all over Zangskar), she had higher dreams. She was convinced that seeing the Dalai Lama would solve her dilemma: perhaps she'd be offered a seat at a nunnery in Dharamsala. She returned from her pilgrimage pregnant and has since had two more children by the same man. He does not provide for their clothing or schooling, but she hopes he will assist them when they are older through his position as a wealthy government contractor. She still brings offerings to the nunnery frequently and maintains close friendships with her "sisters" at the nunnery to which she can never return in this lifetime.

The younger of two sisters born in the Zangla palace, Lhadzom is one of the few aristocratic women to have become a nun. Lhadzom explained that she was sent to the nunnery after her own mother died so that her father's greedy mistress could claim her mother's dowry jewels. Lhadzom's father, the king of Zangla, had abandoned Lhadzom's mother and taken up with a commoner woman when Lhadzom was still a child. Without petitioning for divorce, Lhadzom's mother took her two daughters and her dowry jewels back to her natal home, the noble house of Testa. When Lhadzom's mother died of grief shortly afterward, Lhadzom's father came to fetch his two daughters, whom he would raise according to Zangskari customary law. He also laid claim to his late wife's famous turquoise headdress *(pe rags)*, stating that she had never divorced him, and he would need the headdress to marry off his eldest daughter. Yet he did not pass the headdress on to his eldest daughter when she was married into the royal house in Padum, using the clever excuse that she only had a small wedding *(bag ston chung tse)*. She was divorced and soon thereafter married off again to the royal house of Henaskut in Ladakh, but again failed to receive the jewels, this time because it was her second wedding.

Seeing her mother's and sister's trials, Lhadzom eagerly joined the Zangla nunnery. Yet because of her half brother's dubious parentage, several Zangla villagers proclaimed Lhadzom as the rightful heir to the Zangla throne. Villagers gossiped that her half brother—a monk—was the son of a commoner woman, and perhaps not even the king's own son. Although Lhadzom grudgingly gave up her nun's robes to marry a younger son from the royal house in Padum, she was disqualified from a large wedding because of her previous status as a nun. As such, she could not claim her mother's jewels, which were her rightful dowry. In the meantime, Lhadzom's half brother had fallen in love with a Tibetan woman in Banaras and abandoned his monastic robes. Taking over his father's throne, he married three women in rather rapid succession. His first two wives, the queen of Mulbekh and the daughter of the Zangla Minister, were aristocratic but childless. His third wife, an educated commoner who bore him several children, now wears the precious turquoise headdress which once belonged to Lhadzom's mother. Lhadzom and her family live in a dank lower half of the palace, while her half brother has claimed the choicest rooms for his wives and children. Lhadzom regrets her decision to leave the nunnery every time she tells her story.

The Transfer of Allegiance: Brides and Nuns

Although women become nuns to avoid marriage, they cannot escape the pain of being sent away from their natal homes. Because villages are not exogamous, some brides find husbands within their villages. Most brides are sent to distant villages where it may be difficult to get permission to visit their homes. In Zangskar, as elsewhere in North India, many new brides spend the first few years after marriage living in their natal homes.[19] As such, they may delay the inevitable transition to their husband's villages. Both brides and nuns experience a significant psychological adjustment in their new residences. It may take years to replace their filial attachments with trust in a new "family" and residence. While brides are subject to their husband's family, nuns are subordinate to older nuns. Adapting to the will and whim of these new communities is hardly easy. Even the most basic needs—sufficient food and warm bedding—are not guaranteed in their new homes. Both nuns and brides must relearn the most basic domestic tasks, such as where and when to fetch water, cook tea, or prepare meals. Nuns must learn that they can no longer share their cup or plate with laypeople, while brides learn to eat their husbands' leftovers. Any signs of discomfort or reluctance are held against nuns and brides. They will be judged relentlessly on how generously they serve others and how sparingly they serve themselves. It is thought that they should endure tribulations without complaint in order to prove themselves worthy of their new homes. It is not uncommon for young women to break down under this pressure.

While North Indian brides undergo the trauma of transition with sickness, possession, or suicide, Zangskari brides may be depressed but are rarely suicidal. Marriage is as much a social contract as an affective bond. The Buddhist ethic looks down on suicide, while social norms allow women more independence and ability to travel outside their marriage home, unlike the customs of seclusion or purdah in North India which severely restrict a young bride's movement. Divorces are not difficult to obtain, and a bride's return to her natal house is hardly shameful in cases of abuse. Because there is no emphasis on virgin brides in Zangskar, divorced women are almost as likely to find a new husband as older but never married women. A woman's procreative power signals a transition in her status at her husband's home. After having her first child, a bride is treated with more dignity, even as her mobility is reduced.

Weddings reflect a lengthy set of exchanges over a long stretch of time. Although there is no clear hierarchical relationship between the bride's and groom's house, the bride's house maintains an upper hand because they have the power to delay the wedding for as long as they like, once the bride's hand in marriage has been asked. Most marriages are patrilocal and negotiations are initiated by the groom's house, although matrilocal, or so-called *mag pa* marriages are possible if a house has no sons but only daughters.

A number of matrimonial alliances are possible, depending on the time and wealth available. The quickest form of marriage is known as "stealing the bride" *(bag ma sku byes)*, which is followed by "putting on the head cloth" *(sgo ras rgyab byes)*. In these cases, the groom may have gotten impatient with the delays by his fiancée's family. If the groom's request to hold the wedding is repeatedly turned down by the bride's side for several years, he may take matters into his own hands by "stealing" his own fiancée. Alternatively, some grooms who are not wealthy enough to host a formal wedding may decide to steal their brides with minimal ceremony. The relatives of the girl may tacitly prefer such an arrangement because it avoids the expense of a dowry and extended festivities, although formal weddings can be and often are held years later if both families so choose. In most of these cases, the bride is abducted by friends of the groom with the tacit consent of the bride or her father or brother. If she is abducted without any foreknowledge, her parents or relatives have a right to sue for her immediate return and the wedding may be annulled.

Abduction is common enough to be a standing fear in a young unmarried girl's life. Most abductions are undertaken when the girl in question is traveling alone, because she either has gone to water her fields or is en route to a religious festival. In the more distant past, such abductions were accomplished under the cover of night but nowadays brides are being stolen in broad daylight, to the shock of village elders. The bride is often stuffed into a jeep, frequently kicking and screaming, before being taken to nearby quarters, where the groom and several male representatives of his family, and possibly hers, have gathered. The bride and groom are then given an auspicious white cloth to wear on their heads—hence the name "putting on the head cloth" for this type of wedding. After beer and food are served to all present to seal the marriage, gifts are sent to the bride's family as a reparation. A young man joked that so many brides had been stolen recently from Karsha that the riverbed had run dry. His quip related the current drought to the loss of fertile women, implying a connection between water, women, and fertility.

Depending on the amount of barley, beer, and silver exchanged and the size of the wedding, more formal alliances are termed a "grand wedding" or "minor wedding" *(bag ston chen mo, bag ston chung rtse)*. In grand weddings, every household in the hamlets under a single headman's authority must be invited to a number of feasts, while those holding minor weddings may choose to invite only the households in their immediate hamlet or neighborhood. The exchanges leading up to grand weddings may take years, as both the bride's and the groom's households send their envoys *(don mi)* with a "begging beer" to negotiate the size of the wedding, dowry, and bride-price. The bride's and groom's house must each feast the other's entire village several times in the course of these negotiations to mark the formal stages of agreement. The wedding begins when a party of seven or nine groomsmen, called "partisans" or "witnesses" *(gnya' bo pa, gnya' po)*, set out to fetch the bride on horseback or, more recently, by minivan. Having ritually prepared for the journey with an evening of "dream catching" *(mi lam 'gug byes)*, rehearsal of wedding songs, and heavy drinking, the groomsmen set out for the bride's house without the groom after being formally sent off with gifts from the entire village. Every household in the village sends a flask of beer, while the groom's house and immediate relatives serve breads and yoghurt or vegetables to the circle of dancing groomsmen. The groomsmen, resplendent in their glorious silk brocades, take their cues from their seniormost singer, who is best versed in the traditional wedding songs.[20] The villagers disperse long after the groomsmen have mounted their steeds or their Maruti minivan and departed from the village center.

As they ride across Zangskar to the bride's village, the groomsmen are hosted at nearly every village they encounter en route. As such, they usually reach the bride's house late in the evening, where they do not immediately receive a meal, but must take part in a singing duel to prove their mettle. A series of riddles is exchanged between representatives of the groom's and bride's households to display the sincerity, integrity, wit, and flair of the former. The bride's "inner partisans" *(nang gnya' bo pa)* offer elaborate riddles, each of which requires a set answer from the groom's "outer partisans" *(phyi gyna' bo pa)*. The groomsmen's approach to the bride's household is punctuated by a series of eight stops at makeshift stone cairns *(tho lo)*. At each cairn, the groom's party must successfully negotiate the riddles put to them and face a gauntlet of the bride's age-mates *(ya do pa)*. The latter desist from beating them back with willow staves in exchange for small cash bribes. At the last cairn, the bride's father comes out of the house to hear the groomsmen's final, lewd song, which is accompanied by much sexual innuendo involving dough figurines of the lingam and the yoni.

When the groom's party is finally let inside the house, they deliver their bride-price, which often includes a cow and possibly a horse. Known as the milk price (*'o ma'i rin*), the cow represents symbolic thanks to the bride's mother for nursing and raising the daughter who is given to the groom. A horse must be provided as well if the bride's family has included a jeweled necklace (*khyid bu*) in the bride's dowry. The assemblies of monks and nuns are invited to recite auspicious prayers and hosted with the same lavish meals served to all visiting relatives and dignitaries. The whole village turns out to see the evening's performance and receive an obligatory gift of breads which are provided by the bride's household.

While the bride's household is busy feeding the entire village as well as the groomsmen, relatives, and monastics, the bride herself is nowhere to be found. Her closest friends or age-mates have spirited her away to another house long before the groom's party arrives. While the bride stays hidden and alone, her bridesmaids go out in her defense. Although the bridesmaids seem to oppose the capture of the bride, they are bribed by the groom's party during the elaborate singing duel and later in the evening, when the groom's negotiators come to inquire about the bride's whereabouts. An elaborate fiction is maintained regarding the bride's location, as the bridesmaids regale the negotiators with food, song, and dance, but refuse to deliver the bride. After singing for hours about the joys and sorrows of marriage, the bridesmaids eventually cave in and promise to deliver the bride in return for a tidy bribe. When the groom's party has departed, the bride comes forth, bemoaning her imminent loss of friends. The bridesmaids wash and comb her hair, dress her, and fix the turquoise headdress (*pe rag*) she has received from her mother as dowry. In the shadowy darkness of dawn, they proceed to her natal house.

At the bride's home, they proceed into the symbolic womb of the house, the lower kitchen (*yog khang*), where the bride may well have been conceived or born. The bride and her age-mates cower under a white sheet in the corner of the room to await the arrival of the groom's party from upstairs. By this time the bride's departure has become imminent and the entire party of age-mates is weeping as hysterically as the bride. The groom's party arrives, led by the "auspicious one" (*bkra shis pa, gyna' khri pa*), whose name also alludes to Tibet's first king. Bearing a ritual arrow tied with five colored cloths and a bow, the auspicious one proceeds to the huddle of girls weeping under the cloth, where he raises his arrow above his head before bringing it gently down upon the hidden head of the bride. If he chooses the wrong head, the groom's party must pay a small fine. Now that the symbolic "capture" of the bride is complete, the bride emerges from under her sheet, to join the groom's party in an honorific meal of barley porridge *(ldu ru)*, served by her mother. The mother serves her daughter the last meal with the same calm and collected manner as she pours beer for the groom's partisans, while her daughter is wracked with tears and grief. The bride's headdress is covered in a white sheet to avoid envy. A paternal aunt *(a ni)*, who will escort her to the groom's house, takes her upstairs with the groom's party, where further songs are sung.

By midday, the house is filled with guests and villagers who have come to watch or to contribute to the bride's dowry. The gifts which have been pledged earlier are duly written on a large white scroll or cloth by the scribe. At the appointed hour, the scribe stands up in the middle of the inner courtyard *(tsom)*, which is open to the sky, to read the list of gifts and donors, one by one, for all to hear. The gifts are passed down from the roof through the skyhole into the great room, where they are packed into steel boxes by the groom's party. After every gift is accounted for and packed away, a select group of monks emerges from the offering room *(mchod khang)*, where they have been performing the ritual of "capturing fortune" *(g.yang 'gugs)* to ensure that the household wealth does not depart with the bride. Bearing an arrow from the household altar as well as the shoulder blade of a goat, they circle the courtyard three times, before proceeding back into the altar room to continue their devotions on behalf of the household and wider protective deities. The bride then performs an elaborate leave-taking ceremony, beginning in the household altar room and proceeding to the great room, where she greets every guest, crying and reciting stock phrases about how unlucky she is to be leaving her home. By the time she leaves the house, many of the spectators and relatives have been reduced to tears as well. Outside, a final set of songs and meal is served to the groom's party, who load up the bride's dowry on horseback. When the bride mounts up behind the auspicious one and the aunt mounts up behind another groomsman, the groom's party proceeds off on horseback to the groom's house. Again, they are hosted by every village en route with beer and food, to celebrate their successful capture.

When they reach the groom's house bearing their bride as triumphant booty, the entire village gathers to greet and feast the groom's party. They sing a series of auspicious songs at the entrance to the village before moving in front of the groom's house. A party of monks emerges from the groom's house to perform the "weapon" rite *(zor)*, which wards off envy, jealousy, and malicious gossip that may be tailing the bride to her new home. The senior ritual expert from the monastery smashes a pot of polluted, smelly substances against a rock where the bride's dowry has been piled to cleanse these gifts from any residual envy or attachment. It purifies the bride and her party by allowing her to be safely accepted into the groom's house, which is vulnerable by virtue of opening its doors to a new member. At the door of her new house, the bride is fed barley porridge by her mother-in-law. After the party enters the house, the bride must prostrate to the household deities in the altar room. This signifies the transfer of protection from her natal house deity to her husband's guardian deity. The marriage is consummated when the bride and groom both partake of a symbolic offering cake *('brang rgyas)* which symbolizes their new world and life together. Late in the evening, they are led to their room by the aunt, who then gives the bride some last calming instructions.

The bride and groom, and the groom's parents, dance for the entire village the next night, while the groom's house feasts the entire village to celebrate the arrival of the bride. The bride, her aunt, the groom, and his family are then hosted turn by turn at every house or neighborhood in the village for one week, before they return jointly to the bride's village where they will be hosted in the same fashion. After two weeks of nonstop feasting, the wedding festival is over and village life returns to normal. In the case of a formal divorce, the bride may return to her natal home with her headdress and dowry, although she may be forced to relinquish the latter if she initiates the divorce. If her family protests, the village headmen and their assistants negotiate such divorces as well as the payments of barley owed by each side.

For brides and nuns, the transfers of allegiance to a new residence are symbolized by a ritual break with their natal household deities. Both abandon the protection of their household guardian deity *(pha'i lha)* for a new protective deity at their new residences. When a woman leaves home on her wedding day, she takes leave of her guardian deity, and an arrow brought by the groom's side is placed into her household altar as a substitute.[21] After this point, a woman may no longer approach *(mjal)* the altar of her natal household deity. Upon arrival in her husband's home, the bride is led to the offering room, where she prostrates three times to his household deity. A second arrow, decorated with five colored cloths and a mirror, which the groom's representative had carried back and forth to the bride's home like a talisman, is now placed in the barley pot on the household altar as a symbol of her new arrival under the protective umbrella of her husband's household deity *(pha'i lha)*. Even if new brides spend most of their first few years of marriage in their natal homes, they are obliged to return to their husband's house three times a year when the household deity is worshiped: spring day, autumn harvest, and the wintertime new year festival. The brides' absence at these sacred times is considered to incite the deity's wrath and precipitate household misfortune or disaster.

Unlike the bride, the nun does not abandon her natal household deity when she leaves to join the nunnery. There is no formal ceremony at her household altar to mark her departure into homelessness; however, she must formally prostrate and make offerings to the nunnery's protective deities *(chos skyong)* that she will rely on for protection. These presentations formalize the transfer of spiritual allegiance from the lower, worldly deities of the household and village sphere to the transcendent, otherworldly deities *('jig rten las das pa'i lha)* of the monastic sphere.[22] Although a nun remains far more attached to her natal home than brides do, they transfer their ritual allegiance to Tantric protectors.

Daughters represent a cost regardless of whether they marry or join the nunnery. Most families choose to hold a grand wedding *(bag ston chen mo)* for their eldest daughters, although it may cost them up to one year's income in grain and cash. Younger daughters may be married off with less expensive and smaller weddings *(bag ston chung rtse)* with little stigma. Although the mother will pass her headdress on to the oldest daughter, younger daughters may receive a newly made headdress, if their family has sufficient wealth. Many girls are married initially with the headcloth ceremony until their family has saved up the funds for a grand wedding. Families with several daughters face serious financial constraints by the time they have seen every daughter "out the door" *(sgo mthon byes)*.

Sending a daughter to the nunnery involves far fewer initial costs, although more substantial long-term cost such as feeding daughters who earn little from nunnery endowments or ritual performances. Although nuns first live as apprentices with a relative or neighbor, most families build a cell or rent an unoccupied one near the nunnery's assembly hall on the cliff. Individual residential cells—complete with kitchen, bedroom, and offering room—belong to the household which built them, and they can be bought or sold at will. Building a new cell requires considerable material expenditure of wood, glass, and beams—both hand cut and machine cut—for the doors and windows. Other materials like stones, mud, and water are carried to the site by friends and relatives, while a mason and a carpenter are employed to do most of the skilled construction. After joining the assembly, a nun forfeits some of her time and labor to the monastic community, although her family—if nearby—may still expect her to work at home. For poorer families, the costs of making a daughter a nun are largely offset by the advantages of having a daughter nearby who can be called upon for daily chores on the family farm.

Dutiful Daughters: Celibacy and Subsistence

Besides making merit, one of the most important reasons that parents send their daughters to the nunnery is to benefit from their labor. Unlike elsewhere in the subcontinent, Zangskari households face shortages of labor rather than of food. Sending a daughter to the nunnery is less an issue of having one less mouth to feed than of having more labor around the house. While Yalman (1962) found that poorer families in Sri Lanka sent their sons to the monastery to avoid the burden of feeding them, Zangskari families benefit from daughters living nearby in nunneries who can work on the family estate. The recent migration of young men to urban areas has reduced the pool of adult labor in the agrarian economies in Zangskar and Ladakh. In villages where young men have been joining the civil and military services in droves, parents may choose to make a daughter into a nun so as to keep her at home to run estates short on adult labor. While sons sent away from home earn a cash income, nuns and laywomen run the estates and care for aging parents. Members of the older generation bemoan this trend, saying, "Soon there will be only old folks like ourselves left in Zangskar, when all the young ones have gone away." Poorer households with fewer social networks have a greater incentive to keep a daughter around the home because of the high cost of hiring day laborers for their fields. The daily wage for a field hand has risen from less than twenty rupees in the 1970s to between eighty and a hundred rupees in the year 2000. Nuns toil for their families not only because they choose to but because they must.

Parents do not lose their daughter to the nunnery in the same way that they lose a son to the monastery. Unlike monks, who have few if any domestic labor obligations after they join the monastery, nuns become permanent caretakers for aged parents. Most elderly parents depend for subsistence and succor upon their eldest son who has inherited their house or a daughter living nearby as a nun. Although Sherpa culture gives the youngest son his parents' farm so that he will care for them in old age, Zangskari culture reserves very little for the younger siblings.[23] The customary law of primogeniture still rewards the eldest son with the parents' house and animals, but younger sons have begun to claim their legal share of the family fields. Those nuns who come from more distant villages seek out a local household where they work in exchange for food and other support. Nuns earn their rations by offering their loyal services throughout the year, especially during the busiest harvest and plowing seasons. Yet these relationships must be continually renegotiated as the household membership changes through the marriage or death of its members. After her parents' deaths, a nun may receive less and less support from her brother and his children. A nun may find herself old and forgotten as her parents and siblings pass away one by one. With their siblings dead, nuns rely on distant nephews or their wives, who may have little attachment to an aunt. Yeshe, who has lost the support of her nephew's family but still has usufruct rights to two fields she received from her brother, is too weak to till the fields. She has leased the fields in exchange for grain to a local household. As she grows more and more feeble, it is unclear who besides her fellow nuns will care for her.

Although monks are largely exempt from household labor exchanges, it is common for nuns to represent their family in village or neighborhood work projects. Those nuns who live with an aging mother are most affected by the chronic shortage of adult labor in the village economy. Because such households may have only elderly members and one or two grandchildren, nuns may be called in as able-bodied labor for frequent neighborhood work duties—working as shepherds, repairing irrigation channels, or planting willows. Tsomo's aged mother lives alone in the village with her ailing sister, also a nun. They live in a neighborhood where the houses pool their flocks of sheep and goats, and each house takes them to pasture turn by turn, every day. When it is their turn, Tsomo gets called to spend the day roaming the hillsides with the flock, because her mother and aunt are both too old to race after the nimble animals. She must also go to take her turn watering the fields, according to elaborate schemes of water allocation. The constant demand for nuns as workers conspires to prevent many nuns from fulfilling their ritual duties at the nunnery. During the busiest moments of the agricultural season, all but the most aged nuns may be absent for days on end. Up to one-third of the nun's assembly misses the monthly ritual ceremonies because of labor obligations elsewhere. This is even more surprising considering that such ritual sessions earn both merit and a chance to rest. Garkyid once quipped during a ritual prayer session: "the Precious Buddha has given us a holiday" *(bla ma dkon mchog la chu ti gtangs pin).*

Nuns are in a double bind. If they ignore their family demands, they lose their means of subsistence. If they neglect their responsibilities to the community of nuns, they incur outrage or reprobation. One spring morning just after dawn, Garkyid's elderly mother paid her a rare visit at her cell. The nuns had been out collecting clay to repair their assembly hall since dawn. Garkyid was rather surprised to see her mother, whose age and arthritis had kept her away from the nunnery for years. Her mother desperately asked Garkyid to come home that very minute to read the sacred texts at a ritual her house was supposed to sponsor that day. Garkyid flatly refused, because she would not forfeit her labor obligations at the nunnery. Yet she promised to help her mother and dashed off to the monastery where she found a monk or two in short order. Her mother walked home in peace, and Garkyid arose in the predawn darkness the next day to check that the reading had been completed. By daybreak, she'd returned to help plaster the roofs of the nunnery compound along with the rest of the assembly. The inescapable cycle of reciprocity and guilt binds mothers and daughters in Zangskar as elsewhere in the Buddhist world.

"I can ask my mother for grain, flour, milk, butter, meat, and yogurt, but I'd be ashamed to ask my cousin or anyone else for such food . . . Without my mother and my cousin I'd have nothing," Garkyid once explained. She can ask her mother for food, but can also earn cash as a day laborer *(las byo mkhan)* in the village during the harvest and plowing seasons. Because Garkyid's father had died and her brother earned no salary, Garkyid's mother relied on her granddaughter and Garkyid for help on the family estate until her death. Garkyid used to walk to her mother's house long before sunrise and only return at the end of the day bearing a bit of home-ground flour, butter, milk, or yogurt. She would help her mother sow, weed, irrigate, harvest, thresh, and winnow the crops, or she might roast, wash, and dry the grains, churn butter, spin or card wool, collect dung, repair a leak in the roof, stitch or knead the homespun wool into boots and clothes, bake bread, make barley beer, cook, or feed and milk the livestock.

Although nuns may have usufruct rights to a field in the village, the practice has been declining. For the younger generation of nuns, a field is more a burden than a reward. Many nuns prefer to work for daily wages among their kin networks rather than work on a single field which hardly provides a subsistence. Their preference for wages reflects the tightening labor market as well as the increasing shortage of fields. Those nuns that do till fields will have rights only until their death or retirement, when the field is reabsorbed into the family estate. Garkyid used to till a field owned by her cousin for over a decade. All summer she performed the necessary work, carrying manure, repairing irrigation ditches, watering, weeding, and harvesting the crop. She could do everything herself but plow, which is ritually forbidden for women in Zangskar. She would thresh her crops using her cousin's livestock in exchange for helping him thresh a few days. Her crop was either delivered straight to the nunnery, or she might exchange her grain for other food supplies, if her cousin was willing. Her cousin had a salary working as a peon at the Cooperative Society, unlike her own brother and mother. Yet she had few sources of cash income, besides ritual earnings. With the little cash she saved from ritual donations or as a wage laborer, she purchased rice, wheat flour, salt, sugar, kerosene, oil, matches, ghee, and spices.

Selflessness as Sanctity: How Nuns Serve Monks

Ultimately a nun is engaged in three spheres of service: the nunnery, her home, and the monastery. Serving monks is practical and pragmatic. A nun earns more merit and status in serving monks than in serving lay villagers or even her fellow nuns. Additionally, service is always a reciprocal activity, in which nuns strategically curry favor with more powerful and prestigious monks. Given the power imbalance between monks and nuns, however, such services can be extended at will. Nuns wind up performing the most menial chores at the monastery for monks who offer little in exchange. Although the monastic discipline does not forbid nuns from helping monks in the interest of allowing women to make merit, it also assumes the virtue and honesty of monks. The frequency with which nuns are seduced by monks begs the question of why nuns so willingly subordinate themselves to monks. Why do they place so much trust in men wearing monastic robes when they are so careful to avoid lay advances? The relations between nuns and monks appear to reflect a blatant misrecognition of monastic purity and power. By blindly assuming the sanctity of monks, without being cognizant of their authority, nuns pursue a fundamental Buddhist aim: making merit. Nuns are all too willing to prostrate at the altar of monastic power, in hopes of making merit so that they, too, will be reborn as monks. They justify humiliating services to monks that could spare them a female body in the next life.

Although the monastic code or Vinaya wards off many potential abuses with detailed precepts, it is surprisingly vague about nuns serving monks. The Bhiksuni Pratimoksa, which lists the precepts held by fully ordained nuns, does not have any rules regarding the offering of food by nuns to monks.[24] Depending on the school and its associated Vinaya, or monastic code, fully ordained monks are prevented from accepting food from unrelated nuns. Tibetan monks, who follow the Mulasarvastivadin Vinaya, are prevented from accepting food *in the presence* of an unrelated nun; monks following the Mahasamghika Vinaya are enjoined from accepting food *from the hand* of an unrelated nun.[25] Both Vinayas suggest that nuns who are relatives can serve monks, and neither forbids other domestic services nuns might be asked to perform. In short, the rules reflect a greater concern about regulating food offerings than about preventing nuns from becoming domestic servants.

Did the Buddha intend nuns to be domestic servants for monks? Regardless of what the Buddha may or may not have intended, nuns serve monks across the Buddhist world. One might say that nuns produce a surplus value for the monastic realm, by providing material services for monks at no cost. Nuns thus help perpetuate the concentration of wealth among monks. There are more and less exploitative versions of this relationship. Some nunneries in Ladakh are entirely subordinated as mundane labor reserves for a nearby monastery.[26] Most nunneries in Zangskar are not formally subordinated to monasteries, unless they are nearby, as in the case of Karsha. Although Karsha nuns are not forced to perform daily chores for that monastery, the relationship between nuns and monks is that of servant and master. In terms of the services they perform for monks, nuns resemble wives as much as sisters.

A nun in Zangskar is regularly called to perform a wide range of tasks for a monk: gathering his dung or thistles, working on his construction sites, washing, roasting, or grinding his grain, sewing his hats and boots, fetching his water, baking his breads, cooking his meals, serving his guests, washing his clothes and bedding, and bringing him endless gifts of milk and yogurt. In addition to services rendered to individual monks, Karsha nuns perform customary duties for the monastery, such as carrying several loads of firewood each spring for the monastic kitchen, spending a week washing, drying, and roasting the grain that is collected in rents, and baking thousands of breads for two monastic festivals. Some nuns have told me that their collective duties at the monastery are preferable to the daily tedium of village work.

Monks who serve as abbots or teachers at a nunnery may exact a subtle servitude from humble female pupils. Nuns who are eager to learn ritual or scholastic techniques overlook the asymmetry of power as they willingly care, cook, and tend for such teachers. Yet the nuns I interviewed did not begrudge these services, which they understood to be part of expected hospitality and respect for a teacher, especially if he was a senior monk. Even if the teachers contributed little or nothing to the nuns' education, they expected and received assistance in countless tedious tasks, all at no cost. The potential for abuse, especially in the case of younger monks or those with illicit intentions, need hardly be spelled out.

One of the most menial tasks nuns perform for monks is collecting their cow dung. Dung, or *lca* in local idiom, is one of the most precious fuels in the treeless Zangskari landscape. Significantly, dung is one of the few items in the Zangskari economy which is difficult to buy. It can be bartered or traded at the high-pasture camps, which are swimming in the stuff. Yet the villagers whose yaks and cows have been tethered at these all summer long take most of the dung as their share. Because dung is such a valuable fuel, every village has its own dung-collecting region, which is off limits to persons from another village. All nuns at Karsha nunnery have rights to collect dung on the Karsha hillsides, yet visitors and other temporary residents in Karsha do not have similar rights. Although monks also have rights to collect dung, I have never seen a monk collect dung. This expresses more than a gender divide. Although young men rarely collect dung, older men who have nobody to do it for them are not ashamed to collect dung. A monk does not collect dung because it is beneath his station and he knows that others will do it for him. Of all Zangskari citizens, only monks receive but never need collect dung.

Many monks shamelessly pester nuns to bring them an obligatory "gift" of dung before the winter sets in. All but the most feeble nuns collect between five and ten bushels of dung for relatives and friends at the monastery. The best seasons for dung collecting are late fall and early spring, when the cows are not at the high-pasture camps but are loose on the hillsides around Karsha. Nuns may make daily forays up to the high pastures above the nunnery until the first winter snowfall comes in November or December. The feverish intensity of such dung-collecting forays reflects the fact that the entire winter's warmth depends on one's skill and perseverance. Garkyid and her companions usually head out to the slopes by 4 or 5 in the morning, without so much as a cup of tea. They want to be the first ones on the slope, because the flock of young girls from the village pick the slopes clean later in the day. By the time the sun is high and hot, we have climbed and descended three thousand feet from the high pastures with heavy baskets and a gnawing hunger. After a quick cup of tea and gruel, we climb up again for a second round while the sun's heat is still bearable. Although I tried to learn the finer points of dung collecting from my companions, I was slow to see the obvious traces. "Reading" the scree slopes for the faint tracks which cows make in their wanderings, and then spotting a small patch of dung from two hundred feet away took practice. The hardiest nuns would go up for a third round later in the day, but I could rarely muster the energy for climbing and descending over nine thousand vertical feet in a single day. The dried dung patties collected are critical to survival in the wintertime when temperatures drop to minus fifty degrees Celsius and there are few other sources of heating.

Another customary duty nuns annually perform for monks is baking breads. During weddings and two monastic festivals, Tsongkhapa's birthday and Spring Day, nuns bake up to five thousand breads in assembly line fashion. One nun fetches the huge tubs of sourdough from the sacks under the straw where they had been put to rise or "sleep," as they say in Zangskari idiom. Two other nuns knead the dough, moistening it with cooking oil as necessary, while others measure out exactly identical finger bowls of dough which are rounded into smooth balls and let rise again. Other nuns sit around the searing dung hearth, over which a thin stone is balanced on several jerry cans, made of military-issue steel to withstand great heat and pressure. Each nun flips and expertly pats the dough ball between her palms into a flat bread and places it on the stone, where it is turned and baked to perfection, before passing it down to the two open ends of the hearth. Here there is no jerry can to shield the scorching heat of the open coals, where the yeasty breads are laid for a final toasting, and the nuns who work the ends of the hearth rotate quickly. Finished breads are laid on a blanket to be polished and counted before being packed in baskets and taken to the locked storeroom, where they remain until the ritual begins.

These baking marathons flow uninterruptedly for thirty-six hours, with no scheduled breaks or time clock. Work proceeds organically: when one nun falls asleep off to the side of the blazing hearth, another takes her place. As day melts into night and night into day, the operation slows, while the giddiness increases. Temperatures are as intense as the female bonding and humor. Although the work is exhausting, it provides an excellent excuse to gossip about recent affairs and scandals which are staple entertainment in Zangskar. The open fire in the room produces a thick smoke which first drove me away nearly blinded, with streaming tears.

"If we didn't do this, who else would? Only women know how to make the dough and bake these breads properly in Zangskar. We nuns must go, since village women can't leave their own kitchens for a day and a half. Their husbands, children, and livestock would go hungry." While several nuns tell me they have "no choice" but to bake bread for their relatives' wedding festivals, I asked why laywomen could not bake the breads instead. Nuns explained that laywomen were tied to overwhelming workloads at their own homes with too little time to work elsewhere. Men are often away trading or working in neighboring regions, while women are expected to be in their place at home at all times. A nun's relative autonomy from husbands serves as the pretext to call upon her for the most demanding or time-consuming jobs.

Yet these local customs of having nuns work for the monastery have been contested in recent years. The recent Tibetan teacher at the nunnery dismissed the provincial custom of nuns baking breads, because it interfered with their studies. Rather than maintain the hypocrisy of local monks who encourage nuns to be servants, the Tibetan teacher forbade the nuns from attending the bread-baking sessions. Yet only some of the nuns obeyed. Others could not avoid their customary duties, especially those from poorer houses who might need village aid in the future. The assembly of nuns is split over the issue, even as villagers and monks have begun to look elsewhere for women to bake their breads. Yet everyone is aware that nuns can relinquish these responsibilities to the village and monastery only at the risk of losing valuable means of support.

The Refusal of Exchange

Although nuns may avoid the trap of marriage and maternity, renunciation does not guarantee them much autonomy. The village, nunnery, and monastery all benefit from the productive services that nuns provide. Vows of homelessness are no guarantee that the mundane sphere can be avoided. Nuns may renounce marriage and procreation, but are called into the spheres of production and consumption. In short, nuns are conscripted to their society as much as to the monastic realm. Although they may retain a certain measure of agency concerning their daily tasks, nuns remain vulnerable to the needs of home and hearth. They cannot avoid obligations to the families who provide their means of subsistence. Rather than becoming submissive wives, they remain dutiful daughters and sisters. Yet they are subjugated to the principles of alliance all the same. New brides exchange their rights and duties at their natal home for those of their new marital home. Yet nuns don't forsake their natal duties when they accumulate an extra set of obligations at the nunnery. In exchange for some autonomy, nuns remain beholden to their families as well as to the monks.

Nuns may elude the patriarchal economy of desire, but they cannot escape the universal principle of exchange. One of Lévi-Strauss's most significant theoretical insights was to relate the exchange of women to the incest taboo. While Freud and Darwin had been intrigued by the social and sexual implications in what they saw as a prohibitive rule, Lévi-Strauss saw the rule as generative because it dictated the exchange of women. In his words, "the prohibition of incest is less a rule prohibiting marriage with the mother, sister, or daughter, than a rule obligating the mother, sister, or daughter to be given to others. It is the supreme rule of the gift."[27] This observation—that women are implicit objects of an exchange—was critical to Lévi-Strauss's theory of kinship. By focusing on alliance rather than on descent, his theory emphasized lateral ties of exchange over vertical ties. If kinship can be described as a set of relationships regulating sexuality for the purpose of exchanging women, celibacy is simply an alternate form of kinship and sexuality. As such, celibacy and renunciation confirm rather than contradict Lévi-Strauss's universal theory of exchange. Although it has become clear that both Buddhist and Hindu renouncers depend on reciprocal relations with the laity, there has been little effort to understand the role of nuns.[28] While nuns depend on their kin for subsistence, families can be seen to earn labor and merit from the women they have sent to the nunneries. In this view, households earn one kind of social capital by marrying off their daughters and another kind by sending them to the nunnery.

Lévi-Strauss notes that the "exchange of women" rarely involves a direct or restricted exchange of women between two groups. It is far more common to find a generalized or circular exchange in which women are sent off in one direction with the hopes of receiving women from another. In Zangskar, women are exchanged for a bride-price, gifts, and other favors, as well as the expectation of a future daughter-in-law. The exchange of women cements affinal relations as well as other socioeconomic relations between households. A marital alliance between two houses signals the wealth and status of each, while facilitating crucial exchanges of labor, goods, and livestock in this agrarian economy. As such, the exchange of women is simply one conduit through which other goods and services later flow.[29] There is no necessary hierarchy between wife receiver and wife giver, in contrast to many North Indian kinship systems where the recipient outranks the donor. Indeed, it is not unusual to send a wife to a family with slighter lower status, especially in the case of aristocrats, who have trouble finding a suitable and unrelated family in the same social strata *(rigs)*. Wife receivers generally initiate most marriage negotiations, although both parties can abrogate them during the lengthy process of negotiation, which may take years. The wife givers have as much leverage as wife receivers in this society, where the virginity of the bride is less an issue than in other North Indian societies. In many North Indian societies, the virginity and purity of the bride is always in danger the longer the family delays a marriage. By contrast, in Zangskar wife-giving households may delay the marriage for years because they recognize the loss of labor incurred by marrying off a daughter. The relative sexual freedom and women's labor power contribute to the greater valorization of women in Zangskar, both before and after marriage. Yet the relative scarcity of women in population figures still leaves lingering doubts about female worth.

"Why exchange women? Because they are 'scarce [commodities] . . . essential to the life of the group' the anthropologist tells us. But why this characteristic scarcity, given the biological equilibrium of male and female birth?"[30] With these words, the French feminist Luce Irigaray mocks Lévi-Strauss's rather sexist assumptions that women are always scarce in any society. Lévi-Strauss makes his point about scarcity by noting that even if there are as many women as men in a given society, there will always be an innate lack of the *most desirable* women. For Lévi-Strauss, the theoretical scarcity of women produces an economy of exchange and the rules of kinship. For Nobel laureate Amartya Sen, the actual scarcity of women reflects an egregious disparity between the sexes worldwide which demands explanation. By carefully collating the distribution of men and women in census figures around the globe, Sen and his associates have produced an astonishing figure. There are literally 100 million "missing" women in the world's population, which can only be accounted for by selective infanticide or systematic female neglect. The extent of this female neglect and the corresponding ratio of women to men range considerably cross-culturally, as well as within the Indian subcontinent.[31] The ratio of women to men in Leh and Kargil districts approaches that found in some of India's least favorable districts. The fact that there are nine women for every ten men in Kargil District suggests that women are as undervalorized in tolerant Himalayan cultures as in other parts of India. Recent figures from India's 2001 census suggest that such population disparities are only getting worse, even in the most affluent cities and districts, an indication of deliberate sex selection against women.

Women are pulled back into the domestic sphere regardless of whether they marry, become ordained nuns, or elderly renunciants. In each case, they uphold the reciprocal relations between households within their society. The narratives of several Zangskari nuns indicate the strength of the pull to escape the marriage market. The nuns' strategies of resistance range from the threat of suicide to flight. Yet they also depict a labor-short society in which families desperate to cement alliances attempt to keep daughters as close to home as possible. In times of drought or disaster, affinal relations are critical to the success or failure of household fortunes. From this perspective, celibacy might threaten the alliances produced by the exchange of women. Yet the order of nuns in Tibetan Buddhist culture perpetuates the exchange of women far more than it abolishes it.

"Women, signs, commodities, and currency always pass from one man to another; if it were otherwise, we are told, the social order would fall back upon incestuous and exclusively endogamous ties that would paralyze all commerce . . . But what if these 'commodities' refused to go to the 'market'?" Irigaray asks in her critique of Lévi-Strauss's theory of exchange.[32] Gayle Rubin uses the term "sex/gender system" as a shorthand to express the reality that kinship systems give men certain rights in their female kin which women do not have in themselves or in their male kin.[33] While men retain rights over their daughters in the worldly realm, monks retain rights over nuns in the monastic realm. Although fathers and uncles make the final decision on whether to send a daughter to marriage or celibacy, it is monks who manage the ritual process by which a woman joins or exits the nunnery, as explained in the next chapter. When a young woman joins the monastic order, she passes from the hands of her father into the hands of the monks. Monks are not casual bystanders in the political economy of sex, but actively regulate the "traffic" in nuns between the secular and sacred realms. The monks' order upholds the principle of exchange as it receives one more servant whose spirituality does not challenge but sustains male superiority in the monastic realm. The order of monks upholds the principles of exchange by which nuns are subordinated to the material needs of monks and lay society.

Whether the Buddha intended to or not, the monastic order was adapted to the prevailing social hierarchies from its inception. Although Buddhist doctrine sought ultimately to transcend gender duality, Buddhist practices have maintained social difference at every turn. The political economy of sex is as prevalent in the monastic order as in surrounding society. Buddhist monks preach an egalitarian ethos while they overlook numerous practices that humble and humiliate nuns as menial laborers. Only when lay society begins to appreciate its women will Buddhist orders do the same.

CHAPTER

5

Becoming a Nun

Monks can secure merit and status in Buddhist society because of the monastic discipline they uphold and the male bodies they inhabit. In Tibetan Buddhism, monks can take full ordination after the age of twenty, while the highest ordination nuns can achieve is that of novices. Although recent decades have undone this inequality somewhat, as a handful of Tibetan Buddhist nuns have taken full ordination with East Asian nuns as officiants, these efforts have yet to be broadly accepted by monastic leaders. What is entailed in ordination and why is it so difficult to change the rules regarding this status?

A finite set of ritual procedures produces ordained novice nuns in Zangskar today. These rites of institution enable the authority of monks as much as they limit the agency of nuns. Although nuns make concerted choices at each ritual stage, they have little say about the terms of their submission to monks within this ritual process. From first tonsure to final cremation, nuns are subject to a ritual process controlled and dominated by monks. Their entrance and exit into the assembly of nuns as well as their disciplinary punishments are often managed by monks from distant monasteries. Although nuns can perform tonsure rites or become abbots at many cosmopolitan Tibetan nunneries, this is not the case in Zangskar. Every Zangskari nunnery has a male abbot, and no nuns have performed tonsure rites as yet. The rites of institution which mark the nuns' passage into the monastic life reinstate the difference and hierarchy between nuns and monks. Although both nuns and monks take and uphold the same novice vows and wear similar sexless robes, the entire assembly of nuns must always be seated below that of monks. Nuns remain subject to the authority and surveillance of monks throughout a religious life supposedly dedicated to transcending gender and other social hierarchies.

The inability of nuns to seek higher ordination may be the single most important demarcation in status between monks and nuns in the Buddhist world. Bourdieu (1991) has argued that rites of initiation are significant not so much because they divide the men from the boys, but because they reify a symbolic division between the group eligible for initiation—the men—and those who are ineligible—the women. In other words, rites of institution consecrate an arbitrary boundary between two subgroups by way of instantiating the difference between those who can undergo the rite and those who cannot. By analogy, Buddhist rites of ordination are significant not so much because they separate full monks from novices, but because they indelibly divide monks from nuns. The question of gender is far more significant than ordination status in most Tantric rites.

Some sects of Tibetan Buddhism actively downplay the importance of ordination in favor of ritual prowess. Many monks who become Tantric adepts need not take full ordination at all. Indeed, Tantra is supposed to reverse the conventional hierarchies upheld in monastic and lay society. In theory, the most elaborate Tantric meditations are open to any individual, monastic or lay, regardless of how many precepts he or she holds. In practice, the monks in Zangskar have done little to erase the gender hierarchy despite their commitment to Tantric practice. Across the Buddhist Himalaya, ordained monks continue to exclude nuns from many spectacular and pragmatic ritual practices. These exclusions are based less on textual interdictions than on the customary sense that nuns are inferior to monks. The root of this inferiority may lie in the nuns' novice status as much as in the impurity of their bodies. Let us consider nuns' status as novices in this chapter before turning to bodies in the next chapter.

The Legacy of Ordination

The right to ordain and thereby transmit the Buddha's discipline is a political as much as a ritual act. Ordination remains one of the most jealously guarded privileges within Buddhism. Monks preserve their authority and power by their ability to legislate and adjudicate ordination. Every school of Buddhism traces its ordination tradition back through successive generations of monks to the Buddha himself. Although monks were given the right to administer their own ordinations after the Buddha's demise, he proclaimed that nuns should be ordained by both orders, nuns and monks. This double subjugation had profound and lasting effects. It seems to have speeded the decline and dissolution of the nuns' order in Asia. In giving monks the authority to ordain nuns, the Buddha took away the rights of nuns to reinstate their order unilaterally when it declined. Without the approval and participation of monks, a body of nuns alone would be insufficient to ordain the next generation of nuns. As such, when the nuns were neglected by laypeople and fellow monks, they could not unilaterally revive their own ordination traditions.

The ruling about what qualifies as a valid ordination goes back to the Buddha's day. The Buddha's decision to found the nuns' order appears to have been accompanied by some degree of ambivalence. Although it is difficult to ascertain his intentions—as the Buddha's words were only written down at least three centuries after his death—the decision left an undeniable legacy. According to most canonical accounts of the founding of the nuns' order, the Buddha overturned his initial reluctance to admit women into his monastic order only after being needled by both his aunt and his foremost disciple. The story concludes with the Buddha establishing a set of eight weighty rules by which nuns are permanently subordinated to monks. Whether or not the story reflects the Buddha's actual words, its impact has been undeniable.

The monastic discipline or Vinaya explains that the Buddha's aunt and stepmother, Pajapati Gotami, was in great distress after having entreated the Buddha for admission into his order.[1] Although thrice denied, she and five hundred other women of the Sakya clan decide to live the chaste life in spite of his rejection. After donning their robes and shaving their heads, they march to see the Buddha, and Pajapati, now in tears and dusty, attempts to make her request one last time. Although she is denied an audience with her now famous nephew, his disciple Ananda intervenes on her behalf. When he too is rebuffed, he asks the Buddha if it is possible for women to gain enlightenment. The Buddha answers that yes, women can gain the highest fruits of the monastic life—namely that of stream-winner, once-returner, nonreturner, and arhatship. While Ananda then convinces him to accept women into the order, the Buddha does so with one significant caveat.[2] All women in the order will be subject to "eight weighty precepts" *(lci ba'i chos brgyad),* also translated as eight chief rules *(garudhamma),* in Pali. In a Tibetan text, the rules appear in the following order:[3]

1. Nuns must receive ordination from monks.
2. Nuns must receive an announcement from monks about the proper

date for the fortnightly confession and recitation of their monastic discipline.
3. Nuns must only undertake rainy season retreats under the supervision of monks.
4. Nuns must attend a ceremonial confession following the rainy season together with monks.
5. Nuns must perform penance before both assemblies of monks and nuns for any transgressions.
6. Nuns must not reveal the corruptions of monks.
7. Nuns must not reproach monks.
8. Nuns must prostrate before all monks, even one who has been newly ordained but a day.

When Ananda conveyed the Buddha's eight weighty rules to Pajapati, she replied that she would treasure them as much as a garland of flowers. Yet there is a subtext of subversion. In the Pali canon, the story continues by noting that Pajapati requested that Ananda convey one last request to the Buddha—that he lift the rule about nuns having to prostrate to monks. Perhaps this rule appeared incongruous in light of the radical status leveling which the Buddha had enacted in his monastic order. He had abolished most other forms of social hierarchy—like wealth or status—within each assembly in favor of a single rule about seniority. Those who entered the order first sat above those who came next. Having leveled the playing field, it seems odd that he upheld a rule about gender in which the seniormost nun of her order would have to stoop to a youthful monk who had just taken his vows yesterday. The Buddha's alleged rationale for sticking by the rule subordinating nuns to monks was that since even the most deluded renunciant orders do not permit this veneration of women, how could he?

The story about admitting women into the order also includes several ominous predictions. Although the list varies slightly in each canon, the prophecies compare the admission of women to the destruction of a rice field, red rust on a sugarcane field, and a household which is susceptible to robbers. The Pali canon adds that the monastic order will last only five hundred years rather than a thousand, but compares the eight rules to a dam or dyke (presumably holding back the flood of destruction that the admission of women might bring). These fault lines within this story reveal a hidden misogyny while also suggesting the possibility that the eight rules were added by the Buddha's interlocutors.[4] The odd prophecy about decline as well as the reference to a household under attack suggests the story's later composition, when the order was in decline and under attack from other renunciant orders. The images of crop blight and destruction made women a convenient scapegoat for the decay and schisms that affected the order in the centuries after the Buddha's death. The Buddha's suspicious defense of the rules is hardly consistent with his concerted critique of other renunciant orders, although it does reflect his concern with social opinion and propriety. While the suggestion that the force of nuns could be a powerful flood proves their strength, the same rules weakened the nuns' order from the start.

Although some of the rules were adapted in the centuries following their implementation, their legacy continues to the present day.[5] While nuns received the right to train probationary nuns, receive confessions, and carry out some disciplinary measures, monks have continued to have considerable authority over the nuns' order. Monks have retained an unambiguous right to admit, censure, and expel nuns, while nuns remain forbidden to officially reproach monks, regardless of the offense. Though not explicitly preventing nuns from teaching monks, the rules forbidding nuns from admonishing or reviling monks have had just that effect. The one-way flow of instruction from monks to nuns has reified the nuns' second-class status in the order and may have precipitated their downfall across South Asia by the end of the eleventh century.

After the Buddha's death the nuns' order spread across Asia, although it later declined in many parts. By the third century B.C.E., the sister of the Indian emperor Asoka traveled to Sri Lanka to institute an order of nuns. Sri Lankan nuns traveled to China to institute the nuns' order in China by the fifth century C.E., from which it spread across East Asia.[6] Although full ordination for nuns had died out in Sri Lanka by the eleventh century and in India shortly thereafter, it has survived in China, Korea, Vietnam, and Taiwan. While Japanese women did take full ordination in Korea, in Japan itself nuns and monks took similar *bodhisattva* ordinations after the rise of the Tendai school in the eleventh century, as Faure (2003) notes. It is unclear whether or not full ordination for nuns was ever established in Cambodia or Thailand.[7] The rise of Mahayana Buddhism in India coincided with the decline of nuns, who do not appear much in donor records after the fourth century. The literary evidence for fully ordained nuns in India continues through the eleventh century, particularly in Buddhist Kashmir and Tibetan borderlands. When the monks' order was threatened with collapse it was reinstated with imported monks, as happened in both Sri Lanka and Tibet.[8] Yet the survival of the nuns order never appears to have been much of a priority.

By the late twentieth century, only one-fourth of the women worldwide holding Buddhist precepts held the maximum number of vows as fully ordained nuns. Most of these fully ordained nuns who follow the Dharmagupta school and its 348 vows live in China, Taiwan, Korea, and Vietnam. Most of the nuns following the Mulasarvastivadin school in the Tibetan tradition are novices holding 36 vows.[9] Finally, women following the Theravada school practiced in Sri Lanka, Burma, Thailand, Laos, and Cambodia hold between 8 and 10 precepts as de facto rather than de jure nuns. These precept holders do not qualify as monastics under civil or Buddhist law, although they practice lifelong celibacy and live in monastic institutions. Recently there have been a series of initiatives to ordain women in the Tibetan and Theravada traditions, using East Asian nuns following the Dharmagupta school.[10] Only a handful of Himalayan nuns but quite a few Western nuns who follow Tibetan Buddhism have received full ordination vows as *dge long ma* in Tibetan or *bhiksuni* in Sanskrit. Although the Dalai Lama has permitted Tibetan nuns to travel afield to receive full ordination, he does not have the authority to speak for the entire assembly of monks in the Tibetan tradition. Many monks and some feminists remain opposed to instituting full ordination for women albeit for different reasons. Senior monks in the Tibetan tradition argue that the formal structures to train nuns are not yet in place, while feminists hold that female renunciants are better off outside the disciplinary gaze of monks. Yet the Sri Lankan monks who oppose the revival of full ordination for women using East Asian nuns neglect to mention that it was Sri Lankan nuns who formally instituted the ordination of women in China.

The Rites of Passage for Nuns

Arnold Van Gennep describes the life of an individual in any society as "a series of passages from one age to another and from one occupation to another . . . For every one of these events there are ceremonies whose essential purpose is to enable the individual to pass from one defined position to another which is equally well defined."[11] The rites of passage a woman undergoes to become a nun both produce and sustain her identity within both monastic and secular society. At each stage, such rites demarcate both a social and a ritual role in determining the relations a nun maintains with her society and other nuns. Tonsure, ordination, and admittance to an assembly of nuns consecrate the passage of a nun from lay to monastic life. Although these three basic rites are hardly universal for all Buddhist women, they are mandatory for every Buddhist nun. Furthermore, as rites of institution, they reify and sacralize arbitrary distinctions between apprentices and nuns at the same time that they confirm the broader and irrevocable difference between nuns and monks.

The three rites discussed below—tonsure, ordination, and admittance to an assembly—follow a classic tripartite schema specified by Van Gennep and Victor Turner: separation, transition, and reintegration.[12] Tonsure separates a young girl from a licentious and libidinous adolescence. Ordination signifies the transition from fertility and worldliness to celibacy and asceticism. Finally, admittance into the assembly of nuns or *sangha* marks a reintegration as she assumes a set of obligations to her assembly and society. Although the order of the second and third stages can be reversed, her final integration culminates when she is both ordained and a member of an assembly. Each stage moves a woman from one status to the next in an irrevocable manner. Ordination can be reversed but its effects can never be undone. In Zangskar, ex-monastics are forbidden from taking ordination vows again in this lifetime. In theory their chances for a human rebirth are severely compromised.[13] These rites of passage do far more than affirm an obvious status. Tonsure and ordination rituals create the status they sanctify.

Understanding the ritual passage to the nunnery helps to correct many errors of omission regarding Tibetan Buddhist nuns in Zangskar and Ladakh. Numerous scholars have simply ignored nuns in this region because they had a doctrinal image of nuns. In 1913 the Italian scholar Dainelli made a common mistake when he observed that Ladakh was devoid of nuns, stating, "there are no nunneries, as in Tibet, but a certain number of female attendants called chomos are attached to the most important of monasteries, where they perform the task of servants."[14] In the scholarly literature, nuns are confused with elderly renunciants, because both are called by the same name, *jo mo (jo mo)*, in local idiom. It is often overlooked that renunciants are actually called "household nuns" *(grong pa'i jo mo)*, and only *jo mo* as a shorthand. The two groups—novice nuns and female renunciants—perform very different roles in village life. While nuns conduct ritual prayers for laypeople and have formal village duties, elderly renunciants usually live at home and do not perform any public rituals. They are labeled with derogatory epithets such as "self-willed woman" *(mo rang mo)* and targeted by unkind proverbs: "a woman without a husband is like a stable without a door."[15] The conflation of ordained nuns and female renunciants in local and scholarly discourse elides the nuns' lengthy apprenticeship and training. In local idiom, ordained nuns are rarely spoken of using the honorific term for nun, *dge tshul ma,* while the equivalent term for a male novice, *dge tshul,* is commonplace. The subtle denigration of ordained nuns is probably due to the familiarity of seeing them as servants in the village as well as monastic realm. By agreeing to work in the mundane realm, nuns are considered to be forsaking their ritual and religious goals. The nun's life remains torn between two spheres—domestic and religious—and it can never fully belong to either.

Although first tonsure marks a ritual moment when a young girl first takes vows of celibacy, she is marked for the nun's life years earlier. Parents begin the process of dedicating a daughter to the nunnery by sending her to serve a distant relative who is a nun or, failing that, a monk at a nearby monastery. Most nuns recall these apprenticeships as nurturing relations as kindly older aunts taught them their first letters and religious prayers, stanza by stanza. Others, like Yeshe, recall more difficult apprenticeships, in which beatings and verbal abuse were frequent reminders to study. Yeshe's apprenticeship with her uncle was peppered with soft but frequent blows, which expressed her uncle's attentiveness more than his anger. These days, most girls are sent to live with a tutor between the ages of five and ten, in order to gauge if they have some interest in the monastic life. Their tutor will concentrate on memorization and ask the apprentice to perform countless menial tasks such as fetching water, washing dishes, and cleaning her tutor's rooms. After the apprentice has expressed some interest and shown facility at learning texts, she takes the first formal rite of shaving their hair in front of a monk.

The youthful apprentice who takes tonsure is known as "one who has gone forth fully" *(rab 'byung ma, anagarika).*[16] This term refers to the original meaning of renunciation: going forth into homelessness. She may also be called a "virtuous devotee" *(dge bsnyen ma, upasika),* a term applied to laywomen who take up the five precepts. Both tonsured initiates and laypeople take up the same five precepts—avoiding killing, lying, stealing, sexual misconduct, and intoxicants—albeit in different ritual contexts.

When laypeople take up these five precepts, they neither shave their heads nor adopt celibacy, as tonsured initiates do. Both laypeople and tonsured initiates vow to "cast off impure actions" *(mi tshang spyod spong ba)*, but only tonsured initiates must maintain total celibacy. In short, lay devotees are not renouncing the world in the way that future monastics are. Indeed laypeople commit themselves to the five precepts just as easily as they break them. Laypeople take the precepts to signal an *intention* to be virtuous. There are six types of virtuous devotees *(dge bsnyen drug)*, but only the tonsured candidate qualifies as a fully chaste devotee *(tshangs spyod dge bsnyen)*. Laypeople are also called virtuous devotees when they observe a ritual abstention *(bsnyen gnas)* of eight vows for a single day or during a three-day fasting rite known as Nyungnäs *(smyung gnas)*.[17]

Girls with strong religious inclinations may undergo tonsure without much training or even permission. The candidate is asked to note if she knows anyone who objects to her taking tonsure. If her parents do not know she is taking tonsure, they cannot have any objections, strictly speaking. Yet the initiate does require some ritual instructions from a monk or nun in her community. A single fully ordained monk is sufficient to perform the tonsure rite in Zangskar, although high-ranking nuns performed the rite in Tibet before 1959.[18] The initiate offers the officiating monk a blessing scarf, some money, or some butter to propitiate the local deities. She also undergoes a ritual ablution *(khrus)* in which she is cleansed of the mental defilements *(sgrib)* due to mistaken actions or ignorance. She will make merit simply by offering her body to the path of renunciation which was the Buddha's main legacy.

One ex-nun who told me her tonsure story explained that her parents had never intended for her to become a nun. Although Angmo came from a poor household, her parents had given her the finest earrings and jewels, in hopes of finding her a rich if not kind husband. She was their last hope, for they had lost their only son when he died in a truck accident years earlier while on leave from the army. Angmo loved to dance and sing with her girlfriends, who gained a reputation for being the finest dancers in Karsha village. One year, when an esteemed reincarnate monk, Lotsa Rinpoche, came to visit the village, the young women offered to dance in his honor. Dancing for the youthful monk, Angmo and her companions were delighted with his sparkling wit. Angmo reckoned she must be making merit by the smile on his handsome face. Angmo was so thrilled that she asked him to shave her head after the performance. He refused at first and then scolded her, pointing out that such an act required more than such a hasty decision; moreover, her parents' permission was essential. Although her mother cried, Angmo took her father's silence as consent. When she went to see the Rinpoche the following day and offered him a white blessing scarf, Angmo stood before him with her head bowed. He gently asked for her motivations. She responded that dancing was fine, but that "I'll never get ahead in life by just dancing" *(rsted byes la mgo 'thon byes med)*. He ritually cut a tuft of hair from her head, blessed her, and sent her on her way.

Although the tonsure rite may be quick, its consequences are profound and enduring. Tonsure signals a lifelong intention to reject the call of sexual desire. The initiate is transformed from a potentially fertile and sexual woman into a voluntarily infertile and asexual woman. The ritual transmutes the latent sexual imagery of shorn hair into a purified Buddhist offering *(mchod pa)*. It is also a form of disciplinary control by which the apprentice is brought under the monastic gaze. The initiate will be scrutinized by her parents and tutors at the nunnery to determine whether she has sufficient inclination for the spiritual life. Lifelong celibacy remains an elite path open only to the few and the diligent.

Van Gennep comments that "to cut the hair is to separate oneself from the previous world; to dedicate the hair is to bend oneself to the sacred world."[19] Cutting hair has both symbolic and pedagogic import around the world. Some scholars have placed tonsure under the rubric of "ceremonial mutilation," along with circumcision, bloodletting, and cutting off finger joints; others see a link between tonsure and castration, and still others see tonsure as discipline or monastic control.[20] In Buddhist idiom, the shorn hair can be a vehicle of meditation on impermanence. Coming from the most sacred part of the body, the head, the hair is secured in the chinks of a wall so that its owner is not defiled by its being stepped over.[21] Hair is also a potent symbol of sexuality and its removal signifies a turning away from fecundity. The young woman who shaves her head may mourn the absence of hair inwardly if not publicly. In local idiom, hair is a signal of a woman's health and fertility. The darker and glossier a woman's hair, the better her prospects for marriage and maternity. When older women dress up for festivals, they often weave false braids made from yak hair into their own stringy tresses. Hair binds agemates together, especially on the bride's wedding day. It is her girlfriends who braid her hair one last time before she is taken away by the groomsmen to her new marital home. Several nuns pointedly told me that they did not cry when their heads were shaved, unlike the brides who cry hysterically at marriage. They claimed to have rejoiced at the cutting of their hair and their ties to society.

After tonsure, the apprentice remains in a fluid or liminal realm between household and monastery. She may remain at home with her parents before beginning her more formal training for ordination. During this time, she may participate fully in village life, even as she adopts the androgynous dress and shorn locks of a future nun. She is both a girl and not a girl, as she slips into and out of village and monastic life. Her ears and neck no longer drip with coral, turquoises, and pearls, and her cropped hair signals her liminal status betwixt and between genders. She discards the characteristic pleated dresses with embroidered triangles of red and green and her swishing tie-dye shawl *(ling zed)* in favor of a boyish coat *(gon che)*, because she cannot yet don full monastic robes. Over the next years, she learns to be a nun by unlearning everyday feminine graces. She may still go to the water pipe to fetch water for her household, but no longer flirts and gossips as she used to. Although she can attend drinking parties *(chang dud)* with her agemates, she keeps a restrained etiquette. She may serve but not drink barley beer; she may play the drum but rarely dances to the romantic songs her girlfriends croon before sneaking off for a secret tryst in the fields. She will watch as romances are kindled and smothered by parents negotiating her girlfriends' futures. She must maintain an inward purity *(gtsang ma)* in the midst of unfolding worldly dramas in which she can play little part.

Eventually, she undertakes a more intensive study of religious texts with an elder nun whom she has chosen to be her tutor. This period of apprenticeship can seem unduly harsh. The apprentices may spend days on end locked inside their tutor's cell at the nunnery, memorizing a basic text page by page. They may be left inside a dark room for hours at a time to read the same page of a single ritual text over and over until they can recite it by heart. Every evening, their tutor returns to her cell to prepare dinner and quiz them on pages they have memorized that day. After they have mastered the alphabet and their first prayers, apprentices begin to churn their way through basic Buddhist texts that are recited in daily meditations or monthly assembly.[22] When I asked their teachers if their disciples cried or protested this treatment, I received a laugh as a reply. Ani Putid explained that her niece Namdrol hardly wanted to go home anymore, although her house in Yulang was in plain sight from the nunnery. On the rare occasions when she had taken Namdrol home, the girl soon tired of her elder siblings' rough play. Although Namdrol was too shy to say much, it was clear that she loved her aunt Putid like a mother, clinging to her robes whenever she left her solitary confinement in Putid's cell. When they went to visit Putid's sister in Zangla on Namdrol's first excursion away from the monastic cell in a year, Namdrol had no qualms about traveling down the Zangskar valley for the first time in her life in the care of her aunt and tutor.

Another apprentice from Karsha was kept under strict wraps by her tutor, the head nun, Lobsang Anmo. In fact, both girls often spent their days together, memorizing texts which they recited in unison in the evening to their teachers. When either Angmo or Putid went away to work in the village, they left their disciples with each other to minimize the disruptions in their studies. Both disciples had spent virtually the entire winter locked inside, only coming out once or twice for Tibetan New Year and the celebrations surrounding the Great Prayer Festival and fasting rite at the monastery. As a special exception, Angmo decided to take her charge to visit her own family up the Zangskar valley. The short ride to Padum in a jeep was a first for Kundzom. After attending wedding festivities in Padum, Kundzom, who had missed her daily study routine, was sent off to finish her recitations in the storeroom of the house where we all spent the night. When I went to collect my flashlight in the dark storeroom later that evening, I was shocked to feel Kundzom's face beneath my outstretched fingertips. She was hardly as perturbed as I was by the encounter. When I interrogated Angmo about the excessive cruelty of leaving her disciple in the dank storeroom, Angmo replied that it was for her own benefit. She knew her disciple would be far too distracted by the excitement of strangers in Tsomo's kitchen, where we would spend the night. She had decided to have her pupil finish her daily recitations in the storeroom. When the food was served hours later, she called Kundzom in to eat, before the girl promptly fell asleep from the day's excitement.

By the time Kundzom takes novice ordination, the daily chants will be as familiar to her as the sound of her mother's voice. Every apprentice must memorize several of the prayers that nuns recite or read every day. She learns every daily devotion a nun must perform. Accompanying her teacher to the chapel every night and morning, the apprentice learns to perform prostrations, light the butter lamps, and fill the seven offering bowls from left to right according to a specified ritual regimen. By repeating these actions every day, she comes to absorb them physically as part of her monastic habitus.[23] She may barely know the meaning of the prayers she recites, even as she begins to bend her body and thoughts toward others. She strives to embody a lived compassion in which others take precedence over the self, not by following rules so much as by imitating the actions of the nuns around her. She may begin to take a more active role in the nunnery, helping her teacher prepare the butter tea for the assembly and going to the roof to bring huge bushels of prickly thorn for fuel. She may assist her teacher in gathering dung and thistles for the monastic hearth or in gathering chalk for whitewashing from the limestone deposits high above the village. She may have to lug twenty-liter jerrycans of water from the frozen streambed up to her teacher's room day after day, all winter long. She has adopted a physical regimen of ritual and mundane duties that she can perform in her sleep.

Ordination as Transition

A woman dedicates her life to the discipline of detachment when she finally ordains as a novice (S. *sramanera, dge tshul ma*). The vows taken at tonsure become permanent through ordination. Unlike Theravada monks who come and go from the monastery, Tibetan novices are not supposed to rejoin the monastic order after they have broken their ordination vows. In the Tibetan Buddhist tradition, novice nuns are ordained by monks alone, often in generic ceremonies including male novices. For border regions such as Tibet, a quorum of six fully ordained monks including the preceptor *(mnga' ba)* is required to officiate the rite. The few Tibetan Buddhist nuns who have been acquired full ordination must wait ten years until they are authorized to perform ordinations themselves. Senior monks willing to perform ordinations are rare, and apprentices may have to wait years before taking ordination. Since lay observers are excluded from ordination rites in Tibetan Buddhism, there are no first-hand accounts of these rites. There are numerous translations of the novice and full ordination vows *(bhiksuni pratimoksha)* included in the Vinaya or monastic discipline of various Buddhist schools, but little thick description on the ordination rite itself.[24] This account relies on first-person accounts by nuns who were ordained either in Tibet or in Zangskar.

On the day of the ordination, a nun washes her body and has her head freshly shorn. For the first time she will wear the robes and carry the monastic seating rug *(gding ba),* which she does not yet own but may have borrowed from a fellow nun or even a monk, although the latter action contradicts the Vinaya. After a ritual purification *(khrus)* using blessed saffron water stored inside a sacred vessel, candidates receive a brief teaching on the novice precepts. The candidates are asked to repent the innumerable transgressions they have committed in this and previous lifetimes. The preceptor then asks the initiates a series of questions to determine their qualifications for ordination.[25] The questions are read out loud, and silence indicates assent. The candidates are required to be beholden to neither spouse nor king, to be neither slave nor concubine, neither demon nor deity, neither hermaphrodite nor impotent, but a free and fertile human. Interestingly, they are not questioned about their motivation, education, previous occupation, or family background. While the Buddha allowed lower-caste women, dissatisfied wives, and even ex-prostitutes to join the order, Zangskari monasteries exclude women and men from the lowest caste *(rigs ngan)* from taking ordination or joining the assembly.

Before the close of the ritual, the candidates for ordination are called up in front of the officiant and preceptor to answer the last two questions—their name and the name of their preceptor. The candidates offer their blessing scarves on the officiant's throne and place a small handful of sweetened barley dough and sweet rice *('bras sil)* into the replica of the Buddha's begging bowl. The candidates then place one hand on top of the begging bowl and one below the begging bowl, around the shaft of the ritual staff *(mkhar gsil)* to consecrate the initiates.[26] The officiant gives each candidate his blessing *(byin rlabs)* by pinching the three sacred robes they are wearing—upper, lower, and outer *(gzan gos, sham thabs,* and *chos gos)*—between his fingers and reciting a brief prayer. As one monk explained, when the officiant pinches or even ties his own robes to the new novice's robes, he is symbolizing the unbroken lineage of the Buddha's teachings which the monastic discipline represents. The ceremony is concluded when the candidates return to their seats and recite their novice vows.[27]

The key traits of ordination include many of the classic attributes of what Turner called liminality: total obedience, suffering, simplicity, sacred instruction, silence, unselfishness, obedience, androgyny, anonymity, homogeneity, equality, uniform dress, disregard for personal appearance and wealth, suspension of kinship rights, and mystical powers.[28] As the questions concerning disqualification are read out, initiates remain silent, indicating their qualification for the monastic vocation. They are accepting pain and suffering as they take vows to fast, maintain lifelong celibacy, and eschew any romantic or sentimental attachments to members of the opposite sex. Absolute obedience is enjoined, although the officiant explains the meaning of the vows. Breaking one of the four root vows (*rtsa lhung bzhi*)—to kill, steal, lie, or commit sexual misconduct—involves immediate expulsion from the monastic order. Indeed even thinking about breaking a vow consists of a breach of contract, requiring penance. Anonymity and androgyny are expressed by the uniform maroon robes. The initiates are required to disregard personal vanity and wealth; several of the novice vows expressly forbid adornments, makeup, body-paint, perfume, saffron, and flowers, as well as gold and silver. Novice nuns take up a discipline that will regulate most waking acts of body, speech, and mind. Although there is considerable agency and freedom in what nuns do every day, their habits and thoughts are not supposed to transgress certain boundaries. The vows may be worn lightly, but they can never be forgotten. Turner comments:

> It is as though [initiates] are being reduced or ground down to a uniform condition to be fashioned anew and endowed with additional powers to cope with their new station in life.[29]

The anonymous and androgynous robes signal the candidates' new life and commitment. As a uniform of celibacy, they are supposed to erase sexual attraction and all other gendered signals. They represent the ascetic ideals of poverty, chastity, and selflessness. Merit is made simply by wearing the robes, by giving laypeople a chance to prostrate inwardly to the ideals they signify. Although novice nuns may not wear their robes much for the first few weeks after their ordination and some nuns wear lay clothes when working in the village, all nuns are required to wear their robes during monastic assembly or other ritual events. There are many myths associated with their origin, and special rules apply to their dimensions and use. Fashioned out of pieces of cloth, they remind the wearer that the Buddha and his first disciples sewed their robes from scraps left behind at cremation grounds. In fact, the robes were intended to signal the impurity that the Indian Brahmans rejected but that Buddhist monks relished as teachings about impermanence. While the Sanskrit word for robe (*kayasa*) originally meant impurity, the Zen master Dogen has specified the four ideal types of cloth for making robes: cloth burnt by fire, eaten by oxen, gnawed by mice, or worn by the dead.[30] Robes are worn according to strict rules with the folds piled up in triplicate on both sides of the waist. The upper robes (*gzan gos, chos gos*) should never touch the lower extremities, nor should one step over them. These upper shawls may be used as tumplines worn around the forehead to carry baskets piled high with moist yak dung, but they should never be allowed to touch an "unclean" shoe.

Both male and female novices wear similar robes, which symbolize both asceticism and androgyny. The bold and simple maroon tunic and wrap signify little else in the way of fashion, gender, wealth, or nationality. They are masterpieces of form but not necessarily of function. Although the upper tunic, shawl, and lengthy lower wrap keep out the weather, they are awkward to fold and wash. Since the cloth which is bound around the waist has little structure and neither pockets nor zippers, the ubiquitous keys, spoons, and other accessories are dangled from the waist sash. The simplicity of the outfit makes every detail symbolic. The richness, texture, and color of the cloth all signal the importance and wealth of the bearer. The classic, almost Hellenistic lines of the robes contrast sharply with the rustic baroque of laywomen's clothes. The colors and shapes of feminine dresses—billowing silks and brocades in cobalt blue, lime green, and stately purple, topped by thick woolen homespun and tie-dyed shawls or goatskins—contrast sharply with the oxblood monochrome of monastic dress. Although the austere and sexless robes promote androgyny, they are complemented by bright vests in a range of shocking colors. The sensuous orange, shocking pink, and blushing peach in sheer, translucent rayon or smooth silks and satins give youthful novices a chance to display an understated flamboyance and sensuousness. Older nuns, by contrast, avoid these exaggerated displays by sporting the same drab maroon flannel shirts or faded woolen robes until they are black with soot and grease.

When the head officiant calls the novices in front of him to bless the robes, he reminds them of the ritual sanctity and significance of the vows they are about to take. During the rite, the novices receive sacred instruction and items—vows and robes—which have been forbidden up until this moment. Novices may receive instructions about the form and flow of the rite, but most have never heard the novice vows recited until the ceremony itself. The act of repeating the vows after the officiant is a performative act, in which saying is doing. As such, their reading cannot but have a lasting effect.[31] Ritual transmits highly condensed forms of knowledge about the monastic discipline to the next generation of lineage holders. Tibetan Buddhist rituals emphasize rituals as containers of information, for many esoteric knowledges are only transmitted orally during rituals. This method allows the teacher to evaluate if the student is ready to receive the ritual knowledge and has completed the necessary meditations and austerities. Students are only permitted to study advanced texts and visualizations after having received the oral explanation *(lung bstan)* from a qualified teacher. This practice has enabled monks to control the highest ritual knowledges, while disciplining the ranks of students.

"At the time you hold the vows, you don't know the Vinaya. By the time you know the Vinaya, you may no longer hold the vows" *(sdom pa yod dus, 'dul ba med. 'dul ba yod dus, sdom pa med).*[32] The Vinaya is largely inaccessible to monks and nuns before they take ordination vows. Even after their ordination, most nuns and monks in Zangskar receive little instruction in the vows they must hold for the remainder of their lives. Nuns are excluded from the study of the Vinaya because they are not eligible to hold full ordination vows. Yet even monks—who can and do take full ordination—will not study the Vinaya to any extent unless they undertake advanced theological studies at the Tibetan exile colleges in South India. For the run-of-the-mill monks in Zangskar who do not undertake this elite education, the most common encounter with the Vinaya is during the ritual reading of the Tibetan canon, or Kangyur, whose first 13 books make up the Vinaya. The reading of the canon is intended to make merit for donors rather than foster the study of the central text of Buddhist monasticism. An entire congregation of monks gathers and divides up the pages of the canon, randomly. Every monk recites his pages of the text simultaneously, at top speed. The resulting cacophony does not lend itself to reflective study of words supposedly dating to the Buddha himself. Because the Tibetan canon—written in an archaic Tibetan—has yet to be translated into regional vernaculars, most rural monastics remain unfamiliar with its precise contents.

As Bourdieu makes clear, "concessions of politeness always contain political concessions."[33] Long before they take ordination, nuns have learned to bow and scrape before the monks. Nuns greet most unknown or senior monks in public with stooped shoulders or bowed head. Those monks who are close friends or agemates are still treated with respect, although nuns may engage in more familiar jokes or teasing when not in public. Finally, the youngest monks may not command much deference, but they will still be respected and treated politely, even as scruffy little boys. The only monks that a nun may treat in truly familiar fashion are her own relatives. Even in familial situations, where seating orders are often abandoned, it is almost unthinkable for a monk to be seated below a woman. Even in private, I have never seen a nun served before a monk. A nun cannot share her food with a monk, nor should she be seated on the same rug or at the same table on most public occasions. If nuns and a monk are sitting near one another, nuns must be seated below the monk, preferably at a lower table and on inferior rugs. As one nun, Dechen, described it, "With a monk present, we cannot place our cups on the same table . . . [and] our table cannot be the same height as his." She added that this deportment was critical once she started to wear her robes. I have seen nuns supplicate themselves to monks at every opportunity, in order to make merit. They are eager to perform any number of menial and domestic tasks for monks, cooking, cleaning, and collecting dung as wives do. They submit to patronizing comments and humiliations that they would reject from any other male. I once watched a nun stoop down again and again to pick up the matches a monk was idly tossing to the floor. A patience inculcated by countless Tantric prostrations serves equally well in reproducing the gender hegemony in the monastery.

"Every social order," says Bourdieu,

> systematically takes advantage of the disposition of the body and language to function as depositories of deferred thoughts that can be triggered off at a distance in space and time by the simple effect of re-placing the body in an overall posture which recalls the associated thoughts and feelings . . . Adapting a phrase of Proust's, one might say the arms and legs are full of numb imperatives.[34]

The practice of deference literally inscribes the message of inferiority over and over again. In other words, nuns come to understand that they are "lower rebirths" not so much by reading texts as by bodily practices. Subordination is inscribed on the body far more enduringly than it could ever be on the mind. When I asked nuns why they must sit below monks, some referred vaguely to "religious law" *(chos kyi khrims)*, but many explained that "this is our custom" *(nang tsho lug srol)*. None of my informants mentioned the eight special rules which legislate that nuns must prostrate to monks. Nuns have reproduced these rules for subsequent generations without knowing their content. This physical habitus seems to have provided a durable means of inculcating subjectification over generations.

Bourdieu insists that the significance of momentary interactions emerges from a repetition which outweighs their original ephemerality: "The language of the body, whether articulated or in gestures . . . is incomparably more ambiguous and more over determined than the most over determined uses of ordinary language."[35] Many informants explained that they began to learn the minute rules of deference as soon as they became apprentices. By careful imitation and by frequently having their ears boxed, apprentice nuns learn that disobedience to elders or monks is dangerous. As children, they learn to inhabit a social world in which male is incontrovertibly superior to female in public as in private. Laywomen do sit below men, and defer to them by serving food first and eating later. Young girls get beaten up by their brothers and they see men being served first, while their mothers and aunts move over to let men take the seat nearest the hearth. By the time they join the nunnery, the little apprentices are hardly surprised to see nuns sitting below monks at ritual events, regardless of age or seniority. After a while they do not even think about the deference that monks deserve. At the nunnery, they learn to treat a monk with respect as quickly as they learn never to step over texts or monastic robes. After a few years at the nunnery, the young nuns learn to give up their old ways of walking or gesturing. They no longer swing their hips or toss their heads like their girlfriends in the village below, but use their limbs in a restrained and decorous fashion. In fact, nuns used to get a great kick out of imitating my vigorous style of walking and talking, because it clashed so clearly with the subdued style they'd incorporated. Yeshe once mimicked my style of walking, joking that "while walking, we should not swing our arms like this." She paused and placed her arms stiffly along her sides and added, "We should place them like this while walking."[36]

Bourdieu observed that "practical belief is not a 'state of mind' still less a kind of arbitrary adherence to a set of instituted dogmas and doctrines ('beliefs'), but rather a state of the body."[37] He saw that people act in regularized or repetitive ways, not so much because they are following a precise set of rules, but because they are following what he called the *habitus*. He used this notion of durable but regulated improvisation to explain how action is confined, almost unconsciously, by prior experience. In his view, action is always innovative and constrained in accordance with the limits and possibilities of agency. Bourdieu's theory does not describe how this habitus is inculcated, except to specify that it relies on unconscious, rather than conscious, imitation. As such, it ignores religious deportment or ritual disciplines which are practiced consciously but repeatedly until they become second nature.[38] By contrast, nuns wished to embody virtue and deference so completely that they would become automatic. Ani Putid told me that nuns bow to monks less because they think that every individual monk is superior, but more because they are paying homage to the Buddha and his discipline. She said that all Buddhists should prostrate toward a person in robes, regardless of whether the monastic was a saint or a sinner. The Buddhist notion of *karma* requires both intention and completion of an act. Deference without the proper intention is simply empty or incomplete. As such, nuns must believe in the deference they show.

Bourdieu helps us to understand how this pattern of deference can be systematically misunderstood. Do nuns resent their inferiority as they bow before the monks? It was difficult to find much resistance against the monks' privileges. Some nuns said it was impossible to imagine any nun sitting above a monk. Others could not understand why the tradition of monks sitting above nuns should be changed now. Yet although each act of deference appears insignificant on its own, cumulatively, they provide a self-replicating pattern of subservience. As Bourdieu notes, "it is because agents never know completely what they are doing that what they do has more sense than they know."[39] The external pattern of uniform deference which is reproduced produces an unambiguous message of subordination. This action shapes and is shaped by the social and cultural milieu which conditions experience. All of this bowing and scraping begs the question of where, if any, resistance can emerge. How does a religion of self-effacement also promote feminist questions about discrimination? Although Western feminists may reject the authority of the eight rules, they still bow and humble themselves in front of venerable monks.

Bourdieu comments that "what is 'learned by the body' is not something one has, like knowledge that can be brandished, but something one is."[40] In Buddhist practice, the body's sex is not so much something one has but something one is. While doctrine argues against the notion of an enduring self, bodies reflect existential and enduring moral qualities. Put another way, bodies express a fundamental truth about their occupants. The total stockpile of merit determines where and in what body an individual is reborn. By definition those who inhabit female bodies are considered morally inferior to those inhabiting male bodies. For the same reason, nuns are inferior to monks not because of how much they do or do not meditate but because of their innate bodily disqualification. In local idiom, "female bodies are inferior because they are polluted." In short, even after they take the same novice ordination as monks, nuns are considered to have less merit. Only by striving to make as much merit as they can in this life, can they hope to advance into a higher body in the next life.

Yeshe once repeated a canonical Buddhist parable to explain why the human body is so precious:

> Imagine the entire world is covered with a stormy ocean. Deep in this vast ocean, long before the continents emerged, there was a single tortoise who only surfaces once every hundred years for air. Along with the tortoise, there was one other object in this ocean: a wooden yoke, like you'd put on a yak. The probability of the tortoise surfacing so that it puts its neck through the yoke is greater than the probability of our attaining a human rebirth in our next lifetime.

Given the rarity of the human rebirth, merit making is both imperative and desirable. Those who do not add to their stockpile of merit face a fall into the lower realms. Because women are already defiled and have a low stockpile of merit, they are most likely to drop into one of these lower realms. While every realm besides the human is filled with suffering, only the human realm allows an opportunity for making merit. Like most nuns, Yeshe prays to be reborn as a human and preferably a man in a Buddhist land. Yeshe has told me that the beings in hell and hungry ghosts suffer torment, hunger, and thirst, while animals suffer heavy burdens without thought or speech. Even the gods suffer because pleasures cannot last. As she approaches death, Yeshe thinks about her fate more than she used to. Since suffering is inescapable, Yeshe feels she must make as much merit as she can before she dies. Like most nuns, Yeshe meditates every morning and evening in order to maintain a mental clarity in which only "perfectly good thoughts" *(kun slong bzang po)* arise. She explained the meaning of such thoughts as follows:

> To say perfectly pure thoughts means good thoughts, white thoughts. We do not send others evil thoughts or black thoughts. "Perfectly cleansed thoughts" means the following: we feel only a so-called Bodhisattva mind, a straight mind, which doesn't wish harm upon others, doesn't feel jealousy, doesn't feel anger and pride, and doesn't covet another's wealth. And even while staying within one's own faith, one considers all other sentient beings of the six realms as one's father or mother and one says, "may they be reborn in the Buddha fields."

Joining the Monastic Assembly

The final rite of passage which confers full status as a nun is admission to the monastic assembly (*dge bdun*, S. *sangha*). While tonsure and ordination involve a state of liminality in which a woman is separated from lay society through the pursuit of ascesis, joining the monastic community reintegrates her into collective social life. Each member of the nuns' assembly participates in a set of reciprocal duties and rights. These relations address the mundane minutiae of life which bind the members of this community to one another—including daily chores, property, inheritance, and even death rites. In colloquial idiom, joining the nunnery is called "dwelling on the cliff" *(ri la bzhugs byes)*, signaling the transition of the novice nun, who has lived partly with her tutor at the nunnery and partly at home until now. Once she joins the assembly, a disciple will continue to live with her tutor until she builds or borrows a cell of her own where the nunnery is locates. Like the earlier tonsure and ordination, entrance to the assembly consists of ritualized procedures.

Any woman who wishes to join the nuns' assembly at Karsha must first petition the nuns' abbot, who is usually a monk in Zangskar. Bearing a thermos of butter tea and a blessing scarf, the young girl and one or both of her parents seek an audience with the abbot. As they are welcomed in the abbot's room with tea and perhaps some food, the abbot makes basic inquiries about her studies and motivation for joining the assembly. She may or may not have taken novice ordination, but she must have apprenticed herself to an elder nun for some time by this point. After the initiate has departed, the abbot calls the community of nuns to a session where they are asked to register any doubts they may have. Although there is no formal entrance examination, most apprentices have been under observation for some time by the community of nuns and their abbot. As long as an initiate has exhibited some sign of progress in her studies, she is usually accepted unanimously, for it is a clear offense to hinder a willing disciple's aspiration to take up the monastic life. The candidate will be contacted and told to return on a ritually auspicious day. When the day arrives, the candidate and her parents arrive at the nunnery bearing butter, salt, a basket of breads for the assembly of nuns, and nominal gift of cash to be distributed to the assembly. The candidate may assist the cook in making the communal tea, while her parents are hosted in the guest room with an honorific meal of sweet tea and buttery barley dough *(phye mar)*.

When the assembly of nuns has gathered, the candidate and her parents are ushered into the assembly hall, where they prostrate themselves three times to the altar. Through her prostrations, the new nun now places herself under the protection of the assembly's major Tantric deity, Vajrayogini. From this time onward, the nun is no longer beholden to her household guardian deity and is free to enter any household offering room without fear of pollution, as long as she is not menstruating. If she has not done so already, the new candidate should attend a Tantric empowerment dedicated to the protective deity of her nunnery. She will be initiated into the appropriate meditations, visualizations, and *mandalas* associated with her chosen Tantric protector *(yi dam)*. After such an empowerment, she can recite the liturgy for this deity at the public fire sacrifice, and renew her private collection of offering cakes made of barley *(gtor ma)* which symbolize the deity and its entourage.

In the assembly hall, the candidate sits in the juniormost spot in the long rank of nuns, while her parents, as laypeople, are accommodated on a separate rug against the rear wall of the assembly hall. When the tea and breads are served, the parents may refuse out of politeness because they are not members of the monastic assembly. They may be pressed to have a small cup, while their daughter drinks a cup of the "Vinaya tea" *('dul ja)*, thereby joining the assembly. The play of exchange continues to unfold as the parents offer a sum of money *('gyed)* which is efficiently distributed among the nuns by the nuns' treasurer, who carries change for just this purpose. The abbot replies with a short speech of thanks and offers the parents blessing scarves and a blessing cord. The parents then receive a small payment called an "empty exchange" *(stong deb)*.[41] This sum is a symbolic compensation for the daughter they have given up and for the periodic donations they are expected to make for ritual services. After the nun dies, the parents will return this sum, which amounts to fourteen rupees at the nunnery and twice that sum at the monastery. Shortly afterward, the parents leave the hall and retire to the guest room to drink and chat. Later that evening their daughter's tutor may host a small party for friends and relatives to celebrate the addition of a new nun in the assembly.

The young nun may continue to live with her tutor until her parents build or acquire a cell for her. Building a new cell takes considerable time, energy, and resources, although the resultant building will belong to the nun's family, to be used by subsequent generations of nuns. When a household no longer has a member at the nunnery, it may rent or even sell the building to a new member of the nunnery whose household has no cell on the cliff. In the 1990s, cells were sold for between four thousand and six thousand rupees, the cost of a female cow or yak-cow cross-breed *(mdzo mo)*. Ani Angmo, the first nun to build on the cliff above Karsha village, received little support from her stingy brothers while building her own cell. Ani Yeshe, who spent several winters apprenticing at Sani monastery and Dorje Dzong nunnery, first moved into Ani Angmo's rooms. After a few years, her father and mother held a "begging beer" in Karsha to raise supplies they could not afford, like wooden beams. "Nowadays," Yeshe says, "villagers are too rich and embarrassed *(khrel byes)* to hold a begging beer for an individual monastic cell. We were much poorer in those days."

The Rights and Responsibilities of Being a Nun

Nuns do not flee society so much as join an alternative or transcendent form of society. The society of monks and nuns has a lengthy and well-established tradition in India. The early peripatetic disciples of the Buddha soon settled into more cenobitic communities in which reciprocal relations with the laity were essential to survival. In this context, monasticism developed a vast set of practices or codes by which to regulate the behavior of monastics in relation to the laity. These duties included individual deportment, obligations owed laypeople, as well as rules for accepting and managing the goods and properties that the monastic assembly acquired. Moreover, every monastery had its own rules and customs *(bca' yig)* which specify the succession of offices and other rules a monk must follow.[42] In the Karsha assembly, every nun has certain rights and responsibilities. Her rights include a share *(skal ba)* of the donations in cash or kind which the assembly receives. In exchange, she is supposed to be present at any collective ritual performance, although in her absence her share of food and cash may be set aside or sent down to her in the village. Apprentice nuns may join the monthly ritual sessions to study the texts, but they are not entitled to receive any donations until they formally join the assembly. Every nun is also entitled to an equal share of the nunnery's crops, if there is any grain left over at the end of the three-year period when the position of head nun is rotated.

Membership in the assembly obligates every member to perform both ritual and mundane duties. A nun's ritual and religious obligations include attendance at the trimonthly prayer sessions and annual rituals like the Great Prayer Festival, the auspicious offering rite, the Tara recitations, the *Prajñaparamita*, and other textual readings, the fire sacrifice to Vajrayogini, and the wintertime Losar festivities. She must also attend any ad hoc rites such as recitations of the Tara prayer or a compilation of blessings and prayers which donors may request to honor a death, a birth, or other household occasion. Weddings and funerals are the two major household rites for which the entire assembly of nuns is called to be present. Additionally, the assembly of nuns is called by the village to attend the springtime virtuous offerings for the ancestor *(dge tsha)* and the annual purification and circumambulation of the fields *('bum 'khor)*. While monks are invited to perform household and village rites almost daily, nuns are rarely called upon for such rituals and if so, only for the most basic textual recitations. Most villagers preferred monks as ritual officiants because they were unaccustomed to calling nuns. When pressed, however, they admitted that nuns were less desirable because of the innate impurity and lack of merit which the female body represented as well as nuns' lack of Tantric empowerments and full ordination status. In the case of a severe illness where Tantric prowess and ritual skill were of utmost importance, nuns would be disqualified on both counts. Similarly, monks were more desirable in high-profile rituals, where donors sought merit and/or status.

Mundane duties at the nunnery are hardly an antithesis to enlightenment; they form the very foundation which makes ritual activity possible. Every nun must steward her share of the nunnery's rites. The trimonthly rites and the Great Prayer Festival are stewarded by individual nuns on rotation, while most other rites in the annual calendar are funded from the nunnery's general coffers. Stewards collect donations of cash, butter, and grain for ritual use and communal consumption from villagers as well as from member nuns, if necessary. In the case of the nunnery's largest ritual expense, the Great Prayer Festival, a single nun spends a year organizing begging beers and collecting donations of cash, food, and firewood by going door to door throughout Zangskar. Smaller rituals require less onerous but more frequent and ad hoc collections. Every nun must provide a set quota of fuel to the collective and serve her time on the nunnery's numerous work teams. All nuns under a certain age must collect and deliver several bushels of dung and thistlewood, and those who have not yet been head nun must serve their time as nunnery cook or tea server. All nuns, regardless of seniority, must work on communal projects such as whitewashing, repairing, and tending the nunnery compound and its resources. Simply maintaining and repairing the nunnery, its walls, and paths; shoveling snow off the roof all winter; assembling and dismantling the water pipe every spring and winter; emptying the compost toilet every spring; and tending to the willow groves and flower gardens every summer involve many days of work. In the past decade, the Karsha nuns have helped to build and maintain a willow plantation, a successful water pipe, a toilet, a greenhouse, numerous vegetable and flower plots, a grass compound for debate and teachings, as well as extensive walls to keep wandering livestock out of all of the above. Although the nuns have sharecropped the nunnery's collective fields since 1998, there are always more projects than time or energy to complete them.

After she joins the assembly, a nun is expected to take up a number of ritual offices which rotate among the member nuns according to seniority. At Karsha nunnery, each nun serves as conch blower *(dung ma)*, ritual assistant *(chos g.yog)*, sacristan *(dkon gnyer)*, steward *(gnyer pa)*, assistant chantmaster *(dbu chung)*, and chantmaster *(dbu mdzad)*, with the chantmaster doubling as head nun. Most of these positions involve a three-year tenure, except that of sacristan. The ritual assistant is responsible for making butter sculptures, offering cakes *(gtor ma)*, arraying the altar, and procuring any special ritual substances necessary for esoteric rites. The sacristan goes to the assembly hall every day to light and refill butter lamps, fill and empty offering bowls, and polish or clean the butter lamps. Every day at dawn and dusk, the protective spirits are offered a litany of sounds and smell—juniper incense, a shake of the bell, a short twist of the hand-held drum, and a crescendo of beats on the larger drum, which hangs from the ceiling by a knotted blessing scarf.

The most important post at Karsha nunnery is that of head nun or chantmaster. Every nun must take her turn in this position, after she has completed all the other positions at the nunnery. The nun who is next in line to serve as head nun serves as an assistant chantmaster for three years, to give her time to learn the chants and other administrative duties. Over this period she must apply herself to memorizing over twenty hours' worth of ritual texts to be recited on call. The head nun does more than lead the assembly rituals. She is the CEO, principal shareholder, and office manager of the nuns' corporation. The head nun is in charge of the nunnery's finances, resources, works and projects, ritual calendar, and annual investments and expenditures. If necessary, she may cook the tea and prepare a meal from the supplies a donor has provided before leading the assembly to chant the prayers requested. The head nun keeps track of every sum that comes in or out of the monastic coffers, while recording the ritual or devotion upon which sums are spent. When she rotates out of her post after three years in late December on Tsongkhapa's birthday, she must clear all the outlying accounts by performing a public audit in front of the entire assembly of nuns. She is the unofficial arbitrator of internal politics and complaints registered by any nuns. She may call for a vote of the assembly in case of dispute; however, she often defers the adjudication of the most serious disputes to the abbot, who is usually male.

The Authority and Discipline of Monks

The nunnery, like the monastery, is a disciplinary realm in the service of other powers, be they the state, social hierarchy, or other forms of the status quo, including gender hierarchy. Although the larger Tibetan nunneries in exile are often ruled by female abbots, all of the nunneries in Zangskar have male abbots either in situ or in absentia. These abbots may live at the nunnery and be cared for into old age by the nuns, or reside in absentia in their own monasteries. In the latter case, they may only appear on special ritual occasions or other pressing political occasions. Besides admitting and expelling nuns, abbots may be responsible for limited scholastic or ritual training. The abbot will usually hear from both parties in a dispute and mediate a discussion of the dispute by the full assembly. After consultation with the assembly, the abbot delivers the verdict and punishment for those involved. While the abbot's decision is final in cases of expulsion, a nun may appeal the assembly's decision in the case of a minor dispute. In one case regarding a physical fight between two nuns, the abbot decided to punish both nuns, although the one who first had resorted to fists received additional penances to be performed in front of the entire assembly of nuns. This nun eventually left the nunnery because of the public humiliation she endured and the antagonism she felt from the other nuns. In a case of theft, where the head nun was largely to blame because she kept a communal sum in her own room and spread the news of this sum through the village, the abbot mediated the internal proceedings in a rather aloof manner. Although he made no attempt to find the thief or help bring him to justice, the nuns eventually took the advice of the equally unhelpful village headman and fined the head nun a nominal sum. She left the nunnery a few short years later in shame, when it became clear that her own relative had absconded with the money.

Both monks and villagers place nuns under constant disciplinary surveillance. In the panopticon of village life deviance spells disaster. Nuns are held accountable for standards of purity and piety that monks disregard with impunity. Although monks may be notorious for their indiscretions, only the female body bears the proof of sexual infidelity to the monastic code. Women who get pregnant are thrown out of the monastery, while monks can and do develop traditions of homosexuality and other libertine behaviors.[43] At the same time, Buddhist ideology views any woman, monastic or lay, as a potential threat to the monks' purity and sanctity. This ideology portrays men as the passive victims of insatiable female lust. In this view, nuns are given far less latitude than monks in bending the rules of celibacy. As a local anecdote from Ladakh suggests, nuns are presumed guilty until proved innocent. Having discussed this incident with several informants, I reconstruct it as follows.

It was hot and still in Thikse, Ladakh. It was the day after a monastic festival and some tourists had visited the monastery. When three young nuns passed the jeep on their way back from irrigating their fields, the driver chatted them up rather amiably. Since he was going back into Leh, he agreed to take them to a neighboring village, where they visited with relatives and caught up on news. By early dusk, the nuns hastened to the road and hailed another jeep back to Thikse. In their haste to get back to the nunnery before dark, they jumped into a taxi which was driven by a Muslim, ignoring the social boycott. When they reached Thikse, the same jealous monks who had seen them depart that morning were watching from their clifftop perch. They had also seen the jeep stop in the fields before the village to pick up something the nuns had left behind earlier that morning. Growing somewhat suspicious, the monks became incensed when they heard that the driver was a Muslim. They sent a delegation to the nunnery the next day to demand an explanation for the events they had observed.

When the three nuns were questioned by the head nun and their assembly, they protested their innocence. They resisted the accusations, claiming ignorance of the driver's faith and their desire to get back to the nunnery as excuses. The assembly of nuns took up their case and refused to pay an atonement (*bshags pa*) to the monastery. Insisting that no vows had been broken, the nuns refused to pay the monks' assembly a cash donation, several kilos of butter, and a blessing scarf, and to make obligatory prostrations in front of the full assembly of monks. The nuns' refusal was the turning point in the affair, according to one local informant. By refusing to "plead guilty," the nuns were seen as unrepentant. They might have been absolved by the village if they had made amends at the monastery. In this rare example of a dispute between nuns and monks, the village headman was called in to adjudicate. A village assembly was called soon after, as one representative from each household gathered on the village commons along with the three nuns and several senior monks. They would deliberate until a consensus was achieved.

Young men who had returned home for the festival and holidays were adamant in their desire to punish the nuns. As local students they seized this opportunity to spread the message about the imperative of the social boycott. If word got back to the Buddhist leaders in Leh that even nuns were breaking the boycott, there would be hell to pay. The nuns' fathers could do little in the face of the young men's polemic. A senior monk spoke on the women's behalf, pointing out that nobody had witnessed the nuns breaking their vows. Yet other monks argued that they should be punished at all costs. The nuns silently watched their fates rise and fall in the endless debate. Their testimony seemed hardly relevant to the villagers' cry for justice. Eventually, the villagers reached a decision. The nuns would not be expelled from the nunnery, but would be punished with the maximum fine—beating—for breaking the political boycott by riding in a Muslim jeep. Each nun was led to the village poplar grove and tied to a tree. The village headman and his assistants took turns beating the nuns with willow rods. The nuns endured the whipping for nearly an hour.[44] For each nun, either a father or head of household came to fetch her home. As one informant recalled, villagers had insisted upon this provision so that they could not be blamed if the nuns committed suicide. As one villager recalled, it was said that "if they jump in the river, it's not our doing." One of the nuns' fathers reportedly had spit in the dust before his daughter, saying, "These nuns are without shame." Each family was fined by having to offer a full tea ceremony to the congregations of both nunnery and monastery. The nuns were barred from entering the monastery and nunnery for a few months.

The nuns' public punishment performed and produced a social truth. An otherwise decentralized system of village justice crystallized with terrifying swiftness. The public beating of the nuns displayed the crime as much as its punishment. What was at stake for the actors involved in this conflict? The disaffected and marginalized rural youths were able to assert some agency in pursuing a social boycott that urban politicians had foisted upon them. The headman's actions could send a strong signal to his urban patrons about his cooperation with the boycott. For village elders, the nuns were convenient scapegoats that might teach others a lesson about transgressing village laws. The punishment was carefully chosen after public debate. The nuns' bodies served as a public slate upon which to inscribe communal anger and impotence. Corporal punishment is rarely used in rural disputes. Although some elders I interviewed noted that repeated theft of collective goods like firewood or water could be punished corporally, these threats are rarely enacted. Nuns were expected to be paragons in their adherence to a boycott that laypeople in the cities broke with impunity. It was their female and their celibate status which led to the immediate assumption that they had been defiled by the Muslim touch.[45] Although that defilement might be purified through their suffering, their punishment was a vindication of the local authority of the monks. The innocence or guilt of the nuns was less at stake than the reassertion of local patriarchal authority. Monks administer local justice through their moral guidance as much as through ritual practices explained in the next chapter.

6

Why Nuns Cannot Be Monks

In the predawn stillness, before even the birds were awake, a solitary monk attended to the obligatory ritual routine which would occupy him every day for the entire year that he served as sacristan at Phughtal monastery. He climbed many flights of stairs until reaching the uppermost and holiest spot in the monastery, the cave where the monastery's founder is believed to have meditated in the fifteenth century. Before he could complete his ritual routine of filling the offering bowls in the monastery's offering room for the guardian deities, he went to fetch water from the sacred spring which lies in the gloomy recesses of the cavern. He was dumbfounded when he realized that the small pool carved into the cavern floor was only half full. At first he thought he was dreaming, before he saw that the sacred spring had stopped running. In shock, he stood there, frozen, before returning swiftly down the hundreds of steps he had just climbed. After he climbed back up with a fellow monk in tow, both monks pondered the mystery of the silent pool. The spring had never run dry in their lifetimes, nor, as far as they knew, had it ever ceased to flow since the cavern was first occupied some five centuries earlier. Eventually an assembly of monks was called to discuss the matter. The monks agreed that the spring might have been polluted by a woman attending the monastic festival earlier in the month. They reasoned that she might have drunk from the spring in hopes of benefiting from its curative and fertile powers, disregarding the sign they'd posted nearby for pesky foreign tourists. The assembly of monks shifted into emergency ritual action. Prayers were held all day long to purify the spring, juniper incense was offered, and a series of effigies were made for the subterranean spirits who govern springs and are offended by female pollution. By the next morning, the spring was running again and monastic calm was restored.

The monk who told me this story admitted that the assembly of monks had never been entirely sure what had caused the spring to run dry years ago. "Surely, there could have been other explanations," I asked. "What about demonic influence? Ritual lapses? The wrath of the protectors? The decline of ages known as Kali Yuga? Global warming?" The monk answered that he believed female pollution to be the most likely scenario, although he admitted that other factors could have been involved. His assurance that the prohibition against women drinking at the spring "had always existed" only made me more suspicious. Why was he so certain that this calamity was due to female impurity alone? I reasoned that the belief in the power of female impurity gave monks an easy scapegoat, if and when the spring ever ran dry. The rule prohibiting women from approaching the spring offers meaning as much as method. It can explain a natural disaster in meaningful terms even as it prescribes the appropriate ritual cure. Unlike the more complex multivalent idiom of demonic interference, which requires an extensive astrological hermeneutic simply to identify the particular demon involved, female impurity is diagnosed and remedied by a straightforward process. The injunction against female bodies legitimizes monastic control over ritual space even as it reinforces the goal of cosmic harmony. More broadly, rules about purity and pollution provide ethical and practical schemas for manipulating human disorder.

The Ideology of Purity and Pollution

Purity and pollution are less a matter of fixed categories than of a strategic relationship of two terms. Like sacred and profane, purity and pollution offer collective representations which can maintain and subvert social authority. The two categories imply a symbolic system of local morality and cosmic justice. They highlight the critical cultural fault lines by emphasizing the social boundaries and transgressions that can upset the gods as much as the social order. Yet the categories offer symbolic maps more than territory, to recall Jonathan Smith's (1978) famous dictum. Purity and pollution beliefs offer expressive and instrumental maps which can highlight the critical tensions in a given society. Ritual pollution is often associated with ambiguity, rupture, and repercussion. Yet the nature of these symbolic boundaries is highly mediated and rarely self-evident. Mary Douglas (1966) has argued that ritual pollution is simply matter out of place. Extending this view, it is possible to argue that rules about purity and pollution express a creative attempt to order the chaos of mundane experience. Pollution and purity are symbolic idioms for healing individual and social dis-ease or discomfort. More significantly, the two categories enable the agency and efficacy of local ritual experts—in this case, monks. By its association with impurity as well as purity, the female body offers a perfect medium for monks to practice ritual efficacy.

Gender is as significant a fault line in Buddhist discourse as it is in the Hindu or Muslim one. In each of these discourses, women are conceptualized either as *dangerous* because of their impurity or *in danger* because of their purity.[1] Each of these three cultures conceptualizes women as in need of protection because of their purity, even as they are dangerous because of their potential or temporary impurity. In the Hindu and Muslim culture of North India, women are protected and secluded through *purdah*, because they represent the purity or honor *(izzat)* of the caste or group. Elaborate rules relate caste purity to the chastity of women across the Indian subcontinent.[2] Women—the symbolic vessel for the group's honor or status—must be protected at all costs from degradation or attack. At the same time, women are considered impure by virtue of biological processes like menstruation or childbirth. Orthodox Hindus and upper castes have elaborate rules to prevent accidental defilement from menstruating women. Yet even Shia Muslims isolate women during and after childbirth, a period of extreme pollution. In Kargil, women are sent to the stables to give birth so houses are not defiled. In Zangskar's Buddhist culture, women are dangerous because of their impurity as well as their sexuality, while they are also in danger because their purity can be defiled. Buddhist women are considered to have a fiery and dangerous sexuality, at the same time that they are in danger of being defiled by sexual desire. Monks rectify the danger of female impurity with ritual cleansing. But they also protect women's moral purity through their teachings and example. Their skillful manipulation of the purity and pollution dynamic has enabled Buddhism to flourish on Indian soil for over two millennia.[3]

Teachings of the Buddha firmly disavowed the power of the Brahman priests to purify others in early Indian society:

> By oneself is wrong done, by oneself is one defiled
> By oneself wrong is not done, by oneself, surely, is one cleansed.
> One cannot purify another,
> Purity and impurity are in oneself [alone].[4]

One of the Buddha's most radical injunctions was that the self could only be liberated or purified by its own actions. In arguing that nobody can purify another, the Buddha made an entire vocation—that of Brahmanic priest—obsolete. In the end the radical message was subverted, as the Buddha's disciples began to perform purification rituals for their donors. Purification rites are a central aspect of monastic ritual in Zangskar as elsewhere in the Himalayan realm. Even the radical nonduality of Tantra, which defies the distinction between impure and pure, has been co-opted in the service of Tantric ritual. In Tibetan Buddhism, most Tantric liturgies require some form of purification. The standard Tantric meditation (*sadhana*) is prefaced by ablution, and includes a stage for the confession and purification of defilements. In short, only those with sufficient purity gain access to the highest Tantric knowledges and rituals. In practice, Tantric discourse exalts the purity of the monk even as it subordinates those who are impure, namely nuns.

Both space and society are ordered along an axis of purity and pollution. The hearth or altar represents purity, while the door or exit represents impurity. Guests are seated along rows at any private or public function according to four basic principles: monastic over lay, male over female, aristocratic over commoner, and age over youth. In some political instances, gender is the primary basis of division, so that nuns are seated with laywomen, well below monks and even laymen. Most broadly, society is ordered into three major strata, aristocrats, commoners, and untouchables, ranked according to their presumed purity.[5] Untouchables, who are deemed most impure, experience a kind of "social death," as they cannot share utensils or cooked food with the other two strata. Should they be required to host a seasonal village festival, they give the raw materials over to another "clean" household, which cooks the beer and food and supplies the utensils for the collective feast, which is held inside or outside the untouchable's home. In all contexts, the serving and cooking of food are conducted so that individual saliva or other impurities never touch the food and utensils that are served to others. Because saliva is considered polluting, food and cups are only shared among members of the same strata. Laymen or laywomen of the same strata may pass a cup of beer to one another, but aristocrats will stick to their own cups. Food polluted by high monks is considered to have auspicious blessing power, while food contaminated by a woman is fit only for her own child.

Pollution signifies dirt or darkness in the Tibetan vernacular. Two related terms for pollution, *grib* and *sgrib*, combine obscured states of mind, body, and nature into a single term. Moral obscuration is conflated with the most mundane forms of physical darkness, the shadow and the eclipse.[6] This Buddhist notion of "defilement" as a black stain or shadow recalls the Jain ideology of impure actions as dirt which weighs down the soul *(Jiva)* as well as the medieval European notion of sin as a stain which pursues the criminal as described by Dante or Spencer. In the Tibetan Buddhist ideology, women, corpses, outcastes, adultery, childbirth, death, menstruation, urine, feces, sweat, blood, pus, phlegm, spit, hair, skin, fingernails, and placentas all present a potent impurity.[7] In local idiom defilement is conceptualized as a transgression, excess, or imbalance of the spiritual, psychic, or moral order. While ritual pollution arises in a myriad of inexplicable ways, purity can only be restored by precise measures which include ritual, astrology, medicine, and customary law.[8]

Defilement is addressed by each of the major healing discourses in Zangskar—monastic, medical, oracular, and astrological. All of these discourses share a notion of ultimate and secondary causality. Ultimate causality *(rgyu)* is dictated by *karma,* while secondary or proximate causes *(rkyen)* determine the nature of a given event. The proximate causes of illness include behavior, diet, season, astrology, defilement, demons, or witchcraft *(gong mo b bzhug byes).* While medical and ritual techniques appear to stress the physicality of invasive forces, Buddhist doctrine recognizes such forces as psychic illusions. They are as empty of inherent and independent existence as the phenomenal reality known as the self. Although dirt, blood, pus, excrement, urine, and crowds are all examples of pollution, these beliefs do not simply express rustic public health measures. Such medical materialism seeks to rationalize the irrational by overlooking the arbitrary nature of these rules. Weddings are polluting while Tantric empowerments are purifying—yet both involve proximity to sneezing strangers.

The comprehensive theory of purity and pollution is subsumed by the doctrine of *karma.* While merit or demerit requires intentionality, pollution is perpetuated unwittingly. Yet while merit and *karma* extend over infinite lifetimes, the effects of pollution are experienced much more immediately in this life.[9] Purity and pollution beliefs regulate and relate the endless chaos of human activity to a world of invisible beings. A highly specific cultural discourse defines which acts are polluting or transgressive. Theft, adultery, excessive violence, anger, obsessions, and other human faults are all causes of pollution. Washing, urinating, and defecating near sacred markers like stupas *(mchod rten),* village altars *(lha tho),* or prayer walls *(ma ni)* defile the guardian deity of the village, while burning unclean substances like milk, hair, or other angers the hearth deity *(thabs lha).*

Human acts like plowing and construction are threatening, but the "natural" burrowing of marmots is not. Disturbing the soil near sacred springs, bushes, groves, or other spaces guarded by subterranean spirits *(sa bdag, gzhi bdag, klu)* is harmful. To avoid offending these sprites, all major constructions require ritual preparation and careful use of materials. At a consecration rite *(sa'i cho ga)* before the construction of a stupa, wooden stakes were pounded into the earth without any ritual ado. Yet the first swing of the metal pickax was prefixed by extensive ritual activity. The ax was rubbed with all manner of ritual substances—gold, silver, turquoise, and coral—before a young man of an auspicious birth year whose parents were still alive struck the ax into the spot specified by the astrologer to pin down the resident earth deity *(sa bdag)*. Likewise, harvesting crops using human hands requires no ritual intervention, while the metal scythe can only be wielded after the autumn ritual offering first fruits *(srub lha)* for the village deity.

As Ortner notes, "the core of village religion is essentially a war of purification."[10] The Buddhist principle of dependent origination argues for the interrelatedness of every action and being in the universe.[11] This ethos is premised upon a relationship between visible human and animal realms and a set of invisible realms populated by a host of spirits. The placid harmony of this universe of beings is under a constant threat of imbalance, which can cause personal or communal dis-ease. Ritual defilements as well as moral faults like stealing and adultery can all offend a variety of worldly spirits *(lha, klu, sa bdag, gzhi bdag)*. Because these spirits are beings trapped within the cycle of birth and rebirth which Tibetan Buddhism depicts as the six realms of existence *('gro ba rigs drug)*, they are subject to human vices like jealousy, spite, anger, and intransigence. Unlike Buddhist deities which have transcended this wheel of rebirth and show only compassion, worldly spirits attack humans if not ritually appeased. A victim is said to be "struck by pollution" *(grib 'phogs song)* in the same manner or spot where he or she has struck the offended spirit. Running sores represent a symbolic wound to an invisible being yet to be healed. Pollution from certain inauspicious planets *(gza' grib)* involves cosmic retaliation or attack by even more distant and unknown forces, the stars. Sudden and inexplicable ailments like catatonia, paralysis, muteness, epilepsy, strokes, retardation, or psychosomatic disorders are explained as defilement or offenses against hidden beings.

Moral and behavioral faults are punished with an allegory of misfortune. The discourse about purity and pollution offers meaning without eliding empirical evidence. Like the Azande witchcraft famously described by Evans-Pritchard (1937), Zangskari villagers use pollution to explain why a misfortune strikes a particular place, time, or individual. They recognize that famine, pestilence, drought, hail, floods, landslides, and avalanches have natural causes. Yet they explain coincidences or accidental tragedies using the idiom of pollution. In short, the discourse of defilement relates human and cosmic justice. Human beings attempt to appease or fend off angry spirits through ritual purification. Household and village rites both ensure that the gods and spirits continue to protect humans, despite accidental insolence. When communities or individuals are struck by misfortune *(lan chags)*, monks are quick to blame the guardian deity of the village or house *(yul lha, pha'i lha)*. These guardian deities often flee the village or household they are supposed to protect due to human mistakes, ritual pollution, or the failure to perform purificatory rites. The relationship between humans and their gods is as fraught with struggle as that between the gods themselves.[12] Yet it can be managed by ritual intervention. The connection between microcosm and macrocosm relates individual and social demise. Individuals who transgress against society by excessive violence or adultery are also said to have offended the guardian deities. Rituals of purification help mend visible social relations as much as invisible cosmic ones. In the battle for cosmic order, Buddhist ritual provides peace as much as prosperity.

The discourse of purity and pollution makes meaning out of suffering by identifying a scapegoat. Monks are called in to diagnose and heal drought or disease, just as a doctor is called in to interpret an illness.[13] If the monks decide a village has lost its guardian deity *(lha)*, they may perform a ritual to call back this deity which resembles the rite to call back a sick person's individual soul *(bla)*. Misfortune is a spiritual infection which eats away at village harmony or prosperity. At the same time, the guardian deity—like the proverbial soul of the village—must be appeased and nurtured, so that it does not flee. The power to perform villagewide purifications or supplications to village gods usually falls to monks, especially if the village or its deity is in crisis. Female impurity is a common scapegoat for suspected pollution, because it draws attention away from other ritual or moral lapses. By blaming drought on women who have washed their menstrual cloths in the streambed—as did happen one year—monks downplay social disharmony or lack of devotion. The emphasis on female impurity reinforces an ambiguous moral claim over village purity and fertility. Monks reify their hold on the invisible world even as they are losing their hold on the visible one.

Pollution beliefs and practices make meaning as much as they enable human agency. By calling monks into battle against the seething realms of demons and spirits, villagers shore up the discourse and reality of ritual efficacy. In the war of village purification, monks come out as victors every time. Despite the fact that death and disease continue to occur, monks maintain their ritual prowess. The seamless law of *karma* offers an unfalsifiable account of every event even as it explains the allure of ritual activity. While even the finest ritual and most skilled monk cannot prevent the inexorable wheel of *karma,* the prospect of making merit through ritual is the most optimistic solution available. Purity and pollution are in a symbiotic relationship which require constant ritual intervention. Indeed, purification rites cannot provide permanent purification because that would make the ritual obsolete.[14] One monk alluded to the codependence between monks and demons when he noted that the West has no demons because there are no monks to feed them there. Monasteries would lose their major source of income if they abandoned purification rites. Modernizing politicians attempt to eliminate or curtail this reliance on monastic ritual in Sri Lanka and Ladakh. Yet as elsewhere in the Buddhist world, there is considerable resistance from rural monks and the populace.[15] Both merit making and purification confirm and consolidate monastic control, ritual agency, and religious sanctity.

Gender and the War of Purification

The Tibetan discourse of purity and impurity is strongly gendered. The male body is a clear template for a conception of space that is bounded and sacred. Unlike the terrifying, leaky, and ambiguous female body, the male body is both unambiguous and bounded.[16] Buddhist temples are as masculine as the primordial male Buddha they enclose. Although Tantric imagery also includes female Buddhas and feminine consorts *(yum),* it emphasizes masculine ideals of conquest, violence, and penetration. Applying the homology between the body, temple, and territory, the male body or temple appears to have subdued a landscape conceptualized as female and chaotic in local mythology.[17] The founding myths of Zangskar, Tibet, Mustang, and Bhutan each envision the native landscape as a wild demoness *(srin mo)* who was immobilized in order for the land to be civilized by heroic Buddhist saints.[18] Their violent Buddhist conversion involved building temples which nailed down the fierce demoness at specific points such as her outstretched limbs and sexual organs. These Buddhist constructions are phallic markers which pin down a primordial but feminine nature. The ongoing process of ritual violence and subdual requires an energy conceptualized as feminine as much as a masculine Buddhist civilization.

Unlike the goddess traditions of South Asia which celebrate the primordial female energy known as *shakti*, Tibetan Buddhism uses repeated symbolic violence to subdue the dangerous and primordial female energy of the landscape. This landscape is only subdued through seasonal Buddhist rites that celebrate the conquest over the feminine. Annual rites of subdual literally and figuratively re-member the demoness's dismembered parts.[19] Her female energy is recognized as a primordial energy which must be tamed but cannot be destroyed. The demoness is never killed off but merely repressed. Her chaotic form may be supine, but is hardly passive, as Gyatso (1987) notes. Monks are engaged in constant but necessary struggle with this feminine foe. Their ritual expiations, purifications, and propitiations can only expel the impure and demonic for a temporary period.

Zangskari imaginary is filled with recurring images of envious wives, crazed witches, and seething female ghosts who are subdued or deactivated by powerful priests or Tantric *siddhas*. Women are said to specialize in witchcraft and poisoning, although men can also dabble in these feminine evils. Women both represent and subvert the social ideal of reciprocity. As good hosts, they maintain society's reciprocal relations, but as dangerous poisoners or jealous witches they can destroy sociality and society itself. Yet their negative energies are rarely expelled, but are rather subdued. Unlike in Africa, where witches are routinely killed, Zangskari witches are generally not attacked or expelled from the village.[20] The discourse of exorcism is less about killing the witch than about healing the patient. The witch is made to speak through the victim and forced to retreat through symbolic violence. After she is identified, a bit of her clothing may be burnt. Yet it is the victim rather than the witch who is beaten, if the witch is intransigent and does not reveal her identity. In short, the ritual discourages the destructive paranoia which can inflame witchcraft accusations. The ideology of witchcraft rites involves a relational calculus which emphasizes remedy over destruction. The social fabric is ritually repaired by exorcisms which allude to the intersubjective nature of illness and possession. These rites also produce heroic monks who defeat female scapegoats and reestablish social harmony.

Although the Buddha admitted that women can gain enlightenment, his followers have perpetuated and produced endless rules of stratification within the monastic order. Women have been allowed to renounce homes and husbands, but only if they subordinate themselves to monks. As in caste society, where the status of the group depends on the purity of its women, the prestige of the order of monks relies on the purity of the nuns.[21] Purity and pollution practices have developed in coordination with the stratification of Buddhist society. Monks rose as nuns fell in the social ranking. The radical import of the Buddha's stance on purity was quickly diluted. The Buddha's disciples soon performed the very purification rites the Buddha had disavowed. In Zangskar today, Buddhist monks practice Buddhist equivalents of the Vedic fire sacrifice *(homa, sbyin sreg)* and ablution rite *(abhisekha, khrus)*. A plethora of rites exist to purify the body, the household, and the cosmos. The Buddhist discourse of purification reifies the very social difference that doctrines of nonduality deny. The monks' monopoly on purification has sustained their status and their power. Despite the lack of textual interdictions, nuns are rarely taught the most spectacular Tantric rites like *mandala* making or sacred dance. Although nuns do practice Tantric visualizations, they are rarely if ever called upon to perform many household and village rites.

Monks dominate the major pragmatic rites of purification at every level—body, household, territory, and temple. In times of illness, it is monks who are called to purify bodies and space with ablutions *(khrus)* and cremations. In case of wider household misfortune, monks exorcise noxious spirits through expiations *(bskang gsol)*, the tossing of firebrands *(me tho)*, ransom rites *(nam mkha', mdos, be le)*, or pacifying rites *(brgya bzhi, lha gsol)*. Only monks perform the seasonal rites of purification for the subterranean spirits and guardian deities, including the rites to bring snowfall, to protect crops, to ensure fertility, to cleanse or purify fields, to honor the village deity thrice a year, to honor ancestors, to give thanks for first fruits and harvest, and to expiate wintertime negativity. Nuns and laypeople may help monks by carrying books or relics during the springtime circumambulation of the fields, or Bumkhor *('bum skor, bum 'khor)*. Yet only monks perform the ritual ablution *(khrus)* that cleanses and appeases the spirits which secure fertility and prosperity. In Zangskar, only monks perform ritual ablutions that are a central and powerful part of many Tantric rites—consecrations, ordinations, transmissions, and empowerments—excluding nuns from many types of ritual action.[22] While nuns may perform the basic incense offering rite *(lha bsangs)* when and if no monks can be found, they tend to assist rather than supplant monks in many rites. As such, the nuns of Karsha may assist their abbot in chanting a ritual liturgy to purify the mountains and valleys *(ri khrus lung khrus)*, but they never perform the ablution itself.

The Impurity of Women

Why is it women who can cause springs to run dry but men who are called to purify them? Biology is not neutral in the Tibetan Buddhist ethos. Women's bodies are associated with the intensely polluting activities of menstruation, childbirth, miscarriage, and abortion. These biological activities rupture the symbolic boundaries between nature and culture, to use Sherry Ortner's much debated analogy. While the separation of nature and culture is hardly as universal or monolithic as once thought, the body is clearly a prime locus for this negotiation in many cultures.[23] The female body in particular mediates both natural and cultural activities, through childbirth and through nurturing. Women are bound up with natural processes of life as well as death and decay—in the form of abortion or menstruation and stillbirths. The ambiguous nature of these powers of creation is signaled by the following story about how women came to have the power of menstruation.

As Ani Yeshe, the founding nun at Karsha, once explained, it was men who had the power of menstruation at the beginning of time. She related a story about a primordial pair of humans, a brother and sister, who lived during the era of the first Buddha. Whenever the brother was menstruating, he would stride along, completely oblivious to the blood dripping down between his legs. He wore pants with an open seam between the legs like those worn by Zangskari children today while being potty trained. Although he seemed unconcerned about leaving his blood on the path, his sister would walk behind him, carefully scooping dust over every drop of blood he spilled. When the Buddha observed this human pair, he decided that the wrong sex was menstruating. He rewarded the sister's cleanliness and care by giving her the power of menstruation henceforth. And from that day onward it was women and not men who menstruated. For Yeshe, this tale was one more proof of why women were honored by the gods.

Culturally, however, women's ability to menstruate and bear children causes the stigma of impurity.[24] Menstruating women are excluded from many ritual spaces and activities, although not the mundane chores of hearth and home. Unlike upper-caste Hindu culture, which forbids women from cooking while menstruating, Zangskari women perform their regular household chores during their menstrual periods and forgo a ritual bath. Tantra reverses the conventional purity and pollution dialectic by venerating menstrual blood, albeit not in all cases.[25] In Zangskar, all women must avoid village and household altars (lha tho) and temples while menstruating. One nun explained these interdictions by saying: "Women's bodies are distasteful and give off a bad smell [when menstruating] . . . Thus, they shouldn't enter divine places." Because of a latent impurity, all women are excluded from the triannual worship of clan and village deities (pha'i lha, yul lha) and from approaching the chapels where Tantric protectors are housed. Even women who may have ceased to menstruate or are celibate remain excluded from Tantric places of power in the landscape. Whether this is due to pre-Buddhist notions of sacrality or the advent of Buddhist patriarchy is difficult to tell.[26] While the subterranean spirits ensure fertility in the form of water and snowfall, they are especially offended by female impurity. Women are excluded from chapels where Tantric protectors (mgon po, chos skyong) are worshiped for two reasons, I was told. Either the women might become sick or infertile when they confront fierce Tantric statues with their erect phalluses, or the protectors are offended through being contaminated by women. In sum, women are as much in need of protection as they are a danger against which monks seek protection.

Childbirth transforms both the mother and her newborn into social outcastes, who are confined in order to avoid polluting the village space. The postbirth seclusion ('bang ba) can last between a week and a month, depending on the village deity. The mother must stay inside the house and stoop when passing a window that faces the village altar or temple. Inside the house, she must avoid the hearth and eats from a separate cup and plate. In extreme cases, she may be a virtual prisoner in her room, where she is passed food and drink through the door. The husband or a male affine who cuts the umbilical cord is the only other person who may face some ritual seclusion. The husband's seclusion is less stringent; he can roam outside the house but must avoid village altars, springs, monasteries, and festivals where he might drink from and pollute a common cup. The rules of male seclusion are rarely enforced in urban areas or in the wintertime, when the subterranean spirits are asleep. In the villages of Zangla and Pishu where drought is common and local spirits are held to be especially finicky, female seclusion is extended up to a month, while the husband is barred from crossing any major irrigation leats *(ma yur)* for one week after the birth.

The house itself becomes polluted during the seclusion period, and other villagers—except clan members—avoid eating there. One week after the birth, the household itself can reopen its doors and resume reciprocal relations. It will invite a monk to perform a purification rite using juniper incense *(bsangs)* at the household altar, the offering room, the hearth, and perhaps the village altar.[27] In the case of an illegitimate birth, an additional purification must be held at the village altar. The timing, frequency, and location of subsequent purification rites during the first month after the birth depend on the deity being propitiated. These purifications include an offering of juniper incense and a propitiatory prayer *(lha bsangs)* for local and monastic protectors.[28]

Pollution rules mark out who comes under the protection of a village or clan deity. Strangers who don't belong to a village or those individuals who no longer belong by virtue of marriage are especially offensive to village or household deities. A visiting Nepalese couple in Karsha could not remain with their conservative host after the wife became pregnant, because of their host's clan deity *(pha'i lha)*. When they moved to a house owned by a more progressive local official *(naib tehsildar)*, they were thrown out once again. The official's conservative wife insisted that the Nepalese couple move to the unheated health clinic in Padum in the dead of winter rather than risk polluting her household deity. Married women, who are believed to have forsaken the protection of their natal guardian deities, must take care not to offend them. If married women return to give birth in their natal home, they may face the wrath of their natal guardian deity in the form of miscarriage or other complications. These explanations elide the reasons that a married woman may return home to give birth, such as the sadness of her husband's affair or other marital woes.

While women are connected with birth, they are excluded from the central rites of death. Only men of the clan *(pha spun)* are supposed to minister to the corpse by washing and rubbing it with butter, binding it into a fetal position, and wrapping it in a white shroud on the second day after death. Only monks and never nuns can perform the ritual *(pho ba)* which enables the soul to leave the body, and the funerary prayers *(cho ga)* which transfer merit to the deceased. Although many women assist the household in feeding the mourners—who are often women—men perform most ritual duties associated with the corpse. The cremation itself—held on the fourth day after death—is attended by monks and laymen alone. On the morning of the cremation, a male clan member carries a basket of the deceased's clothes to the nearest monastery with a willow frond or "life wood" *(srog shing)*. The abbot burns this frond to extinguish the deceased's connection with the world. The corpse becomes a ritual vessel *(bum pa)* as it is dressed in a Five Buddha crown *(rgyal ba rigs lnga)*, ritual topknot, and silk cape. When the corpse is carried outside the house, all family members—including women—prostrate and circumambulate the basket three times. The assembly of monks as well as a host of laymen proceed with the corpse to the cremation ground. The corpse is carried by clan members, who are followed by a procession of village laymen carrying wood for the cremation pyre and holding a white sheet to prevent the village deity from being polluted by a view of the corpse. Once the corpse is placed on the pyre, the assembly of monks purifies the corpse by offering prayers and tossing mustard seeds *(yungs dkar)*. Most of the younger monks and laymen then return to the village, while the senior officiants stay behind to perform the burnt offering *(sbyin sreg)* that dissolves the corpse into the five purified elements from which it arose—air, fire, water, earth, metal.[29]

Before or after the cremation, several monks perform an abbreviated *g.yang 'gugs* ritual to ensure that the household prosperity does not depart with the corpse. Women, though absent from the cremation, do attend the funerary feast which is cooked outside and consumed outside the deceased's house on the day of cremation. One member of every household and the entire assemblies of both monastery and nunnery are invited to partake of this feast. The monks and nuns chant prayers on behalf of the deceased, while laymen gather to read a bit of the Diamond Sutra or the condensed Perfection of Wisdom Sutra. A traditional meal of wheat bread, barley dough *(pa ba)*, and melted butter is served, of which a symbolic portion is fed to the hungry ghosts and the deceased, who remains in the intermediary zone *(bar do)* before rebirth. The meal is consumed entirely outside the house, and any remains are fed to invisible and visible scavengers. Finally, select clothes and utensils of the deceased are auctioned off to the monks and nuns, who divide the proceeds of the auction among themselves. A few monks will remain at the house to perform rites transferring merit to the deceased for the next few days, while the household enters a period of death defilement *(ro nga)* and seclusion. The spouse of the deceased is secluded for a week, until a purification ritual of juniper incense is held which allows the household to resume its normal intercourse.

The Woeful Body: Sex and Sin

The female body is more than impure; it is a calamity and a punishment. The Tibetan terms for woman, "lower rebirth" *(skye dman)* or "black one" *(nag mo)*, make explicit her lower or stained status. The first term literally implies that women are lower than men in the hierarchy of possible rebirth. In this theory, women need more merit than men because they are more likely to fall into a lower rebirth—as an animal—in their next lifetime. This view suspends women between the realms of culture and nature, nicely illustrating Ortner's (1974) famous argument about women occupying a mediating position between nature and culture. Another word in the Tibetan lexicon reinforces the conception that women are somehow less than human or at least not fully grown. The word for man, *skyes pa*, which literally means "birth," also means "adult" or "growth." These semantics suggest that women are somehow a lesser or not fully grown rebirth, which is illustrated by the Tibetan proverb that women are at least seven lifetimes behind men.

If the female body is seen as a punishment for previous misdeeds, its specific forms of suffering must be endured without complaint. My informants described the female body as polluted *(grib can)* because it suffers childbirth and menstruation. It is miserable or woeful *(lan chag can)* because it is more vulnerable to rape and adultery. Finally, it is called sinful *(sdig pa can)* because women have more desire. These terms reflect a direct relationship between the polluted female body and its miserable state. Menstruation, literally "body breaking down" *(lus zhigs byes)*, suggests an image of the female body as in a constant state of disrepair. Whether menstruating, giving birth, or delivering miscarriages, the female body is an enduring source of pain and misery. The multiple associations of the Tibetan term for woeful—which include destiny, disaster, misfortune, adversity, calamity, punishment, unlucky accident, and retribution— illustrate the overdetermined view of the female body.

In the words of Kisagotami, one of the Buddha's early female disciples *(theri)* to gain liberation,

The Guide of a restless,
passionate humanity has said—
to be a woman is to suffer.[30]

The local discourse about women's bodies being a locus of suffering is supported by medical and sociological evidence. The Buddhist aversion to abortion and the scarcity of contraceptives results in a surfeit of pregnancies. In some rural regions of Zangskar, women average eleven pregnancies, and 90 percent of women suffer from anemia. Contraception is underutilized in urban areas and nonexistent in the most rural and remote locations. Although there has been some improvement in women's health services, infant and maternal mortality rates remain shockingly high. In local idiom, men are said to have "hardened bodies" (lus bsran te) which have more endurance and greater imperviousness to illness. As one informant said, "men just don't seem to die." The female body is a locus of suffering because it perpetuates anguish and attachment. As one nun explained, "motherhood always involves suffering. First there is pregnancy, then miscarriage, or childbirth. The child may be stillborn or it may die soon after birth. Even if it lives, it causes its mother pain by abandoning her." Buddhist doctrine makes birth the first stage in the Twelve Stages of Dependent Origination (rten 'brel bcu gnyis), which traps sentient beings in the cycle of suffering. Mothers directly contribute to the endless cycle of suffering known as samsara by producing another sentient being who experiences and perpetuates suffering. At the same time, because the human rebirth is so precious and rare, abortion is usually discouraged. Ironically, motherhood is a vehicle of pain and liberation. The Dalai Lama has noted that humans learn compassion experientially—at the mother's breast—rather than intellectually. Mothers exemplify perfectly detached compassion because they give of themselves without demanding much in return. As such, mothers are a powerful symbol of compassion in Tibetan Buddhism.[31] Monks often explain that since all beings have been one's mother in a prior life due to the endless cycling of birth and rebirth, all deserve the same love owed to one's mother.

Women well versed in Buddhist doctrine might explain that although women are lesser rebirths, they can excel in making merit through generosity. Garkyid's mother explained that women can excel at daily generosity (sbyin pa) by giving alms or hosting strangers, even though men can read texts and build temples. Ani Yeshe explained that laywomen who learn to offer the best food they have even if it is their last morsel practice true detachment. Ani Yeshe and Ani Putid both told me about the legendary tale of Lingzed Choskid, who was in hell when a monk named Lama Chozang came to rescue people out of hell. Having been granted his wish that people who had a previous connection with him could escape, Chozang opened the doors of hell wide to let everyone escape. Yet only women managed to escape, while the men were all stopped by guards or trampled underfoot. In the end, not a single man escaped; only women escaped because they had offered the monk alms in the past. The Buddha's own life story mentions that the laywoman Sujata—who brought him a meal of milk-rice after his austerities—later becomes foremost among women who take refuge in his precepts.

Informants disagreed about whether men or women accumulate more demerit. Some insisted that men were less sinful than women in spite of the fact that men butchered, killed, and fought. One informant noted that while men do the actual butchering it is women who force them to kill when they say "there is no meat in the house." Such impeccable Buddhist logic can also justify men who kill openly, but atone for their deeds, as opposed to women who kill secretly and without remorse using poison or witchcraft. When I asked about the unspeakable sins committed during warfare, I was told that violence may be justified to save Buddhism from destruction. Some villagers assumed that if men sin, it must be for a good cause, while women sin only for themselves. Others admitted that men are more liable to anger and abuse. In this economy of merit, women—who have less merit—are urged to perform private acts of merit like praying, prostrating, spinning prayer wheels, and fasting, while men, who already have merit, can generate even more permanent sources of merit by building religious constructions or making endowments that will outlast their death.[32] I was told that women participated in the fasting rite far more than men did, because women are in need of both merit and purification. Most of the women I interviewed at several fasting rites explicitly noted that they fasted to gain a male body in their next rebirth. The perspective that the female body is a punishment was clearly expressed by one female informant:

Oh yes, women are sinful and impure. We are more miserable than men because, as we say, wherever you look, men seem to be having a better time than women. Most men work less than women do, the men's work is easier, and men can spend all day sleeping while women hardly get a chance to rest for an instant. We women have to cook the meals, do all the housework, wash clothes and things, take care of the kids, and then go to the fields, and again in the evening cook another meal. We women are just plain unlucky; because as they say we still have not removed prior bad *karma*.

Fear of Females and Fairies

Women are dangerous and polluted because of their potent sexuality. The fear of female sexuality appears in many sources, including a Tibetan myth of origins. This myth explains that a mountain ogress, who was an incarnation of the female *bodhisattva* Tara, who vowed to take rebirth only in the female form, came to the Tibetan plateau in search of a mate. Feeling compassion for the lonely ogress, the *bodhisattva* Chenrezig (Avalokitesvara) took incarnation as a monkey and married the ogress. They had six children, whose descendants became the six original clans of Tibet. These descendants took human form gradually, though with serious consequences for the two genders. Men, who take after Avalokitesvara, have inherited mercy, intelligence, and a calm, judicious nature. Women, who take after the ogress, inherited lust, hatred, and greed as well as laughter, courage, and restlessness.[33] Tibetan refugees who were interviewed about this myth explained that women most resemble the ogress—impetuous, violent, witchlike—while men have inherited the cleverness of the monkey. In Zangskar, women are said to be plagued by jealousy, greed, anger, and desire, while men are more driven by ambition, logic, and power. In the local vernacular, men have "big hearts" *(snying chen mo)*, while women have "small hearts" *(snying chung)*.[34] Women are said to be fearful, bashful, and wicked, while men are brave, brash, and good.

A Zanskari proverb about why polyandry is preferable to polygyny illustrates the belief that women have more desire or passion than men:

> A husband with two wives burns like wood on the funeral pyre,
> A woman with two husbands is like a wild rose blossom.

The saying also suggests that women's uncontrollable desires sap male strength. Women are seen as insatiable sexual predators who can drain the men they arouse. One monk explained that women are fierce *(srong can)* and hot *(tshad can)* like demons and the desert. A layperson explained that a woman's sexuality can deplete a man's life force or dry up his lungs *(lo'a skam po 'gyur).* Cultural idiom suggests that women initiate many sexual dalliances, while reality shows men to be the sexual predators in most cases. Yet male fantasies are most vividly expressed in a mysterious belief in beautiful fairies or *mämo (sman mo)* whose voracious sexual appetites bring disease or destruction. Living on distant glaciers, these fairies are intensely beautiful women who seduce unwary men. Known for their insatiable sexual hunger and tight vaginas, they are forever on the lookout for human husbands. Although they are ravishing, it is unwise to unite with these mämo. Ani Yeshe reports what she has heard:

> The *mämo* live in houses just like people, have children, and keep ibex instead of goats and sheep. They milk them each day after letting them out to the highest pastures just below the snow fields. This is why when we see a herd of ibex come down to a village, we always suspect that a *mämo* must be nearby. I wonder if they have fields . . . ? They like salt just like ibex, but if they lick you, you will get sick.[35]

Men who succumb to the sexual advances of the *mämo* may become ill, go mad, or die if they lose enough of their life force *(srog).* Geshe Ngawang Tharpa once told me a tale he had heard in Ichar village. A young man, who had gone out hunting alone, had killed an ibex. While returning to the village, carrying the ibex upon his back, the hunter met a woman who looked just like his wife, although she was a *mämo* in disguise. Exhausted from his long day hunting, the hunter put down his load. Wordlessly, the woman picked up the ibex, put it in her basket, and set off behind the hunter, who sped off in the darkening gloom down the precipitous trail. After marching silently along for some time, they got to the outskirts of the village. The sound of the dogs barking frightened the fairy, who dropped her load and fled. When the hunter heard the thud of the ibex hitting the ground, he turned and was surprised to find himself alone. He called out for his "wife," but got no answer. When he reached the kitchen, he berated his wife for disappearing so suddenly. She looked at him in surprise and replied that she'd been home all day. He said no more, but fell slightly ill the next day.

The abbot who told me this story compared the fairies with visions of hidden places *(sbas yul)* that only appear to highly realized individuals. The Karsha Lonpo explained that the fairies were simply a trick of the mind, like mirages or a lustful fantasy. Ani Yeshe gave a more traditional gloss when she said that meeting a *mämo* is like meeting a witch or a demon—a sign of impending misfortune or bad luck.[36] Urban tales from Ladakh tell of people being lost for days who are found unconscious and prone, with their mouths full of silt, but no recollection of meeting the *mämo*.[37] Those who boast about meeting such a fairy are said to flirt with death. There was a tale about a man from Kazar village who went to collect dung on the upper pastures when he saw a woman in the streambed, washing wool. He called out, but she seemed not to hear him. When he returned and told people what he'd seen, someone died in his household. Only powerful Tantric saints have enough ritual power *(dbang)* to overcome the advances of the *mämo*. There is a tale of a meditator who once lived in the now ruined "northern temple" *(byang dgon pa)* near Karsha. He was visited daily by *mämo* bringing gifts of milk, yogurt, and dung. Yet he always placed his rosary over the breads outside his hut at night to prevent them from being stolen.

The tales of a dangerous female sexuality occur across South and Central Asia. Libidinal fantasies of fairies populate myths found in a broad mountainous arc stretching from the Hindu Kush in Pakistan through the Himalayas of India, Nepal, and Bhutan. In the Hindu Kush, the Kalash people have tales of *succhi,* fierce fairies who guard wild sheep and ibex on the mountain summits.[38] If properly propitiated with juniper incense and celibacy on the night before the hunt, the fairies assist hunters by "allowing" them to kill ibex and giving them supernatural powers. Hunters who fail to make the offerings have accidents or return empty-handed. In Ladakh, the hunters who neglect offerings to the *mämo* see the prey dissolve before their eyes and turn into beautiful women.[39] Further east, in Burma, a classical text notes that a woman's libido is eight times as strong as a man's.[40]

Sex is draining in both Eastern and Western folklore. The American football player, the Kalash hunter, and the Vedic priest all dedicate themselves to celibacy before the Big Game, Big Hunt, or Big Sacrifice. This pervasive fear is a hidden tribute to a powerful female sexuality. The qualities assigned to female fluids—life giving as well as defiling—extend the ambiguous nature of female sexuality.[41] In Hindu culture, Puranic sources are replete with foreboding about the disastrous consequences of uncontrolled female sexuality *(shakti)* or lust *(kama)*. Dangerous or unhealthy sexual liaisons are ones in which the woman might be more lustful or potent than the man. Men who partake of this danger by having sex with younger women even court illness or death. The *Kama Sutra* offers women agency as initiators of sexual advances, but it, too, carefully preserves rather than ruptures social boundaries.[42] The more conservative or Brahmanic discourses perpetuate the threat of sex which always includes the risk of betrayal. Hindu myth is replete with paradoxical images of female sexuality. Goddesses can be both dangerous and life giving, wrathful and peaceful, subdued or terrifying.[43] In classic myth and images, consorts are usually subordinated to their male counterpart—Sita/Ram, Laxmi/Vishnu, Saraswati/Brahma, and Radha/Krishna. Tantric imagery reverses the position in placing Parvati as Kali on top of Shiva, or displaying the wrathful Durga in the act of destruction or conquest. Goddesses can be both erotic temptress or devouring mother, but their uncontrolled energies are terrifying to behold.

South Asian religions have allowed women to attain sanctity but not purity. Buddhist Tantra reproduces social hierarchy and difference. Tantric doctrine and imagery may valorize the female, but Tantric practice retains a puritan aversion to impurity. Although some Tantric doctrines and iconography appear to reverse the dominance of the male, much Tantric ritual practice reasserts difference. Despite doctrinal allusions about the ultimate need to abandon distinctions like male and female, Tantric rituals of purification and expiation just examined repeatedly reassert the division between monks and nuns. The fire of asceticism may burn off temporary pollution, but it cannot erase the permanent stigmata of female impurity. If this is true, how can nuns gain enlightenment?

7

Can Nuns Gain Enlightenment?

Under a colorful Tibetan tent in New Delhi on the eve of the millennium, I finally was able to ask the Dalai Lama if women could gain enlightenment. Unlike the pushy mobs of dharma seekers I'd encountered in New York or Boston, the crowd in Delhi appeared calm, almost gentle. The slow passage of people through the unplugged metal detectors that seemed to be serving merely a decorative function betrayed the importance of the speaker. As the cymbals and quavering reeds heralded the Dalai Lama's arrival, the crowd of Tibetans, Indians, and foreigners got to its feet. When Tendzin Gyatso appeared to discuss his most recent book, exuding his usual irrepressible mirth, he seemed almost ordinary. Yet the automatic response of the Tibetans to his entrance—three rapid prostrations that the crowd performed as a wave—reminded me that he was a living incarnation of Tibet's patron deity, Avalokitesvara. The Dalai Lama spoke that night of the need for compassion and peace at the close of a turbulent and violent millennium. Deftly alluding to the global paranoia about computer failures, he assured his audience that the millennium was nothing but an elaborately wrapped parcel, which would prove—when unwrapped—to be empty. He deflated capitalist anxiety while offering the elliptical lure of emptiness. During the question period at the end of his talk, I had the long-awaited chance to ask him: "Is it possible to gain enlightenment in the female body?" When he heard the question, he began to chuckle before responding with enthusiasm. Of course women can gain enlightenment, he said emphatically, but admitted that not every Buddhist school had explained this clearly. The Dalai Lama allowed that each of the three major vehicles (*yana*) of Buddhism had responded differently to this issue. He noted that the earliest Hinayana teachings gave women rather short shrift, even as subsequent Mahayana teachings accorded women a somewhat better status.[1] His own Vajrayana school had the best record because it used gender as a tool on the path to enlightenment. He added that the highest yoga Tantras made use of the distinction between male and female to express qualities of enlightenment rather than innate characteristics.

The Dalai Lama's response is only the most recent in a debate that goes back to the Buddha himself. Yet the Buddha's words were hardly definitive in a conversation that has persisted over two millennia. While scholars of every era have wrestled with the issue of gender and enlightenment, they have rarely come to agreement. Buddhist literature illustrates a myriad of views on the female body, but little consensus. This body has been the site of repression, aggression, and attraction in every era, by texts which treat the very same body with aversion and then awe, desire then disgust. Yet the very evidence of this ongoing debate about the female body suggests that gender is hardly irrelevant to the question of enlightenment.

Scholars have spilt much ink over the question of whether misogyny has been rising or declining over the centuries. Contrary to Bernard Faure's (2003) most recent assertion that there is a clear consensus that the trajectory has been one of progress, there have been impassioned defenses as well as critiques of every era. Although some have documented an early inclusiveness giving way to institutional androcentrism, others have found the Mahayana a liberating rebuttal to early bouts of misogyny.[2] Nineteenth- and early-twentieth-century feminists were overly optimistic about the Buddha's radical decision to invite women into his monastic order. Later scholars corrected this initial euphoria by calling attention to the overt misogyny and androcentrism which pervades Pali texts and Mahayana literature.[3] Overall, a split remains between those who seek to deconstruct Buddhism for its innate sexism and those who search to recuperate its most usable aspect. This book is an effort to parse a middle way between a blind optimism and the defeatist attack. It does not shy away from identifying sexism in practice yet it refuses to reduce those same practices into a static or simplistic scapegoat. Rather than surveying the Buddhist literary canon as most of the previous scholarship has, I consider Buddhist monastic practices in Zangskar. These Tantric practices are a reflection of local culture as well as broader Indian and Tibetan contexts.

Tantra offers one of the most liberating ideologies found within Buddhism. Yet its practices have reified the social hierarchy and exclusion within the monastic setting. Although dedicated to antinomian and anti-authoritarian goals, Tantra reproduces social and symbolic difference on many levels. Coming from a peripatetic background, Tantra was a threat before it was co-opted by the monastic establishment. As Onians (2003) notes, the pursuit of a single norm—the rejection of all norms—was soon institutionalized within the monastic setting. The use of male and female to represent essentially perfected qualities has not always liberated nuns in the Tibetan monastic tradition. Although Tantric iconography celebrates symbols of male and female, its ritual practices continue to exclude nuns in Zangskar as elsewhere in the Himalayas. Monks in Zangskar have discarded Tantra's liberatory theory of gender in favor of its pragmatic and esoteric techniques for a ritual monopoly. In the Gelug nunneries and monasteries of Zangskar, Tantra is often used in the service of purification, protection, and expiation. Zangskari monks and nuns have institutionalized the very practices the first Tantric adepts sought to overcome.

Tantra and Women

What is the use of austerities?
What is the use of going on pilgrimage?
Is release achieved by bathing in water? . . .
Without meditating, without renouncing the world,
One may stay at home in the company of one's wife.
If it's already manifest, what's the use of meditation?
And if it is hidden, one is just measuring darkness . . .
I have visited in my wanderings shrines and other places of pilgrimage,
But I have not seen another shrine blissful like my own body.[4]

This ninth-century poem by the Tantric saint *(siddha)* Saraha represents a new strain of Buddhist practices known collectively as Tantra. Strictly speaking, Tantra is the English word used to refer to a tradition that Sanskrit texts knew as Vajrayana, Mantrayana, or Mantramahayana. Intellectually, these movements extend the Mahayana critique of the Hinayana in applying a discourse about the limits of even the Mahayana. Socially and historically, the practices we now label Buddhist Tantra are believed to have flourished on the margins of the Indian subcontinent—Kashmir, Uddiyana, Bengal, Assam—between the eighth and twelfth centuries. Some scholars have characterized Tantra as a monstrous inversion heralding the inevitable decline of Buddhism in its Indian homeland. Others have viewed Tantra as a final Buddhist innovation along India's frontiers which only reached its culmination inside Tibet.[5] Although we know relatively little about Tantra's social sphere, its radical techniques suggest open contempt for the arrogant scholasticism and sexism of monastic Buddhism. If we read against the grain of apparently elitist texts, Tantra appeared to embrace a range of ritual and symbolic energies. The texts offer insight into popular voices and vocations, when its saints become wine sellers, arrow makers, and fishmongers in order to gain insight.

Known as the "path of no meditation," Tantra rejects the meditator's obsessions with gradual purification. Its adherents seek awakening in the midst of everyday life, both within and without the confines of the monastery. Taking Nagarjuna's insistence that there is no distinction between *samsara* and *nirvana* to its logical conclusion, Tantric ideology recommends an ethics which claims to lie beyond the distinctions of pure and impure.[6] What earlier texts had defined as conditioned, impure, or imperfect, Tantric texts recognize as unconditioned, luminous, and perfect. Seeing all things—including male and female, as well as sex and celibacy—without discrimination opens a Pandora's box of possible techniques. The very discipline and discrimination which had aided the disciple on the path toward enlightenment now appear as obstructions. The Tantric ethos applied the underlying Mahayana ideals of compassion, wisdom, and purification to a broader conception of liberation. As the liberation of others took precedence over the liberation of the self, so too transgressive actions which might appear harmful to the self could be validated if they benefited others.

From the *Cittavisuddhiprakarama,* a Tantric text:

> Love, enjoyed by the ignorant, becomes bondage.
> That very same love, tasted by one with understanding,
> Brings liberation.[7]

Physical desire is one of many forbidden attitudes to become the vehicle and ground for Tantric awakening. Tantra harnesses powerful energies, like desire and aggression, which are rejected in Hinayana and Mahayana ideologies. It relies on esoteric practices of the body *(mudra),* speech *(mantra),* and mind *(sadhana)* to construct and deconstruct perfected reality. Ritualized bodily gestures or *mudra* symbolize deeper philosophical and physical goals. The repetitious recitations offer a means of purification and access to protective and divine powers. Applying Vedic ideas about ritual efficacy, Tantric mantras call forth the very reality they invoke.[8] Meditations or "means of attainment" *(sadhana)* involve the creation and dissolution of elaborate universes. These mental visualizations allow the devotee to project or become a perfected expression of enlightened awareness. Such meditations realize "a non-duality of action and awareness" by fusing the path with the goal of the practice.[9] The practitioner generates and becomes the deity and its perfected qualities, which are invoked by the visualization. Such Tantric practices are supposed to break down the conventional duality of subject and object, worshiper and worshiped.

From the *Candamaharosana Tantra:*

> The man [sees] the woman as a goddess,
> The woman [sees] the man as a god.
> By joining the diamond scepter and the lotus,
> They should make offerings to each other.
> There is no worship apart from this.[10]

The union of the diamond and lotus is a multivalent symbol. It can signal ritualized intercourse or other abstractions such as the union of self and other, or the fusion of method and wisdom. The momentary bliss of sexual union is a means for experiencing nonduality and interdependence. The ritual route to nondual awareness combines emptiness and compassion through the radical unification of opposites rather than through a false suppression of negatives. Tantra valorizes many actions explicitly forbidden by the precepts held by Buddhist laypeople and monastics. Just as the Buddha prescribed meditations on human corpses to instill revulsion for the human body, Tantric initiations *(abhisekha)* use sex as a tool of awareness. Tantric practices take experience to be the ground of knowledge. In fighting fire with fire, or using passion to counter pleasure, Tantra is often misunderstood. Its transgressions are intended as a means of subverting false or rigid discrimination. By undoing the simplistic distinction between right and wrong, Tantric practitioners seek a subtle immanence of enlightenment. Tantric teachers advocate lurid or dangerous practices as the speedy path to enlightenment. At the same time, they reject the slow or gradual path to perfection and its attendant disparagement of women.

From the *Candamaharosana Tantra:*

In all the discourses and Abhidharma texts, women are disparaged,
Spoken for the sake of disciples of various capacities—

> The real truth is taught secretly . . .
> 'Why do the early disciples and others slander women?'
> The Lord answered: 'That is common to the early disciples and others
> Who live in the realm of desire,
> Not knowing the path of liberation
> That relies on women and bestows everything.'[11]

Tantra urges its practitioners to see the goddess in every mortal woman. Although earlier scholars read Tantra as having exploited women with shameful sexual practices, recent scholarship restores female agency to these texts.[12] This re-reading sees women less as passive subjects than as active agents who require male supplication, if not subordination. Unlike goddesses who changed their female form in prior Mahayana texts, Tantric heroines did not have to become male but could use males on the path to liberation. The practice of male abjection was supposed to undo a corrosive male ego. Indian saints like Tilopa, Atisa, and Naropa each received some of their most valuable teachings when they humbled themselves to divine female figures known as *dakini*. Appearing in disguise as hags and lower-caste women, these teachers outwit Tantric adepts too proud to see such unlikely females as a source of teaching. They offer a telling antidote against the adept's lingering androcentricism.

> The male aspirant, with all his possessions,
> Should worship the female partner.
> This worship is supreme, but
> If he is scornful, he will surely burn [in hell].[13]

Although the *dakini* rose to prominence in Tantra, her imagery has less to do with a valorization of the female than with the valorization of emptiness. Some have regarded her as a Jungian anima for the male meditator; others see her as a valorization of female agency.[14] Yet strictly speaking the *dakini* represents ultimate nonduality or emptiness. The Sanskrit term *dakini* is translated into Tibetan as a "female being moving through space, covering everything" *(nam mkha'i khams su khyab par 'gro ma)* usually shortened to "female sky goer" *(mkha' 'gro ma)*. This definition exemplifies the nonduality of space which encompasses two endpoints of a journey as well as all the points in between. She represents many of the contradictory aspects of space *(nam mkha')* and emptiness *(stong pa nyid)*, which are physically infinite but conceptually singular. Doctrinally, she stands for the generative nature of emptiness, which is the womb or matrix of enlightenment. She also exemplifies the primordial purity and freedom of non-duality. Iconographically, she is often portrayed as a naked woman, holding aloft a skull filled with blood, often at a cremation ground or other meditation site. Her naked female body signifies an unmediated and blissful experience of emptiness. As Padmasambhava explained to his consort, Yeshe Tsogyal:

> The basis for realizing enlightenment is a human body.
> Male or female—there is no great difference.
> But if she develops the mind bent on enlightenment,
> The woman's body is better.[15]

Tantra seems to have been most liberating for women outside the monastic realm. In Tibetan literature, women were more likely to find enlightenment outside the monastic walls than inside them. A wide range of liberation stories *(rnam 'thar)* celebrate women who escaped or avoided monastic celibacy.[16] Machig Labdron only achieves success after abandoning her monastic vows. Both Yeshe Tsogyal and Nangsa Obum achieve their liberation as sexual consorts outside the lawful gaze of the monastery. Princess Mandarava achieved enlightenment when she abandoned her ordination vows and became Padmasambhava's consort. For each of these women, monasticism, like marriage, was a constraint on female spirituality. Although Tantric practices may encourage male supplication, society does not. As such, most Tantric heroines struggled against patriarchy and other social norms. As one of Tibet's most famous female adepts, Yeshe Tsogyal, explains:

> I am a woman—I have little power to resist danger.
> Because of my inferior birth, everyone attacks me.
> If I go as a beggar, dogs attack me.
> If I have great wealth and food, bandits attack me.
> If I do a great deal, the locals attack me.
> If I do nothing, the gossips attack me.
> If anything goes wrong, they all attack me.
> Whatever I do, I have no chance for happiness.
> Because I am a woman, it is hard to follow the Dharma.
> It is hard even to stay alive![17]

Despite the power of its poetry and its imagery, the Tantra practiced in monasteries today does little to promote female agency. While Tibetan Tantra bridges the individual and the collective, the shamanic and the scholastic, its practices have barely eroded the hierarchy between monks and nuns.[18] Although all major Tibetan schools draw on Tantric sources, each addresses the contradiction between Tantric nonduality and monastic hierarchy in its own fashion. The fifteenth-century founder of the Gelugpa school, Tsongkshapa, favors a conservative approach to Tantric sex in his essay on the gradual stages of moral purification. Yet even he notes that it is exceedingly difficult to gain enlightenment without Tantric union. Later commentators observed that it is possible to maintain monastic vows by privileging subtle or symbolic union over gross or physical union. Sex rather than the liberation of both male and female became a central scholastic topic. Tsongkhapa's (2000) text on the graduated path simply reified the subordination of female to male. Its chapters on *karma*, as noted, specify the female body as undesirable and of lesser merit. The monks and nuns who practice Tantric meditations in Zangskar today use its symbolic techniques daily in their ritual and meditative practices. However, the radical import of these symbols has been lost in the pragmatic rites of propitiation and expiation which the symbols fuel. These ritual practices have used purification as a means to acquire prosperity, while overlooking ongoing gender inequalities.

Tantric Practices in Zangskar

Most of the nuns in Karsha have been initiated into the highest yoga Tantra of Vajrayogini. Although they meditate and visualize the female form of their personal protector *(yi dam)* every evening, they rarely speak explicitly of her female imagery. Although laywomen know that Vajrayogini is the main protective deity *(chos skyong)* at the nunnery, they seek out little special ritual attention from her. Indeed, laywomen were more likely to visit the nunnery to request ritual performances for a mundane reason, such as a kinship bond, rather than because of the female protector. In the case of fertility issues, laywomen look for blessings *(byin rlabs)* and power *(dbang)* from famous monks or by circumambulating sites associated with magical power.[19] When I questioned nuns directly about the female iconography of *dakini* more generally, nuns referred me to monks. Monks often emphasized the abstract qualities of emptiness and compassion rather than the *dakini*'s female form, as Simmer-Brown (2001) confirmed in urban Tibetan settings. The nuns' reticence may have been due to the fact that I had not taken the Vajrayogini empowerment. Vajrayogini was usually placed alongside the standard Gelug trinity of Tantric meditational deities, Vajra Bhairava *('jigs byed)*, Guhyasamaja *(sangs ba 'dus pa)*, and Chakrasamvara *(bde mchog)*. Given that Tantra is an ideology which aims to overcome gender duality, it was logical for monks not to dwell on Vajrayogini's female form.

The esoteric path of Tantra demands physical as well as mental discipline. The initiate first encounters the body, speech, and mind of his or her meditation deity during Tantric empowerments *(dbang)*. Ani Yeshe recalls that when she took the Vajrayogini empowerment, she was required to swallow a flaming barley ball *(ting lo)* in order to acquaint herself with the lightning dance of this female Buddha. The visual instructions for meditating on this deity make reference to the swallowing of this lightning-like deity:

From the heart of the Venerable Vajrayogini before me comes a similar Venerable Vajrayogini, the size of only a thumb. She enters through my mouth and dances like lightning from the crown of my head to the soles of my feet. Finally, she dissolves into the letter Bam at my navel. This completely transforms and there arises an eight petaled lotus of various colors with a sun Mandala at its center. Upon this arises Venerable Vajrayogini. Her outstretched left leg treads on the breast of red Kalarati. Her bent left leg treads on the head of the black Bhairava, which is bent backwards. She has a red-colored body which shines with a brilliance like that of the fire of the aeon. She has one face, two hands, and three eyes looking towards the Pure Land of the Dakinis. Her right hand, outstretched and pointing downward, holds a curved knife marked with a Vajra. Her left hand holds up a skullcap filled with blood which she partakes of with her upturned mouth.[20]

In their daily meditations, Karsha nuns visualize Vajrayogini's terrifying skullcap as a symbol for the primordial clarity of the mind, while the polluted substances in the skullcap are imagined as divine nectar. Her female characteristics are but another trap of the duality they are trying to transcend. Durkheim once said that asceticism "is a necessary school where men form and temper themselves, and acquire the qualities of disinterestedness and endurance without which there would be no religion."[21] Tantric exercises known as preliminary practices *(sngo 'gro)* literally write the abstract truths of suffering on the human body. These practices—which every nun undergoes as part of her training in asceticism—involve solitary confinement, continual chanting, and constant visualizations. Preliminary practices prepare nuns for further Tantric initiations by disciplining body, speech, and mind. Asceticism empties and purifies the three doors of perception from distractions or obscurations. The one-pointed concentration on the breath, the voice, and the image helps transcend the distinction between pain and pleasure. Although the bodily scars of repeated prostrations heal quite quickly, the underlying mental effects of the ritual endure. These rigors prepare nuns for the psychological and physical intensity of lifelong celibacy. To abandon sexual intimacy, marital companionship, and the comfort of producing children requires considerable fortitude. The preliminary practices which nuns undergo after joining the assembly are only a foretaste of their lifelong bodily mortifications. They prepare the self to dedicate its own suffering to the wider universe of suffering.

"But abstinences and privations," Durkheim comments, "do not come without suffering. We hold to the profane world by all the fibres of our flesh . . . So we cannot detach ourselves from it without doing violence to our nature and without painfully wounding our instincts."[22] For the Buddha, asceticism was a means, rather than an end in itself. Nuns talk about their ascetic experiences in a manner not unlike athletes talking about training routines. Yet pedagogic issues are more at stake than personal pride. The oldest nun at Karsha, Ani Yeshe, once displayed the full-length prostrations (rgyang phyag) she had performed during her first retreat some forty years earlier. With surprising nimbleness for someone over seventy, she leapt off her cushion and threw her full body down, sliding her hands along the floor until her arms were fully extended above her head. She grimaced and said she was getting too old for this sort of thing as she pushed herself back up on her knees. Yet she could recall her former sensations and feelings as if they had occurred yesterday. She explained how her elbows, palms, and knees were rubbed raw during her repeated prostrations years ago. She told us that the blood stains had dotted her freshly plastered floor, because she had refused to wear the customary leather aprons and wooden forearm shields that many Tibetans wear while doing preliminary practices. She reported the same experience as other nuns: "Although I felt pain at first, after a while I didn't even notice the bleeding anymore." Yeshe's reminiscences of her pain were not intended as exaggerated bravado. They reminded younger nuns what is required to train in the arts of detachment.

Ascetic training, including the preliminary practices, develops a corporal habitus of detachment. Nuns abstain from food, drink, and sleep so that further abstentions can be borne automatically and without conscious reflection. They abandon food, sleep, and other distractions so as to prepare themselves for the concentration required during lengthy Tantric rituals. Most nuns can perform their daily ritual recitations almost unthinkingly, regardless of whether they are cooking a pot of tea or carrying a forty-pound can of water up the cliff. Yet unlike Bourdieu's habitus, which is borne unconsciously and unreflectively, the ascetic habitus is the product of the highest consciousness and reflections. It is made up of symbolic acts which express a bodily praxis as well as philosophical principle. Buddhist detachment requires a constant mindfulness, in which bodily desires are registered and then transcended, rather than simply repressed. Yet Tantric detachment is highly conscious. Even the most mundane acts are infused with profound symbolic import.

Every night after dinner, as Yeshe completes her evening prayers and visualizations, she mixes the last sip of tea in her cup with a pinch of barley flour. The dough cleans out the butter left in her cup and serves as a bedtime snack. She then turns her cup upside down, because it would be inauspicious to leave an empty cup facing upward. This cup would suggest both desire and lack—in the sense of poverty—if found the next morning next to her dead body. Her actions signify both humility and the awareness that death can come at any moment. Yeshe's actions give real meaning to the cliché "Live each day as if it could be your last." In her nightly meditation, she contemplates the transience of life:

> By next morning, if I open my eyes, it is by the mercy of the Three Jewels as well as my root teacher that I have not died, that I am not sick, and that I have a sound body . . . By tomorrow morning will my consciousness return or not return? By tomorrow morning will I return to arise again or not? If I die then it is because of the Precious Buddha's mercy. If we die then it is all right for us old ones.

Yeshe's nightly Tantric meditation also includes a simple practice known as *gtong len,* in which she strives for perfect generosity. In thought as well as deed, she must learn how to give up everything for others. She practices the doctrine of universal compassion by giving away everything she has, including not only physical comforts but even her mental happiness. She thinks to herself every day:

May the suffering of all those who are hungry come to me. May all of my happiness go to them . . . May those without clothes receive from those who have clothes . . . Just as we are now drinking tea and eating bread, we should think, may all those without food receive as well . . . If I go hungry it is okay. If I have no clothes and am cold, it is no problem.

This practice of enlightened thought *(sems skyed, bodhicitta)* was championed by the eighth-century Indian saint Shantideva. His guide to the *bodhisattva*'s perfect compassion explains what it means to dedicate one's entire being to the welfare of others:

May I be the doctor and the medicine and may I be the nurse,
For all sick beings in the world, until everyone is healed . . .
And during the era of famine may I turn myself into food and drink.
May I become an inexhaustible treasure
For those who are poor and destitute;
May I turn into all things they could need
And may these be placed close beside them . . .
May I be a protector for those without one,
A guide for all travelers on the way;
May I be a bridge, a boat, and a ship for all those who wish to cross.[23]

Many Tantric meditations are concerned less with withdrawal than with developing an awareness of universal interdependence. They are far more reciprocal and relational than has been suggested. Doctrinally, Tantric retreats are conducive to both individual and collective liberation. In practice, such retreats link personal welfare to the wider community and universe. Tantric retreats foster both communalism and individualism. While undergoing a process of spiritual individuation, Tantric initiates engage in building solidarity with their wider community. Their meticulous construction and deconstruction of the sacred and profane unleash a powerful set of effects on themselves as well as on their audiences. In fact, the initiates are far less solitary than ordinarily imagined.

Most nuns prepare for their retreats through a communal apprenticeship at the nunnery. Furthermore, they may choose to undertake preliminary Tantric practices in joint retreats with other nuns.[24] Joint retreats allow nuns to conserve material expenses by sharing the cost of food and fuel with other members of their collective. Oddly enough, withdrawing from society requires nearly as many resources and reciprocities as living within society. Meditative seclusion requires careful preparation. The nascent meditator may solicit resources and labor in exchange for merit and blessing. The most advanced meditators do not solicit such support but simply await its arrival. In either case, the meditator engages in a free-flowing and creative reciprocity. Senior monks may ask for little while distributing their blessings. However, nuns with far less Tantric potency are compelled to beg for alms long before they begin their retreat.

Many of the nuns at Karsha have performed their preliminary practices in communal retreats. The nuns who engage in such collective retreats pool their resources in order to withdraw from their monastic and secular communities. A group of several nuns will require only one retreat room and assistant, and somewhat less fuel and food to stay warm and fed for the entire retreat, which is usually performed in the dead of winter when their domestic duties are minimal. During meditation retreats, nuns do not leave their designated cell, which is equipped with an interior compost toilet. For the duration of the retreat, they may not receive any visitors, but will only see two other individuals, the meditation assistant (mtshams g,yog) and the meditation instructor (mtshams rgan). The meditation assistant, usually a niece or an apprentice nun, cooks, fetches water, and goes to the village whenever the stockpile of food supplies runs low. The nuns on retreat forgo all communal obligations to the assembly, such as ritual attendance or collective work projects. However, they must find a substitute to steward any rituals in the monastic calendar for which they are responsible. For nearly eighteen hours a day, over a period lasting up to three or four months, nuns visualize, meditate, and prostrate in a ritualized manner. Every movement, breath, meal, and nap in retreat are regulated by ritual procedure.[25] Yet the illusion of solitariness can only be maintained by the surrounding community of nuns and villagers, who provide the goods and services which enable the retreat from society.

Preliminary practices can be performed in one's own monastic cell or by traveling to Buddhist sacred sites across India. Traveling "abroad" with other pilgrims offers nuns an alternate opportunity to cut themselves off from domestic obligations. Like many other Zangskari nuns, Skalzang collected enough funds to travel to Bodhgaya, in North India, to perform her preliminary practices. Although the trip by plane, bus, and rail was costly, the cheap cost of fruits and vegetables on the Indian plains was a welcome relief. Joining Buddhists of numerous nationalities who had flocked to the site where the Buddha once gained enlightenment, Skalzang set forth to procure her rooms for the period of her "retreat." Although she had been invited to share a room with an elderly Ladakhi couple she'd met on the train, she declined the offer, knowing that she would be too busy cooking for them to perform her retreat. Although she decided to concentrate on finishing the hundred thousand prostrations, she confessed that she felt a bit guilty for abandoning the couple when she took a room attached to a nearby Tibetan monastery.

After stocking her kitchen with the basic foodstuffs to last a few months, Skalzang began her ascetic exercises. She prostrated for seventeen hours a day, in two lengthy sessions—from three A.M. until noon, and then from two until ten P.M. She slept less than five hours a day and spent the remaining time preparing food or walking to and from the stupa to her room. She performed her prostrations using pads to protect her elbows and knees. However, her entire body was swollen with discomfort from the repeated act of throwing herself lengthwise on the ground. Shooting stabs of pain accompanied every prostration for the first three weeks. Yet once she finished the first ten thousand prostrations, she noted, "My body no longer felt the pain or lack of sleep." She believed that the merit of her prostrations had taken effect. The number of prostrations she could perform increased dramatically during this period. While she could only do between five and six hundred prostrations daily for the first few weeks, by the end of the month she was doing more than two thousand prostrations a day.

Tantric visualizations can empower nuns even as they exclude them. Nuns may visualize themselves as Vajrayogini, their protective deity, for several weeks of retreat. However, when they emerge from such retreats, they are not authorized to perform the burnt offering *(sbyin sreg)* to this deity. As nuns, they may dissolve and create endless images of themselves as a perfected deity. However, because they are not monks, they cannot complete the ritual communion of burnt offerings with that same deity. While their meditations may remove mental defilements, they cannot remove the physical taint of the female body. The burnt offering is supposed to remove ritual faults while pacifying the universe, but it cannot undo the innate fault of their sex.[26] Even those monks who have failed to complete the Vajrayogini meditation the nun has just completed are empowered to perform the burnt offering—as long as they have received a Vajrayogini initiation. In Zangskar, I have witnessed monks called to perform the burnt offerings for a deity that they rarely visualize or honor as nuns do each day.

Unlike select nuns in Kathmandu, who have received instruction in many sacred arts, Zangskari nuns are not taught the most spectacular Tantric practices like *mandala* making and fire sacrifices. Customary denial rather than textual interdictions has been the main reason for denying nuns this kind of ritual training in Tibet as elsewhere across the Buddhist Himalaya. These are the practices by which monks have gained fame and wealth when traveling abroad. As scores of foreign feminists began asking why there were no nuns performing such rites, monks began to look into their own tradition for answers. There was no simple reason for denying women training in an art form supposedly dedicated to the pursuit of nonduality and enlightenment for all. By the mid-1990s, a select group of elite monks in Kathmandu began to teach nuns these sacred arts. Since then, nuns from Kopan and Kyirong have performed these arts in the West.[27]

In Zangskar today, nuns may study the most esoteric Tantric doctrines, but they are unable to transmit them to their students. There are no teachings passed down exclusively among women and no famous female adepts within the monastic realm. Laypeople seek out Tantric initiations or blessings from accomplished monks and spiritual leaders who are recognized reincarnations or Tulku *(sprul sku)*, whose very touch may remove obscurations and defilements, but nuns and laywomen remain marginalized and associated with lesser Tantric potency. Although Tantric ideology rejects discrimination, its practices have sustained a real gender duality.[28] Within the monastic realm of the Gelug sect, Tantra has absorbed rather than eroded discriminatory attitudes toward the feminine. It has elaborated an essentialized image of the female body. Its doctrines may speak of nonduality between male and female, but its rituals continue to discriminate against nuns. The Tantric practices undertaken by Zangskari monks perpetuate the distinctions between monks and nuns. The collective inferiority of nuns is maintained in public rituals by segregated and demoted seating areas for nuns. One rarely sees any signs of the Tantric goal of gender reversal, as monks rarely relinquish their superior position relative to nuns. At the same time, Tantra does allow for some status leveling within the assembly of monks. Both novice and fully ordained monks have equal access to ritual initiations or retreats. Even laypeople perform the preliminary practices, albeit not in solitary retreat like nuns. However, such devotional disciplines do not confer the same status and power which monks have by virtue of their membership in the monastic assembly.

Yet the fire of asceticism may transmute mundane dross into a higher or enlightened reality. The Tantric meditations that a nun undertakes enables physical and psychological detachment. Meditation may transmute the petty injustices and aggravations of her domestic life into an endless play of wisdom and compassion. While performing her worldly duties as cook, washerwoman, field hand, or nanny, a nun may be practicing advanced Tantric visualizations. In short, she may be performing the union of opposites even as she labors in the conventional realm. Nuns may appear to be mired in the mundane even as they practice the highest Tantras. Why then are there so few women and no nuns at all in the stories of Tantric adepts known as *Mahasiddha?* Why are the nuns' devotions barely acknowledged while Tantric feats of *siddhas* like Tilopa and Virupa are still recounted? Why are the rich and corpulent monks who sit in comfort atop vast spiritual empires the most likely to draw Buddhist devotions and donors? Given Tantra's piercing message of looking for unlikely female teachers, why are humble nuns or elderly female renunciants so rarely honored? Although Tantric saints like Naropa were instructed by divine females, modern Zangskari monks are mired in conventional distinctions. The lessons of nonduality have been long forgotten since the rise of monastic distinctions. Domesticity may have been liberating for male saints, but not for female renunciants.

The selfless and passionate detachment of nuns is overlooked or misrecognized as mindless devotion. Nuns practice a more profound poverty and compassion, while monks speed on to higher spiritual learning. Although the Vinaya was supposed to transcend differences in gender and caste, the monastic order has preserved a pervasive discrimination. The most radical aspects of Tantra—the liberating potential of sexuality and the ultimately illusory nature of gender—are often ignored by monks in Zangskar today. A profound egalitarianism has been diluted by culture and custom. When I asked several nuns if women gain enlightenment as easily as men, they gave a variety of answers. Some said that women could, but only after making merit or overcoming bodily defilements. Others said that women can't gain liberation until they take rebirth as a male.

Yet everyday acts of resistance against the patriarchal authority of monks do appear. Urban nuns and Western feminists have challenged the most sexist aspects of Buddhist monasticism, as we shall see in the final chapter. Radio, film, and television have added to a wider appreciation of gender equality among Buddhists in Jammu and Kashmir as in other Indian communities. One nun reported that she had heard on the radio that men and women are equal. If Indira Gandhi and Benazir Bhutto could become head of their countries, she wondered, then why should women not have the same chance at enlightenment that men do? This statement was delivered in a half-convinced voice, as if reporting news from a distant front she had not yet visited. The idea that nuns can be as capable as monks of attaining liberation has yet to be accepted, even among the most strident nuns. The regularized repetition of subordination is only just beginning to be undone.

8

Monasticism and Modernity

"I was shocked . . . I didn't realize how bad it was. Some nuns didn't have enough to eat or decent clothes to wear. Many had never had a single Dharma teaching," said Tsering Palmo, one of Ladakh's foremost nuns.[1] She was discussing her own reactions upon visiting Ladakhi nunneries after having lived outside Ladakh for several years. Born in one of the aristocratic houses of Matho in 1966, Palmo's birth horoscope as a fire horse signaled a fiery temperament, strong will, and disregard for convention. Her parents and villagers should have been forewarned, but they thought she was spinning yarns as a child when she told them that she was going to become a nun one day. As there were no nuns in her home village of Matho and never had been as far as anyone could recall, her statement seemed preposterous. Palmo spent her early years rather placidly, attending the village school during the day while memorizing prayers from her grandfather's religious texts by night. She admits that she barely understood the profound significance of the texts she chanted. Yet because the devotions gave her deep satisfaction, she pursued the study of Tibetan grammar and Buddhist history with her uncle, an instructor at Leh's Central Institute for Buddhist Studies (CIBS).

When she had passed tenth grade, Palmo's parents took her on a pilgrimage to visit the monasteries throughout Ladakh. At Rizong—where a community of nuns performs economic services for the monastery—she begged her parents for permission to join the nuns. Her parents were shocked and saddened by their daughter's wish to pursue the ascetic life. They sent her back for more schooling in Leh, in hopes that she would become a government servant and marry. They were no exception to other parents of their class in seeking to dissuade their children from monasticism. Palmo told me that renunciation is still regarded as shameful for highly educated children of the elites. Those families who can afford it send their kids to study and get jobs. Girls who stay behind and choose celibacy are looked at rather suspiciously. Once she completed her post-secondary schooling, Palmo won a drama competition which proved to be a turning point in her life. She earned the role of Rigdzin Angmo, a woman born in Matho's royal family at the beginning of the twentieth century. As Palmo traveled, performing the play all over Ladakh, women cried openly and identified with her role in the play. For Palmo herself, "Although it was just a drama, it felt like real life. It was at this point that I decided I would do something different with my life."[2]

Rigdzin Angmo's drama begins when her father, the king of Matho, betrothes her against her will to a nobleman in nearby Spiti. Upon reaching her new home, Rigdzin Angmo suffers under mean and spiteful parents-in-law who scold her without reprieve. After enduring countless humiliations at the hands of her in-laws and the villagers, she escapes to join her uncle, the abbot of the nearby Skye monastery. Her uncle tells her she cannot stay in the monastery with him and marries her off to a Tibetan nobleman from Tshurpu. Her Tibetan in-laws treat her even more roughly than those in Spiti, but she cannot flee because she has two children. One day, two of her fellow villagers arrive on pilgrimage. When she begs them to take her home, they agree and tell her to slip out to their camp the next dawn. The princess gets up at the first light and creeps silently to the pilgrim's camp, but they have already left in fear of their king's wrath. She is so devastated that she dedicates any merit gained to a vow that she and all other women might not be reborn as women. She then commits suicide by jumping in the river. A passing monk who observes that her body floats upstream rather than downstream realizes that she must be a *dakini* or a divine emanation. After collecting her body and performing an elaborate cremation, the monk finds twenty-one Tara images inscribed on one of her ribs, which drops unscathed from the funeral pyre.

Palmo's performance in this drama left her with a burning ambition to avoid the fate of ordinary women. Although she first went to Kashmir to study medicine, she abandoned this course after hearing a rumor that she would have to dissect recently killed animals. When her uncle told her about the Tibetan Astrological and Medical College *(sman rtsis khang)* in Dharamsala, the Dalai Lama's home in India, she began to study day and night for six months so as to pass the rigorous entrance exam, which no

Ladakhi woman had ever passed. After gaining admission into this medical college at the age of twenty-one, she undertook a six-year course that would change her life irrevocably. While studying medicine, she began attending the Dharma classes held for foreigners at the nearby Tibetan Library. She recalls, "The atmosphere in Dharamsala was so pure and holy. I felt from the beginning that this was the place I had been looking for since childhood." Her principal at the Medical College forbade her from attending any more Dharma teachings so that she would redirect her attentions to her medical studies. Yet she continued to pursue her religious instruction with a learned Tibetan monk, Geshe Sonam Rinchen, in secret, flouting her principal and the library rules. When Geshe Rinchen told her that he hoped that she would become a teacher in Ladakh, she thought she had misunderstood his Tibetan or that perhaps he was making fun of her. It was still inconceivable to her that a nun could become a teacher.

Palmo described her own meetings with her teachers using the classic Buddhist imagery of ripening seeds:

> The seeds of Dharma which were born in my mind from my grandparents, father, and uncle, they were brought to fruit in Dharamsala by this Geshe . . . Meeting his Holiness and receiving teachings were like flowers which led to the ripening of the seeds.

While in Dharamsala, Ani Palmo began to attend teachings from the Dalai Lama. She dedicated all her merit toward accomplishing the goal of becoming a nun. Yet when she petitioned her teacher to allow her to take ordination, he advised her to wait and suggested that she take the five lay precepts instead. After spending three years in self-examination, she upheld the vows and had her head shaved by Khamtrul Rinpoche in 1991 and took novice ordination from the Dalai Lama in 1993. Her religious training was rather eclectic. Although she was born into a Sakya household, she received her spiritual training from monks in three other schools—Nyingma, Kagyud, and Gelug. On her way home to Ladakh in 1994, she attended an academic conference in Jispa, Lahaul, where she was shocked to hear a lecture on nuns by a scholar from Leh's CIBS. Having observed the high status of nuns among Tibetan refugees, she was horrified to learn that Ladakhi nuns worked as wage laborers on roads and fields or as household servants. In Leh, she challenged the young lecturer about his findings, but recalls how the institute's librarian confirmed the fact that nuns in lower Ladakh frequently ran estates largely abandoned by wealthy families who had moved to Leh. Although Palmo had planned to pursue a doctorate at the Buddhist Institute of Dialectics after taking up a prestigious medical post offered by the Tibetan government, she decided it was time to stop learning and start acting.

When Palmo first returned home, her parents, relatives, and friends cried and tried to dissuade her from the celibate life. She was outraged that they understood so little of Buddhism, and became all the more convinced that her efforts on behalf of nuns would be worthwhile. She spent three months in retreat at Matho monastery during her first winter, completing her preliminary practices of 100,000 prostrations, prayers, and visualizations. The following year she opened a thriving private medical clinic in Leh. She began to work on behalf of Ladakhi nuns for two local nongovernmental organizations, the Students Educational and Cultural Movement of Ladakh (SECMOL) and the Mahabodhi Foundation. Soon after, during Sakyadhita's Fourth International Conference on Buddhist Women in 1995, she had the chance to meet and network with nuns, precept holders, and laywomen from throughout Asia. Many of the speakers had been agitating on behalf of Buddhist nuns for nearly a decade.[3] Ordained nuns and precept holders from Thailand, Burma, Korea, Bhutan, Europe, and North America converged in Leh to electrify local audiences with their impeccable deportment and teachings. Ani Palmo brought the Ladakhi nuns to tears with a speech about their plight.[4] Although the Dalai Lama did not attend, he sent an encouraging statement indicating that a new era was dawning for Buddhist women: "Especially heartening, as this, your fourth conference clearly demonstrates, Buddhist women are casting off traditional and outmoded restraints to dedicating themselves to implementing and promoting Buddhist practice."[5]

The Cutting Edge of Buddhist Feminism

The energy generated by the Sakyadhita conference galvanized local and foreign advocates for nuns to begin constructing or renovating several nunneries in Ladakh and Zangskar. Between 1995 and 1998, four nunneries—Timosgam, Tia, Mahabodhi, and Lingshed—were built, while two others—Rizong and Wakkha—were substantially expanded. Palmo's Ladakh Nuns Association (LNA), which was established in 1996, spearheaded a number of projects which increased the education, visibility, and material status of nuns in Ladakh. Initially, Palmo took care not to antagonize local monastic authorities, by steering clear of pan-Buddhist issues like the reintroduction of full ordination. She took a more conservative route by urging novice nuns to study their precepts and strengthening monastic discipline. Yet she could not ignore the fact that Ladakhi nuns had little time to practice the very precepts they upheld. Although the male monastic community at Rizong was renowned for its strict adherence to monastic discipline, it could only sustain this religious ascendancy by requiring indentured services of nuns and laypeople. Rizong monks might not eat after noon and followed strict rules of poverty, but they required nuns to labor all day on behalf of the monastery's economic enterprises.

While most Ladakhi nunneries are independent institutions not directly attached to a monastery, Julichen is subordinated to Rizong monastery. Lying in lower Ladakh, Julichen nunnery takes its name, "Great Apricots," from the rich crop of apricots that nuns process and sell on behalf of the monastery. Julichen effectively serves as the factory floor of the monastic corporation.[6] While the nunnery sustains profane needs of subsistence, the monastery engages in sacred ritual. The nuns serve as the worker bees in the monastic hive, which is overseen by monks engaged in their ritual ministrations. Nuns work from dawn to dusk processing the monastery's vast wealth of grain, apples, apricots, and wool. While the monastery soars skyward at the end of a secluded valley, far above the distractions of human livelihood, the squat and ramshackle nunnery sits amid the monastic fields and orchards. The nuns' quarters are bursting with odd heaps of barley sacks, drying apricots, woolen homespun waiting to be dyed, abandoned looms, and plowshares in various states of disrepair. Nuns spend most of their waking hours working or cooking for the monastic estate, while living in rooms bereft of religious images. When Palmo returned to the nunnery she had thought of joining, she was disheartened to see its sad decline. Although Rizong had housed over forty monks and twenty nuns in the early 1970s, the monastic population had dropped to eighteen monks and six nuns by the 1980s.[7] There were only four nuns left in the mid-1990s; they worked side by side in the fields with local sharecroppers. The nunnery had not had a new recruit for several decades.

Overcoming the subtle opposition of Rizong monks, Palmo expanded the nunnery and quintupled its membership by 1999. With the permission of the abbot of Rizong and the assistance of local nuns, foreigners, and wage laborers, she began to construct a new nunnery complex. When Palmo and her companions first arrived at Rizong, the local monks and villagers made fun of them, joking, "They have come as tourists, and they will leave after a few months." After a few years, they had built eleven residential cells, four teaching rooms, a meditation hall, a toilet, and a conference hall. The construction was interrupted for fund-raising and the ordination of several new nuns, all of whom were secondary-school graduates. These highly educated and outspoken new young recruits had little desire to perform menial tasks like the ones their elders continued to do faithfully. As a result, the community of nuns is split. The younger recruits have adopted a religious curriculum of meditation, Tibetan, and philosophy, while the elders continue to slave on the monastic estates.

The Rizong monks blocked Palmo's plan to turn Rizong into a training institute for Ladakhi nuns, so Palmo found a building in Leh to house her new foundation, the LNA. After 1997 she held a series of conferences on monastic discipline for nuns across Ladakh and Zangskar.[8] In the course of these conferences nuns from throughout the region met to exchange ideas and address common problems. The most common problems that nuns complained of were a lack of residential or assembly space, a lack of teachers, and too little ritual training. Finally, there was the problem of no permanent endowments, which forced most nuns to work as domestic or wage laborers rather than devoting themselves to spiritual study. Palmo described these nuns as "hanging in the middle, between two worlds," because they were neither laywomen nor fully able to be nuns. She was heartened when nuns began to express a desire for more study and less domestic drudgery. She stressed the importance of study and monastic discipline but was also conscious that nuns would come under the gaze of the Ladakhi public. In one conference address, Palmo spoke of a nun's virtue being like a white robe: "Just as a stain cannot be removed from this robe, so too a broken precept can never be undone." She continued by noting that the monastic vows were not only a refuge but also the eyes with which nuns might find their path through an existence still trapped in delusion and desire.

Initially, Palmo encountered considerable resistance from laypeople and local monks. Some laypeople complained that nuns were no longer available for domestic chores. There were also the pragmatists who said that withdrawing nuns from rural areas already short of labor would be disastrous. Some monks thought she was crazy to try to educate "illiterate" nuns who would just be corrupted by coming to Leh or overeducated for life in the rural nunneries. Lastly, the nuns themselves thought she was mocking them when she described the advanced philosophical training they should receive. Palmo's biggest complaint was that people refused to take her seriously. She suspected that they saw her as a newly ordained imposter with little concept of monastic life in Ladakh after her extensive sojourn among the Tibetans. Many who were sympathetic to Palmo's message were fearful of openly subverting the privileges of monks. Palmo listened to their complaints and refuted them as best she could. She carried on day after day, even when people were laughing at her. Recalling the vow of the Matho princess she had once played so many years ago, she told me she would dedicate whatever merit she had earned toward the nuns and happily die for her cause.

When the highest-living Tibetan Buddhist authority spoke out on behalf of women, Ladakhi people finally took note. Although the Dalai Lama's office had ignored Palmo's numerous requests for a public meeting, he accepted her invitation to give a public talk on women during his 1998 visit. His Holiness spoke to a thronged audience about how men and women have an equal capacity for enlightenment. Local attitudes toward nuns shifted noticeably after the local media picked up the Dalai Lama's speech. In 1999 and in 2000, the Dalai Lama's office contributed sums totaling half a million rupees for the construction of a Ladakh Nuns Institute. As of 2003, the LNA had yet to receive these funds. They were still being held by the Ladakhi Buddhist Association (LBA), which accepted the sum on behalf of the nuns.

Disregarding typical obstacles like the failure of the LBA to relinquish these funds, Palmo has begun to build her institute with foreign funding. She envisions a place where nuns can attend teachings or workshops and train to work in a number of fields—as maternal health workers, traditional doctors, painters, tailors, or handicrafts experts. She wants the nunneries to become self-sufficient enterprises as well as educational institutes. She has convinced the principal at Leh's CIBS to open branch schools at some of the larger nunneries in Ladakh, although there are numerous delays due to the lack of qualified female teachers. A pilot school begun at Timosgam has begun to offer the standard Buddhist curriculum to young nuns and village girls. Those who graduate from CIBS can become teachers throughout Ladakh, Zangskar, and Nubra. The best and brightest students from Ladakhi nunneries have been sent to Tibetan institutes in India in Dharamsala, Mungood, Darjeeling, and Varanasi, where they are studying philosophy, Buddhist studies, and Tibetan medicine.

Although she appears to have multiple emanations given the amount of territory she covers, Palmo is not the only one working on behalf of nuns in Ladakh. The synergy between Buddhism and feminism in Ladakh dates back to the early 1990s, when a group called the Ladakh Women's Alliance was founded by Swedish development expert Helena Norberg-Hodge, to "counter the negative consequences of development and the increasing participation of Ladakh in the global economy."[9] Although the Women's Alliance is dominated by Leh's aristocratic and wealthy elites, its members helped organize the Sakyadhita conference in 1995 and the largest-ever gathering of nuns to perform a Tara Puja in Leh's holiest temple, the Jokhang, in 2001. The Women's Alliance has also worked with prominent Ladakhi politicians, like Stogdan Rinpoche and Thikse Rinpoche, who have promised to uplift the status of nuns. While these politicians have yet to deliver on their promises, they have not actively obstructed Palmo's reforms either.

One of the first nunneries to be overhauled, long before Palmo arrived on the scene, was Wakkha nunnery in Kargil District. When the Tibetan Geshe Sonam Palzang was first sent to Wakkha in 1976 by the office of the Dalai Lama, he eschewed foreign donors to build his nunnery, but relied only on funds from local villagers and Tibetan refugees. Although a monk who had spent decades earning his title of Geshe—a Ph.D. in the Gelugpa Monastic Colleges—he spent loving energy on every detail of the nunnery's layout. The colorful mosaics, beautifully proportioned flowerbeds, tidy and egalitarian residential cells, functional classrooms, and neatly stacked kitchen woodpile are all a tribute to his skillful design. As his school for young girls gained a reputation for being better than the local government schools, village girls flocked to the nunnery. Within the space of two decades, Wakkha became one of the largest nunneries in Ladakh.

Of the four new nunneries constructed in Ladakh between 1995 and 1998, women were catalysts in only one case. The blessing and approval of senior monks were essential, given that their hegemony in the religious sphere remains unchallenged.[10] Ani Palmo worked with a Dutch nun from the Chomo Foundation to build a new nunnery complex at Timosgam, which was completed in 2000. After the completion of a residential complex and assembly hall, the nunnery had enrolled thirty members by 2001, who were studying at the new school under the tutorship of a young monk from CIBS. Tia nunnery, by contrast, was built without the help of LNA. The head of Hemis monastery, Drugchen Rinpoche, established his new nunnery in the nearby village of Tia in the mid-1990s, when thirteen women, all of whom had passed their tenth-class exams, requested ordination. Oddly enough, Drugchen Rinpoche has not permitted his community of nearly fifty nuns to participate in Palmo's seminars on monastic discipline.

The ground for the new nunnery at the Mahabodhi complex outside of Leh was broken during the Sakyadhita conference in 1995. Three years later, a new nunnery was completed under the direction of a charismatic Ladakhi monk, Bhikku Sanghasena. Sanghasena was trained as a Theravada monk in Bangalore after leaving his home in Timosgam, first joining the Indian army and then dropping out in disgust.[11] Sanghasena receives ample funds from the Mahabodhi Society, an international Buddhist foundation which includes wealthy Taiwanese and Korean donors. He sponsored the first four nuns of Ladakh ever to receive full ordination, at a ceremony in Bodhgaya, India.[12] Three of the Mahabodhi nuns have been sent to Taiwan for further studies, while the fourth one, along with five novice nuns, remains in Leh. The nuns in Leh seemed somewhat despondent after their teachers, two Spanish nuns, were dismissed in 2000. Yet the nuns at Mahabodhi have since taken up leadership roles, after their whirlwind tour of Buddhist monuments in Nepal, Singapore, Thailand, and Taiwan—where they had ample opportunity to see what East Asian nuns have accomplished.

Ngawang Changchub is another charismatic and tenacious Ladakhi monk who has advocated for nuns in his home village of Lingshed for the last decade. Having left his remote home at the age of 6 to enroll in the prestigious Tibetan monastery of Drepung in South India, he spent the next 23 years studying, before becoming the first non-Tibetan in exile to receive a first in his Geshe Lharampa degree. This distinction—the Tibetan equivalent of a summa cum laude—can be awarded to one Geshe among those who debate one another for the honor. After receiving his degree and having the honor to debate for the Dalai Lama, Geshe Changchub returned to Leh to attend the Sakyadhita conference, where he became impressed with the work done on behalf of nuns across Asia. He began recruiting foreign sponsors to fund a nunnery in Lingshed. He has pursued a wide range of other projects as well—including a new school, annual conferences on Tibetan medicine and religion, and a hostel for over a hundred children who study in Leh—although his grandest ambitions, a radio station and a helicopter landing pad in Lingshed, have yet to be realized. Completed in 1998, the Lingshed nunnery houses over two dozen nuns from the remote villages around Lingshed. The nuns study under the tutelage of local monks, while two of the brightest nuns have been sent to Dharamsala to study dialectics. For all his charms, the Geshe was unable to convince local villagers to sell a parcel of wasteland to the nunnery for the construction of a trekking lodge.[13] Local elders seem to have balked at the idea of nuns acquiring either landed wealth or power in the local community, a pattern which was to repeat itself in Zangskar.

Over one hundred nuns gathered at the Leh Jokhang to say prayers for the female Buddha, Tara, for one week in 2001, under the auspices of the Women's Alliance, the Ladakh Women's Association, and the LNA. The event was remarkable for a number of reasons. It was the first time that a congregation of nuns was invited to perform a ritual within the city's central monastery. It was also the first time that Ladakhi laypeople participated in a ritual empowerment (dbang), partly orchestrated by nuns. Finally, it was the first time I have observed two of the most venerated monks and political leaders of Ladakh, Bakula Rinpoche and Sras Rinpoche, conduct a ritual in conjunction with an assembly of nuns. The ritual preparations for the eminent Rinpoches were conducted largely by monks, as nuns were deemed unqualified to prepare the ritual ground for the upcoming Tantric initiation. The mundane preparations for the ritual had been organized mostly by nuns and laywomen, working months in advance. Both Ladakhi and Tibetan laywomen had solicited vast sums to house and feed over a hundred nuns for over a week in Leh. The lay volunteers who came to the temple thrice daily to feed the nuns seemed to welcome the rare pleasure of serving monastics of their own sex. The laywomen I interviewed admitted that they were impressed by the nuns' ritual performance, but very few admitted that they might consider calling nuns for a household ritual.

Too Much Reform?

The reforms in Zangskar have kept abreast of those in Ladakh, although the emphasis has been more on the education of nuns rather than on construction. Despite being more remote, Zangskari nunneries received foreign sponsorship for nuns earlier than most Ladakhi nunneries did.[14] An American nun, Karma Lekshe Tsomo, has devoted considerable effort to improving educational conditions at two nunneries in Zangskar since the mid-1980s. Before tampering with a Gelugpa monastic curriculum that had excluded nuns for centuries, she obtained the approval of the Dalai Lama as well as of the renowned Namgyal Institute of Dialectics. She founded the Jamyang Choling Institute, which supports nunneries in Dharamsala and other Himalayan sites, and has advocated giving nuns permission to pursue the advanced Geshe *(dge bshes)* degree at the Dalai Lama's own Namgyal Institute.[15] She then began to design fledgling philosophical programs further afield, in Zangskar.

Lekshe raised enough money to build classrooms or supply books at three nunneries in Zangskar—Karsha, Zangla, and Pishu. She recruited two senior Geshes as teachers at Karsha and Zangla, although she was unable to find a teacher for Pishu. Despite the lack of basic amenities like heat, proper vegetables, and communication for at least six winter months, these venerable monks taught nuns the rudiments of philosophy. Two successive teachers have died at Karsha since 1995. The first Geshe was a Zangskari monk named Ngawang Tharpa, whom Yeshe had met in Tibet back in 1956 and who had become their abbot in 1986. After Ngawang Tharpa died in 1995, Lekshe Tsomo hired a second Geshe to live at Karsha, a Tibetan named Sonam Rinchen. After teaching from 1996 until 2001, when he suffered his second stroke, Geshe Rinchen passed away in early 2002 outside of Zangskar. The Geshe at Zangla first arrived in the late 1980s and stayed until his death in 1999. Revered by local villagers and nuns alike, Ngawang Tharpa received an elaborate funeral service, while the Zangla villagers honored their Geshe with a stupa in his name.

A Canadian foundation based in Toronto known as Gaden Choling has been the other major donor for Zangskari nuns. After instituting a pilot sponsorship program to provide material support for Karsha nunnery in 1991, I helped extend this aid to cover three more nunneries—Pishu, Skyagam, and Dorje Dzong—in 1996. By the year 2001, Gaden Choling provided substantial financial assistance to over one hundred nuns at the nine major nunneries of Zangksar. The funds have largely been used to purchase food and other staples so as to allow nuns the time to pursue their ritual training and practice. Every nunnery has used the funds to purchase basic foodstuffs like butter, tea, salt, and flour, supplementing the subsistence rations the nuns earn by working in the fields. The funds have also been used to supplement the material costs of construction—for a classroom in Karsha, a new assembly hall at Skyagam, and residential cells at Sani. Finally, the funds were also used to purchase a set of "smokeless" stoves produced locally out of recycled metal by Ladakhi blacksmiths. Every nunnery decides how to apportion the funds on its own, as nuns learn basic management and accounting skills in addition to their ritual training. These funds have enabled nuns across Zangskar to receive permanent endowments, which has reduced but hardly erased their reliance on daily wage labor in their villages.

Yet the steady trickle of funds, feminists, and tourists has also begun to alter the balance of power in less than benign ways. The theft of over three thousand dollars in foreign donations at Karsha nunnery is but one symptom of the shift in power. By local accounts, the theft was the largest sum stolen in Zangskar in the past hundred years. Even more shockingly, it was stolen from a monastic community considered in local folklore to be under the protection of Tantric protectors. The cash was taken from a box in the head nun's room while she and most of the nuns were off attending a wedding in the nearby village of Yulang. Although the lock on her room had been broken, the cash had mysteriously disappeared from a box inside, which was still locked when she discovered it. The only person who knew the location of the key to the box was her distant relative in Karsha, a young man whom she had looked out for when she had been sent to Karsha village as a teenager. He emerged as a prime suspect, especially after he built a huge hotel with mysterious funds soon after the theft. The head nun had shielded him during the investigation of the theft.

While the nuns pursued justice through all the traditional channels, they were stymied at every turn. After requesting the appropriate divinations from oracles and sending blessing scarves to many of the Tantric deities whose aid they beseeched, they went to the local headman for assistance. Bribed with a bottle of rum by the head nun, he refused to prosecute the prime suspect, her relative. Although subsequent rumors further implicated this suspect, the split within the assembly of nuns and the Geshe's indecision merely compounded the theft. If the head nun was complicit, she would have broken a root vow and should have been dismissed from the nunnery immediately. As it later emerged, she had lied about her handling of the funds, breaking another root vow and earning grounds to be cast out of the assembly and order of nuns. At the same time, the village's customary laws failed completely to address the largest theft in village history. The headman himself discouraged the nuns from pursuing justice by suggesting that if they took their case to the police, further tragedy would result. Police interrogations at nearby Dzongkhul monastery that same summer had left several monks beaten and one monk dead from shock, it was said. In this context, the nuns were unwilling to subject the elderly nuns and Geshe to police interrogations. Yet why did the villagers and nuns not pursue further investigations or strategies of retaliation? The villagers may have felt the nuns had received their due for their hubris. The nuns themselves seem to have accepted that karmic justice will take its effect, considering how little help they received in applying human justice. I cannot imagine a similar theft at the monastery going unpunished.

Although describing nuns in Burma, the following statement applies equally well to nuns in Kashmir:

> Nuns derive their status from association with the monks and from the part they play in enabling the monks to separate from the worldly. Therefore, equality and independence may not be an attractive proposition for them, but rather threatening and confusing to their basic sense of religious identity.[16]

Local laypeople seem to find nuns' increased independence threatening or unwelcome. What do Zangskari villagers make of the foreign sponsorship which has descended upon them without much effort on their part? While the nuns are pleased with donations, there is backlash in Zangskar as well as in Ladakh. The development of nuns has received limited and hesitant support from monks and village elders. Major reforms in Zangskar have required permission if not explicit support from at least one high-ranking monk. Without lobbying local headmen to grant nuns the rights to physical resources like land, water, stones, and mud, not a single construction can proceed. Without village consent, larger projects could have been stalled indefinitely. In Zangskar, as elsewhere in India, the development of women faces both hidden and overt transcripts of resistance. Although nuns are allowed some freedom of movement and speech, their rapid gains in wealth is threatening to local powers. When I first came to Zangskar in 1989, nuns had better facilities there than at those nunneries in Ladakh—like Shergol and Thikse—which lacked residential cells. By 2003 the tide had shifted, as Ladakhi nunneries were growing and Zangskari ones were somewhat stalled.

Some villagers envy the nuns their good fortune; others mock their attempts at advanced study. Many villagers feel the nuns are being pushed too fast and too far. The nuns themselves complain that they still have little time to memorize their texts because of their continuing domestic duties. Privately, villagers and monks admit that the focus on philosophy is a bit misplaced, given that many nuns still lack basic Tibetan literacy. Villagers are concerned that if the nuns focus too much on dialectics, they will neglect to memorize basic texts recited at funerals or weddings. Some villagers jibed that the cacophonous sound of nuns debating would hardly guide the deceased to its next rebirth as traditional prayers are believed to do. Such jokes send a clear message that nuns should stop trying to learn new tricks. They also point to the unshaken belief that monks but not nuns are most fit to study advanced philosophy.

A memorandum of 1996 summed up the views of Ladakhi politicians and monks:

> After new monasteries are established, the nuns should not go to town anymore . . . Nuns need to be very careful of their actions of body, speech, and mind, when associating with laypeople and monks, and also to prevent attraction to men/monks from arising . . . H.H. The Dalai Lama has repeatedly said that the time for nuns and monks to sit in the monasteries and only pray is over. We should become trained as doctors, lawyers, and nurses to serve society, taking as our example the social activities of Christian monks and nuns.[17]

Those who endorsed this recommendation seem ambivalent about the proper roles for nuns. What was Palmo supposed to make of these mixed signals, which favor a this-worldly asceticism but also fear the growing worldliness of nuns? Palmo recalls that this meeting, called to discuss the status of nuns, was critical to getting the support of the Rizong abbot for further education for the nuns at Julichen. Yet the patronizing tenor of the message implies a group of monks who are trying to protect their power by confining nuns to a "proper" place. It is not clear why nuns should be prevented from coming to town, when monks have been coming and going from town and market for centuries. The attempt at secluding nuns violates the Buddha's intention that monastics wander through towns giving teachings and collecting alms. Indeed the idea that nuns should be cloistered recalls medieval Christianity more than Buddhist doctrine. Just as in the Middle Ages, when the alarming rise in nuns led to their being secluded, Ladakhi monks may simply be responding to nuns' increased visibility in the local landscape.[18] Monks have good reason to feel threatened by growing numbers of nuns in Ladakh. By 2001, there were over 300 nuns and over 500 monks resident in Ladakh, along with 110 nuns and 300 monks residing in Zangskar. Unfortunately there are no statistics on earlier populations of nuns, because nuns were rarely mentioned in the scholarly literature on Buddhist monasticism. The population of monks is declining—as the example of Rizong suggests (a drop from forty monks in 1970 to eighteen monks by the late 1980s). The rising proportion of nuns in Ladakh and Zangskar along with sharp declines in resident monks may be growing cause for concern among the monastic leadership.

The efforts to train nuns in more practical pursuits, like medicine, have been beset with obstacles. Palmo and Lekshe Tsomo both tried to train nuns as local Tibetan doctors *(am chi)* or maternal health workers. Yet they have received almost no support and much grief from existing government agencies. Palmo was shunned by local *am chi* organizations before she managed to recruit a female *am chi* from nearby Kinnaur—in the neighboring state of Himachal Pradesh—to train several nuns in Tibetan medicine. Some of these nuns have enrolled at prestigious Tibetan medical institutes like Chakpori, located in Assam, Northeast India. Lekshe convinced a Ladakhi gynecologist, Dr. Lhadrol, to train several Zangskari nuns in maternal health at the Leh Hospital. Yet the nuns were unable to serve as community health workers in Zangskar because the medical bureaucracy of Kargil District argued that they lacked the proper training. Although nuns lack Urdu literacy, so do some of the most basic communal health workers. Furthermore, nuns are less likely to be bound by familiar duties than married women and far more able to travel and sustain wider social networks. As such it is a real loss that nuns have been prevented from becoming health workers in Zangskar.

Feminism, Celibacy, and Globalism

The collision and collusion between local and global forms of feminism and Buddhism in eastern Kashmir are far from complete. Although the reigning hegemony of monks has been disrupted, centuries of patriarchy cannot be overturned quickly. It is not immediately clear whether the East or the West is driving the recent reforms in the monastic realm. While both foreign and local feminists have been colluding in these reforms, has the impetus toward egalitarianism come mainly from the foreigners or the locals? Buddhist modernist movements in Sri Lanka and Nepal suggest that Orientalism is rarely a uni-directional flow as Said presumed. Local reformers construct images of decayed or corrupted Buddhism as much as

Western reformers have.[19] The recent reforms of Buddhist monasticism in Kashmir draw on a number of intersecting discourses which are both foreign and indigenous. When the Dalai Lama explains that men and women have equal capacity for enlightenment, he is referring to doctrinal assumptions as much as responding to recent feminist critiques. The Ladakhi reforms might have occurred without foreign feminists. But they would have had a different shape and trajectory without the influx of foreign culture and capital. The shifting nature of Buddhist institutions and practices is intertwined with feminism, doctrinal beliefs, and late capitalism. Religious practices are moored in a shifting set of locations, including local culture, the pan-Buddhist ethnoscape, and global flows of capital.

The field of Buddhist monasticism has seen an immediate struggle for power and agency which resists a teleological script of progress. Neither the dominant nor the subaltern groups are as monolithic as they appear. On the subaltern side, scheming politicians, educated nuns, and well-meaning Geshes jostle for their portion of power. Locally, monks and nuns compete to channel the new forms of social and symbolic capital into their monastic ventures. On the foreign side, feminist donors, aging dharma bums, and development experts compete for the favors of the locals. Although gender alliances may cut across the local/foreign divide, class and rural/urban divides are hardly obsolete. The competition for land and wealth has only intensified, while the diverse definitions of social justice and gender equality have made collaboration difficult. While foreign and local feminists may share a goal of revalorizing nuns, they may disagree on the actual methods. Petty competition between differing sets of do-gooders undermines overall development efforts. Every group follows its own leadership, often resisting collaboration and a single hierarchy of power. Strategies of divide and rule have prevented radical progress. As a result, local nuns and even foreign feminists continue to bow and scrape before the local Rinpoches in hopes of a blessing or favor. Although feminists may wish to rebuild Buddhist institutions from the ground up, monastic hegemony remains largely undisturbed. The resulting scenario of resistance and reform is beset with multiple starts and stumbles.

Both Buddhism and feminism have always been deterritorialized and wandering ideologies. Alan Watts once called Buddhism "Hinduism for export" because it transported central ideas like *karma* and *dharma* beyond the local Hindu landscape of caste and community. Yet Buddhist practices were adapted to cultural and social conditions wherever they spread. Ideologies of merit and purity have served to perpetuate enduring gender differences. In their heady days, Western feminists dreamed of a worldwide revolution of the second sex. Yet they were soon forced to adapt to local culture and politics, after being attacked for privileging a white, Western, and bourgeois perspective at the expense of color and class.[20] Indian feminists have created a separate discourse of women's liberation, less dependent on European humanism or colonial imperialism. For Himalayan and Buddhist feminists, untangling the postcolonial discourse on gender inequality within their own traditions is one priority.

A critical issue remains. Is it possible to transcend religiously sanctioned inequality by calling on authentic sources within the tradition itself? Or must scholars go outside the tradition to legitimize an alternate model of gender norms? Textual scholars have argued that the status of women in Buddhism has been far more contested than previously thought.[21] Yet the debate has foundered over what counts as authentic or inauthentic within a given tradition. Those with the authority to speak for a tradition—be they male scholars or monks—have excluded or denigrated those who contest this right, like feminists and nuns. Bourdieu once noted that academic as much as religious institutions have equally elaborate methods by which to authorize who has the right to speak. The pursuit of authority is even more contested outside than inside the academic realm.[22] Like scholars, monks refuse to accept opposing arguments about the ordination of women, on sectarian or scholastic grounds. There are many sources of dissension on how to raise the status of nuns. Sri Lankan monks disagree with the Dalai Lama's tentative support for nuns' ordination or education, because they prize their own Theravada school's reputation for purity and faithfulness to the Buddha's supposed intentions. Even within a single tradition, there is little consensus. Senior Tibetan monks may disagree on whether or not nuns should pursue full ordination.

Foreign funding and local initiatives between monks and nuns have led several avant-garde nunneries in India and Nepal to sponsor programs permitting nuns to study advanced philosophy and the spectacular ritual arts—like *mandala* making, fire sacrifices, and sacred dances. After 1994, monks were invited to teach a select group of young nuns how to create the elaborate sand *mandalas* and perform the burnt offering rite which accompanies the deconstruction of a *mandala* at Kyirong and Kopan nunneries in Kathmandu. In Dharamsala, India, Lekshe Tsomo secured the admission of nuns to the Namgyal Institute of Dialectics, after 1985. The nuns who graduate from this twenty-year program of philosophical study will receive a Geshe degree and be eligible to teach the next generation of student nuns. While the Dalai Lama has been supportive of these efforts, he has warned that they must be conducted under proper monastic authority with the necessary spiritual discipline.

The politics of diaspora have led to a more intense negotiation over what counts as Tibetan culture and Buddhism. Tibetan culture is contested in exile for a number of reasons, not least of which is the pressing claim for a Tibetan homeland.[23] This contestation can take violent forms, as it did in 1998, when several Tibetan youths immolated themselves on the streets of New Delhi to protest the Dalai Lama's pacifist stance. The struggle over Tibetan identity is overshadowed by two powerful and pervasive images: the Dalai Lama and Tibet. The rapid, widespread, and systematic circulation of mechanically reproduced images of both Tibet and the Dalai Lama have dictated their purity and simplicity.[24] The Dalai Lama's timeless message of wisdom and compassion holds a dreamlike fascination for spiritually impoverished audiences in the West. His personal charisma captivates advocates as well as agnostics. At the same time, commodified images of Tibet which pervade American culture ignore the complexity of the diaspora and historical spread of Tibetan culture in the Himalayas.[25] There are costs of peddling simplistic or anachronistic images of a Tibetan Shangri La. The reification of Tibet ignores important fault lines between Tibetans in exile and those within Tibet, as well as the usual suspects of class and gender. The Hollywood seekers who flock to hear the Dalai Lama must overlook these divisions in order to perpetuate their static image of a harmonious and perfect Tibet. Their images elide the problems of patriarchy, caste, and other forms of religious discrimination.

Many academics celebrate the hybridity and confusion within Tibetan Buddhism. Some busily deconstruct contesting images of Tibetan Buddhism, while others collude with image makers in the diaspora to privilege the "most authoritative" voices of monks. The politics of diaspora and androcentric scholarship fuel each other in overlooking a sustained feminist critique of Tibetan Buddhism. The first group of Tibetan nuns invited to construct a *mandala* in America was stymied by the suspicions of diaspora Tibetans. Kyirong nuns had been studying *mandala* making for years and had received the explicit blessing of the Dalai Lama on their journey to America. Nevertheless, Tibetans at the office of Tibet in New York were wary of the nuns' ritual skills, especially as they were due to participate in a ritual with the Dalai Lama.[26] Only after presenting visual documentation of *mandalas* they had produced in Nepal were the nuns permitted to create a *mandala* for the Dalai Lama's visit to Brandeis University. The watchdogs of religion in exile were more concerned with policing gender roles within ritual arts than their fellow monastics in Asia. Even women highly trained in ritual expertise face consistent disbelief or an assumption of ritual inferiority.

The global community of Buddhist feminists continues to include diverse national, political, ethnic, and sexual orientations. This imagined community of Buddhist feminists may share a broad goal of raising the status of nuns, yet rarely agree on methods for implementing that goal. The major agendas for reform have been ritual empowerment, reviving full ordination, and increased education. Yet many doctrinal and national barriers must be overcome. Globe-trotting nuns sidestep sectarian debates by promoting nuns' ordination in the Theravada and Tibetan traditions using nuns from a separate lineage, the Dharmagupta. The World Wide Web has facilitated the communication and alliance of nuns in disparate social, cultural, and political settings. Yet it cannot overcome biases and differences between schools and sects. The names Greater Vehicle and Lesser Vehicle (Mahayana and Hinayana) continue to signify the patronizing attitude the former school exhibits toward the latter.

The recent Buddhist reforms are the latest incarnations of processes that have been developing for centuries. Kashmir has been the site of cultural flows of goods, people, and practices for centuries, given its strategic position at the juncture between Central and South Asia. So what is new about feminist reforms of Buddhism in Jammu and Kashmir today? Although global flows are as old as trade and warfare, the modern collapse of time and space has fundamentally altered the frequency and scale of the exchanges. The recent reforms of Buddhist monasticism have been unique in terms of their speed, iteration, and geographic extent. The collapse of time and space through technological innovations has yielded new forms of super-modernity and hyper-reality in which transience is celebrated over rootedness, disruption over continuity. The influx of new flows of media, militarism, culture, and capitalism has upset traditional networks of sociality, trade, information, and governance.

Buddhist institutions in Jammu and Kashmir today are produced through a complex conjunction of social, political, and economic forces. The militant struggle for political autonomy in Jammu and Kashmir has brought religious identities to center stage. Buddhists and Muslims in Ladakh and Zangskar are fighting their battle for autonomy and recognition within the state. Feminists, tourists, and donors in search of Shangri La continue to swamp the summer landscape of Ladakh. The heady mix of donors and dharma seekers has revamped the local face of Buddhism in many ways. Local politicians urge a return to a purer, primordial form of Buddhism, disregarding youthful monks who absorb Indian culture through the films of Bollywood—Bombay's version of Hollywood. Monastic festivals are thronged with tourists and fewer Ladakhis, while teenagers fill the film and video parlors in Leh. Monks with television sets and VCRs are too busy for Tantric retreats. Young monks sport Yankee baseball caps in the bazaar, while teenage girls prefer Punjabi dress and headscarves over the traditional dress that the Women's Alliance makes mandatory.

The fragmentary and imaginary communities of Buddhists have transcended many conventional scholastic categories.[27] Himalayan Buddhist nuns are less bound by territory, ethnicity, and culture than a century ago. Yet new and enduring differences of class, nationality, and region continue to separate communities, despite the global flows that link them. Nuns in Zangskar rarely travel to Kathmandu or elsewhere in India. Interactions between Buddhists in Kathmandu and Dharamsala have intensified, as have those between the feminist coffee houses in Holland with nunneries in Jammu and Kashmir. These links, however, are both tenuous and transient. The postmodern tendency to flatten differences in search of the simulacrum overlooks enduring cultural divisions which do not succumb to blurred boundaries. The fantasy of globalism cannot hide pervasive ruptures of class and region, as well as the threat of religious communalism. The Himalayan realm has no special purchase on bliss or harmony in the dystopian subcontinent. The good Buddhist ascetic and the corrupted Western seeker will feed on each other as long as each believes ultimate happiness to lie on the other's inaccessible shore.

We live in an era in which celibacy is under deep attack if not in crisis. Catholic priests and Thai monks are caught in deeply disturbing cases of perversion and fraud, while biographies deconstructing Gandhi or Mother Teresa are all the rage. Voices within the Catholic Church are calling for it to reconsider a millennia-old policy: priestly celibacy. At the same time, learned scholars are defending the historical origins and theological claims in support of this increasingly conflicted practice. Regardless of the outcome, religious asceticism is no longer sheltered under the aura of sanctity it once commanded. The practice of celibacy continues to inspire prurient curiosity, cynical disbelief, and wondering incomprehension. The initial impetus for celibacy in both Buddhism and Christianity was to foster contemplative seclusion from the world. Yet Buddhist monasticism was premised upon an essential engagement with the world. Unlike Christian ascetics who went to the desert to seek solitude, Buddhist monks were enjoined to teach in North India's rapidly developing urban culture. Although they soon abandoned their peripatetic ways and settled into permanent institutions, monks continue to follow a discipline which limits property, undertakes seasonal retreats, and emphasizes reciprocal relations with the laity. Buddhist monasticism required patronage and permanent endowments to survive. These exchanges maintain the economy of merit which provides monks subsistence and security. The quest for merit fuels social difference between monks and nuns. What began as an escape from difference has led to its reinforcement.

Celibacy must be reimagined as an engagement with the world rather than its rejection. Buddhist monks as much as nuns depend on their exchanges with laypersons. These exchanges will be maintained only if laypeople continue to honor and respect the monastic vocation. The upholding of monastic vows becomes ever more difficult given the modern impetus of worldly asceticism. Upholding precepts is the critical condition for the division of labor between sacred and profane. For nuns as well as monks, upholding the Buddha's moral discipline is critical to the continuity of the monastic order. Yet nuns can only hope to perpetuate their discipline if they are granted the material endowments, ritual patronage, and respect historically reserved for monks. This support, accompanied by changing attitudes in the laity toward nuns, will spell the difference between victory and defeat for Buddhist monasticism in the coming years.

NOTES
REFERENCES
INDEX

Notes

1. Gendering Monasticism

1. Some scholars (Ahearn 2001; Butler 1999; Knauft 1996) have noted that Bourdieu's version of practice theory precludes a rational or conscious agent. The theory has also been attacked for failing to show how the habitus is inculcated or operates (Mahmood 2001; Farnell 2000). While Bourdieu's (1977, 1988, 1990, 1991, 1999) practice theory may preclude a conscious agent, it does not fail to recognize the strategic deployment of culture, contrary to Appadurai's (1996) critique. Ortner (1989b, 1996) attacks the major proponents of practice theory (Sahlins, Bourdieu, and Giddens) for their lack of engagement with feminist and subaltern critiques of power, while supplying her own definition of practice as serious games.

2. Spiro (1970) divides Buddhism into its nibbanic, kammatic, and apotropaic aspects, while Samuel (1993) argues for an analogous schema of pragmatic, *karma*, and bodhi orientations in Tibetan Buddhism. Compare the division of Newar Buddhism into the path of disciples, householders, and priests explored by Gellner (1992). Gombrich (1971), Tambiah (1968, 1970), Obeyesekere (1968), and Southwold (1983, 1985) describe the dialectic between precept and practice in Theravada Buddhism but rarely manage to transcend the binary oppositions they impose, as Gellner (1990) astutely notes.

3. Previous approaches often characterized monks as isolationist or asocial. Tambiah (1970: 68) characterizes the Buddhist monkhood as "an initiation that offers a man a way out of reciprocity" while Ortner (1978, 1989) describes monks as asocial and antirelational, even as their data suggests otherwise. Lewis (2000) offers a new approach which emphasizes the relations between laypeople and monastics among the Newar.

4. Several key monographs which explore the new ethnographic imperative to see both culture as both more fluid and unstable include Appadurai (1996), Marcus and Fisher (1986), Clifford and Marcus (1986), Marcus (1998), Knauft

(1996), Fox (1991), and Behar and Gordon (1998). Russell McCutcheon (1997, 1999, 2001), Fitzgerald (1999), Masuzawa (1993), Smith (1982), and Guthrie (1993) are leading critics in the movement to destabilize the category religion.

5. Dirks (1994) and Asad (1993) break with Geertz's hermeneutic in their analyses of ritual and power, while Ortner (1996, 1999b, 1999a) faults the subaltern approach for ignoring thick description and the semiotic approach for overlooking power.

6. Lopez (1995, 1998) analyzes the orientalist and colonialist legacies within Buddhist studies, while Eckel (1994), Lewis (2000), and Schopen (1997) have uncovered many of the Protestant presuppositions of Buddhist scholarship.

7. Scholars who focus heavily on the economic and political relations of monasticism include Carrasco (1959), Goldstein (1971a,b, 1986, 1989), Tsarong (1987), Aziz (1978), and Gelek (1984, 1986). Goldstein's and Miller's debate on the validity of the term "serf" spans a few issues of the *Tibet Journal*.

8. The Princeton series on Buddhism in practice (Lopez 1995, 1997) unwittingly reinstates texts at the center of its analysis. Although the volumes are dedicated to foregrounding practice, they reinstate the centrality of textual translations, which Simmer-Brown (2001) has also criticized.

9. Lopez (1998), Korom (1997), and Bishop (1989) deconstruct the genealogy of discourses on Tibetan Buddhism, while Diehl (2002) and Dodin and Räther (2001) explore the reinvention of Tibetan traditions and culture in exile.

10. Gellner (1990, 1998) is one of many scholars who ignore the presence of Buddhism in Zangskar and Ladakh in Mughal India after the twelfth century.

11. Snellgrove (1989), Ramble (1990), Mumford (1989), and Samuel (1993) depict Himalayan Buddhism as a more shamanic form of Tibetan Buddhism, while Kornman (1997) denigrates the Ladakhi version of the Gesar epic as "primitive." The practice of assuming that the peripheral is archaic or primitive is criticized by Aggarwal (1994, 1997) and Gutschow (1998, 2002).

12. Local and foreign scholars who mostly ignore nuns while describing Buddhist monasticism in Ladakh and Zangskar include Crook and Osmaston (1994), Dendaletche (1985), Desideri in Fillipi (1932), Dargyay (1980, 1987, 1988), Dollfus (1989), Friedl (1983), Kaplanian (1981), Petech (1977, 1998), Schuh (1976, 1983), Snellgrove and Skorupski (1980), Gergan (1976), Tsering (1979), Paldan (1982), Zodpa and Shagspo (1979), and Shakspo (1988a, 1993). Scholars who do describe the nuns in Ladakh and Zangskar include Green (1997), Grimshaw (1983a,b, 1992), Gutschow (1997a, 1998a, 2000a,b, 2001a,b, 2002), Reis (1983), and Riaboff (1997a).

13. An elderly monk in Karsha overlooked the presence of a nunnery in the village of Zangla when he once told me, "There is no *dgon pa* in Zangla."

14. Despite his careful attention to deconstructing stereotypes about Tibet, Lopez (1998:211) repeats a common trope when noting: "unmarried daughters often

became nuns (sometimes remaining at home). Other women became nuns to escape a bad marriage, to avoid pregnancy, or after the death of a spouse." March (1976), Ortner (1983, 1989a) Aziz (1976), Furer-Haimendorf (1976), Kerin (2000), Tsomo (1989, 1988, 1996), and van Ede (2002) characterize many of the inhabitants of Sherpa and Tibetan nunneries as lifelong celibates. While Ortner (1996:147) admits to having "virtually no information on the day to day life in the nunnery" she draws broad conclusions about how nuns and monks occupy similar subject positions in Sherpa society.

15. Randi Warne (2001:150) notes that en-gendering religious studies is hardly confined to the proposition "add women and stir." She calls for a radical decentering of the discipline in which gender becomes a fundamental unit of analysis, which is as sweeping as Joan Scott's (1999) re-envisioning the nature of historical analysis or Carol Gilligan's critique of developmental psychology. Nita Kumar (1994) explores the implication of seeing women as subjects in South Asian studies.

16. Arai (1999) and Havnevik (1990) offer published monographs on contemporary life in a Buddhist nunnery, which largely ignore the social and economic relations between nuns and laypeople, as well as nuns and monks. These works are complemented by Grimshaw's unpublished dissertation and memoir (1983a, 1992) and Bartholomeusz's (1994) monograph on female renunciants in Sri Lanka.

17. Haraway's (1991:192) phrase "passionate detachment" refers to a perspective that deconstructs the conventional balance of power, while discussing the virtues and pitfalls of feminist standpoint theory.

18. For a detailed account of how Tibetan Buddhist ethics builds on the earlier ethical paths of Mahayana and Theravada, see Kontgrul (1998), Tsongkhapa (2000), Dudjom Rinpoche (1966), and Keown (1992).

19. Samuel (1993:203) argues that the Mahayana ethics "inevitably somewhat weakened" Theravada ethics, without addressing the Mahayana and Tantric focus on purification and merit making.

20. Lopez (1997) depicts the standard seven steps of the Tantric *sadhana* as homage to the assembled deities, symbolic offerings, purification via confession of sins, admiration of the deities, entreaty to the teachers to stay in the world, supplication to the bodhisattvas, and the dedication of merit to all sentient beings.

21. Onians (2003:20–23) clarifies the ethical debate about antinomian acts which the bodhisattva is authorized and enjoined to perform. She builds on and elucidates Keown's (1992) arguments about how Tantric ethics supersede Mahayana ethics.

22. The list of virtuous and nonvirtuous acts can be broken down into acts of body, speech, and mind. The varying interpretations of the Buddhist theories

and practices of *karma* are outlined in monographs by Keyes and Daniel (1983), Neufeldt (1986), O'Flaherty (1983), and Reichenbach (1990).

23. Rigzin (1993) identifies the Tibetan list of four ways to collect merit (*bsod nams su bya ba'i dngos po bzhi)*, while Spiro (1970:94) and Gombrich (1971) cite the Digha Nikaya (III, I, 218) on making merit.

24. The Tibetan ethicist Tsongkhapa (2000:252–258) implies on the one hand that complete *karma* can never be undone, yet on the other lists the four basic actions which can eradicate *karma* before it becomes "complete": contrition, ritual remedies, turning away from faults, and taking refuge.

25. Lichter and Epstein (1983) analyze both ultimate and secondary causality in terms of Tibetan ritual practice and beliefs.

26. The relationship between virtue and wealth, and its implications for a Buddhist ethics, are explored in Sizemore and Swearer (1990).

27. The ideology of sati offers a fascinating parallel, for it is said that a woman who commits sati (self-immolation) on her husband's funeral pyre for seven lifetimes is purified of the female rebirth, as Weinberger-Thomas (1999) notes.

28. Tsongkhapa (2000:243) lists the eight bodily effects of good *karma:* long life span, good color, good lineage, power, trust, fame, being male, and having strength. Tsongkhapa (2000:243) defines consummate color and lineage as "having an excellent body by way of its good color and shape; being pleasant to look at because you do not have incomplete sensory faculties . . . having been born with a good lineage that is esteemed and famed in the world." Recalling the Pure Land Sutra, it also states that a male rebirth is caused by recognizing the failings of the female body, causing others to reject it, and rescuing those about to be castrated.

29. Bowie (1998) notes that Thai villagers gave to the poor, but does not tell us if such gifts earn more or less merit than those to monks. Her data suggests that while the poor may give a greater portion of their income to monks than the rich do, they do not necessarily earn more merit thereby. As such, her conclusion that giving to the poor makes more merit than giving to monks is not warranted.

30. Buddhadasa's words are translated in Swearer (1995:400).

2. Locating Buddhism in Zangskar

1. The Treaty of Lahore in 1846 forced the Sikhs to cede the territories between the Indus and Beas rivers to the British, which the latter simply sold to their Dogra ally. The newly anointed Maharaja Gulab Singh paid a mere 8.5 million rupees for Kashmir and its environs under the Treaty of Amritsar, as Datta (1972) notes.

2. Anderson (1991), Richards (1992), Cohn (1990, 1996), and Appadurai (1996)

describe the colonial forms of knowledge that manipulate the power and legitimacy of the imperial state, while Hopkirk (1991, 1997) describes the race for Tibet in the Great Game. In 1921, the population of Srinagar (141,735) was just under half that of Delhi (304,420).

3. Schofield (1996, 2000) summarizes the questions of legitimacy and illegitimacy in the Kashmir conflict as debated by Jha (1996), Ganguly (1995), Lamb (1966, 1991, 1994), and Wirsing (1998).

4. Kaul and Kaul (1992), Dani (1991), Chibber (1998), Prasad and Dal (1987), Khan (1970), and Sen (1969) provide fascinating and first-hand details on the Indo-Pak war in Ladakh, yet only the first two mention the invasion of the Gilgit raiders into Zangskar.

5. The role of the Zaildar *(ziladar)* in collecting taxes and administering the Permanent Settlement under Dogra and British administration is illustrated in Barkley (1875), Douie (1899), and Douie and Johnstone (1890).

6. The Indian census of 2001 *(www.censusindia.net)* reports the population of Leh district as 117,637, and the population of Kargil district as 115,227. In 1979 Kargil and Leh districts were newly created out of a district formerly known as Ladakh—a term still used to describe Leh district.

7. Benedict Anderson (1991) fails to account for the paradoxical rise of religion as a supranational identity which has spread through the same channels as nationalism, as Van der Veer (1994) and Van der Veer and Lehman (1998) explore.

8. The 183,963 persons identified as eligible for ST status made up only 2.5 percent of the population of Jammu and Kashmir but 88.7 percent of the population in Leh and Kargil districts. Thanks to Martijn van Beek for this information.

9. Fedarko (2003) reports on the prisoner's dilemma that has left Indian and Pakistani soldiers stranded on the world's highest killing fields. The influx of militants trained in Pakistani terrorist camps into Kashmir and the violence they have wrought on the local landscape are described in Hewitt (1995), Wirsing (1994:120), and Stern (2001).

10. Van Beek (1996, 2000, 2001) and van Beek and Bertelsen (1997, 1995) have detailed the conflict and complexity inherent in the Ladakhi autonomy movement. Van Beek and Bertelsen (1995:12) cite a local Shia leader from Suru, Agha Hyder, who noted, "We are all Ladakhis. We all suffer under Kashmiris. We should fight them together, instead of each other."

11. The *Indian Express* (12/9/95) reported "Foreigners Taken Hostage By Zanskar Activists"; an Islamabad daily, *The News* (9/13/95), reported "Buddhists Release Foreign Hostages."

12. Compare efforts to modernize Buddhism in Sri Lanka and Nepal as described by Gombrich and Obeyesekere (1988) and Sarah Levine (2000).

13. Grist (1998), Aggarwal (2001, 1994), and Dollfus (1995) detail the politics and poetics of Muslim identity in Kargil and Leh districts, yet none address Zangskar specifically.

14. There were roughly 125 nuns and 325 monks residing in Zangskar's monastic institutions in 2002. In the village of Karsha alone, there are 440 laypeople but 100 monks and nuns. By contrast, in the Thai village where Tambiah (1970) worked in 1966, there were only 10 monks residing in a village of 932 laypeople. Monastics accounted for about 15 percent of Ladakh's population in the nineteenth century, according to Cunningham (1873).

15. Tambiah (1976:355–60) and Bunnag (1973) describe rural Thai monks who move to Bangkok to acquire social networks before disrobing.

16. The travel sections in the *Boston Globe* (6/25/00) and the *Financial Times* (4/21/01) have featured Karsha's nunnery and monastery, while Zangskar's trail from Darcha to Padum and Lamayuru was hailed as one of the world's "Ten Classic Treks" by *Outside* magazine in 2001.

17. Personal communication, Tahsil Education Officer in July 1992.

18. Sonam Wangchug reported in 1999 that only one-tenth of all public school students reach the tenth grade matriculation exam. Of those who took the exam, only 4 percent passed in 1998 and 7 percent in 1999. By contrast, nearly 100 percent of the private school students passed the same exam those years.

19. Crook and Osmaston (1994:259) report Zangskar's child mortality while a French nongovernmental organization (Aide Medical Zanskar, personal communication) reported an infant mortality rate of 250 per 1,000 in 2001. Wiley (1992, 1994) reported an infant mortality rate of between 117 and 180 per 1,000 at Leh hospital in 1991.

20. The largest allopathic clinic in Zangskar had exhausted its supplies of penicillin, cough medicine, and oral rehydration packets in December of 1995. The next shipment of medicines arrived nine months later in September.

21. Osmaston (1994:42) estimates the annual precipitation in central Zangskar as 200–250 mm, while Hartmann (1983:136) reports an average annual precipitation of 115 mm for Leh and 306 mm for Kargil. Only two districts in India—one in Rajasthan and one in Gujarat—have a lower average precipitation than Ladakh in their driest month. Yet their wettest months have five times the precipitation that Ladakh does. Using Landsat imagery, Crook and Osmaston (1994:54) report that only .25 percent of Zangskar is cultivated.

22. Local medical censuses recorded the population of Zangskar to be 10,253 in 1996 and 10,861 in 2000.

23. The passes to the east and south of Zangskar include the Morang La (5,300 m), Shingo La (5,096 m), and the Phirtse La (5,350 m), while the Omasi La (5,342 m), Poat La (5,490 m), and Kang La (5,468 m) take traders west to Paldar and Kishtwar. Routes to the Indus Valley must traverse the Charchar La (4,900 m)

or Ruberung La (4,700 m), or a set of seven passes: the Parfi La (3,900 m), Hanuma La (4,710 m), Senge La (4,970 m), Bumtse La (4,200), Sirsir La (4,680), Nyigutse La (5,000), and Yogma La (4,700 m). Kargil is reached due north over the Pentse La pass (4,400 m).

24. Gutschow and Gutschow (2003) describe the patterns of field ownership and irrigation in Zangskar. They specify that only a handful of Rinam's 180 fields and only two of Karsha's over 1,000 fields are owned by nonresidents.

25. While Drew (1875) reported a total population of about 2,500 people living in 45 hamlets when he visited Zangskar in the late nineteenth century, the Permanent Settlement of 1908 recorded a census of 4,441 people (Muhammad, 1909). In 1908, the religious breakdown was 97 percent Buddhist and 3 percent Muslim. There were roughly 51 hamlets in 1908 but I counted more than 100 hamlets by 1995.

26. The total cultivated land increased from 3,217 acres to 4,178 acres between 1908 and 1971, but had jumped to 5,124 acres by 1981. In one older village, Rinam, only 18 out of 182 fields were built in this century, as Gutschow and Gutschow (2003) report. This validates the finding that many new fields were built in entirely new settlements rather than in already existing hamlets.

27. Although Huber and Pedersen (1997) critique the popular conception of a Tibetan environmental ethic, they fail to note the common property schemes described by Gutschow (1997c, 1998a) and Crook and Osmaston (1994).

28. Lansing (1991) coined this term to explain how Balinese temples articulate a common interest in irrigation management without the use of an external bureaucracy.

29. Agrarian practices in Zangskar are described in extensive detail in Crook and Osmaston (1994) and Friedl (1983). Those villages with more grazing areas and thus larger herds of livestock produce surplus butter, which is traded internally for surplus grain. The largest grazing areas usually lie at higher altitudes or along the major riverbeds.

30. Per month, the family may expect three kilos of butter per hybrid *(mdzo mo)* and two kilos of butter per cow *(ba shi)*.

31. Moore (1996) finds diagnostic events critical to understanding the durable and the improvised nature of practice, which Bourdieu (1977) has called the habitus.

32. Like the Nyinba houses discussed by Levine (1988:111), Zangskari households represent classic corporate groups.

33. Bourdieu (1977:183) states that "symbolic capital, a transformed and thereby disguised form of physical 'economic' capital, produces its proper effect inasmuch, and only inasmuch, as it conceals the fact that it originates in 'material' forms of capital which are also, in the last analysis, the source of its effects." Elsewhere Bourdieu (1980:118) notes that "symbolic capital is this denied cap-

ital recognized as legitimate, that is misrecognized as capital . . . is perhaps the only possible form of accumulation when economic capital is not recognized."

34. The monastery runs on a fixed, sacred calendar of thirty-day months, while village and nunnery follow the same intercalated astrological calendar which uses solar and lunar cycles.

35. Day (1989), Dollfus (1989), Phylactou (1989), Riaboff (1997a,c), and Kaplanian (1981, 1989) describe rites dedicated to the spirits in the three realms, which are also detailed in Mumford (1990).

36. The houses visited include major sharecroppers *(chun pa)* for the monastery, headman's houses, or other significant houses.

37. The circumambulation during *Bum skor* involves transporting Buddhist relics such as a statue, a vessel of blessed water, and perhaps a volume of the Prajñaparamita *('Bum).*

38. Each village section receives a number of volumes depending on its size. Phyikar gets five volumes, Nangkar gets four volumes, while Tiur, Sendo, and Yulang each receive one volume. In Yulang, only households which receive irrigation water from Karsha participate, suggesting the rite is related to fertility.

39. Nebesky-Wojkowitz (1969) and Kohn (2001) describe the *'chams* dances, while the latter depicts the role of the old couple at the Mani Rimdu dance in Nepal.

40. *Srub lha* is the first day when the scythe *(zor ba)* may be used in the fields.

41. I estimate that 12,200 kg of grain goes up in smoke each year in Zangskar. Each of the 2,000 households in Zangskar uses about 5 kg of grain during its fire sacrifice (consisting of 1 kg of raw barley, wheat, peas, and buckwheat, and 1 kg each of barley flour and other grains), while the monasteries and nunneries burn an additional 200 kilos in their rituals.

42. The Padum Skurim festival involves corvee labor *('u lag),* drawn from six households each in Gyapag, Nyerog, Yulang, and Karsha.

43. The document that contains the monastic regulations *(chos khrims)* includes many rules frequently broken, such as the one against beer drinking.

44. Both village and household altars are renewed three times a year: New Year (X.29), Spring Day (II.1), and Harvest Day (VII.?). The new year celebrations in Ladakh are described by Day (1989), Dargyay (1989), Dollfus (1989), Phylactou (1989), and Kaplanian (1981).

45. The offering cakes *(lha bon mchod pa)* eaten at Losar and springtime plowing ceremonies seem connected with fertility, as is the dough or butter ibex.

46. One Karsha resident recalls that a live goat was sacrificed annually to the village deity in upper Zangskar in her childhood. The local deities invoked at one house included the household guardian deity *(Pha'i lha gser lha),* the village god *(Jo bo dgra lha),* Six-Armed Mahakala, a local protector *(Shar Phyogs),* and a legendary dwarf *(Ba lu ma).*

47. In Zangskari, the deities honored include: guardian god, hearth god, the golden ibex, the iron post, the golden mother beam, the pearly rafters, the

doughy ceiling, the starry window, the eight cross-beams, four posts, the subterranean spirits, gods, lords of the earth and place.

48. For fear of bad luck, a firebrand is not tossed if one of the household members
is absent, unless he or she is far enough away (that is, in Delhi) to be immune.

49. Mumford (1990) and Turner (1969, 1974) describe the creative liminality of
the new year rites when hierarchies are first reversed and then reaffirmed.

50. The barley beer drunk communally during the New Year festival is paid for by
the fines collected by the village shepherd *(lo ra pa),* chosen each year to prevent village livestock from grazing in the fields. Several tax fields sharecropped
by a local household also provide additional barley for the beer that is stored
throughout the festival in the monastery's largest vat.

51. The girl dancers are called Khatunma, possibly after the legendary queen
from Skardu, Gyal Khatun, wife of the Ladakhi king Jamyang Namgyal. Other
Ladakhi kings who took Muslim wives include Nyima Namgyal (1694–1720),
who married Zizi Khatun from Khapalu, and Tsewang Rabtan, who married
Zora Khatun.

52. I was told that post-solstice rites are believed to give the sun a ritual push, so
that it does not get stuck—like a truck going into reverse—when reversing its
path across the horizon at solstice time.

53. The use of fire in solstice rituals in the Hindu Kush and Indo-Tibetan realms is
described by Khoo (1997), Loude and Lievre (1987), and Vohra (1995a).

54. The altar includes three ritual cakes *(gtor ma),* offered to the religious protectors *(chos skyong),* the guardian deity *(yi dam),* and the "lords of the site" *(gzhi
bdag).* Smaller offering cakes *(zhal zas)* represent food for the deities and demons or obstacles *(bgegs).*

55. Aziz (1976) portrays a nunnery kitchen among the Sherpa in Nepal.

56. The monks renew their Vinaya vows in a more relaxed manner, without fasting. The Karsha nuns are the only monastics in Zangskar who perform this
rigorous renewal of their Vinaya vows.

57. Daniels (1994), Klein (1985), Miller (1980), Aziz (1978), and Brauen (1994) all
attest to women's economic agency in Himalayan and Tibetan households.
Brauen describes the Bumthang valley of eastern Bhutan, where women own
most of the property.

58. Among Tibetan nomad populations east of Zangskar, women are expected to
weave, as Ahmed (1997) notes.

59. The kinship terminology is largely symmetrical and classificatory. Consan-
guine kin *(gnyen)* are differentiated from affinal relations *(spun, tshan),* just as
cross-cousins *(a zhang a ni'i phrug gu)* are distinguished from parallel cousins
(a ma che chung gi phrug gu, a pha che chung gi phrug gu). Dollfus (1989),
Gutschow (1995), and Prince Peter (1963: 335–394) review the Ladakhi and
Zangskari kinship terminology.

60. Gutschow (1995a), Desideri (in Fillipi, 1932: 192), Prince Peter (1963:327–

328), Brauen (1980a:23; 1980b:54, 55), Levine (1981), and Carrasco (1959:39) each define bone as an idiom of patrilineal descent.

61. The *pha spun* was originally a lineage group, although it has become a neighborhood group with less reference to kinship in Ladakh according to Phylactou (1989), Dollfus (1989), Day (1989), Prince Peter (1956), and Brauen (1980a,b, 1982).

62. Bone and deity are interconnected, but not interchangeable, terms. The fact that houses may take on a new guardian deity but keep their old bone, or keep their deity while changing their bone, has not been discussed extensively in the *pha spun* literature.

63. Riaboff (1997a,b) and Day (1989) describe the hierarchy of protective deities and gods in Zangskari and Ladakhi cosmology.

64. Erdmann (1983) and Brauen (1980a) distinguish royalty from aristocracy, although the two strata intermarry and do not have any commensality restrictions.

65. Yalman (1962) notes that while monasteries are ambivalent about accepting members of the lowest castes, renunciation is a "safety valve" of social mobility in rigidly stratified societies.

66. Yalman (1963:41) cites a common Sri Lankan saying in an essay that argues that the purity of caste is dependent on the purity of its women, in response to Gough (1955).

67. Goldstein's (1971c, 1978, 1987) groundbreaking work on the Tibetan systems of polyandry and its "monomarital principle" is discussed by Aziz (1974, 1978), Dargyay (1980, 1988), Crook and Osmaston (1994), Gutschow (1995a), Levine (1981, 1988), Phylactou (1989), and Prince Peter (1963, 1980).

68. My survey (Gutschow, 1998a) of 398 marriages in two Zangskari villages yielded 7 percent (26) as polyandrous, 8 percent (30) as polygynous, and 85 percent (339) as monogamous. Crook and Osmaston (1994) reported that in Shade village 40 percent of the marriages were polyandrous, while in Stongde village only 18 percent (10) of the marriages were polyandrous and 15 percent (8) were polygynous.

3. The Buddhist Economy of Merit

1. A standard Tantric initiation ceremony involves empowerment *(dbang bskur),* oral transmission *(lung),* and secret meditation instructions *(khrid)* as described in K. Gyatso (1996) and Trungpa (1982).

2. The nuns wove Tsetan's wool and built his house in Karsha, which villagers quip should be called the "Nuns' Treasury." In local idiom, treasury *(bla brang)* is a term ordinarily reserved for a monastic treasury and its separate endow-

ments. The term is never used to describe a private house, nor is it commonly associated with nunneries, who have so few permanent endowments.

3. Tambiah (1970) divides the "total religious field" in Thailand into four quadrants, specifying that monks perform collective merit making and death rites, but avoid the more pragmatic or expiatory rites performed by diviners, mediums, and other ritual specialists. His artificial distinction between monks and other, more pragmatic ritual specialists elides the slippage between ritual experts and their services for lay patrons in practice. Although Tambiah's analysis offers a useful heuristic device, it ignores the overlapping complexity of ritual roles in practice. As Samuel (1993) notes, Tibetan Buddhist monks often perform the duties that diviners, mediums, and exorcists perform in Southeast Asian Buddhist societies.

4. An introduction to the vast Tibetan literature on emptiness includes several key translations by Jeffrey Hopkins (1984, 1987a,b, 1999).

5. Paul (1979, 1985) and Wayman (1974) describe the Tathagathagarba theory.

6. Paul (1985:189) translates the Lotus Sutra, which specifies that women are not able to gain five critical types of status, including that of irreversible bodhisattva.

7. Cited from Paul's (1985:308) translation of the "Sutra on Changing the Female Sex." Nancy Schuster Barnes (1981, 1985) analyzes the Mahayana sources about changing the female body which debate the issue of whether it is possible to gain enlightenment in the female body.

8. The hierarchy of giving is explained in several of the articles in Sizemore and Swearer (1990:13–16), while Bowie (1999), Kirsch (1977:249), and Keyes (1983a,b) address the issue of whether the amount of merit accumulated by an act of generosity is proportional to the donor's wealth.

9. Spiro (1970) and Tambiah (1984) observed that the most ascetic monks were the object of the greatest devotions and ritual requests.

10. Keyes (1983a:858) outlines the connection between wealth and merit in Thai ethics.

11. Spiro (1970:110) describes how Burmese calculate the amount of merit received by an act of generosity or *dana*.

12. Even this story suggests that sheer quantity of gifts is the ultimate measure of merit. Strong (1990) argues that the story of Asoka and the myrobalan fruit implies that a single fruit can be worth as much as a kingdom. Yet even Asoka's tiny gift of a fruit takes meaning from all he has given. More important, once his power is restored, Asoka gives away all but the state treasury. This kingdom is then ransomed back by the ministers, using the state treasury, with a final payment that proves Asoka's gifts to be equal to those of the venerable Anathapindika, the greatest lay donor in the Buddha's lifetime.

13. Powers (1995:99) translates the Sutra Explaining the Thought *(samdhinir-*

mocana sutra, dgongs pa nges par 'grel pa'i mdo) from the Stog Palace edition of the Tibetan Kangyur.

14. Ortner (1978, 1999) concludes that Sherpa Buddhism is more selfish and asocial than Thai Buddhism. Her argument overlooks the elaborate reciprocities required to stage widespread and popular rites like the exorcisms, fasting rites, and hospitality rites for the gods.

15. While Ortner (1989, 1999a) relates how monastic institutions are founded, she does not detail the ongoing economic relations which fund monasteries and nunneries, as do Furer-Haimendorf (1964, 1976) and Aziz (1976, 1978), and Tsarong (1987). Tsarong (1987) and Crook and Osmaston (1994) each detail the economic arrangements for funding monastic rituals and other enterprises for Ladakh and Zangskar, respectively.

16. Tambiah (1970:147, 1968:68), Spiro (1970:103), and Kaufman (1960:183–184) show how informants rank various forms of merit making. In Tambiah's list, building a temple *(wat)* ranks the highest, while Kaufman's list places taking full ordination first and building a temple second. Each act receives a proportional amount of prestige or legitimacy for the donor as Keyes (1983a, 1990) and Kirsch (1977) note.

17. Schopen (1994:529ff.) translates the applicable part of the Tibetan Vinaya *(Derge 'Dul ba,* cha 154b.3–155b.2) and provides a lengthy analysis of the Sanskrit notion of permanent endowments or "that which is not exhausted" *(aksaya nivi, mi zad pa).*

18. Schopen (1994:533) translates the inscription from Sanci.

19. Schopen (1994:548) cites Horner's (1992:347) translation of the Vinaya: "When, monks seeds belonging to an order are sown on ground belonging to an individual, having given back a portion, [the rest] may be made use of. When seeds belonging to an individual are sown on ground belonging to an Order, having given back a portion, [the rest] may be made use of."

20. Schopen (1997:229–231) offers a lengthy exegesis on the Tibetan and Sanskrit glosses *(daksinam adis, yon bsngo ba)* used to describe the process of directing a spiritual reward or merit to a named beneficiary, while Gombrich (1971, 1975) explores the ways in which merit transfers are justified by canonical apologetics and current informants.

21. Schopen (1997) and Barnes (2000) both mention the decline in nuns as donors after the rise of the Mahayana in the fourth century C.E., but neither offers a certain explanation of why this occurred. Schopen (1996a) shows how nuns may have been forbidden to build stupas, a sign of the monks' attempt to control or contain them. Schopen (1994, 1996a,b, 1997) unpacks the Protestant presuppositions which privileged textual sources and thereby ignored a host of fascinating issues like the transference of merit and the pervasiveness of the stupa cult.

22. Gombrich (1971) elucidates the doctrinal debates within canonical sources about the transfer of food and merit to hungry ghosts and gods. The doctrinal answer that merit is earned by those who rejoice in an act of virtue maintains the primacy of *karma* while encouraging donors to believe that they are "transferring" the merit of their good deeds to deceased relatives.

23. Geertz (1968, 1980, 1999) describes the Balinese theater state; Tambiah (1976, 1978, 1987, 1989), Carrithers (1987), and Spiro (1977, 1978) debate the contradiction between Buddhist detachment and pragmatic kingship.

24. Hirakawa (1990:87–94) argues in favor of the northern sources which place Asoka's reign and the spread of Buddhism into Kashmir about a century after the Buddha's death. Pandit's (1935:19) translation of the *Rajatarangini* lists the monastery founded by King Surendra in Sauraka, which Ganhar and Ganhar (1956:16) identify as the Suru Valley.

25. Zangskar's earliest petroglyphs—including ibex, horses, archers, and deer—are dated to the eighth and sixth centuries B.C.E. by Ebert (1994), Francefort et al. (1990), Orofino (1990), and Linrothe (1999). Osmaston (1994, 1985) speculates that Zangskar's first inhabitants were pastoralists who migrated from the Indus Valley, while later settlement required the development of irrigation, suitable crops, and domesticating the wild yak *('brong)*.

26. The Kushan empire spread Buddhism across Central Asia in the first centuries C.E., although its exact outlines remain under debate even today. Petech (1977) records Kusan influence in Ladakh, but Snellgrove and Skorupski (1980:9) dismiss Zangskar's Kanishka stupa as "an exaggerated claim."

27. Huge rock carvings of standing Maitreya figures dated roughly to between the seventh and ninth centuries are found along a route connecting the Indus Valley, the Suru Valley, and Zangskar, at Mulbekh, Chigtan, Kartse Khar, and Karsha (Sneelgrove and Skorupsky 1977, 1980; Vohra 1988; Toricelli 1994; Fontein 1979). The fifteenth-century *Zangskar Chronicle (Zangs dkar chags tsul lo rgyus)*, which is translated by Franke (1926), reports that Zangskar lay under Kashmir during the time of a seventh-century revolt near Drangtse, which was suppressed by Tibetan forces from Guge. Snellgrove (1986:388), Petech (1977:9), and Vitali (1996:283) mention the revolt at Drangtse, which either refers to a site in southern Zangskar—near the border with Spiti—or to the eastern end of Pang gong Lake, both of which are strategic sites for controlling routes into Zangskar and Ladakh.

28. Tsering and Russell (1986) note that the lineage of fully ordained nuns was never transmitted to Tibet, while Snellgrove (1987), Shakabpa (1967), and Tucci (1988) say nothing about the nuns' order when they describe the transmission of the monks' order into Tibet. Tsai (1994, 1981) reports the arrival of the order of nuns in China during the fourth century C.E.

29. Even careful scholars like Swearer (1995:52) mistakenly place the dissolution

of the nuns' order in India at least three centuries too early, in 456 c.e. follow-ing Jordt (1988:31). Skilling (1994) describes the copper plates found which confirm the presence of fully ordained nuns in Gujarat in 723 c.e., while the Chinese pilgrim Hsuan Tsang (600–664) recorded hundreds of nuns residing in Kashmiri nunneries (Nadou 1980:39–41). Literary evidence for nuns in the Indo-Tibetan borderlands continues through the eleventh century, although further research is sorely needed.

30. The Ladakhi chronicles (Francke 1914) report that Thon mi Sambhota came to Kashmir. There are households along the Zangskar river in Chilling and Trahan, Zangskar, which still bear the clan name Thonmi Sambhota. The clan names, place names, and names of village deities offer tantalizing historical ev-idence which has been ignored by most scholars until now.

31. Padmasambhava's exploits in the mythical lands known as Uddiyana and Zahor are discussed by Nadou (1980), Gyatso (1998), Francke (1926), and Roerich (1949). Contemporary Ladakhi pilgrims believe his birthplace to be the Lotus Lake *(mtsho pad ma)* found near Rewalsar, in Mandi district. Some scholars disagree about whether his birthplace is located in what is today Swat, in Paki-stan, or in modern Bengal.

32. Demievelle (1952), Haarh (1969), Tucci (1988:2–7), Snellgrove (1987:429–433), and Nadou (1980:34–37) describe the founding of Samyas.

33. Snellgrove (1987:431) and Tucci (1988:9) describe the annual endowment for Tibet's first monastery, Samyas, as including 150 estates providing an annual allowance of 75 bushels of barley, 9 changes of clothes, 108 ounces of seasoned butter, 1 horse, 4 packs of paper, and 3 pieces of dry ink, and salt for the abbot; 35 bushels of barley, 800 ounces of butter, 1 horse, and 6 changes of clothes for each of the 25 monks in retreat; 50 bushels of barley, 6 changes of clothes, 800 ounces of butter for each of the 13 teachers; 8 bushels of barley, 2 packs of pa-per, and 1 piece of ink for each of the monks in retreat; and 25 bushels of bar-ley and 3 changes of clothes for each of the 25 students.

34. Vitali's (1996) translation of a fifteenth-century chronicle from Guge offers startling new insights into these nascent Himalayan kingdoms. Nyimagon's queen is spelled Zhang kha ma by Petech (1997:232) but Cog ro Zangs kha ma by Vitali (1996:172). The latter spelling suggests that Nyimagon's wife may be from Zangskar, and of the Cog Ro clan which Vitali places in Spiti. There is no reason that the clan could not also have spread to Zangskar.

35. Petech (1998:232–233), Vitali (1996:156–159), and Tucci (1956) summarize the conflicting Tibetan sources regarding the division of Nyimagon's empire among his three sons. Vitali (1996:160) notes that "by far the most problem-atic of the three skors [kingdoms] is Guge." I follow the detailed account given by the Ladakhi historian Gergan (1976:182; my translation from Ladakhi): "The youngest [son] lDe gtsug mgon was given: from the lower portions of the

Kage River to the upper head of the Pentse Valley, the land of Lahaul, the three realms of Zangskar, the Spiti ladle, the common subjects [it] contains, the turquoise earrings [like a] treasured eye in the peacock feather, the armor of sapphires, tiny stones and powder of that same [sapphire]: these were the lands and jewels which made up the dominions. A footnote: Lungnag, Stod, and gZhung all together [comprise] three separate valleys, known generally as the 'three doors of Zangskar.'"

36. The gap between the death of Detsugon in the late tenth century and the subsequent kings of Zangskar is interpreted by historians such as Crook and Osmaston (1994:445–446), Snellgrove and Skorupski (1980), Vitali (1996), Petech (1977), and Dargyay (1987). The Zangskar chronicle (Francke 1926) implies Detsugon's son, named Senge Lde, was raised in Kashmir, where he married the king's daughter, before inheriting the kingdom of Kishtwar. While his sons then returned to retake the throne of Zangskar, there is a considerable gap in the subsequent chronology until the fifteenth century.

37. Tucci (1988) and Snellgrove and Skorupski (1980:86) both translate an eleventh-century biography of Rinchen Zangpo written by his disciple, Pal Yeshe. The text describes Rinchen Zangpo's sister, Yogini Light of the Doctrine, as a highly accomplished Tantric adept and a probationary nun *(dge slob ma).*

38. Tsering and Russell (1986:28) explain that between the fifteenth and seventeenth centuries individual monks seem to have performed full ordination rites for a few nuns in Tibet, although such ordinations are invalid, in canonical terms.

39. The fifteenth-century text by the abbot of Tholing monastery translated by Vitali (1996:51, 60, 107, 110, 114, 178, 274–251) has numerous references to nunneries founded by King Yeshe Od and his daughter. The text repeatedly refers to nuns as *btsun mo,* but does not specify whether the nuns held novice or full ordination vows. It also mentions a thirteenth-century woman who is a fully ordained nun.

40. Klimburg-Salter (1998:85) assumes that the women in the Tabo frieze are nuns, but does not dwell on the nature of their ordination vows.

41. The fifteenth-century Tibetan historian who wrote the *Blue Annals* devotes two lines to Gelongma Palmo, but devotes ten pages to the male disciples who wrote liturgies for the rite she founded. Roerich (1949:1007–1018, 1044), Zopa and Churinoff (1995), Ortner (1989:181; 1999:297–305), March (1979:277ff.), Shaw (1994:126–130), Tsomo (1989:120), and Vargas-O'Brian (2001) offer versions of Gelongma Palmo's life story.

42. Vargas-O'Brian (2001) does not specify Palmo's birthplace. Nadou (1980:188) clearly situates her in Kashmir, because her disciples included Jnanabhadra, who ordained Rinchen Zangpo in 971 C.E. Vargas-O'Brian (2001) and Dowman (1985:372–375) note that Gelongma Palmo (Bhiksuni Lakmi) from Kashmir

should not be confused with Laksminkara from Uddiyana, the sister of King Indrabodhi.

43. Ortner's (1999a) oral biography of Palmo closely matches that told by Ngawang Tharpa in Zangskar. The one detail that Tharpa adds is that Gelongma Palmo is refused admission to the nunnery until the abbot reads a letter from her famous brother, who is King Indrabodhi in this version.

44. The Candamaharosana Tantra is translated by Shaw (1994:48), who argues that Tantric adepts had to respect and honor women, especially those from whom they sought teachings.

45. In comparing the narratives of medieval men and women, Bynum (1991) overturns Turner's conclusion about liminality by arguing that women experience continuity rather than reversal in their ritual dramas.

46. Princess Mandarava, Yeshe Tsogyal, and Lakminkara are enlightened female adepts whose biographies are translated in Chonam and Khandro (1998), Tulku (1983), Dowman (1984, 1985), Shaw (1987), and Gross (1987).

47. My translation of a thirteenth-century inscription from the walls of the Avalokitesvara temple in Karsha village.

48. The history of Zangskar can be culled from rock carvings, wall paintings, petroglyphs, royal chronicles, monastic tax records, colophons of religious texts, and oral legends. Translations of local texts are found in Francke (1926), Gergan (1976), Tsering (1979), Zodpa and Shakspo (1979), Crook and Osmaston (1994), Gutschow (1998), Petech (1977, 1998), Roerich (1949), and Snellgrove and Skorupski (1980).

49. Historical research on and archeological evidence (Linrothe 1999, 2002) of Kashmiri-style stone sculptures and stupas found near Karsha and elsewhere in the Northern Realm reinforce local legends attributing three temples in Zangskar's Northern Realm—at Karsha, Langmi, and Dechiling—to Rinchen Zangpo.

50. Phagspa Sherab (1012–1097) is mentioned in Crook and Osmaston (1994), Karmay (1980), Roerich (1949:233, 354–55), Snellgrove and Skorupski (1980:42), and Vitali (1990).

51. Gutschow (1998) describes a local Zangskari history *(man ngag gi slob dpon brgyud pa'i rtogs pa brjod pa nyung ngu rnam par gsal ba zhes bya ba bzhugs so)* which records the exploits of Zangskari doctors who became personal physicians to two Panchen Lamas, Lozang Chökyi Gyaltsen (1569–1602) and Palden Yeshe, as well as the great fifth Dalai Lama, Lozang Gyatso (1617–1682).

52. In 2002 Zangskar's ten nunneries housed roughly 125 nuns: Karsha (22), Zangla (18), Skyagam (14), Shun-Satak (14), Dorje Dzong (13), Tungri (11), Pishu (11), Bya (6), Manda (3), Sani (14). Its eight monasteries housed roughly 325 monks: Karsha (100), Stongde (45), Phugthal (65), Rangdum (25), Bardan (30), Stagrimo (25), Dzongkhul (20), Mune (15).

53. Petech (1977) reports that a young Zangla prince, Tsondüs Gyaltsen, valiantly

defended his kingdom during this Ladakhi invasion but later fled to Guge where be became a disciple of the abbot of Tholing monastery in 1618.

54. The Pishu nuns learned the *gcod* practice from a Tibetan monk whose father was called Khampa Lugong. He may have been one of the human ransoms *(glud 'gong)* who were expelled from Lhasa during the new year celebration to remove negativity, as Richardson (1993) notes.

55. Petech (1977: 99, 109) describes how Tanzin Angmo, princess of Padum, was first a nun, but was later married to the Ladakhi king Deskyong Namgyal (ruled 1720–1739).

56. Gutschow (1998) and Riaboff (1997) interpret the settlement reports authored by Muhammad (1909, 1908). Carrasco (1959:86) confirms that in the Tibetan province of Sakya, monasteries held 42 percent of land, while aristocrats held 21 percent and commoners held 37 percent.

57. Kaul and Kaul (1992) describe the land reform act promulgated in the 1980s, which affected only a handful of Zangskari households.

58. Bakula Rinpoche, a friend of Pandit Nehru's, served as the minister of foreign affairs in Jammu and Kashmir before becoming ambassador to Mongolia, as Kaul and Kaul (1992) and Shakspo (1988b) note.

59. One such monastic estate is known as Khang 'Gog, or literally, "ruined house," possibly because it was so difficult to maintain. Its owners, several of whom left in the last century, included migrants from Tibet.

60. Osmaston (1990) and Mankelow (1999) record the crop yields in Zangskar, which compare favorably with those of small farms in North America.

61. The inner retinue includes the posts of: disciplinarian *(dge skos)*, assistant disciplinarian *(dge g.yog)*, sacristan *(dkon gnyer)*, butcher *(bsha' pa)*, cook *(byan ma)*, and hearth assistant *(thab g.yog)*. The outer retinue includes: two conch blowers *(dung pa)*, two long horn blowers *(dung chen pa)*, and two oboe players *(rgya gling pa)*. The Labrang sacristan performs offerings to the Tantric deities and local protectors, including Pehar and other king spirits *(rgyal po)*.

62. The total amount of grain collected is a rough figure at best. Riaboff (1997a) enumerates the various amounts of grain used to sponsor each monastic ritual.

63. Besides managing endowments, the four Labrang stewards each have specific assignments: the treasurer *(lde pa)* and assistant treasurer *(lde pa'i g.yog po)* handle the loans and rents, the sacristan *(dkon gnyer)* is in charge of ritual items and offerings, while the cook *(byan ma)* manages ritual donations and the distribution of food. The Labrang stewards collect taxes from the following villages: Karsha, Yulang, Rinam, Sendo, Abran, Chibra, Kushul, Lungmur, Hamiling, Skyagam, Remala, Manda, Phye, Rantagsha, Shamoling, Tungri, Cangri, Trahan, Rabnyod, Nawaphal, Rizhing, Langmi, Testa, Kazar, Hongshet, Gyapag, Nyerog, Rurug, Pipiting, Tshazar, Zangla, Marutse, Aksho.

64. The twelve houses in Karsha pay a total of 78 *khal* in tax, one house in Yulang

pays 7 *khal*, the ten houses in Rizhing pay a total of 30 *khal*, the seven houses in Kumig pay a total of 21 *khal*, and the fifteen houses in Stongde pay a total of 42 *khal* tax, for a total of 178 *khal*. Riaboff (1997a) reports a total of 170 *khal* in taxes from similar houses; the discrepancy may be due to our monastic informants. The measure used for grain since at least the thirteenth century is the *khal*, which is made up of 20 cups *('bre)* or roughly 10–12 kilograms.

65. Every monk must serve as a manipa steward on rotation.

66. Each household received a silver rupee coin known colloquially as a *dolo*, after the Hindi *tola*, the standard weight of the British rupee after 1833, according to Yule and Burnell's (1886:563, 807, 928) popular lexicon. In 1960 a *dolo* could purchase 5 *khal* (50 kg) of grain, while a sheep could be bought for 2–3 *dolo*, a cow for 6–7 *dolo*, and an ordinary work horse for 8–9 *dolo*.

67. Several houses pay the "interest" in butter rather than grain, and some houses pay only half as much interest as others, and some households of three villages—Abran, Tzazar, and Rgyapag-Nyerog—pay their interest directly to the monastic treasury.

68. One steward recalled that at least five nuns were needed for two weeks to roast the grain. While the nuns often work for free, laywomen demand a wage.

69. The titular head of the monastery, Ngari Rinpoche, gets five shares; the Labrang treasury gets ten shares; the abbot gets three shares; the ex-abbots, Vajra master, chantmaster, assistant chantmaster, disciplinarian, Labrang managers, and Labrang assistant each get an additional share. French (1995:4) reports that monks in one Tibetan monastery annually received 110 kg of grain (80 kg in raw grain and 30 kg as flour).

70. Compare the Tashi Gonpa nunnery in Nepal, where each nun received 84 kg of grain annually (roughly one-fifth of her grain consumption). The total grain disbursed was 2,025 kg per year according to Fürer Haimendorf (1976:127).

71. Tungri, Dorje Dzong, and Pishu nunnery merely host the bi-monthly prayer sessions and the Great Prayer Festival, while the newest and least well endowed nunneries like Skyagam, Bya, Manda and Sani only celebrate a brief Prayer Festival.

72. Each of these monthly rituals requires: 1.3 kg of butter for tea and butter lamps, 7 kg of roasted barley flour for the communal offering cakes *(tshogs)*, 10 kg of wheat flour for the breads (except on the tenth), one bottle of buttermilk as a leavening agent, a handful of salt, two handfuls of loose green tea, and a plateful of sweets known as *tshogs zas*.

73. The food provided during the Great Prayer Festival is a rich repast. In addition to the thick butter tea, a typical menu might include: breakfast of sweet tea, fried bread *(ku ra)*, butter porridge *(du ru)*, sweet barley dough *(phye dmar)*; lunch of rice and lentils or stew *(pag thug)*; snack of flat breads and apricot

stew *(pha ting);* and a dinner of pea flour paste *(bag pa),* butter, and chili paste *(tsha mig).*

74. The donations a single nun earns have risen sharply due to the increased length of the festival as well as inflation. In 2000, each nun earned 350 Rs (or $9), in 1995 the sum was 200 Rs, in 1990, the sum was barely 100 Rs, and in the early 1980s a nun might earn 30 rupees. When the festival began in the 1960s each nun earned only 5 rupees.

75. Gutschow (1999), March (1979), and Ortner (1978) describe the ritual sequence of the *smyung gnas* fasting ritual. A single meal is eaten on the first day of the festival, while the second day is a total fast, and the third day involves the breaking of the fast and a communal meal *(tshogs).*

76. Gutschow (1997) compares the economics and attendance of the 1994 fasting rituals held at Karsha monastery and nunnery. The monastery's fast had over 350 participants and required the following goods: 1,500 kg of grain for the beer, 7,000 Rs worth of meat, 930 kg of butter, 1,700 kg local flour, 700 kg baking flour, 400 kg rice, and 2,000 flat breads. The nunnery's fast had 28 participants and required: 60 kg of grain for beer, 1,000 Rs worth of meat, 31 kg of butter, 200 kg local flour, 20 kg baking flour, 20 kg rice, and 100 flat breads.

77. Gutschow (1999) describes the interdependent cycle of fasting and feasting which accompanies the fasting rite and is dominated by female participants in Zangskar.

78. Geertz (1973:112), in his classic description of the Balinese cockfight, notes, "What, as we have already seen, the cockfight talks most forcibly about is status relationships, and what it says about them is that they are matters of life and death."

79. Bourdieu (1977: 179) emphasizes the power of symbolic capital in agrarian society when he explains, "thus we see that symbolic capital, which in the form of prestige or renown attached to a family name is readily convertible back into economic capital, is perhaps the most valuable form of accumulation in a society in which the severity of the climate . . . and the limited technical resources . . . demand collective labor."

80. Aggarwal (1994:267–268) describes the religious syncretism in the border village of Achinathang, where local legend of a sibling pair that stole from the prophet ascribes a joint origin to Ramazan and the Buddhist fasting ritual.

81. Bourdieu (1990:96).

82. Phylactou (1989) and Day (1989) describe the annual cycle of household rituals in Ladakh.

83. Bourdieu (1990:97).

84. The dialectic between ascetic forest monks and the urbanized or worldly monks is described by Tambiah (1984), Carrithers (1983), Gombrich and Obeyesekere (1988), and Yalman (1962).

85. Cited from Irigaray (1987:120).

4. The Buddhist Traffic in Women

1. Rosaldo (1986), Steedly (1993), and Jackson (1998) theorize how narratives can serve as models of and for social reality while Kakar (1989) and Doniger (1973, 1980, 1984, 1999) explore the Indian use of myths, dreams, and narratives to reflect cultural paradoxes.

2. Arendt (1973:107) is cited in Jackson (1998:34) to show how storytelling shapes experience without attempting necessarily to explain it away.

3. The tale of Nangsa Öbum belongs to a didactic genre known as "returned from beyond" *('das log)* tales, in which heroes or heroines use near-death experiences to offer moral teachings, as outlined in Epstein (1982), Havnevik (1995, 1998), and Pommaret (1989). Nangsa's tale is translated by Allione (1984) and Waddell (1895).

4. Faure (1998:20) notes that while beauty may be a blessing for monks it is a curse for women who seek to become nuns.

5. Quoted in Allione (1984:122).

6. Only one nun out of a hundred I interviewed was an eldest daughter. She had to flee Zangskar and has never returned.

7. According to Crook and Osmaston (1994), nearly half of all adult women (ranging in age from fifteen to thirty-one) were unmarried in Kumig village, where the mean age of marriage was 20.5 for women. I found that one-sixth of women over twenty-five were unmarried in Tashitongdze in 1992.

8. Customarily, illegitimate children *(nal bu)* are raised by the mother for the first few years and sent to the father's house where they may stay until death or marriage.

9. Tsomo (1996:25) translates the nun's discipline, which states: "Just as a person whose leg is injured is unable to walk; similarly those who have broken the precepts cannot be reborn as a god or a human."

10. In Zangskar, fate or luck is colloquially known by the name "forehead" *(stod pa)* after the place where it is believed to be written. Compare the Tamil notion of karma called "headwriting" which Daniel (1983) describes.

11. Durkheim (1965:351).

12. There were four women raped in Karsha—a village of 438 inhabitants—during a seven-year period. Daniels (1994) reports that one-seventh (three out of twenty) of the female pilgrims she interviewed in Nepal had been raped along their journey.

13. Legitimate children under the age of six are buried without a formal cremation, either in the winter kitchen—the symbolic womb of the house—or outside the village. An illegitimate child is never buried in the house, because it would be inauspicious and defiling.

14. The search for female community as a rationale for joining a monastic com-

munity has been largely ignored in the literature, although Faure (2003) addresses it in his account of medieval Japanese nunneries. Ortner (1996:130), for example, admits that "the data are unavailable to indicate whether such expectations [for sisterhood] are widespread among women contemplating becoming nuns, and/or whether, in practice, such 'sisterly' supportiveness actually crystallizes."

15. The neologisms for homosexuality are reported in Goldstein (1984:203). Goldstein (1964:134) describes homosexuality as "sinful but widespread" among bodyguard monks called the *ldab ldobs*.

16. Aku Tonpa's escapades are translated and illustrated in Dorje (1975).

17. Women may send out signals inviting an affair, but men are the agents of seduction who carry out the daring escapades of adultery.

18. A disrobed nun *(jo log)* owes her congregation a blessing scarf, 10,000 rupees ($250), and a full tea service to the congregation, while fallen monks *(grva log)* must pay their congregation between 1,000 and 10,000 rupees ($25–$250), depending on which monastic post they have abandoned.

19. Bennet (1983) and Raheja and Gold (1992) describe the depression and abuse new brides suffer far from their natal homes in Hindu and Rajput culture.

20. The term for the groom's party *(gnya' bo pa)* derives from partisan *(gnya' ba)* or buyer *(nyo pa)*, as they are seen to be bartering for the bride.

21. Day (1989), Dollfus (1989), and Phylactou (1989) discuss the symbolism of the arrow in Ladakhi marriage.

22. Day (1989) and Kapferer (1991) describe the rise and fall of deities and demons within the Ladakhi and Sinhalese religious imaginations.

23. Ortner (1989a) describes how youngest sons and nuns offer aging parents assistance on family estates in Sherpa societies.

24. Lekshe Tsomo (1996) translates the monastic discipline in the Dharmagupta and the Mulasarvastivadin schools, while Horner (1992), Kabilsingh (1984, 1998), and Hirakawa (1999) translate other recensions of this discipline from Pali and Chinese texts.

25. Prebish (1996:94–95) compares the Pratimoksa sutras in the Mahasamghika and Mulasarvastivadin schools.

26. Grimshaw (1983a, 1983b, 1992) explores the economic relations and subservience between Julichen nunnery and Rizong monastery at Rizong in Ladakh.

27. Cited from Lévi-Strauss (1969:481).

28. Dumont's (1976) classic essay suggests that world renunciants aim to separate themselves from society, which proves impossible in the case of Buddhism. Khandelwal (1996, 1997, 2001) and Phillimore (2001) confirm the reciprocal ties that female renunciants retain in Hindu orders, while Mills (1997), Lewis (2000), and Swearer (1995) do the same for Buddhist orders, without exploring the gendered nature of such exchanges.

29. Rubin (1975:174) defines marriage as one in which women are the conduit of a relationship but not in control of it. Strathern (1988:339) cautions that both men and women may be objects and agents of the marital exchange at different times and that "it is as agents that they suffer domination."

30. Irigaray (1985:170) deconstructs Lévi-Strauss's premise that men acquire sociality through the exchange of women by questioning his underlying premise of heterosexuality. Butler (1990), Irigaray (1985, 1987, 1994), MacCormack and Strathern (1980), Rubin (1975), Steedly (1993), and Strathern (1988) each criticize Lévi-Strauss's (1969:496) famous assertion that "the emergence of symbolic thought must have required that women, like words, should be things that were exchanged."

31. Dreze and Sen (1994) note that the female-male ratio in India (.93) is lower than that of China (.94) and Africa (.96), but higher than that of Pakistan (.91). The ratio of women to men in Leh (.805) and Kargil districts (.900) are reported in the 2001 Census of India, while Vasudev (2003) reports on the shocking rise of female infanticide and sex selection in some of India's affluent cities, suburbs, and states.

32. Irigaray (1987:192).

33. Rubin (1975:177) argues that "'exchange of women' is a shorthand for expressing that the social relations of a kinship system specify that men have certain rights in their female kin, and that women do not have the same rights either to themselves or to their male kin."

5. Becoming a Nun

1. The narrative describing the founding of the nuns' order and the eight special rules varies across different recensions of the Vinaya, or monastic discipline. Blackstone (2001:9) lists most of the translations of this narrative, which include Horner (1952) and Warren (1885) from the Pali, Wilson in Paul (1985) and Rockhill (1884) from the Sanskrit and Tibetan Mulasarvastivadin canon, and Nolot (1991), Strong (1995), and Hirakawa (1999) from the Sanskrit and Chinese Mahasamghika canon. Sponberg (1992:14–15) explicitly contrasts the Pali and Mulasarvastivadin versions of the narrative.

2. Findly (1999:59) notes that Ananda was made to pay for his insolence in standing up for nuns by having to confess a wrongdoing after the Buddha's death.

3. The Tibetan version of the eight rules is translated in Jamgön Kongtrul's *Buddhist Ethics* (1998:364), who cites Gunaprabha's *One Hundred Formal Procedures.* The order and wording of the eight rules vary slightly depending on the Buddhist school, although the overall effect remains the same: nuns are subordinate to monks. The most important difference is that in the

Mulasarvastivadin Vinaya, the eight rules prevents nuns from scolding or censuring even those monks who break their precepts, while the Mahasamghika Vinaya substitutes a rule that nuns cannot receive food or gifts before monks do.

4. Scholars who have questioned the validity of the eight rules include Barnes (2000), Horner (1930), Nattier (1988), Sponberg (1992), and Yuichi (1982).

5. Both Wilson (1997) and Willis (1985) argue that the rules effectively forbid nuns from teaching monks. Horner (1930) and Findly (1999) argue that the early order of nuns abandoned several of the eight rules when they began to arrange their own absolutions, confessions, and rainy season retreats.

6. Tsai (1994) reports that by the fourth century, Kashmiri monks began ordaining women in China, although such ordinations were deemed invalid because they lacked a quorum of fully ordained nuns. The procedure of monks ordaining novice nuns is valid in Tibetan Buddhism.

7. Skilling (1994) and Gunawardana (1988) provide literary references for the order of nuns in South Asia and Sri Lanka up through the late tenth century, in Siam during the seventh century, in Burma between the eleventh and fifteenth centuries, in Cambodia during the twelfth century, and in Java during the fourteenth century. Schopen (1997), Barnes (2001), and Falk (1980) depict the nuns' powerful presence in India up through the fourth century, while speculating on its later decline.

8. Gombrich (1971) notes that when the Sri Lankan monks' order fully collapsed in 1065, and was threatened with extinction in 1596, 1697, and 1753, Burmese and Thai monks were brought in to revive the tradition.

9. Fully ordained nuns hold a different number of vows in each school, yet all vows are organized into the same seven groups: Parajika, Sanghavasesa, Nisargika-payantika, Payantika, Pratidesaniya, Saiksa, and Adhikarana samatha, although the last group, which concerns rules regulating disputes, is often omitted. The complete list of 311 vows of the Theravada canon, the 348 vows of Dharmagupta canon, and the 371 vows of the Mulasarvastivadin canon are translated in Hirakawa (1999), Kabilsingh (1985, 1998), and Tsomo (1998).

10. Tsomo (1988) notes that 60,000 women hold Buddhist precepts throughout the world: 15,000 are fully ordained nuns, 5,000 are novices or probationers, and 40,000 hold a varying number of precepts (five, eight, or ten). The debate over reestablishing full ordination for nuns is discussed in Bartholomeusz (1992, 1994), Gombrich and Obeyesekere (1988), Levine (2000), Li (2000), and Tsomo (1988, 1996).

11. Van Gennep (1960:2–3).

12. Victor Turner (1967:94) interpreted Van Gennep's tripartite scheme as phases of a single ritual or social process. For Turner, transition or liminality became

the centerpiece of a theoretical schema which explained the dual necessity of static social order and creative, antinomian reversal.

13. In Tsomo's translation (1996:25), the Dharmagupta school warns nuns who break their vows that "just as a person whose leg is injured is unable to walk, similarly those who have broken the precepts, cannot be reborn as a god or a human." An ordination manual from this school warns that breaking the four root precepts *(parajika)* is like "a man who having his head cut off cannot come to life; a tree with dead root cannot be alive again; a needle cannot be used without a head; nor a broken rock can come back to its original shape anymore." Sarah Levine supplied this manual from Lumbini.

14. Dainelli's observations about the absence of nuns in Ladakh are recorded by Fillipi (1932:111).

15. Dollfus (1989) reports the Ladakhi proverb. In the Himalayan and Tibetan realm, unordained women can form peripheral communities or attach themselves to nunneries, as Klein (1985) and Ortner (1989a, 1996:116) describe.

16. *Rab 'byung ma* is a condensation of *rab tu 'byung ba,* which derives from *rab tu* (thoroughly, fully) and *'byung ba* (go forth, set out).

17. While the two terms, *bsyen gnas* and *smyung gnas,* are often mistaken, Gutschow (1999) clarifies the ritual process of the fasting rite.

18. Havnevik (1998) reports that nuns in Tibet like Ani Lochen administered first tonsure.

19. Van Gennep (1960:166).

20. Scholars who debate the symbolic import of hair include Tylor (1873), Berg (1951), Leach (1958), Hershman (1974), Obeyesekere (1981), Lang (1995), Hallpike (1969), and Eilberg-Schwartz and Doniger (1995). Bartholomeusz (1994) and Salgado (1996) describe the tonsure ceremony for female renunciants *(dasa sil mata)* in Sri Lanka, in which the shorn hair is used as a meditation vehicle.

21. Like Zangskaris, Sherpas toss hair, old clothes, and amulets into trees so they cannot be defiled, as Adams (1999) notes. The idea that luck *(spar kha)* resides in physical substances like hair or clothes is related to the Indian notion of bodily substances which Marriot (1989, 1991) explores. Van Gennep (1960:166) notes that shorn hair is often "buried, burned, saved in a sachet, or placed in a relative's keeping."

22. Such texts may include standard canonical works such as the Diamond Sutra, Heart Sutra, and Offering to the Lama, and a local text by Dragom Rinpoche (1992).

23. Bourdieu (1977) borrowed the notion of habitus from Marcel Mauss (1935) to describe the habitual but generative activities of the body. While Mahmood (2001) and Farnell (2000) reject Bourdieu's account for failing to explain how the habitus is embodied, it does reflect how nuns adopt the monastic discipline through their bodies rather than merely through rote memorization of rules.

24. Gutschow (1998a, 2001b) provides a second-hand account of a novice ordination in Tibet. Thurman (1995) and Dagpa, Tsering, and Chophel (1975) translate ordination manuals and novice vows in the Tibetan tradition. Tambiah (1968, 1985), Spiro (1982:234–254), and Keyes (1986) depict monks' ordination in the Theravada tradition.

25. A Dharmagupta ordination manual lists thirteen major obstacles which prevent an individual from taking ordination: (1) having committed one of the Four Root Downfalls, (2) having defiled a nun, (3) having received precepts through deceit, (4) apostasy, (5) being not fully female, (6) having committed patricide, (7) having committed matricide, (8) having killed an Arhat, or fully enlightened being, (9) having caused a schism in the monastic assembly, (10) having shed the blood of the Buddha, (11) being nonhuman, (12) being an animal, and (13) not having proper male and female characteristics. The ten minor hindrances are: (1) not knowing one's name, (2) not knowing the name of one's proposer, (3) being under the age of twenty, (4) not having the three robes and an alms bowl, (5) the disapproval of one's mother or father, (6) being in debt, (7) being a slave, (8) holding a government post, (9) having neither male nor female characteristics, (10) having one of the five sicknesses (leprosy, epilepsy, retardation, eczema, and manic depression). Horner (1930:140–151) and Wijayaratna (1990:120–121) list the ten minor obstructions in the Pali canon.

26. The ritual staff, which is illustrated in Waddell (1895:211), is only held by monks and used during rites which dedicate merit *(sngo ba)* while collecting fall alms.

27. In the Tibetan tradition, novices hold thirty-six vows which are abbreviated to ten precepts that specify the ten nonvirtuous acts to be cast off *(yan lag bcu):* not killing, not stealing, no sexual misconduct, avoiding lies, avoiding intoxicants, avoiding dancing, avoiding garlands, avoiding high beds or seats, avoiding untimely food, avoiding taking gold and silver.

28. The ordination ritual exemplifies the ritual liminality exhaustively described by Turner (1969, 1974).

29. Turner (1969:95).

30. Heirman (1997:52–54) describes the five Buddhist robes to which nuns are entitled. She explores the various interpretations of the two additional robes nuns wear, which include a breast covering/support and a bathing cloth.

31. Tambiah (1985), calling on Austin (1962), finds rituals to be illocutionary acts in which saying is doing, while Bell (1996) synthesizes the theories describing ritual as performance and practice.

32. The Tibetan proverb about monks and their discipline was recited by Geshe Ngawang Jordan.

33. Bourdieu (1997:95).

34. Bourdieu (1990:69).

35. Bourdieu (1977:120).

36. Among the 113 rules of training *(saiksa dharma)* which a fully ordained nun should follow are a number about the swaying and swinging of arms, legs, head, shoulders, as Kabilsingh (1998:242) notes. Tsomo (1996:120) translated the rules as follows: "train in going to other households without keeping hands on hips, without twisting the body, without swinging the arms, without twisting the head, without touching the shoulders. Train in not holding hands when going to other households."

37. Bourdieu (1990:68).

38. Mahmood (2001:837–838) faults Bourdieu for failing to address conscious attempts to inculcate ritual disciplines so thoroughly that they become automatic or unconscious.

39. Bourdieu (1990:69).

40. Bourdieu (1990:73).

41. French (1995:110–114) discusses the death payments *(stong)* which are paid to the family of a person who has been murdered.

42. Cabezon (1997) translates a set of customary rules from Sera monastery; Schopen (1997, 1994, 1995, 1996b) describes the legislative prescriptions regarding property, inheritance, transfer, and possession found in canonical texts.

43. Zwilling (1992) explores homosexuality in Tibetan monasteries; Faure (1997) describes the permissive attitudes toward homosexuality in Japanese and Chinese monasteries.

44. While villagers take an interest in prosecuting monks who commit adultery or rape, I have never heard of a nun or monk being beaten in any other context. The degree of the punishment in this case may have been affected by the fact that youth gangs were beating up people who broke the boycott in Leh.

45. Menon and Bhasin (1998), Kakar (1996), and Das (1995) explore the social and psychological rationale for using women as scapegoats in communal conflicts between Hindus and Muslims in India.

6. Why Nuns Cannot Be Monks

1. Ortner (1996, chap. 3) theorizes that women were dangerous because they were considered impure in earlier, band societies. Only later were they held to be in danger because of their purity, with the advent of state societies.

2. Dumont (1980:21) derives the English word "caste" from the Portuguese *casta,* or not mixed, which goes back to the Latin *castus,* or chaste. Yalman (1963, 1971) and Gough (1955) explore the classic question of why the purity of women is essential to the purity of the caste.

3. Dumont (1960, 1980) argued that the discourse of purity and pollution would pervade any ideologies of renunciation born on Indian soil. He was partly cor-

rect—as both Buddhist and Hindu renunciant orders granted women lesser status, in part due to their impurity.

4. The *Dhammapada* (verse 165) is translated in Carter and Palihawadana (1987:31).

5. Aggarwal (1996, 2000), Mills (1997), and Gutschow (1998a) describe the ordering of the Ladakhi space and society around purity and pollution.

6. Das (1902:244, 333) defines *grib* as "defilement, stain or spot, filth, [religious] contamination" and *sgrib* as "sin, mental and moral, defilement, the state of being obscured, darkened . . . to eclipse, to cover over." Pollution is to be distinguished from and yet related to other ritual idioms like fault *(skyon)*, harm *(gnod pa)*, obstacle *(bgegs pa)*, demonic evil *(gdon)*, or sin *(sdig pa)*.

7. Day (1989), Kaplanian (1981, 1983), Mills (1997), and Vohra (1989a,b) examine purity and pollution in Ladakhi culture, while Daniels (1994), Havnevik (1990), Lichter and Epstein (1983), March (1979), Ortner (1973a,b, 1978), Paul (1970), and Schicklgruber (1992) describe its role in Tibetan and Sherpa culture.

8. Srinivas (1952) notes that in Hindu culture pollution arises quite casually, while purity is attained through precise actions. Analogously, Tambiah (1968) found that in Thai Buddhism, virtue is precisely delineated, but its fruit (merit) is left vague. Yet sin is sketched in the broadest brushstrokes while its punishments are carefully detailed.

9. Lichter and Epstein (1973) suggest merit and demerit extend over numerous lifetimes, while secondary causality *(rkyen)* like pollution only affects a single life.

10. Ortner (1973:54).

11. The doctrine of dependent origination is made concrete by an image from Tibetan cosmology, the wheel of existence *(srid pa'i 'khor lo)*. All sentient beings are born into one of six families of existence *('gro ba rigs drugs)*: gods *(lha)*, demi-gods *(lha ma yin)*, humans *(mi)*, animals *(dud 'gro)*, hungry ghosts *(yi dvags)*, and hell-beings *(myal ba can)*. French (1995:197–203) and Nebesky-Wojkowitz (1975) relate the moral principles behind this Tibetan cosmology, while Huber and Pedersen (1997) deny its environmental ethos.

12. Riaboff (1997c) translates a Zangskari legend about a love spat between three guardian deities *(yul lha)*, while Kapferer (1991) sees the struggle between demons as a morality play for class struggle.

13. Kleinman (1978, 1980, 1988, 1995) has elaborated the role of the doctor and patient in constructing meaning through illness narratives.

14. The scholars who discuss the pragmatism of Buddhist purification rites rarely explore the connection between the purity and prestige of monks and the subordination of nuns (Gombrich 1971; Samuel 1993; Spiro 1982; Tucci 1980; and Tambiah 1970, 1984).

15. Bertelsen (1997) and Aggarwal (2000) discuss the modernization of Ladakhi

Buddhism, which has attempted to expunge purification and other unorthodox rites just as the Buddhist modernists have done in Sri Lanka and Nepal
(Gombrich and Obeyesekere 1988; Levine 2000).

16. Wilson (1996) clarifies the leaking impurity of the female body compared with
the more bounded virility of the male body in Buddhist literature.

17. Douglas (1991, 1982) has proposed that pollution beliefs suggest an analogy
between body, temple, and territory. The individual body is a map for the social body, just as concern over social boundaries is reflected in concern over
bodily emissions.

18. Gyatso (1987) and Marko (1990) describe the Tibetan myth of the landscape
as a primordial demoness who must be subdued but not killed off. Aris (1979),
Francke (1926), Gutschow (1997a), and Dujardin (1998:72) describe similar
legends about the landscape as a demoness across the Indo-Tibetan cultural
realm. The demoness remains nailed down with twelve temples in Tibet and
Bhutan, three temples in Zangskar, and five stupas in Mustang.

19. Most basic Buddhist ritual includes meditation, which is glossed in Sanskrit
as right recollection *(samyak smrti)* to indicate the recollection of scattered
thoughts.

20. Jackson (1999) explains the category of witch, while Comaroff and Comaroff
(1999) detail the relationship between witchcraft and violence in South Africa.

21. While Yalman (1963) and Gough (1955) have debated the link between
women's purity and caste status in Indian culture, Ortner (1996, chap. 3) notes
that the purity and control of women were means to secure honor, status, and
power.

22. Kohn (1997) and Bentor (1997) both describe the importance of purification
during consecration rites.

23. Ortner (1996, chaps. 2, 7) reframes her theory about the universality of the na-
ture/culture divide but stands by her original hunch that the symbolism of
male/female often speaks to the existential encounter between nature/culture.
Her theory has been criticized by, among others, MacCormack and Strathern
(1980), Ortner and Whitehead (1981), and Collier and Yanagisako (1987).

24. Day (1989) and Reis (1983:225) confirm the Ladakhi belief about the impurity
of menstrual blood, while Nebesky-Wojkowitz (1975:344) reports that menstrual blood is as noxious as blood from corpses, diseased cows, and mad dogs.

25. Doniger (1980:32–43) notes the symbolism of menstrual blood in post-Vedic
thought, Hershman (1974:286) describes this blood as cleansing, while Marglin
(1982, 1983) and Shaw (1994) note its uses in Tantric ritual.

26. Huber (1994) confirms that women are prevented from entering the most sacred circuit on the Lhari pilgrimage.

27. Aziz (1978:251–252), Havnevik (1990:167–169), and Ortner (1973a) offer evidence that Tibetan and Sherpa cultures remove birth pollution with a liquid

ablution *(khrus)*. By contrast, postpartum rites in Ladakh and Zangskar purify with juniper smoke, which is also found among the Dardic and Kailash cultures of the Hindu Kush (Loude and Lievre 1987).

28. The propitiatory text addresses numerous protective deities, including the lama, yidam, Buddha, *dakinis,* local protectors, local guardians, protectors of wealth, treasures, earth protectors, subterranean spirits, king spirits, and named regional protectors.

29. The liturgy of the burnt offering rite is detailed in Tulku and Perrot (1987). The mustard seeds are purifying and remind the hearers of the parable concerning Kisagotami and the Buddha. Kisagotami, who is terribly distraught over the death of her son, is instructed by the Buddha to find one household which has not experienced death. Unable to do so, she realizes the universality of her suffering.

30. Kisagotami is one of the female elders *(theri)* from the Buddha's day, whose song *(gatha)* of enlightenment appears in a canonical text known as the *Therigatha* which is translated by Murcott (1991:87).

31. Gross (1999) and Klein (1995) suggest that the doctrinal definition of compassion does not have much to do with relational empathy in a Western sense.

32. Compare Ortner's (1989a) account of the way in which wealth and power enable Big Men to build monasteries and temples among the Sherpa of Nepal. Gutschow (1999) discusses the overwhelming participation of women in one of the most popular lay rites, the fasting ritual *(symung gnas)*.

33. Shakabpa (1967), Aris (1979), Miller (1980), and Havnevik (1990) each present versions of the Tibetan origin myth. Miller (1980:160) reports that her Tibetan informants clearly described male and female natures in relation to the myth.

34. Bourdieu (1980:70) describes gender roles in Kabyle society: "The opposition between male and female is realized in posture, in the gestures and movements of the body, in the form of uprightness between the straight and the bent, between firmness, uprightness, and directness (a man faces forward, looking and striking directly at his adversary), and restraint, reserve, and flexibility."

35. The *sman mo* are mentioned in Day (1989), Dollfus (1988: 133–5), Nebesky-Wojkowitz (1975:199–202), and Tucci (1949, 2:752). They should not be confused with wrathful female demons *(ma mo, mamoo)* described as having snakes instead of hair and riding astride a tiger.

36. The Tibetan astrological notions of luck *(spar kha)* and life force are explained by Cornu (1997).

37. Rebecca Norman, pers. comm.

38. Loude and Lievre (1987, 1997) explore the role of fairies in Kailash culture.

39. Dollfus (1988) relates the connection between hunting and mämo in Ladakhi culture.

40. Kawanami (1995:3) cites a Burmese treatise of didactic tales, the *Dhammaniti*, which notes that "women's appetite is twice that of men, their intelligence four times, their assiduity six times, and their desires eight times."

41. Doniger (1980) and Marglin (1982, 1983) describe the symbolism of sexual and bodily fluids in the Hindu imagination. Yalman (1963:30) notes that milk is the most pure substance and serves as a direct antidote to menstrual pollution in Sri Lanka, while Loude and Lievre (1987) report that milk is a sacred substance which is only handled by men—who are pure, versus women who are not—at the high pastures in the Kailash culture of northwest Pakistan.

42. Doniger (1985, 1980, 1999) explores Hindu myths for controlling the dangerous catastrophe of a potent female sexuality. Her new translation of the Kama Sutra (Vatsyayana 2003) restores a female agency and social complexity elided in previous translations.

43. The Hindu ambivalence toward female sexuality and its goddesses is outlined in many monographs, including Doniger (1973, 1980, 1995), Hawley and Wulff (1996), Kakar (1989), Kinsley (1988), and Obeyesekere (1984).

7. Can Nuns Gain Enlightenment?

1. The Dalai Lama ignored the fact that the terms "Lesser Vehicle," or Hinayana, and "Greater Vehicle," or Mahayana, clearly express the latter school's view of its own superiority. The term "Nikaya Buddhism" is a less derogatory way of referring to the eighteen schools of early Buddhism that are often glossed collectively as Hinayana.

2. Faure's (2003) brilliant study of gender and agency in Japanese Buddhism misrepresents the current debates in feminist scholarship on Buddhism, by failing to elucidate the debate on whether Buddhist literature has progressed or regressed in terms of its misogyny. While Rhys-Davids (1909), Horner (1930), and Waters (1995) describe the Theravada sources as reflecting an egalitarian ethos, Falk (1974), Kloppenborg (1995), Lang (1982, 1985), and Wilson (1994, 1995a,b, 1996) depict their sexism. Similarly, while Yuichi (1982) and Paul (1985) emphasize the misogyny of the Mahayana record, Barnes (1981, 1985), Dargyay (1995), Dowman (1985), Gross (1993, 1999), Shaw (1994), Sponberg (1992), and Willis (1985) celebrate the liberating aspects of Mahayana discourse.

3. Both Cabezon (1992) and Conze (1951:124–125) argue that Tibetan and Mahayana literature downplay the importance of wisdom, the feminine symbol, while privileging the male symbol of skillful means or compassion. Both of these authors use rather circular arguments to confirm an androcentric stance which contradicts the centrality of wisdom in Mahayana and Tibetan literature.

4. Saraha—one of the eighty-four illustrious Tantric saints known as the

Mahasiddha—writes a poem about his awakening, translated by David Snellgrove in Conze et al. (1954:224–239) as well as by Robinson (1979) and Dowman (1985).

5. Onians (2003) offers a subtle summary of how Tantric theory responds to Mahayana concerns about morality and antinomian practices. Dutt (1962) describes Indian Tantra as a movement of historical decline, but Cozort (1986) and Hopkins (1984, 1987a,b, 1999) describe Tantric and Tibetan Buddhism as a culmination of earlier Buddhist philosophies.

6. In his *Mulamadhyamakakarikah,* Nagarjuna argues that "there is no distinction whatsoever between *samsara* and *nirvana* and there is no distinction whatsoever between *nirvana* and *samsara*," as translated by Strong (1995:148).

7. Shaw (1994:140) translates from the *Cittavisuddhiprakarama.*

8. In Vedic thought, sacred speech could cause the very reality being invoked, as Gonda (1975:65–70; 1963:63–64) has observed. This theory denies the arbitrary nature of the relationship between signifier and signified. The privileging of orality over literacy as a more powerful and precise form of language contradicts Goody's (1985) theory of the universal displacement of orality by literacy.

9. Cited from Guenther's (1989:85) analysis of yoga.

10. Shaw (1994: 153) translates the *Candamaharosana Tantra.*

11. From Shaw's (1994: 145) translation of the *Candamaharosana Tantra.*

12. Although accused by critics of glorifying women's roles in Tantric practice, Shaw (1994, 1996) offers a powerful and persuasive reversal of the androcentric interpretation of Tantric texts. The translation of textual meaning into lived practice is fraught with ambiguity, in Shaw's work as much as in that of her androcentric critics. Perret's (1997) insightful review clarifies the mistaken assumption that normative views express social reality.

13. Shaw (1994:176) translates the *Cakrasamvara Tantra.*

14. Simmer-Brown's (2001) careful review of the literature on the Dakini rejects the two poles of Jungian and feminist interpretation in favor of a Tibetan scholastic view. Klein (1995), Willis (1987), Gross (1987), and Gyatso (1998) provide further exegesis of the Dakini. Klein (1995:150) translates Dakini as "lady who journeys pervasively in the element of the sky," while Das (1903:158) translates *khyab par 'gro ba* as "to move, covering everything in the way."

15. Tulku (1983:102) cites Padmasambhava's words of advice to Yeshe Tsogyal.

16. There are far fewer female teachers than male ones in the Tantric tradition. Yet the female liberation stories are no less exemplary, as translated by Allione (1984), Chonam and Khandro (1998), Dowman (1984, 1985), Edou (1996), Gross (1987, 1993), Gyatso (1985, 1987), Ray (1980), Shaw (1994), Tulku (1985), and Willis (1987).

17. Tarthang Thulku (1985:105) translates from Yeshe Tsogyal's biography.

18. Samuel (1993) describes the synthesis of shamanic individualism and clerical communalism in Tibetan Buddhism. In her translation of a classic spiritual autobiography, Gyatso (1998) astutely considers how an autobiographical emphasis on ego is to be reconciled with a doctrine of selflessness.

19. Both Phugthal and Nawaphal are sacred sites where women circumambulate a temple or stupa carrying a large smooth rock in hopes of achieving fertility. The sites may have some pre-Buddhist significance.

20. K. Gyatso (1996:359) translates a Tibetan liturgy used to visualize Vajryogini, also discussed in Trungpa (1982:226–242).

21. Durkheim (1965:355).

22. Durkheim (1965:351) described asceticism as an "unnatural act" that necessarily inflicted pain and other forms of violence.

23. Santideva's eighth-century poem is translated by Batchelor (1979:23).

24. The preliminary practices may include 111,111 repetitions of: prayers for refuge *(skyabs 'gro)*, full-length prostrations *(phyag chen mo)*, making a *mandala (dkyil 'khor)*, and visualizations of the meditational deity, who is Vajrayogini *(rdo rje rnal 'byor ma)* for the Karsha nuns. The additional 11,111 of each practice over and above the prescribed hundred thousand account for ritual mistakes or lapses in attention.

25. Retreat practices involve four elements *(bsnyen pa bzhi):* (1) a complete ritualization of all movements and posture of the body, or *lus kyi bsnyen pa*, (2) counting the mantras, or *grangs kyi bsnyen pa*, (3) visualizing and dissolving oneself into the deity, or *mtshan ma'i bsnyen pa*, and (4) the generation and completion stage as one becomes the deity, or *sems brtan gyi bsnyen pa*.

26. Ötrul (1987) and Tulku and Perrot (1987) describe the Tibetan liturgy and practice of burnt offerings *(sbyin sregs)*.

27. Kerin (2000) describes the training in ritual arts at Kyirong Thukche Choling in Nepal, which the Dalai Lama has supported. Thubsten Jinpa, the Dalai Lama's main translator and an ex-monk from Dzongkha monastery (which has been rebuilt in exile in Kathmandu), explained that it was Dzongkha monks who first decided to teach the Kyirong nuns the sacred arts. The monastery and nunnery had had some affiliations in Tibet before 1959, due to their proximity.

28. The Tantric valorization of female has not led to noticeable improvement in women's rights or status. The presence of feminine symbols does not imply a necessary valorization of women, as Bynum (1992) has argued.

8. Monasticism and Modernity

1. Tsering Palmo, personal interview, August 1, 2001.

2. Ibid. One of Palmo's audience members was the late princess of Matho, the

younger sister of Rigdzin Angmo and older sister of one of the most powerful men in Ladakh, Thubstan Tsewang, who is head of Ladakh's autonomous governing body, the Hill Council.

3. Gutschow (1995b) describes the Sakyadhita conference at Leh, which was the fourth of six international conferences to promote the education and ordination of Buddhist women: Bodhgaya (1987), Bangkok (1991), Colombo (1993), Ladakh (1995), Phnom Penh (1997), and Lumbini (2000).

4. Palmo told me that when she heard my conference paper (Gutschow 1997) about the conditions of Zangskari nuns, she "cried all night" and remained deeply affected for the remainder of Leh's Sakyadhita conference.

5. Part of the Dalai Lama's speech to nuns appears in Gutschow (1995b:19).

6. Grimshaw (1992, 1983a,b) summarizes the monastic economy which binds nunnery to monastery at Rizong, while Rizvi (1999) details the extensive trade in apricots which links lower Ladakh to Tibet.

7. Paldan (1982) and Grimshaw (1983a) detail the numbers of nuns and monks at Rizong and Julichen.

8. Ani Palmo held a series of Vinaya training seminars with financial assistance from sponsors. The seminars were held in Ladakh in October 1997 and September 1998, in Zangskar in July 1997 and in Nubra in June 1998.

9. Ladakh Women's Alliance brochure.

10. Ortner (1989:170–172, 1993) describes the founding of Devuche nunnery in Nepal, which could not have proceeded without the support of the abbot of Tengboche monastery. His gift of three relics—a statue, book, and stupa— symbolize the body, speech, and mind of the Buddha.

11. Dodin (1994) describes the history and rise of the Mahabodhi Society in Ladakh.

12. Taiwanese nuns from Foguangshan organized and officiated at a full ordination ceremony at Bodhgaya in 1998 for nuns from India, Nepal, and Sri Lanka, which is described in Li (2000).

13. The Geshe's supporters have a website *(www.lingshed.org)* and a 1998 newsletter which reported: "We found that our earlier proposal of having land/building and renting rooms was not feasible because of the present status of tenancy relationships. We have to find out another way of making ourselves self-sufficient."

14. Karma Lekshe Tsomo has spent the last two decades promoting the status of Buddhist nuns throughout Asia and America. She has taken full ordination vows twice—in both Taiwan and Korea—but follows the Tibetan Buddhist tradition.

15. A brochure describes Jamyang Choling's explicit aim as: "to preserve and revive Buddhist culture in areas where it is declining dangerously due to secularism, cultural infringement, and economic hardship." Jamyang Choling has

supported seven nunneries—two in Dharamsala, three in Zangskar, and two in Spiti—which house over 180 nuns of Tibetan, Mongolian, Bhutanese, and Indian nationalities.

16. Cited from Kawanami's (1995) paper from the Sakyadhita conference in Leh.

17. Cited from a memorandum issued to commemorate a meeting held in Leh, Ladakh, on May 14, 1996, to discuss the status of Ladakhi nuns. Participants included the president of Ladakh's governing Hill Council, Thubstan Tsewang, members of the Ladakhi Gonpa Association, and senior incarnates Thikse Rinpoche, Sras Rinpoche, and Stagna Rinpoche.

18. Southern (1970:309–328) and Lynch (1992:212–215) note that when the number of nuns increased dramatically during the High Middle Ages, monastic officials tried vainly to limit their influence as well as their membership. As a result, a movement of women known as beguines took up celibacy without joining a monastic community.

19. Lopez (1994) addresses the dual construction of Buddhism by Western scholars and Asian reformers in Sri Lanka. Gombrich and Obeyesekere (1988), Gellner (1992, 2001), Spiro (1982), and Lopez (1994) depict variations on Buddhist modernism in South and Southeast Asia.

20. Visweswaran (1997, 1998) and Aggarwal (1999) summarize the so-called third wave of international feminism, which emphasizes the cross-cutting cleavages of class, race, nationality, and ethnicity in deconstructing the category "woman."

21. Scholars like Rita Gross (1999, 1994) and Miranda Shaw (1994) seek to revalorize Buddhism and Tantricism from within by arguing that androcentricism is untrue to the inner vision of these movements.

22. Bourdieu (1991:109–110) notes: "the authorized spokesperson is only able to use words to act on other agents and, through their action, on things, themselves, because his speech concentrates within it the accumulated symbolic capital of the group which has delegated him and of which he is the authorized representative."

23. Baumann (1997), Dodin and Räther (1997), Korom (1997a,b), Lopez (1995, 1998), and Venturino (1995) have analyzed how Tibetan culture has been salvaged and reified during the process of diaspora. Bishop (1989) explores the complex genealogy of images about Tibet which led to its idealization as Shangri La in the twentieth century.

24. Lopez (1994, 1998) deconstructs the myth making surrounding images of Tibet as Shangri La, which offends authors like Thurman (1998) who consider such efforts counterproductive to supporting the Tibetan cause.

25. The flood of images about Tibet and Buddhism in the popular press and on the Hollywood screen (*Time*, 10/13/97; *Der Spiegel*, 4/13/98; *Seven Years in Tibet; Kun Dun*) and in advertisements has both popularized and commodified

Tibetan culture, as Korom (1997a,b) explains. Tibetans reflexively construct more hybrid images of Tibet, but they are often as reductive in the interest of political expediency.

26. Kerin (2000) and Gordon Fellman (pers. comm.) describe the visit of the Kyirong nuns to the United States in 1998 to perform a set of *mandalas* at Trinity College and Brandeis University. Exiles often perpetuate a conservative approach to gender issues in the interest of avoiding further discord or sectarian division.

27. A new type of ethnography and cultural analysis is required by re-envisioning the fluidity and transience of modern life in terms of ethnoscapes or nonspaces, as described by Appadurai (1996) and Auge (1999, 2001) among others.

References

Adams, Vincanne. 1999. *Tigers of the Snow and Other Virtual Sherpas: An Ethnography of Himalayan Encounters.* Princeton: Princeton University Press.

Aggarwal, Ravina. 1994. From Mixed Strain of Barley Grains: Person and Place in a Ladakhi Village. Ph.D. dissertation, Department of Anthropology, Indiana University.

——— 1997. From Utopia to Heterotopia: Towards an Anthropology of Ladakh. In *Recent Research on Ladakh 6: Proceedings of the Sixth International Colloquium on Ladakh,* ed. Henry Osmaston and Ngawang Tsering, 21–29. Bristol: Bristol University Press.

——— 2000. At the Margins of Death: Ritual Space and the Politics of Location in an Indo-Himalayan Border Village. *American Ethnologist* 28(3): 549–573.

Ahearn, Laura. 2001. Language and Agency. *Annual Review of Anthropology* 31: 109–137.

Ahmed, Leila. 1992. *Women and Gender in Islam: Historical Roots of a Modern Debate.* New Haven: Yale University Press.

Ahmed, Monisha. 1997. We Are Warp and Weft: Nomadic Pastoralism and the Tradition of Weaving in Rupshu (Eastern Ladakh). D.Phil. thesis, Faculty of Anthropology and Geography, Oxford University.

Akbar, M. J. 1991. *Kashmir: Behind the Vale.* New Delhi: Viking Press.

Allione, Tsultrim. 1984. *Women of Wisdom.* London: Arkana.

Anderson, Benedict. 1991. *Imagined Communities.* New York: Verso Press.

Appadurai, Arjun. 1996. *Modernity at Large: Cultural Dimensions of Globalization.* Minneapolis: University of Minnesota Press.

Arai, Paula. 1999. *Women Living Zen: Japanese Soto Buddhist Nuns.* Oxford: Oxford University Press.

Arendt, Hannah. 1973. *Men in Dark Times.* Harmondworth: Penguin.

Aris, Michael. 1979. *Bhutan: The Early History of a Himalayan Kingdom.* Warminster, England: Aris & Phillips.

Asad, Talal. 1993. *Genealogies of Religion: Disciplines and Reasons of Power in Christianity and Islam*. Baltimore: Johns Hopkins University Press.

Auge, Marc. 1999. *An Anthropology for Contemporaneous Worlds*. Trans. A. Jacobs. Stanford: Stanford University Press.

———— 2001. *In the Metro*. Trans. Tom Conley. Minneapolis: University of Minnesota Press.

Austin, J. L. 1962. *How to Do Things with Words*. Cambridge: Harvard University Press.

Aziz, Barbara. 1974. Some Notions about Descent and Residence in Tibetan Society. In *Contributions to the Anthropology of Nepal*, ed. Christophe von Fürer-Haimendorf, 23–49. Warminster, England: Aris & Phillips.

———— 1976. Views from the Monastery Kitchen. *Kailash* 4(2): 155–167.

———— 1978. *Tibetan Frontier Families*. New Delhi: Vikas Publishing House.

———— 1988. Women in Tibetan Society and Tibetology. In *Tibetan Studies: Proceeding of the Fourth Seminar of the I.A.T.S.*, ed. Helga Übach and Jampa Panglung, 25–34. Munich: Kommission für Zentralasiatische Studien, Bayerische Akademie der Wissenschaften.

———— 1989. Buddhist Nuns. *Natural History* 98(3): 41–48.

Barkley, D. G. 1875. *Directions for Revenue Officers in the Punjab Regarding the Settlement and Collection of the Land Revenue and the Other Duties Connected Therewith*. Lahore: Central Jail Press.

Barnes, Nancy Schuster. 1981. Changing the Female Body: Wise Women and the Bodhisattva Career in Some Maharatnakutasutras. *Journal of the International Association of Buddhist Studies* 4(1): 24–69.

———— 1985. Striking a Balance: Women and Images of Women in Early Chinese Buddhism. In *Women, Religion, and Social Change*, ed. Yvonne Haddad and Ellison Findly. Albany: SUNY Press.

———— 2000. The Nuns at the Stupa: Inscriptional Evidence for the Lives and Activities of Early Buddhist Nuns in India. In *Women's Buddhism, Buddhism's Women: Tradition, Revision, Renewal*, ed. Ellison Findly, 17–36. Boston: Wisdom Press.

Bartholomeusz, Tessa. 1992. The Female Mendicant in Buddhist Sri Lanka. In *Buddhism, Sexuality, and Gender*, ed. José Cabezon, 37–64. Albany: SUNY Press.

———— 1994. *Women under the Bo Tree*. Cambridge: Cambridge University Press.

Batchelor, Stephen. 1979. *A Guide to the Bodhisattva's Way of Life*. Dharamsala: Library of Tibetan Works and Archives.

Bauman, Martin. 1997. Shangri La in Exile. *Diaspora* 6(3): 377–404.

Beek, Martijn van. 1996. Identity Fetishism and the Art of Representation: The Long Struggle for Regional Autonomy in Ladakh. Ph.D. dissertation, Department of Sociology, Cornell University.

———— 1997. The Importance of Being Tribal; or the Impossibility of Being

Ladakhis. In *Recent Research on Ladakh 7: Proceedings of the Seventh International Colloquium of Ladakh Studies,* ed. Thierry Dodin and Heinz Räther, 21–42. Ulm: Ulmer Kulturanthropologische Schriften.

———— 2000. Lessons from Ladakh? Local Responses to Globalization and Social Change. In *Globalization and Social Change,* ed. Johannes Dragsbaek Schmidt and Jacques Hersh. New York: Routledge.

———— 2001. Beyond Identity Fetishism: "Communal" Conflict and Ladakh in the Limits of Autonomy. *Cultural Anthropology* 15(4): 525–569.

Beek, Martijn van, and Kristoffer Brix Bertelsen. 1995. Ladakh: 'Independence' Is Not Enough. *Himal* 8(2): 7–15.

———— 1997. No Present without the Past. In *Recent Research on Ladakh 7: Proceedings of the Seventh International Colloquium of Ladakh Studies,* ed. Thierry Dodin and Heinz Räther, 43–66. Ulm: Ulmer Kulturanthropologische Schriften.

Behar, Ruth. 1993. *Translated Woman.* Boston: Beacon Press.

Bell, Catherine. 1996. *Ritual Theory, Ritual Practice.* New York: Oxford University Press.

Bennet, Lynn. 1983. *Dangerous Wives and Sacred Sisters: Social and Symbolic Roles of High Caste Women in Nepal.* New York: Columbia University Press.

Bentor, Yael. 1997. The Horseback Consecration Ritual. In *Religions of Tibet in Practice,* ed. Donald Lopez, 234–254. New Delhi: Munshiram Manoharlal Publishers.

Berg, Charles. 1951. *The Unconscious Significance of Hair.* London: George Allen & Unwin.

Bertelsen, Kristoffer. 1997. Early Modern Buddhism in Ladakh: On the Construction of Buddhist Ladakhi Identity and Its Consequences. In *Recent Research on Ladakh 7: Proceedings of the Seventh International Colloquium for Ladakh Studies,* ed. Thierry Dodin and Heinz Räther, 67–88. Ulm: Ulmer Kulturanthropologische Schriften.

Bishop, Peter. 1989. *The Myth of Shangri-La: Tibet, Travel Writing, and the Western Creation of Sacred Landscape.* Berkeley: University of California Press.

Blackstone, Katherine. 1999. Damming the Dhamma: Problems with the Bhikkhuniis in the Pali Vinaya. *Journal of Buddhist Ethics* 6. <jbe.gold.ac.uk/6/blackstone991.html>

Bourdieu, Pierre. 1977. *Outline of a Theory of Practice.* Trans. Richard Nice. Cambridge: Cambridge University Press.

———— 1988. *Homo Academicus.* Stanford: Stanford University Press.

———— 1990. *The Logic of Practice.* Stanford: Stanford University Press.

———— 1991. *Language and Symbolic Power.* Trans. Gino Raymond and Matthew Adamson. Cambridge: Harvard University Press.

———— 1999. *The Weight of the World: Social Suffering in Contemporary Society.* Stanford: Stanford University Press.

Bowie, Katherine. 1998. The Alchemy of Charity: Of Class and Buddhism in Northern Thailand. *American Anthropologist* 100(2): 469–481.

Brauen, Martin. 1980a. *Feste in Ladakh.* Graz: Akademische Druk und Verlagsanstalt.

———— 1980b. The Pha Spun of Ladakh. In *Tibetan Studies in Honour of Hugh Richardson: Proceedings of the International Seminar on Tibetan Studies,* ed. Michael Aris and Aung San Suu Kyi, 53–58. Warminster, England: Aris & Phillips.

———— 1982. Death Customs in Ladakh. *Kailash* 9(4): 319–332.

———— 1994. *Irgendwo in Bhutan: Wo die Frauen (Fast Immer) das Sagen Haben.* Frauenfeld: Verlag im Waldgut.

Braun, Willi, and Russell T. McCutcheon, eds. 2000. *Guide to the Study of Religion.* London: Cassell.

Bunnag, Jane. 1973. *Buddhist Monk, Buddhist Layman: A Study of Urban Monastic Organization in Central Thailand.* Cambridge: Cambridge University Press.

Butler, Judith. 1990. *Gender Trouble: Feminism and the Subversion of Identity.* New York: Routledge.

———— 1993. *Bodies That Matter.* New York: Routledge.

Bynum, Caroline Walker. 1986. The Complexity of Symbols. In *Gender and Religion: On the Complexity of Symbols,* ed. C. Bynum, S. Harrell, and P. Richman. Boston: Beacon Press.

———— 1992. *Fragmentation and Redemption: Essays on Gender and the Human Body in Medieval Religion.* New York: Zone Books.

Cabezon, José. 1992. Mother Wisdom, Father Love: Gender-Based Imagery in Mahayana Buddhist Thought. In *Buddhism, Sexuality, and Gender,* ed. José Cabezon, 181–202. Albany: SUNY Press.

———— 1997. The Regulations of a Monastery. In *Religions of Tibet in Practice,* ed. D. Lopez, 335–354. Princeton: Princeton University Press.

Campbell, June. 1996. *Traveler in Space: In Search of Female Identity in Buddhism.* New York: George Braziller.

Carrasco, Pedro. 1959. *Land and Polity in Tibet.* Seattle: University of Washington Press.

Carrithers, Michael. 1983. *The Forest Monks of Sri Lanka.* Delhi: Oxford University Press.

———— 1987. Buddhists without History. *Contributions to Indian Sociology* 21(1): 165–168.

Carter, John, and Mahinda Palihawadana, trans. 1987. *The Dhammapada.* New York: Oxford University Press.

Census Office of India. 1981. *District Census Office Handbook: Kargil (Village and Town Directory)*.

Chibber, M. L. 1998. *Pakistan's Criminal Folly in Kashmir: The Drama of Accession and Rescue of Ladakh*. New Delhi: Manas Publications.

Chonam, Lama, and Sangye Khandro, trans. 1998. *The Lives and Liberation of Princess Mandarava: The Indian Consort of Padmasambhava*. Boston: Wisdom Publications.

Clifford, James. 1997. *Routes: Travel and Translation in the Twentieth Century*. Cambridge: Harvard University Press.

Clifford, James, and George Marcus. 1986. *Writing Culture: The Politics and Poetics of Ethnography*. Berkeley: University of California Press.

Cohn, Bernard. 1990. *An Anthropologist among the Historians and Other Essays*. New Delhi: Oxford University Press.

——— 1996. *Colonialism and Its Forms of Knowledge: The British in India*. Princeton: Princeton University Press.

Collier, Jane, and Sylvia Yanigasako. 1987. Toward a Unified Analysis of Gender and Kinship. In *Gender and Kinship: Essays Toward a Unified Analysis*, ed. J. Collier and S. Yanagisako, 14–50. Stanford: Stanford University Press.

Comaroff, Jean, and John Comaroff. 1999. Occult Economies and the Violence of Abstraction: Notes from the South African Postcolony. *American Ethnologist* 26(2): 279–303.

Conze, Edward. 1951. *Buddhism: Its Essence and Development*. New York: Harper & Row.

Conze, Edward et al., trans. 1954. *Buddhist Texts through the Ages*. Boston: Shambhala Publications.

Cornu, Phillippe. 1997. *Tibetan Astrology*. Trans. Hamish Gregor. Boston: Shambhala.

Cozort, Daniel. 1986. *Highest Yoga Tantra*. Ithaca, N.Y.: Snow Lion Publications.

Crook, John, and Henry Osmaston. 1994. *Himalayan Buddhist Villages*. New Delhi: Motilal Banarsidass.

Cunningham, Alexander. 1977 [1854]. *Ladak: Physical, Statistical, and Historical, with Notes of the Surrounding Countries*. New Delhi: Sagar Publications.

Dagpa, Lobsang, Migmar Tsering, and Ngawang Chophel. 1975. *The Discipline of the Novice Monk*. Mussorie, India: Sakya College.

Daniel, Sheryl. 1983. The Tool Box Approach of the Tamil to the Issue of Moral Responsibility and Human Destiny. In *Karma: An Anthropological Enquiry*, ed. Charles Keyes and E. Valentine Daniel. Berkeley: University of California Press.

Daniels, Christine. 1994. Defilement and Purification: Tibetan Buddhist Pilgrims at Bodhnath, Nepal. D.Phil. thesis, Faculty of Anthropology and Geography, Oxford University.

Dargyay, Eva, and Lobsang Dargyay. 1980. Vorlaufiger Bericht Uber Zwei

Forschungreisen Nach Zangskar (West-Tibet). *Zentralasiatische Studien* 14(2): 85–114.

———— 1987. The Dynasty of Bzang-la (Zanskar, West Tibet) and Its Chronology: A Reconsideration. In *Silver on Lapis: Tibetan Literary Culture and History,* ed. Christopher Beckwith, 13–32. Bloomington, Ind.: Tibet Society.

———— 1988. Buddhism in Adaptation: Ancestor Gods and Their Tantric Counterparts in the Religious Life of Zanskar. *History of Religions* 28(2): 123–134.

———— 1995. Buddhist Thought from a Feminist Perspective. In *Gender, Genre, and Religion: Feminist Reflections,* ed. M. Joy and E. Neumaier-Dargyay. Calgary: Calgary Institute for the Humanities Press.

Das, Sarat Chandra. 1902. *A Tibetan-English Dictionary.* Calcutta: Bengal Secretariat Book Depot.

Das, Veena. 1995. *Critical Events: An Anthropological Perspective on Contemporary India.* New Delhi: Oxford University Press.

Datta, C. L. 1972. *Ladakh and Western Himalayan Politics (1819–1848): The Dogra Conquest of Ladakh, Baltistan, and West Tibet and Reactions of Other Powers.* Delhi: Munshiram Maharlal.

Day, Sophie. 1989. Embodying Spirits: Village Oracles and Possession Ritual in Ladakh, North India. Ph.D. dissertation, Department of Anthropology, London School of Economics.

Demiéville, Paul. 1952. *La Concile de Lhasa.* Paris: Imprimerie National de France.

Dentaletche, Claude, ed. 1985. *Ladakh, Himalaya Occidental: Ethnologie, Ecologie.* Pau, France: Acta Biologica Montana.

Denton, Lynn. 1991. Varieties of Hindu Female Asceticism. In *Roles and Rituals for Indian Women,* ed. J. Leslie, 211–232. Delhi: Motilal Banarsidass.

Diehl, Keila. 2002. *Echoes from Dharamsala: Music in the Life of a Tibetan Refugee.* Berkeley: University of California Press.

Dirks, Nicholas. 1987. *The Hollow Crown: The Ethnohistory of an Indian Kingdom.* Cambridge: Cambridge University Press.

———— 1994. Ritual and Resistance: Subversion as Social Fact. In *Culture/Power/ History: A Reader in Contemporary Social Theory,* ed. N. Dirks, G. Eley, and S. Ortner, 483–503. Princeton: Princeton University Press.

———— 2001. *Castes of Mind: Colonialism and the Making of Modern India.* Princeton: Princeton University Press.

Dodin, Thierry. 1994. 'Ecumenism' in Contemporary Ladkhi Buddhism. In *Tibetan Studies: Proceedings of the Sixth Seminar of the I.A.T.S.,* ed. Per Kvaerne, 168–177. Oslo: Institute for Comparative Research in Human Culture.

Dodin, Thierry, and Heinz Räther, eds. 1997. *Mythos Tibet: Wahrnehmungen, Projektionen, Phantasien.* Cologne: Dumont Verlag. Republished as *Imagining Tibet: Realities, Projections, Fantasies.* Boston: Wisdom Press, 2001.

Dollfus, Pascale. 1988. La representation du bouquetin au Ladakh, region de culture tibetaine de l'Inde du Nord. In *Tibetan Studies: Proceeding of the Fourth Seminar of the I.A.T.S.*, ed. Helga Übach and Jampa Panglung, 125–138. Munich: Kommission für Zentralasiatische Studien, Bayerische Akademie der Wissenschaften.

———— 1989. *Lieu de neige et de genevriers: organisation sociale et religiuse de communautes bouddhistes du Ladakh*. Paris: CNRS.

———— 1995. The History of Muslims in Central Ladakh. *Tibet Journal* 20(3): 35–58.

Doniger, Wendy. 1973. *Siva: The Erotic Ascetic*. London: Oxford University Press.

———— 1980. *Women, Androgynes, and Other Mythical Beasts*. Chicago: University of Chicago Press.

———— 1984. *Dreams, Illusions, and Other Realities*. Chicago: University of Chicago Press.

———— 1985. *Tales of Sex and Violence: Folklore, Sacrifice, and Danger in the Jaiminiya Brahmana*. Chicago: University of Chicago Press.

———— 1999. *Splitting the Difference: Gender and Myth in Ancient Greece and India*. Chicago: University of Chicago Press.

Dorje, Rinjing. 1975. *The Tales of Aku Tonpa: The Legendary Rascal of Tibet*. San Rafael, Calif.: Dorje Ling Press.

Douglas, Mary. 1982. *Natural Symbols: Explorations in Cosmology*. New York: Pantheon.

———— 1991. *Purity and Danger: An Analysis of the Concepts of Pollution and Taboo*. London: Routledge.

Douie, J. M. 1899. *Panjab Settlement Manuel*. Lahore: Civil and Military Gazette Press.

Douie, J. M., and D. C. Johnstone, eds. 1890. *Punjab Revenue Circulars: Being a Re-Issue in the Consolidated Form of All Revenue Circulars of the Board of Administration and the Financial Commissioner Which Were in Force*. Lahore: Central Jail Press.

Dowman, Keith, trans. 1984. *Sky Dancer: The Secret Life and Songs of the Laday Yeshe Tsogyel*. London: Arkana.

————, trans. and comm. 1985. *Masters of Mahamudra: Songs and Histories of the Eighty-Four Buddhist Siddhas*. Albany: SUNY Press.

Dragom Rinpoche. 1992. *Zangs skar bslab bya sying gi nor bu* [The precious heart jewel of advice for Zangskar]. Delhi: Jayyed Press.

Drew, Francis. 1875. *Jammoo and Kashmir Territories*. London: Edward Stanford.

Dreze, Jean, and Amartya Sen. 1994. *India: Economic Development and Social Opportunity*. New Delhi: Oxford University Press.

Dujardin, Marc. 1998. *From Fortress to Farmhouse: A Living Architecture*. In *Bhutan: Mountain Fortress of the Gods*, ed. Christian Schickelgruber and Françoise Pommaret, 61–84. Boston: Shambhala.

Dumont, Louis. 1960. World Renunciation in Indian Religions. *Contributions to Indian Sociology* 4: 3–62.

———— 1980. *Homo Hierarchicus.* Chicago: University of Chicago Press.

Durkheim, Emile. 1965. *The Elementary Forms of the Religious Life.* Trans. Joseph Swain. New York: Free Press.

Dutt, Sukumar. 1962. *Buddhist Monks and Monasteries of India: Their History and Their Contribution to Indian Culture.* London: George Allen and Unwin.

Eckel, Malcolm David. 1994. The Ghost at the Table: On the Study of Buddhism and the Study of Religion. *Journal of the American Academy of Religion* 62(4): 1085–1100.

Edou, Jerome. 1996. *Machig Labdrøn and the Foundations of Chod.* Ithaca, N.Y.: Snow Lion Publications.

Eilberg-Schwartz, Howard, and Wendy Doniger, eds. 1995. *Off with Her Head: The Denial of Women's Identity in Myth, Religion, and Culture.* Berkeley: University of California Press.

Elford, Jonathan. 1994. Kumik: A Demographic Profile. In *Himalayan Buddhist Villages,* ed. John Crook and Henry Osmaston, 331–362. New Delhi: Motilal.

Enslin, Elizabeth. 1994. Beyond Writing: Feminist Practice and the Limitations of Ethnography. *Cultural Anthropology* 9(4): 537–568.

Epstein, L. 1982. On the History and Psychology of the 'Das-log. *Tibet Journal* 7(4): 20–85.

Erdmann, Ferry. 1983. Social Stratification in Ladakh: Upper Estates and Low Castes. In *Recent Research on Ladakh,* ed. Detlef Kantowsky and Reinhard Sander, 139–155. Cologne: Weltforum Verlag.

Falk, Nancy. 1980. The Case of the Vanishing Nuns: The Fruits of Ambivalence in Ancient Buddhism. In *Unspoken Worlds: Women's Religious Lives in Non-Western Cultures,* ed. N. Falk and R. Gross, 207–224. New York: Harper & Row.

Farnell, Brenda. 2000. Getting Out of the Habitus: An Alternative Model of Dynamically Embodied Social Action. *Journal of the Royal Anthropological Institute* 6(3): 397–418.

Faure, Bernard. 1997. *The Red Thread: Buddhist Approaches to Sexuality.* Princeton: Princeton University Press.

———— 2003. *The Power of Denial: Buddhism, Purity, and Gender.* Princeton: Princeton University Press.

Fedarko, Kevin. 2003. The Coldest War. *Outside Magazine* 28(2): 38–59.

Fillipi, Fillipo de. 1932. *An Account of Tibet, The Travels of Ippolito Desideri of Pistoia, S. J., 1712–1727.* London: George Routledge and Sons.

Findly, Ellison. 1999. Women and the Arahant Issue in Early Pali Literature. *Journal of Feminist Studies in Religion* 15(1): 57–76.

Fitzgerald, Timothy. 1999. *The Ideology of Religious Studies.* New York: Oxford University Press.

Fontein, J. 1979. A Rock Sculpture of Maitreya in the Suru Valley, Ladakh. *Artibus Asie* 41(1): 5–8.

Fox, Richard, ed. 1992. *Recapturing Anthropology: Working in the Present.* Santa Fe: School of American Research Press.

Francfort, H. P. et al. 1990. Petroglyphes archaïques du Ladakh et du Zanskar. *Arts Asiatiques* 45: 5–27.

Francke, Agustus Hermann. 1914. *Antiquities of Indian Tibet.* Vol. 1. Calcutta: Archaeological Survey of India.

———— 1926. Zangs dkar chags tshul lo rgyus [A record of the inhabitation of Zangskar]. In *Antiquities of Indian Tibet,* vol. 2. Calcutta: Archeological Survey of India.

French, Rebecca. 1995. *The Golden Yoke: The Legal Cosmology of Buddhist Tibet.* Ithaca, N.Y.: Cornell University Press.

———— 1997. The Drug pa bsad pa stong gi zhal che: Stong Death Payments, the Sixth Section of the dGa' ldan Pho Brang Law Code. Paper delivered at the Eighth I.A.T.S. Seminar in Bloomington, Indiana.

Friedl, Wolfang. 1983. *Gessellschaft, Wirtschaft, und Materielle Kultur in Zanskar (Ladakh).* Sankt Augustin: VGH Wissenschaftsverlag.

Fruzetti, Lina. 1982. *The Gift of a Virgin: Women, Marriage, and Ritual in a Bengali Society.* New Brunswick, N.J.: Rutgers University Press.

Fürer-Haimendorf, Christopher von. 1964. *The Sherpas of Nepal.* London: J. Murray.

———— 1976. A Nunnery in Nepal. *Kailash* 4(2): 121–154.

Geertz, Clifford. 1968. *Islam Observed: Religious Development in Morocco and Indonesia.* Chicago: University of Chicago Press.

———— 1973. *The Interpretation of Cultures.* New York: Basic Books.

———— 1980. *Negara: The Theater State in Nineteenth-Century Bali.* Princeton: Princeton University Press.

———— 1995. *After the Fact: Two Centuries, Four Decades, One Anthropologist.* Cambridge: Cambridge University Press.

Gelek, Surkhang. 1984. The Measurement of *Lag 'don* Tax in Tibetan Society. *Tibet Journal* 9(1): 20–30.

———— 1986. Government, Monastic, and Private Taxation in Tibet. *Tibet Journal* 11(1): 21–40.

Gellner, David. 1990. What Is the Anthropology of Buddhism About. *Journal of the Anthropological Society of Oxford* 21(2): 95–112.

———— 1992. *Monk, Householder, and Tantric Priest: Newar Buddhism and Its Hierarchy of Ritual.* Cambridge: Cambridge University Press.

———— 2001. *The Anthropology of Buddhism and Hinduism: Weberian Themes.* Oxford: Oxford University Press.

Gergan, S. S. 1976. *La dvags ryal rabs 'chi med gter* [The Ladakh Chronicles: An everlasting treasure]. Srinagar: S. S. Gergan.

Goldstein, Melvin. 1971a. Taxation and the Structure of a Tibetan Village. *Central Asiatic Journal* 15(1): 1–27.

——— 1971b. Serfdom and Mobility: An Examination of the Institution of 'Human Lease' in Traditional Tibetan Society. *Jounal of Asian Studies* 30(3): 521–534.

——— 1978. Pahari and Tibetan Polyandry Revisited. *Ethnology* 17(3): 325–337.

——— 1984. *English-Tibetan Dictionary of Modern Tibetan.* With Ngawangthondup Narkyid. Dharamsala: Library of Tibetan Works and Archives.

——— 1986. Reexamining Choice, Dependency, and Command in the Tibetan Social System: Tax Appendages and Other Landless Serfs. *Tibet Journal* 11(4): 79–112.

——— 1987. When Brothers Share a Wife. *Natural History* 96(3): 39–48.

——— 1989. *A History of Modern Tibet, 1913–1951.* Berkeley: University of California Press.

Gombrich, Richard. 1971. *Precept and Practice.* Oxford: Clarendon Press.

——— 1975. Buddhist Karma and Social Control. *History of Religions* 17(4): 212–220.

Gombrich, Richard, and Gananath Obeyesekere, eds. 1988. *Buddhism Transformed: Religious Change in Sri Lanka.* Princeton: Princeton University Press.

Gonda, Jan. 1963. *The Vision of the Vedic Poets.* The Hague: Mouton and Co.

——— 1975. *Vedic Literature.* Wiesbaden: Otto Harrassowitz.

Gough, Kathleen. 1955. Female Initiation Rites on the Malabar Coast. *Journal of the Royal Anthroplogical Institute* 85(1): 45–80.

Green, Paula. 1987. Buddhist Nuns in Ladakh. In *Recent Research on Ladakh 6: Proceedings of the Sixth International Colloquium on Ladakh,* ed. Henry Osmaston and Ngawang Tsering, 99–104. Bristol: Bristol University Press.

Grimshaw, Anna. 1983a. Rizong: A Monastic Community in Ladakh. Ph.D. dissertation, Department of Anthropology, Cambridge University.

——— 1983b. Celibacy, Religion, and Economic Activity in a Monastic Community of Ladakh. In *Recent Research on Ladakh: Proceedings of the First International Colloquium on Ladakh Studies,* ed. Dieter Kantowsky and Reinhard Sander, 121–134. Cologne: Weltforum Verlag.

——— 1992. *Servants of the Buddha: Winter in a Himalayan Convent.* London: Open Letters Press.

Grist, Nicola. 1990. Land Tax, Labour, and Household Organization in Ladakh. In *Wissenschafsgeschichte und Gegenwärtige Forschungen in Nordwest-Indien,* ed.

Lydia Icke-Schwalbe and Gudrun Meier. Dresden: Staatliches Museum für Völkerkunde.

———— 1998. Local Politics in the Suru Valley of North India. Ph.D. dissertation, Department of Anthropology, Goldsmiths' College.

Gross, Rita. 1987. Yeshe Tsogyel: Enlightened Consort, Great Teacher, Female Role Model. *Tibet Journal* 12(4): 1–18. Reprinted in Willis (1989).

———— 1993. *Buddhism after Patriarchy: A Feminist History, Analysis, and Reconstruction of Buddhism.* Albany: SUNY Press.

———— 1999. Strategies for a Feminist Revalorization of Buddhism. In *Feminism and World Religions,* ed. A. Sharma and K. Young, 78–109. Albany: SUNY Press.

Guenther, Herbert. 1989. *Tibetan Buddhism in Western Perspective.* Berkeley: Dharma Publishing.

Gunawardana, R. A. L. H. 1988. Subtle Silk of Ferreous Firmness: Buddhist Nuns in Ancient and Early Medieval Sri Lanka and Their Role in the Propagation of Buddhism. *Sri Lanka Journal of the Humanities* 14: 1–59.

Gupta, Samjukta. 2000. The Goddess, Women, and Their Rituals in Hinduism. In *Faces of the Feminine in Ancient, Medieval, and Modern India,* ed. Mandrakarta Bose, 87–106. Delhi: Oxford University Press.

Guthrie, Stewart. 1993. *Faces in the Clouds: A New Theory of Religion.* New York: Oxford University Press.

Gutschow, Kim. 1995a. Kinship in Zangskar: Idiom and Practice. In *Recent Research on Ladakh 4 & 5: Proceedings of the Fourth and Fifth International Colloquia on Ladakh,* ed. Henry Osmaston and Phillip Denwood, 334–346. London: School of African and Oriental Studies.

———— 1995b. The Power of Compassion or the Power of Rhetoric? A Report on Sakyadhita's Fourth International Conference on Buddhist Women. *Himal* 8(6): 18–21.

———— 1997a. Unfocussed Merit-Making in Zangskar: A Socio-Economic Account of Karsha Nunnery. *Tibet Journal* 22(2): 30–58.

———— 1997b. Lords of the Fort, Lords of the Water, and No Lords at All: A Comparison of Irrigation in Three Tibetan Societies. In *Recent Research on Ladakh 6: Proceedings of the Sixth International Colloquium on Ladakh,* ed. H. Osmaston and Ngawang Tsering, 105–116. Bristol: Bristol University Press.

———— 1997c. A Study of 'Wind Disorder' or Madness in Zangskar, India. In *Recent Research on Ladakh 7: Proceedings of the Seventh International Colloquium for Ladakh Studies,* ed. Thierry Dodin and Heinz Räther, 177–202. Ulm: Ulmer Kulturanthropologische Schriften.

———— 1998a. An Economy of Merit: Women and Buddhist Monasticism in

Zangskar, Northwest India. Ph.D. dissertation, Harvard University, Department of Anthropology.

———— 1998b. Hydro-Logic in the Northwest Himalaya: Several Case Studies from Zangskar. In *Culture Area Karakorum Studies: Proceedings of the International Symposium on Karakorum-Hindukush-Himalaya, Dynamics of Change,* vol. 1, *Stellrecht.* Cologne: Rudiger Köppe Verlag.

———— 1999. The *Smyung Gnas* Fast in Zangskar, Northwest India: How Liminality Depends on Structure. In *Ladakh: Culture, History, and Development between Himalaya and Karakorum,* ed. Martijn van Beek and Kristoffer Bertelsen, 153–173. Copenhagen: Nordic Institute of Asian Studies.

———— 2000a. Novice Ordination for Nuns: The Rhetoric and Reality of Female Monasticism in Northwest India. In *Women's Buddhism, Buddhism's Women: Tradition, Revision, Renewal,* ed. Ellison Findly, 103–118. Boston: Wisdom Books.

———— 2000b. Yeshe's Tibetan Pilgrimage and the Founding of a Himalayan Nunnery. In *Innovative Buddhist Women: Swimming against the Stream,* ed. Karma Lekshe Tsomo, 212–228. London: Curzon Press.

———— 2001a. Women Who Refuse to Be Exchanged: Nuns in Zangskar, Northwest India. In *Celibacy, Culture, and Society: The Anthropology of Sexual Abstinence,* ed. Elisa Sobo and Sandra Bell, 47–64. Madison: University of Wisconsin Press.

———— 2001b. What Makes a Nun? Apprenticeship and Ritual Passage in Zangskar, North India. *Journal of the International Association of Buddhist Studies* 24(2): 187–216.

———— 2002. The Delusion of Gender and Renunciation in Buddhist Kashmir. In *Everyday Life in South Asia,* ed. Diane Mines and Sarah Lamb. Bloomington: University of Indiana Press.

Gutschow, Kim, and Niels Gutschow. 2003. Rinam Dissolved: An Analysis of Land and Water in Zangskar, Northwest India. In *Space and Territory in the Buddhist Himalaya,* ed. Niels Gutschow, Axel Michaels, and Charles Ramble. Vienna: Österiche Akademie der Wisssenschaften.

Gyatso, Janet. 1985. The Development of the Gcod Tradition. In *Soundings in Tibetan Civilization,* ed. Barbara Aziz and Matthew Kapstein. New Delhi: Manohar Publishers.

———— 1987. Down with the Demoness: Reflections on a Feminine Ground in Tibet. *Tibet Journal* 12(4): 38–53. Reprinted in Willis (1989).

———— 1998. *Aspirations of the Self: The Secret Autobiographies of a Tibetan Visionary.* Princeton: Princeton University Press.

Gyatso, Geshe Kelsang. 1996. *Guide to Dakini Land; The Highest Yoga Tantra Practice of Buddha Vajrayogini.* London: Tharpa Publications.

Hallpike, C. R. 1969. Social Hair. *Man,* n.s., 4: 256–264.

Haraway, Donna. 1991. Situated Knowledges: The Science Question in Feminism and the Privilege of Partial Perspective. In D. Haraway, *Simians, Cyborgs, and Women.* London: Free Association Books.

Hartmann, Hans. 1983. Planzengesellschaften entlang der Kashmirroute in Ladakh. *Jahrbuch des Vereins zum Schutz der Bergwelt* 48: 131–173.

Havnevik, Hanna. 1990. *Tibetan Buddhist Nuns.* Oslo: Norwegian University Press.

———— 1998. On Pilgrimage for 40 Years in the Himalayas: The Female Lama Jetsun Lochen Rinpoche's (1865–1951) Quest for Sacred Sites. In *Pilgrimage in Tibet,* ed. Alex McKay, 85–107. London: Curzon Press.

Hawley, John Stratton, and Donna Marie Wulf. 1996. *Devi: Goddesses of India.* Berkeley: University of California Press.

Heirman, Ann. 1997. Some Remarks on the Rise of the *bhiksunisamgha* and on the Ordination Ceremony for *bhiksunis* according to the Dharmaguptaka *Vinaya. Journal of the International Association of Buddhist Studies* 20(2): 33–86.

Hershman, Paul. 1974. Hair, Sex, and Dirt. *Man,* n.s., 9(2): 274–298.

Hewitt, Vernon. 1995. *Reclaiming the Past? The Search for Political and Cultural Unity in Contemporary Jammu and Kashmir.* London: Portland Books.

Hirakawa, Akira. 1990. *A History of Indian Buddhism From Skyamuni to Early Mahayana.* Trans. Paul Groner. Honolulu: University of Hawaii Press.

———— 1999. *Monastic Discipline for the Buddhist Nuns: An English Translation of the Chinese Text of the Mahasamghika-Bhiksuni Vinaya.* Patna: Kashi Prasad Jayaswal Research Institute.

Hopkins, Jeffrey. 1984. *The Tantric Distinction: A Buddhist's Reflections on Compassion and Emptiness.* Boston: Wisdom Publications.

———— 1999. *Emptiness in the Mind-Only School of Buddhism.* Berkeley: University of California Press.

————, trans. 1987a. *Tantra in Tibet: The Great Exposition of Secret Mantra* by *Tsong-ka-pa.* New Delhi: Motilal Banarsidass.

———— 1987b. *The Yoga of Tibet: The Great Exposition of Secret Mantra by Tsong-ka-pa.* New Delhi: Motilal Banarsidass.

Hopkirk, Peter. 1982. *Trespassers on the Roof of the World: The Secret Exploration of Tibet.* Los Angeles: Jeremy Tarcher.

———— 1991. *The Great Game: On Secret Service in High Asia.* London: Oxford University Press.

———— 1997. *Quest for Kim: In Search of Kipling's Great Game.* London: Oxford University Press.

Horner, I. B. 1930. *Women under Primitive Buddhism: Laywomen and Almswomen.* London: Routledge & Kegan Paul.

————, trans. 1992. *The Book of the Discipline (Vinaya Pitaka). Vol. V (Cullavagga).* Oxford: Pali Text Society.

Huber, Tony, and Poul Pedersen. 1997. Metereological Knowledge and Environmental Ideas in Traditional and Modern Societies: The Case of Tibet. *Journal of the Royal Anthropological Institute* 3(3): 577–598.

Irigaray, L. 1985. *This Sex Which Is Not One.* Ithaca, N.Y.: Cornell University Press.

———— 1987. *Sexes and Genealogies.* New York: Columbia University Press.

———— 1994. *Thinking the Difference: For a Peaceful Revolution.* New York: Routledge.

Jackson, Michael. 1989. *Paths toward a Clearing: Radical Empiricism and Ethnographic Enquiry.* Bloomington: Indiana University Press.

———— 1998. *Minima Ethnographica: Intersubjectivity and the Anthropological Project.* Chicago: University of Chicago Press.

———— 1999. The Witch as a Category and as a Person. In *The Insider/Outsider Problem in the Study of Religion,* ed. R. McCutcheon, 311–330. London: Cassell.

Jagmohan, Malhotra. 1992. *My Frozen Turbulence in Kashmir.* New Delhi: Allied Publishers.

Jäschke, H. A. 1987 [1881]. *A Tibetan-English Dictionary.* New Delhi: Motilal Banarsidass.

Jha, Prem Shankar. 1996. *Kashmir 1947: Rival Versions of History.* New Delhi: Oxford University Press.

Jordt, Ingrid. 1988. Bhikkhuni, Thilashin, and Mae-Chi: Women Who Renounce the World in Burma, Thailand, and the Classical Buddhist Texts. *Crossroads* 4(1): 31–39.

Kabilisingh, Chatsumarn. 1984. *A Comparative Study of Bhikkhuni Patimokkha.* Varanasi: Chaukhambha Orientalia.

———— 1998. *The Bhikkuni Patimokkha of the Six Schools.* New Delhi: Sri Satguru Publications.

Kakar, Sudhir. 1989. *Intimate Relations: Exploring Indian Sexuality.* Chicago: University of Chicago Press.

———— 1996. *The Colors of Violence: Cultural Identities, Religion, and Conflict.* Chicago: University of Chicago Press.

Kapferer, Bruce. 1991. *A Celebration of Demons.* Washington, D.C.: Berg Publishers.

Kaplanian, Patrick. 1981. *Les Ladakhis du Cachemire.* Paris: Hachette.

———— 1989. Les Mickha au Ladakh et le Mikha Specha (mi kha dpe cha). In *Tibetan Studies: Proceeding of the Fourth Seminar of the I.A.T.S.,* ed. Helga Übach and Jampa Panglung, 209–213. Munich: Kommission für Zentralasiatische Studien, Bayerische Akademie der Wissenschaften.

Kaufman, Howard. 1960. *Bangkhuad: A Community Study in Thailand.* Locust Valley, N.Y.: J. J. Augustin.

Kaul, Shridhar, and H. N. Kaul. 1992. *Ladakh through the Ages: Towards a New Identity.* New Delhi: Indus.

Kawanami, Hiroko. 1995. Buddhist Nuns in Transition: The Case of the Burmese Thil a-shin. Presented in July 1995, Sakyadhita Conference, Leh, Ladakh.

Keown, Damien. 1992. *The Nature of Buddhist Ethics.* London: Macmillan.

Kerin, Melissa. 2000. From Periphery to Center: Tibetan Women's Journey to Sacred Artistry. In *Women's Buddhism, Buddhism's Women: Tradition, Revision, Renewal,* ed. Ellison Findly, 319–338. Boston: Wisdom Publications.

Keyes, Charles. 1983a. Economic Action and Buddhist Morality in a Thai Village. *Journal of Asian Studies* 42(4): 851–868.

——— 1983b. Merit-Transference in the Karmic Theory of Popular Theravada Buddhism. In *Karma: An Anthropological Enquiry,* ed. C. Keyes and E. V. Daniel, 261–286. Berkeley: University of California Press.

——— 1986. Ambiguous Gender: Male Initiation in a Northern Thai Buddhist Society. In *Gender and Religion: On the Complexity of Symbols,* ed. C. Bynum, S. Harrell, and P. Richman, 66–96. Boston: Beacon Press.

——— 1990. Buddhist Practical Morality in a Changing Agrarian World: A Case from Northeastern Thailand. In *Ethics, Wealth, and Salvation: A Study in Buddhist Social Ethics,* ed. R. Sizemore and D. Swearer, 170–189. Columbia: University of South Carolina Press.

Keyes, Charles, and E. Valentine Daniel, eds. 1983. *Karma: An Anthropological Enquiry.* Berkeley: University of California Press.

Khan, Akbar. 1970. *Raiders in Kashmir.* Karachi: Bookpoint Press.

Khandelwal, Meena. 1996. Walking a Tightrope: Saintliness, Gender, and Power in an Ethnographic Encounter. *Anthropology and Humanism* 21(2): 111–134.

——— 1997. Ungendered Atma, Masculine Virility, and Feminine Compassion: Ambiguities in Renunciant Discourses on Gender. *Contributions to Indian Sociology,* n.s., 31(1): 79–107.

——— 2001. Sexual Fluids, Emotions, Morality: Notes on the Gendering of Brahmacharya. In *Celibacy, Culture, and Society: The Anthropology of Sexual Abstinence,* ed. Elisa Sobo and Sandra Bell, 157–179. Madison: University of Wisconsin Press.

Khoo, Michael. 1997. Preliminary Remarks Concerning Solar Observation, Solar Calendars, and Festivals in Ladakh and the Western Himalaya. In *Recent Research on Ladakh 7: Proceedings of the Seventh Colloquium of the International Association for Ladakh Studies* held in Bonn/Sankt Augustin, 12–15 June 1995, ed. Thierry Dodin and Heinz Räther, 235–269. Ulm: Ulmer Kulturanthropologische Schriften.

Kinsley, David. 1988. *Hindu Goddesses: Visions of the Divine Feminine in the Hindu Religious Tradition.* Berkeley: University of California Press.

Kirsch, Thomas. 1977. Complexity in the Thai Religious System: An Interpretation. *Journal of Asian Studies* 36(2): 241–266.

Klein, Anne. 1985. Primordial Purity and Everyday Life: Exalted Female Symbols and the Women of Tibet. In *Immaculate and Powerful: The Female in Sacred Image and Social Reality,* ed. Clarissa Atkinson, Constance Buchanan, and Margaret Miles, 111–138. Boston: Beacon Press.

———— 1987. The Birthless Birthgiver: Reflections of the Liturgy of Yeshe Tsogyel, the Great Bliss Queen. *Tibet Journal* 12(4): 19–37.

———— 1995. *Meeting the Great Bliss Queen: Buddhists, Feminists, and the Art of the Self.* Boston: Beacon Press.

Kleinman, Arthur. 1978. Concepts and a Model for the Comparison of Medical Systems as Cultural Systems. *Social Science and Medicine* 12: 85–93.

———— 1980. *Patients and Healers in the Context of Culture.* Berkeley: University of California Press.

———— 1988. *The Illness Narratives: Suffering, Healing, and the Human Condition.* New York: Basic Books.

———— 1995. *Writing at the Margin: Discourse between Anthropology and Medicine.* Berkeley: University of California Press.

Klimburg-Salter, Deborah. 1998. *Tabo, a Lamp for the Kingdom: Early Indo-Tibetan Buddhist Art in the Western Himalaya.* London: Thames and Hudson.

Kloppenborg, Ria. 1995. Female Stereotypes in Early Buddhism: The Women of the Therigatha. In *Female Stereotypes in Religious Traditions,* ed. Ria Kloppenborg and Wouter Hanegraaff, 151–169. New York: E. J. Brill.

Knauft, Bruce. 1996. *Genealogies for the Present in Cultural Anthropology.* New York: Routledge.

Kohn, Richard. 2001. *Lord of the Dance: The Mani Rimdu Festival in Tibet and Nepal.* Albany: SUNY Press.

Kongtrul, Jamgon Lodrö Taye. 1998. *Buddhist Ethics.* Trans. International Translation Committee. Ithaca, N.Y.: Snow Lion Publications.

Kornman, Richard. 1997. A Tribal History. In *Religions of Tibet in Practice,* ed. D. Lopez, 77–97. Princeton: Princeton University Press.

Korom, Frank, ed. 1997. *Constructing Tibetan Culture: Contemporary Perspectives.* Quebec: World Heritage Press.

Kumar, Nita. 1994. *Women as Subjects: South Asian Histories.* Charlottesville: University of Virginia Press.

Lamb, Alastair. 1966. *Crisis in Kashmir, 1947–1966.* London: Routledge & Kegan Paul.

———— 1991. *Kashmir: A Disputed Legacy, 1846–1990.* Hertingfordbury: Roxford Books.

————— 1994. *Birth of a Tragedy: Kashmir 1947.* Hertingfordbury: Roxford Books.

Lang, Karen. 1981. Images of Women in Early Buddhism and Christian Gnosticism. *Buddhist-Christian Studies* 2: 95–105.

————— 1985. Lord's Death Snare: Gender-Related Imagery in the Theragatha and the Therigatha. *Journal of Feminist Studies in Religion* 2(2): 63–79.

————— 1995. Shaven Heads and Loose Hair: Buddhist Attitudes toward Hair and Sexuality. In *Off with Her Head: The Denial of Women's Identity in Myth, Religion, and Culture,* ed. H. Eilberg-Schwartz and W. Doniger, 32–52. Berkeley: University of California Press.

Lansing, Stephen. 1991. *Priests and Programmers: Technologies of Power in the Engineered Landscape of Bali.* Princeton: Princeton University Press.

Leach, Edmund. 1958. Magical Hair. *Journal of the Royal Anthropological Institute* 83: 147–164.

————— 1968. *Dialectic in Practical Religion.* Cambridge: Cambridge University Press.

Lehman, F. K. 1989. Internal Inflationary Pressures in the Prestige Economy of the Feast of Merit Complex. In *Ritual, Power, and Economy: Upland-Lowland Contrasts in Mainland Southeast Asia,* ed. S. Russell, 89–102. DeKalb: Northern Illinois University Center for Southeast Asian Societies.

————— 1996. Can God Be Coerced? Structural Correlates of Merit and Blessing in Some Southeast Asian Religions. In *Merit and Blessing in Mainland Southeast Asia in Comparative Perspective,* ed. C. Kammerer and N. Tannenbaum, 20–51. New Haven: Yale University Press.

Levine, Nancy. 1980. Nyinba Polyandry and the Allocation of Paternity. *Journal of Comparative Family Studies* 11: 283–298.

————— 1981. The Theory of *Ru:* Kinship, Descent, and Status in Tibetan Society. In *Asian Highland Societies,* ed. Christopher von Fürer-Haimendorf. New Delhi: Sterling.

————— 1988. *The Dynamics of Polyandry.* Chicago: University of Chicago Press.

Levine, Sarah. 2000. At the Cutting Edge: Theravada Nuns in the Kathmandu Valley. In *Innovative Buddhist Women: Swimming against the Stream,* ed. Karma Lekshe Tsomo, 13–29. London: Curzon Press.

Lévi-Strauss, Claude. 1969. *The Elementary Structures of Kinship.* Boston: Beacon Press.

Lewis, Todd. 2000. *Popular Buddhist Texts from Nepal: Narratives and Rituals of Newar Buddhism.* Ithaca, N.Y.: Snow Lion Publications.

Li, Yuchen. 2000. Ordination, Legitimacy, and Sisterhood: The International Full Ordination Ceremony in Bodhgaya. In *Swimming against the Stream: Innovative Women in Buddhism,* ed. Karma Lekshe Tsomo, 168–200. London: Curzon Press.

Lichter, Daniel, and Lawrence Epstein. 1983. Irony in Tibetan Notions of the Good Life. In *Karma: An Anthropological Enquiry,* ed. Charles Keyes and E. V. Daniel, 223–260. Berkeley: University of California Press.

Linrothe, Robert. 1999. A Summer in the Field. *Orientations* 30(5): 57–67.

———— 2002. Invisible: Picturing Interiority in Western Himalayan Stupa Architecture. In *The Built Surface: Architecture and the Pictorial Arts from Antiquity to the Enlightenment,* vol. 1, ed. Christy Anderson, 75–98. Burlington, England: Ashgate Press.

Lopez, Donald. 1994. *Curators of the Buddha: The Study of Buddhism under Colonialism.* Chicago: University of Chicago Press.

———— 1998. *Prisoners of Shangri-La.* Chicago: University of Chicago Press.

Lopez, Donald, ed. 1995. *Buddhism in Practice.* Princeton: Princeton University Press.

———— 1997. *Religions of Tibet in Practice.* Princeton: Princeton University Press.

Loude, Jean-Yves, and Viviane Lievre. 1987. *Kalash Solstice: Winter Feasts of the Kalash of North Pakistan.* Islamabad: Lok Virsa.

———— 1997. *Men between Fairies and Women: The Bipolarity of the Environment of the Hindu Kush,* ed. Alexander W. MacDonald. New Delhi: D. K. Printworld.

Lynch, Joseph. 1992. *The Medieval Church: A Brief History.* New York: Longman.

MacCormack, Carol, and Strathern, Marilyn, eds. 1980. *Nature, Culture, and Gender.* Cambridge: Cambridge University Press.

Mahmood, Saba. 2001. Rehearsed Spontaneity and the Conventionality of Ritual: Disciplines of Sālāt. *American Ethnologist* 28(9): 827–853.

Mankelow, John. 1999. The Introduction of Modern Chemical Fertiliser to the Zanskar Valley, Ladakh and Its Effects on Agricultural Productivity, Soil Quality and Zanskari Society. BSc thesis, Oxford Brookes University.

Marais, Gill. 1991. *Right over the Mountain: Travels with a Tibetan Medicine Man.* Dorset, Great Britain: Element Books.

March, Kathryn. 1979. The Intermediacy of Women: Female Gender Symbolism and the Social Position of Women among Tamangs and Sherpas of Highland Nepal. Ph.D. dissertation, Department of Anthropology, Cornell University.

Marcus, George. 1998. *Ethnography through Thick and Thin.* Princeton: Princeton University Press.

Marcus, George, and Michael Fischer. 1986. *Anthropology as Cultural Critique: An Experimental Moment in the Human Sciences.* Chicago: University of Chicago Press.

Marglin, Frederique Apfell. 1982. Types of Sexual Union and Their Implicit Meanings. In *The Divine Consort: Radha and the Goddesses of India,* ed. J. S. Hawley and D. M. Wulf. Berkeley: Graduate Theological Union.

———— 1985. Female Sexuality in the Hindu World. In *Immaculate and Powerful: The Female in Sacred Image and Social Reality*, ed. Clarissa Atkinson, Constance Buchanan, and Margaret Miles, 39–61. Boston: Beacon Press.

Marko, Anna. 1990. Civilizing Woman the Demon: A Tibetan Myth of the State. *Social Analysis* 29: 6–18.

Marriot, McKim. 1989. Constructing an Indian Ethnosociology. *Contributions to Indian Sociology*, n.s., 23(1): 1–39.

———— 1991. On 'Constructing an Indian Ethnosociology.' *Contributions to Indian Sociology*, n.s., 25(2): 295–308.

Masuzawa, Tomoko. 1993. *In Search of Dreamtime: The Quest for the Origin of Religion*. Chicago: University of Chicago Press.

Mauss, Marcel. 1972 [1935]. Techniques of the Body. Reprinted in *Sociology and Psychology: Essays by Marcel Mauss*. London: Routledge & Kegan Paul.

McCutcheon, Russell T. 1997. *Manufacturing Religion: The Discourse on Sui Generis Religion and the Politics of Nostalgia*. New York: Oxford University Press.

———— 1999. *The Insider/Outsider Problem in the Study of Religion*. London: Cassell.

———— 2001. *Critics Not Caretakers: Redescribing the Public Study of Religion*. Albany: SUNY Press.

Menon, Ritu, and Kamla Bhasin. 1998. *Borders and Boundaries: Women in India's Partition*. New Delhi: Kali for Women.

Miller, Barbara. 1980. Views of Women's Roles in Buddhist Tibet. In *History of Buddhism*, ed. A. K. Narain, 156–166. New Delhi: B. R. Publishing Co.

Mills, Martin. 1997. Religious Authority and Pastoral Care in Tibetan Buddhism: The Ritual Hierarchies of Lingshed Monastery, Ladakh. Ph.D. dissertation, University of Edinburgh.

Moghissi, Haideh. 1999. *Feminism and Islamic Fundamentalism: The Limits of Postmodern Analysis*. New York: Zed Books.

Moore, S. 1987. Explaining the Present: Theoretical Dilemmas in Processual Ethnography. *American Ethnography* 14(4): 727–736.

Muhammad, Chaudri Khushi. 1908. *Preliminary Report of Ladakh Settlement*. Jammu: Banbir Prakash Press.

———— 1909. *Assessment Report of Zanskar Ilaka in the Ladakh District*. Allahabad: Pioneer Press.

Mumford, Stan. 1989. *Himalayan Dialogues: Tibetan Lamas and Gurung Shamans in Nepal*. Madison: University of Wisconsin Press.

Murcott, Susan. 1991. *The First Buddhist Women: Translations and Commentary on the Therigatha*. Berkeley: Parallax Press.

Nadou, Jean. 1980. *Buddhists of Kashmir*. New Delhi: Agam Kala Prakashan.

Nattier, Jan. 1988. The Candragarbha-Sutra in Central and East Asia: Studies in a

Buddhist Prophecy of Decline. Ph.D. dissertation, Harvard University, Department of Religion.

Nebesky-Wojkowitz, Rene de. 1969. *'Chams: The Sacred Dance of the Tibetans.* Leiden: Brill.

———— 1975. Oracles and Demons of Tibet: The Cult and Iconography of the Tibetan Protective Deities. Graz: Akademische Druck und Verlagsanstalt.

Neufeldt, Ronald. 1986. *Karma and Rebirth: Post-Classical Developments.* Albany: SUNY Press.

Obeyesekere, Gananath. 1968. Theodicy, Sin, and Salvation in a Sociology of Buddhism. In *Dialectic in Practical Religion,* ed. E. Leach, 7–40. Cambridge: Cambridge University Press.

———— 1981. *Medusa's Hair: An Essay on Personal Symbols and Religious Experience.* Chicago: University of Chicago Press.

———— 1984. *The Cult of the Goddess Pattini.* Chicago: University of Chicago Press.

O'Flaherty, Wendy Doniger. 1983. *Karma and Rebirth in Classical Indian Tradition.* New Delhi: Motilal Banarsidass.

Onians, Isabelle. 2003. Tantric Buddhist Apologetics, or Antinomianism as a Norm. Ph.D. dissertation, Oxford University.

Orofino, Giacomella. 1990. A Note on Some Tibetan Petroglyphs of the Ladakh Area. *East and West* 41: 173–199.

Ortner, Sherry. 1973. Sherpa Purity. *American Anthropologist* 75: 49–63.

———— 1978. *Sherpas through Their Rituals.* New York: Cambridge University Press.

———— 1983. The Founding of the First Sherpa Nunnery and the Problem of 'Women' as an Analytic Category. In *Feminist Re-Visions: What Has Been and Might Be,* ed. V. Patraka and L. Tilly, 93–134. Ann Arbor: University of Michigan Women's Studies Program.

———— 1989a. *High Religion: A Cultural and Political History of Sherpa Buddhism.* Princeton: Princeton University Press.

———— 1989b. Cultural Politics: Religious Activism and Ideological Transformation among Twentieth-Century Sherpas. *Dialectical Anthropology* 14: 197–211.

———— 1995. Resistance and the Problem of Ethnographic Refusal. *Contributions to the Comparative Study of Society and History* 37(1): 173–193.

———— 1996. *Making Gender: The Politics and Erotics of Culture.* Boston: Beacon Press.

———— 1999a. *Life and Death on Mt. Everest: Sherpas and Himalayan Mountaineering.* Princeton: Princeton University Press.

———— 1999b. Thick Resistance: Death and the Cultural Construction of Agency in Himalayan Mountaineering. In *The Fate of Culture,* ed. Sherry Ortner, 136–164. Berkeley: University of California Press.

Ortner, Sherry, and Harriet Whitehead. 1981. *Sexual Meanings: The Cultural Construction of Gender*. Cambridge: Cambridge University Press.

Osmaston, Henry. 1994. Human Adaptation to the Environment. In *Himalayan Buddhist Villages*, ed. John Crook and Henry Osmaston. New Delhi: Motilal Banarsidass.

Ötrul Rinpoche, Panchen. 1987. The Ritual Fire Offering. *Chö Yang* 1(2): 69–75.

Paldan, Thubstan. 1982. *A Brief Guide to the Buddhist Monasteries and Royal Castles of Ladakh*. Trans. M. Aris. Leh: Ladakh Project.

Paul, Diane. 1979. The Concept of the Tthagatagarbha in the Srimaladevi Sutra (Sheng-Man Ching). *Journal of the American Oriental Society* 99(2): 191–203.

——— 1985. *Women in Buddhism: Images of the Feminine in Mahayana Tradition*. Berkeley: University of California Press.

Paul, Robert. 1970. Sherpas and Their Religion. Ph.D. dissertation, Department of Anthropology, University of Chicago.

Petech, Luciano. 1977. *A Kingdom of Ladakh*. Rome: Instituto Per Il Medio Ed Estremo Oriente.

——— 1998. Western Tibet: Historical Introduction. In *Tabo, a Lamp for the Kingdom: Early Indo-Tibetan Buddhist Art in the Western Himalaya*, ed. Deborah Klimburg-Salter. London: Thames and Hudson.

Peter, Prince of Greece and Denmark. 1956. The Pha Spun of Leh Tehsil in Ladakh, Eastern Kashmir, India. *East and West* 7: 138–146.

——— 1963. *A Study of Polyandry*. The Hague: Mouton & Co.

——— 1980. Comments on the Social and Cultural Implications of Variant Systems of Polyandrous Alliances. *Journal of Comparative Family Studies* 11: 371–375.

Phillimore, Peter. 2001. Private Lives and Public Identities: An Example of Female Celibacy in Northwest India. In *Celibacy, Culture, and Society: The Anthropology of Sexual Abstinence*, ed. E. Sobo and D. Bell, 29–46. Madison: University of Wisconsin Press.

Phylactou, Maria. 1989. Household Organisation and Marriage in Ladakh-Indian Himalaya. Ph.D. dissertation, Department of Anthropology, London School of Economics.

Pommaret, Françoise. 1989. *Les Revenants de l'Au-dela dans le Monde Tibetain*. Paris: CNRS.

Powers, John. 1995. *Introduction to Tibetan Buddhism*. Ithaca, N.Y.: Snow Lion Publications.

Prasad, S. N., and Dharm Pal. 1987. *History of Operations in Jammu and Kashmir (1947–48)*. New Delhi: History Division, Ministry of Defense, Government of India.

Prebish, Charles. 1996. *Buddhist Monastic Discipline: The Sanskrit Pratimoksa Sutras of the Mahasamghikas and the Mulasarvastivadins*. New Delhi: Motilal Banarsidass.

Rabgyas, Tashi. 1984. *Mar yul la dvags kyi sngon rabs kun gsal me long* [History of Ladakh called The Mirror Which Illuminates All]. Delhi: Jayyed Press.

Raheja, Gloria Goodwin, and Ann Grodzins Gold. 1992. *Listen to the Heron's Words: Reimagining Gender and Kinship in North India.* Berkeley: University of California Press.

Ramble, Charles. 1984. The Lamas of Lubra: Tibetan Bonpo Householder Priests in Western Nepal. D.Phil. thesis, Faculty of Anthropology, Oxford University.

——— 1990. How Buddhist Are Buddhist Communities? The Construction of Tradition in Two Lamaist Villages. *Journal of the Anthropological Society of Oxford* 21(2): 185–197.

Ray, Reginald. 1980. Accomplished Women in Tantric Buddhism of Medieval India and Tibet. In *Unspoken Worlds,* ed. Nancy Auer Falk and Rita Gross. New York: Harper & Row.

——— 1994. *Buddhist Saints in India: A Study in Buddhist Values and Orientations.* New York: Oxford University Press.

Reichenbach, Bruce. 1990. *The Law of Karma: A Philosophical Study.* London: Macmillan.

Reis, Ria. 1983. Reproduction or Retreat: The Position of Buddhist Women in Ladakh. In *Recent Research on Ladakh: Proceedings of the First International Colloquium on Ladakh Studies,* ed. Dieter Kantowsky and Reinhard Sander, 217–229. Cologne: Weltforum Verlag.

Rhys-Davids, Caroline, and K. R. Norman, trans. 1989 [1909]. *Poems of the Early Buddhist Nuns (Therigatha) and Elders' Verses II.* Oxford: Pali Text Society.

Rhys-Davids, T. W., and Caroline Rhys-Davids. 1966. *Dialogues of the Buddha. Vol. II (Mahaparinibbanasutta).* London: Luzac and Co.

Riaboff, Isabelle. 1997a. Le Roi et le Moine: Figures et principes de pouvoir et de sa légitimation au Zanskar (Himalaya Occidental). Ph.D. thesis, Laboratoire d'ethnologie et de sociologie comparative, Université de Paris X.

——— 1997b. Les lha, une categorie zanskari a geometrie variable: Ou, Que sont les dieux devenus? In *Recent Research on Ladakh No. 7: Proceedings of the Seventh Colloquium of the International Association for Ladakh Studies,* ed. Thierry Dodin and H. Räther, 335–378. New Delhi: Motilal Banarsidass.

——— 1997c. Notes sur les rituels agraires au Zanskar: Terre, terroirs, territoires. In *Tibetan Studies: Proceedings of the Seventh Seminar of the I.A.T.S.,* ed. H. Krasser, M. T. Much, E. Steinkellner, and H. Tauscher, 803–816. Vienna: Verlag der Österreichischen Akademie der Wissenschaften.

Richards, Thomas. 1992. Archive and Utopia. *Representations* (Winter): 104–135.

Richardson, Hugh. 1993. *Ceremonies of the Lhasa Year.* London: Serindia Publications.

Rigdzin, Tsepag. 1993. *Tibetan-English Dictionary of Buddhist Terminology.* Dharamsala: Library of Tibetan Works and Archives.

Rizvi, Janet. 1999. *Trans-Himalayan Caravans: Merchant Princes and Peasant Traders in Ladakh.* New York: Oxford University Press.

Robinson, James, trans. 1979. *Buddha's Lions.* Berkeley: Dharma Publishing.

Roerich, George, trans. 1949. *The Blue Annals.* Calcutta: Motilal.

Rosaldo, Renato. 1986. Ilongot Hunting as Story and Experience. In *The Anthropology of Experience,* ed. V. Turner and E. Bruner. Urbana: University of Illinois Press.

Roth, Gustav. 1970. *Bhiksuni-Vinaya.* Patna: K. P. Jayaswal Research Institute.

Rubin, Gail. 1975. The Traffic in Women: Notes on the 'Political Economy' of Sex. In *Toward an Anthropology of Women.* New York: Monthly Review Press.

Said, Edward. 1978. *Orientalism.* New York: Vintage Books.

Saler, Benson. 1993. *Conceptualizing Religion: Immanent Anthropologists, Transcendent Natives, and Unbounded Categories.* Leiden: E. J. Brill.

Salgado, Nirmala. 1996. Ways of Knowing and Transmitting Religious Knowledge: Case Studies of Theravada Buddhist Nuns. *Journal of the International Association of Buddhist Studies* 19(1): 61–80.

Samuel, Geoffrey. 1982. Tibet as a Stateless Society and Some Islamic Parallels. *Journal of Asian Studies* 41(2): 215–229.

———— 1993. *Civilized Shamans: Buddhism in Tibetan Societies.* Washington, D.C.: Smithsonian Institution Press.

Schickelgruber, Christophe. 1992. *Grib:* On the Significance of the Term in a Socio-Religious Context. In *Tibetan Studies: Proceedings of the Fifth Seminar of the I.A.T.S.,* ed. S. Ihara and Z. Yamaguchi. Narita: Naritsan Institute for Buddhist Studies.

Schofield, Victoria. 1996. *Kashmir in the Crossfire.* London: I. B. Tauris Publishers.

———— 2000. *Kashmir in Conflict: India, Pakistan and the Unfinished War.* New York: I. B. Tauris Publishers.

Schopen, Gregory. 1994. Doing Business for the Lord: Lending on Interest and Written Loan Contracts in the Mulasarvastivada-Vinaya. *Journal of the American Oriental Society* 114(4): 527–554.

———— 1995. Monastic Law Meets the Real World: A Monk's Continuing Right to Inherit Family Property in Classical India. *History of Religions* 35(2): 101–123.

———— 1996a. The Suppression of Nuns and the Ritual Murder of Their Special Dead in Two Buddhist Monastic Texts. *Journal of Indian Philosophy* 24(6): 563–592.

———— 1996b. The Lay Ownership of Monasteries and the Role of the Monk in Mulasarvastivadin Monasticism. *Journal of the International Association of Buddhist Studies* 19(1): 81–126.

———— 1997. *Bones, Stones, and Buddhist Monks: Collected Papers on the Archeology, Epigraphy, and Texts of Monastic Buddhism in India.* Honolulu: University of Hawaii Press.

Schuh, Dieter. 1976. Urkunden und Zendschreiben aus Zentraltibet, Ladakh, und Zanskar. *Monumenta Tibetica Historica.* Band 2,4. Sankt Augustin: VGH Wissenschaftsverlag.

——— 1983. *Historiographische Dokumenta aus Zans-dkar.* Sankt Augustin: Archiv für Zentralasiatische Geschichts-Forschung.

Scott, Joan Wallach. 1999. *Gender and the Politics of History.* New York: Columbia University Press.

Sen, L. P. 1969. *Slender Was the Thread: Kashmir Confrontation, 1947–48.* New Delhi: Orient Longmans.

Shakabpa, Tsepon. 1967. *Tibet: A Political History.* New Haven: Yale University Press.

Shakspo, Nawang Tsering. 1988a. *A History of Buddhism in Ladakh.* Delhi: Ladakh Buddha Vihara.

——— 1988b. The Revival of Buddhism in Modern Ladakh. In *Tibetan Studies: Proceeding of the Fourth Seminar of the I.A.T.S.,* ed. Helga Übach and Jampa Panglung, 439–448. Munich: Kommission für Zentralasiatische Studien, Bayerische Akademie der Wissenschaften.

——— 1993. *An Insight into Ladakh.* Leh: N. T. Shakspo.

Shaw, Miranda. 1994. *Passionate Enlightenment: Women in Tantric Buddhism.* Princeton: Princeton University Press.

Simmer-Brown, Judith. 2001. *The Dakini's Warm Breath: The Feminine Principle in Tibetan Buddhism.* Boston: Shambhala Publications.

Sizemore, Russell, and Donald Swearer, eds. 1990. *Ethics, Wealth, and Salvation: A Study in Buddhist Social Ethics.* Columbia: University of South Carolina Press.

Skilling, Peter. 1993–94. A Note on the History of the Bhikkhuni Sangha (II): The Order of Nuns after the Parinirvana. *W.F.B. Review* 30(4)/31(1): 29–49.

Smith, Jonathan Z. 1982. *Imagining Religion: From Babylon to Jonestown.* Chicago: University of Chicago Press.

Snellgrove, David. 1987. *Indo-Tibetan Buddhism: Indian Buddhists and Their Tibetan Successors.* London: Serindia Publications.

——— 1989. *Himalayan Pilgrimage: A Study of Tibetan Religion by a Traveller through Western Nepal.* Boston: Shambhala.

Snellgrove, David, and Tadeusz Skorupski. 1980. *The Cultural Heritage of Ladakh: Zangskar and the Cave Temples of Ladakh.* Warminster, England: Aris & Phillips.

Southern, R. W. 1970. *Western Society and the Church in the Middle Ages.* New York: Penguin Books.

Southwold, Martin. 1982. *Buddhism in Life: The Anthropological Study of Religion and the Sinhalese Practice of Buddhism.* Manchester: Manchester University Press.

Spiro, Melford. 1977. Review of Tambiah, 1976. *Journal of Asian Studies* 36(4): 789–791.

———— 1978. Reply to Professor Tambiah. *Journal of Asian Studies* 37(4): 809–812.

———— 1982. *Buddhism and Society: A Great Tradition and Its Burmese Vicissitudes.* Berkeley: University of California Press.

Sponberg, Alan. 1992. Attitudes toward Women and the Feminine in Early Buddhism. In *Buddhism, Sexuality, and Gender,* ed. José Cabezon, 3–36. Albany: SUNY Press.

Srinivas, M. N. 1952. *Religion and Society among the Coorgs of South India.* London: Oxford University Press.

Stacey, Judith. 1988. Can There Be a Feminist Ethnography? *Women's Studies International Forum* 11(1): 21–27.

Steedly, M. 1993. *Hanging without a Rope: Narrative Experience in Colonial and Post-Colonial Karoland.* Princeton: Princeton University Press.

Stern, Jessica. 2001. Meeting with the Muj. *Bulletin of the Atomic Scientists* 57(1): 42–51.

Strathern, Marilyn. 1987. An Awkward Relationship: The Case of Feminism and Anthropology. *Signs* 12(2): 276–292.

———— 1988. *The Gender of the Gift.* Berkeley: University of California Press.

Strenski, Ivan. 1983. On Generalized Exchange and the Domestication of the Sangha. *Man,* n.s., 18(3): 463–477.

Strong, John. 1990. Rich Man, Poor Man, Bhikkhu, King: Asoka's Great Quinquennial Festival and the Nature of Dana. In *Ethics, Wealth, and Salvation: A Study in Buddhist Social Ethics,* ed. Russell Sizemore and Donald Swearer, 107–123. Columbia: University of South Carolina Press.

———— 1995. The Experience of Buddhism: Sources and Interpretations. Belmont, Calif.: Wadsworth Publishing.

Swearer, Donald. 1995. A Modern Sermon on Merit Making. In *Buddhism in Practice,* ed. D. Lopez, 399–401. Princeton: Princeton University Press.

Tambiah, Stanley. 1968. The Ideology of Merit and the Social Correlates of Buddhism in a Thai Village. In *Dialectic in Practical Religion,* ed. Edmund Leach, 41–121. Cambridge: Cambridge University Press.

———— 1970. *Buddhism and the Spirit Cults of Northeast Thailand.* Cambridge: Cambridge University Press.

———— 1976. *World Conqueror and World Renouncer: A Study of Buddhism and Polity in Thailand against a Historical Background.* Cambridge: Cambridge University Press.

———— 1978. The Buddhist Conceptions of Kingship and Its Historical Manifestations: Reply to Spiro. *Journal of Asian Studies* 37(4): 801–809.

———— 1984. *The Buddhist Saints of the Forest and the Cult of Amulets.* Cambridge: Cambridge University Press.

———— 1985. *Culture, Thought, and Social Action: An Anthropological Perspective.* Cambridge: Harvard University Press.

Thurman, Robert. 1995. *Essential Tibetan Buddhism.* San Francisco: Harper Collins.

———— 1998. *Inner Revolution: Life, Liberty, and the Pursuit of Real Happiness.* New York: Riverhead Books.

Toricelli, Fabrizio. 1994. Some Notes on the Maitreya Image in Western Ladakh. *Tibet Journal* 19(1): 3–16.

Trungpa, Chogyam. 1982. Sacred Outlook: The Vajrayogini Shrine and Practice. In *The Silk Route and the Diamond Path: Esoteric Buddhist Art on the Trans-Himalayan Trade Routes,* ed. Deborah Klimburg-Salter, 226–242. Los Angeles: UCLA Art Council.

Tsai, Kathryn [Kathryn Cissell]. 1981. The Chinese Buddhist Monastic Order for Women: The First Two Centuries. In *Women in China: Current Directions for Historical Scholarship,* ed. Richard Guisso and Stanley Johannesen. Youngs-town, Ohio: Philo Press.

———— 1994. *Lives of the Nuns: Biographies of Chinese Buddhist Nuns from the Fourth to Sixth Centuries.* Honolulu: University of Hawaii Press.

Tsarong, Paljor. 1987. Economy and Ideology on a Tibetan Monastic Estate in Ladakh: Processes of Production, Reproduction, and Transformation. Ph.D. dissertation, Department of Anthropology, University of Wisconsin at Madi-son.

Tsering, Ngawang. 1979. *Buddhism in Ladakh.* New Delhi: Sterling.

Tsering, Tashi, and Philippa Russell. 1986. An Account of the Buddhist Ordina-tion of Women. *Chö Yang* 1(1): 21–32.

Tsomo, Karma Lekshe. 1988. *Sakyadhita: Daughters of the Buddha.* Ithaca, N.Y.: Snow Lion Publications.

———— 1989. Tibetan Nuns and Nunneries. In *Feminine Ground: Essays on Women and Tibet,* ed. Janice Willis, 118–134. Ithaca, N.Y.: Snow Lion Publica-tions.

———— 1996. *Sisters in Solitude: Two Traditions of Buddhist Monastic Ethics for Women.* Albany: SUNY Press.

Tsongkhapa. 2000. *The Great Treatise on the Stages of the Path to Enlightenment* [Lam Rim Chen mo]. Vol. 1. Trans. Lamrim Chenmo Translation Committee. Ithaca, N.Y.: Snow Lion Publications.

Tucci, Giuseppe. 1949. *Tibetan Painted Scrolls.* Vol. 2. Rome: La Libreria dello Stato.

———— 1956. *Preliminary Report on Two Scientific Expeditions in Nepal.* Vol. 10. Rome: Serie Orientale Roma.

———— 1980. *Religions of Tibet.* Trans. Geoffrey Samuel. Berkeley: University of California Press.

————— 1988. *Rin-Chen-Bzang-Po and the Renaissance of Buddhism in Tibet around the Millennium.* New Delhi: Aditya Prakashan.

Tulku, Sharpa, and Michael Perrott. 1987. *A Manual of Ritual Fire Offerings.* Dharamsala: Library of Tibetan Works and Archives.

Tulku, Tharthang, trans. 1983. *Mother of Knowledge: The Enlightenment of Ye-shes mtsho-rgyal.* Berkeley: Dharma Publishing.

Turner, Victor. 1967. *The Forest of Symbols: Aspects of Ndembu Ritual.* Ithaca, N.Y.: Cornell University Press.

————— 1969. *The Ritual Process: Structure and Anti-Structure.* Ithaca, N.Y.: Cornell University Press.

————— 1974. *Dramas, Fields, and Metaphors: Symbolic Action in Human Society.* Ithaca, N.Y.: Cornell University Press.

van der Veer, Peter. 1994. *Religious Nationalism: Hindus and Muslims in India.* Berkeley: University of California Press.

————— 2001. *Imperial Encounters: Religion and Modernity in India and Britain.* Princeton: Princeton University Press.

van der Veer, Peter, and Hartmut Lehmann, eds. 1999. *Nation and Religion: Perspectives on Europe and Asia.* Princeton: Princeton University Press.

van Ede, Yolanda. 2000. Of Birds and Wings: Tibetan Nuns and Their Encounters with Knowledge. In *Innovative Buddhist Women: Swimming against the Stream,* ed. Karma Lekshe Tsomo, 201–211. London: Curzon Press.

van Gennep, Arnold. 1960 [1908]. *The Rites of Passage: A Classic Study of Cultural Celebrations,* trans. M. Vizedom and M. Caffee. Chicago: University of Chicago Press.

Vargas-O'Brian, Ivette. 2001. The Life of dGe slong ma dPal mo: The Experience of a Leper, Founder of a Fasting Ritual, a Transmitter of Buddhist Teachings on Suffering and Renunciation in Tibetan Religious History. *Journal of the International Association of Buddhist Studies* 24(2): 157–185.

Vasodev, Shefalee. 2003. The Unwanted Girl. *India Today.* November 10, 2003.

Vatsayana. 2000. *Kamasutra/Vatsyayana Mallanaga.* A new complete translation of the Sanskrit Texts with excerpts from the Sanskrit Jayamangala commentary of Yasodhara Indrapada, the Hindi Jaya commentary of Devadatta Shastri and explanatory notes by the translators, Wendy Doniger and Sudhir Kakar. New York: Oxford University Press.

Venturino, Steven. 1995. Translating Tibet's Cultural Dispersion: Solzhenitsyn, Paine, and Orwell in Dharamsala. *Diaspora* 4(2): 153–180.

Visweswaran, Kamala. 1988. Defining Feminist Ethnography. *Inscriptions* 3/4: 27–46.

————— 1994. *Fictions of Feminist Ethnography.* Minneapolis: University of Minnesota Press.

———— 1997. Histories of Feminist Ethnography. *Annual Review of Anthropology* 26: 591–621.

Vitali, Roberto. 1990. *Early Temples of Central Tibet*. Warminster, England: Aris & Phillips.

———— 1996. *The Kingdoms of Gu.ge Pu.hrang according to mNga'.ris rgyal.rabs by Gu.ge mkan.chen Ngag.dbang grags.pa*. New Delhi: Indraprashta Press.

Vohra, Rohit. 1989a. *An Ethnography of the Buddhist Dards of Ladakh: Mythic lore—household—alliance system—kinship*. Luxembourg: Skydie Brown International.

———— 1989b. *The Religion of the Dards in Ladakh: Investigations into Their Pre-Buddhist 'Brog-pa Traditions*. Luxembourg: Skydie Brown International.

———— 1995a. Early History of Ladakh: Mythic Lore and Fabulation. In *Recent Research on Ladakh nos. 4 & 5: Proceedings of the Fourth and Fifth Colloquia on Ladakh*, ed. Henry Osmaston and Phillip Denwood, 215–234. London: School of African and Oriental Studies.

———— 1995b. Arabic Inscriptions of the Late First Millennium A.D. from Tangtse in Ladakh. In *Recent Research on Ladakh nos. 4 & 5: Proceedings of the Fourth and Fifth Colloquia on Ladakh*, ed. Henry Osmaston and Phillip Denwood, 419–429. London: School of African and Oriental Studies.

Waddell, L. Austine. 1895. The Buddhism of Tibet, or Lamaism. London: W. H. Allen & Co.

Walters, Jonathan. 1995. Gotami's Story. In *Buddhism in Practice*, ed. D. Lopez, 113–138. Princeton: Princeton University Press.

Warne, Randi. 2001. (En)gendering Religious Studies. In *Feminism in the Study of Religion*, ed. D. Juschka, 147–156. London: Continuum Press.

Warren, Henry Clarke. 1885 [1995]. *Buddhism in Translation*. Reprint. New Delhi: Motilal Banarsidass.

Wayman, Alex. 1974. *The Lion's Roar of Queen Srimala*. New York: Columbia University Press.

Weinberger-Thomas, Catherine. 1999. *Ashes of Immortality: Widow-Burning in India*. Chicago: University of Chicago Press.

Wijayaratna, Mohan. 1990. *Buddhist Monastic Life: According to the Texts of the Theravada Tradition*. Trans. C. Grangier and S. Collins. New York: Cambridge University Press.

Wiley, Andrea S. 1992. High Altitude Adaptation and Maternal-Infant Health: Neonatal Characteristics and Infant Survival in the Himalaya. Ph.D. dissertation, Department of Anthropology, University of California, Berkeley and San Francisco.

———— 1994. Neonatal Size and Infant Mortality at High Altitude in the Western Himalaya. *American Journal of Physical Anthropology* 94: 289–305.

Willis, Janice. 1972. *The Diamond Light: An Introduction to Tibetan Buddhist Meditations*. New York: Simon & Schuster.

———— 1984. Tibetan Ani-s: The Nun's Life in Tibet. *Tibet Journal* 9(4): 14–32.

———— 1985. Nuns and Benefactresses: The Role of Women in the Development of Buddhism. In *Women, Religion, and Social Change*, ed. Y. Haddad and E. Findly, 59–85. Albany: SUNY Press.

———— 1987. Dakini; Some Comments on Its Nature and Meaning. *Tibet Journal* 12(4): 56–71.

———— 1989. *Feminine Ground: Essays on Women and Tibet*. Ithaca, N.Y.: Snow Lion Publications.

Wilson, Elizabeth. 1994. Henpecked Husbands and Renouncers Home on the Range: Celibacy as Social Disengagement in South Asian Buddhism. *Union Seminary Quarterly Review* 48(3–4): 7–28.

———— 1995. The Female Body as a Source of Horror and Insight in Post-Asokan Indian Buddhism. In *Religious Reflections on the Human Body*, ed. Jamie Law, 76–99. Bloomington: Indiana University Press.

———— 1996. *Charming Cadavers: Horrific Figurations of the Feminine in Indian Buddhist Hagiographic Literature*. Chicago: University of Chicago Press.

Wirsing, Robert. 1998. *India, Pakistan, and the Kashmir Dispute: On Regional Conflict and Its Resolution*. New York: St. Martin's Press.

Yalman, Nur. 1962. The Ascetic Buddhist Monks of Ceylon. *Ethnology* 1(3): 315–328.

———— 1963. On the Purity of Women in the Castes of Ceylon and Malabar. *Journal of the Royal Anthropological Institute* 93: 25–58.

———— 1971. *Under the Bo Tree: Studies in Caste, Kinship and Marriage in the Interior of Ceylon*. Berkeley: University of California Press.

Yuchi, Kajiyama. 1982. Women in Buddhism. *Eastern Buddhist* 15(2): 53–70.

Yule, Henry, and A. C. Burnell. 1886. *Hobson-Jobson: A Glossary of Colloquial Anglo Indian Words and Phrases, and of Kindred Terms, Etymological, Historical, Geographical and Discursive*. New Delhi: Rupa and Co.

Zodpa, Geshe Lobzang, and Ngawang Tsering Shakspo. 1979. *Zangs dkar gyi rgyal rabs dang chos 'byung* [The Royal Chronicle and religious history of Zangskar]. Leh: Ladakh Buddha Vihar.

Zopa, Lobzang, and George Churinoff. 1995. *Nyung Nae: The Means of Achievement of the Eleven-Faced Great Compassionate One, Avalokitesvara*. Boston: Wisdom Publications.

Zwilling, Leonard. 1992. Homosexuality as Seen in Indian Buddhist Texts. In *Buddhism, Gender, and Sexuality*, ed. José Cabezon, 203–214. Albany: SUNY Press.

Index

deities of, 71; purification rites and, 205; sacred animals and, 61; seating orders, 4; social hierarchy and, 92; in Zangskar and Ladakh, 34, *40. See also* Monks; Nunneries; *specific monasteries*

Mon caste, 30, 71, 128

Mongolia, 96

Monks, 1, 4–5, 12, 13, 68; authority over nuns, 168, 184–187, 194–197, 234; in Buddhist history, 94; declining population of, 250; economic resources and, 49; exchange of women and, 166–167; festivals and, 109–110; funeral rites and, 210–212; gendered economy of merit and, 83–85; hierarchy among, 86–87; homosexual relations among, 144; of Lhasa, 22; merit *(bsod rnams)* and, 2, 17; modernity and, 34; monastic corporation and, 107; nuns' service to, 159–163; in old age, 84; purification rituals and, 204–205, 207–208, 210; ratio of nuns to, 19; ritual calendar and, 55–57, 59, 63; ritual roles for, 119–120; services for laypeople, 83; sexual improprieties of, 18, 144, 145, 146, 159, 195; social mobility of, 103; spiritual authority over nunneries, 101; Tantric practice and, 79, 83; in Thailand, 88; as traditional medical healers, 38–39; wealth and, 74; wedding rites and, 153–154. *See also* Abbots; Monasteries

Morality *(tshul khrims, sila)*, 14, 15

"Mother field," 57, 58

Mulasarvastivadin Vinaya, 74, 89, 160, 173

Mune monastery and nunnery, 99

Musharraf, Pervez, 31, 32

Muslims. *See* Islam

Nagaradza, 95

Nagarjuna, 222

Naib Tahsildar (revenue official), 49

Namdrol (nun), 178–179

Namgyal Institute of Dialectics, 246, 252

Nangkar neighborhood, 50, 60

Nangsa Öbum, 124–127, 225

Naropa, 98, 124, 224, 234

Nepal, 9, 35, 217, 244, 252; Buddhist modernism in, 250; laborers from, 43

New Year rites, 52, 53, 63–66, 179

Ngari Rinpoche, 60, 86–87, 110

Ngawang Changchub, 244

Ngawang Tharpa, Geshe, 21, 22, 216, 246

Ngawang Tsering, 99, 101

Ngowa (bsngo ba) rite, 90, 110, 111

Norberg-Hodge, Helena, 243

Norbu (nun), 133

North America, Buddhism in, 19, 96, 239, 253–254

Nunneries, 34–35, 128, 160; Buddhist feminism and, 239–245; Buddhist school identification of, 99; in economy of merit, 66–69, 113–116; foreign sponsorship and reform, 245–250; land ownership and, 102; in Zangskar and Ladakh, *40. See also* Monasteries; *specific nunneries*

Nuns, 3, 123–124, 146; alms collection by, 111, 115; assembly of, 174, 189–191; in Buddhist history, 93–94, 95–96; celibacy of, 6, 7, 12, 69, 144–145; as dutiful daughters, 156–159; enlightenment and, 230–235; "exchange of women" and, 164; exclusion from Buddhist scholarship, 11; fellowship of women, 142–145; feminist, 5; gendered economy of merit and, 83–85; lay renunciants, 11; livestock herds and, 59; modernity and, 34; monks' authority over, 168, 170–173, 194–197; in old age, 84; ordination and, 11, 68, 184; path to nunhood, 124–127; poverty of, 86, 113; purification rituals, 122, 208; purity of, 207; ratio of monks to, 19; rights and responsibilities of, 191–194; rites of passage for, 173–180; rituals and, 66–69; roles for, 119–120; services for laypeople, 83; social status of, 12; subordination to monks, 5–8, 159–163, 184–187; Tantric practice and, 79; transfer of allegiance and, 148–156; waged work of, 78; women who become nuns, types of, 127–137

Nyima (nun), 143

Nyingma school, 238

Nyungnas *(smyung gnas)* ritual, 96, 176

Offering cakes, 68, 146, 154, 190, 193

Onians, Isabelle, 221